UNDERSTANDING
AND DIVERSITY IN CHILD AND
ADOLESCENT MENTAL HEALTH

UNDERSTANDING UNIQUENESS AND DIVERSITY IN CHILD AND ADOLESCENT MENTAL HEALTH

Edited By

MATTHEW HODES

SUSAN SHUR-FEN GAU

PETRUS J. DE VRIES

ACADEMIC PRESS

An imprint of Elsevier

Academic Press is an imprint of Elsevier
125 London Wall, London EC2Y 5AS, United Kingdom
525 B Street, Suite 1650, San Diego, CA 92101-4495, United States
50 Hampshire Street, 5th Floor, Cambridge, MA 02139, United States
The Boulevard, Langford Lane, Kidlington, Oxford OX5 1GB, United Kingdom

Notices
Knowledge and best practice in this field are constantly changing. As new research
and experience broaden our understanding, changes in research methods,
professional practices, or medical treatment may become necessary.

Practitioners and researchers must always rely on their own experience and
knowledge in evaluating and using any information, methods, compounds, or
experiments described herein. In using such information or methods they should be
mindful of their own safety and the safety of others, including parties for whom
they have a professional responsibility.

To the fullest extent of the law, neither the Publisher nor the authors, contributors, or
editors, assume any liability for any injury and/or damage to persons or property as
a matter of products liability, negligence or otherwise, or from any use or operation
of any methods, products, instructions, or ideas contained in the material herein.

Library of Congress Cataloging-in-Publication Data
A catalog record for this book is available from the Library of Congress

British Library Cataloguing-in-Publication Data
A catalogue record for this book is available from the British Library

ISBN: 978-0-12-815310-9

For information on all Academic Press publications visit our website at
https://www.elsevier.com/books-and-journals

Working together
to grow libraries in
developing countries

www.elsevier.com • www.bookaid.org

Publisher: Nikki Levy
Acquisition Editor: Emily Ekle
Editorial Project Manager: Barbara Makinster
Production Project Manager: Mohana Natarajan
Designer: Matthew Limbert

Typeset by TNQ Technologies

Contents

PART I

UNDERSTANDING DIVERSITY IN DEVELOPMENT AND PSYCHOPATHOLOGY

1. Variations in Pathways Into and Out of Antisocial Behavior From the Perspective of Developmental Psychopathology

ERIC ACQUAVIVA, PIERRE ELLUL, XAVIER BENAROUS

2. Developmental Considerations in Bipolar Disorder

MICHAL GOETZ, MARKETA MOHAPLOVA, ANTONIN SEBELA, TOMAS NOVAK

3. Heterogeneity in Tics and Gilles de la Tourette Syndrome

VALSAMMA EAPEN, AMELIA WALTER, MARY M. ROBERTSON

4. Risk and Protective Factors and Course of Functional Somatic Symptoms in Young People

CHARLOTTE ULRIKKA RASK, IRMA J. BONVANIE, ELENA M. GARRALDA

5. Anxiety and Anxiety Disorders in Young People: A Cross-Cultural Perspective

SELDA KOYDEMIR, CECILIA A. ESSAU

PART II
UNIQUENESS AND RISK IN MARGINALIZED GROUPS

6. Child Developmental Trajectories in Adversity: Environmental Embedding and Developmental Cascades in Contexts of Risk
XANTHE HUNT, MARK TOMLINSON

7. Infant Mental Health in Africa: Embracing Cultural Diversity
ASTRID BERG, ANUSHA LACHMAN, JUANÉ VOGES

8. Mental Health Service Provision for Child and Adolescent Refugees: European Perspectives
JOERG M. FEGERT, THORSTEN SUKALE, REBECCA C. BROWN

9. Sexuality and Gender Identity in Child and Adolescent Mental Health: Some Reflections on Social, Psychiatric, and Mental Health Service Changes

GORDON HARPER, MARI DOMINGUEZ, ANGELS MAYORDOMO-ARANDA, MATTHEW HODES

PART III

SUPPORTING UNIQUENESS AND DIVERSITY THROUGH INTERVENTIONS AND SERVICES

10. Pharmacogenomics in the Treatment of Child and Adolescent Psychiatric Disorders

SALMA MALIK, SOPHIA A. WALKER, SASHA MALIK, LISA NAMEROW

11. Telepsychiatry and Digital Mental Health Care in Child and Adolescent Psychiatry: Implications for Service Delivery in Low- and Middle-Income Countries
SAVITA MALHOTRA, RUCHITA SHAH

PART IV

EUROPEAN PERSPECTIVES ON CHILD AND ADOLESCENT MENTAL HEALTH SERVICES AND TRAINING

12. Child and Adolescent Mental Health: Knowledge, Practice, and Services in Central Europe
HELMUT REMSCHMIDT, MICHAL GOETZ, PATRICK HAEMMERLE

13. Child and Adolescent Psychiatry Training in Europe

BRIAN W. JACOBS, ELIZABETH BARRETT, HENRIKJE KLASEN, PAUL ROBERTSON,
LUCIA VAŠKOVÁ, EVA ŠNIRCOVÁ, EKIN SÖNMEZ

List of Contributors

Eric Acquaviva Hôpital Robert Debré, Paris, France

Elizabeth Barrett University College, Dublin, Ireland

Xavier Benarous Pitié-Salepêtrière Hospital, Sorbonne University, Paris, France; INSERM Unit U1105 Research Group for Analysis of the Multimodal Cerebral Function, University of Picardy Jules Verne (UPJV), Amiens, France

Astrid Berg University of Cape Town, Cape Town, South Africa; Stellenbosch University, Cape Town, South Africa

Irma J. Bonvanie Paediatric Department Martini Hospital, Groningen, The Netherlands

Rebecca C. Brown University of Ulm, Ulm, Germany

Petrus J. de Vries Division of Child & Adolescent Psychiatry, University of Cape Town, Cape Town, South Africa

Mari Dominguez Imperial College London, London, United Kingdom

Valsamma Eapen University of New South Wales, Sydney NSW, Australia; Liverpool Hospital & Ingham Institute, Liverpool NSW, Australia

Pierre Ellul Hôpital Robert Debré, Paris, France

Cecilia A. Essau University of Roehampton, London, United Kingdom

Joerg M. Fegert University of Ulm, Ulm, Germany

Elena M. Garralda Imperial College London, London, United Kingdom

Michal Goetz Charles University Second Faculty of Medicine, Prague, Czech Republic

Patrick Haemmerle FMH, Freiburg/Fribourg, Switzerland

Gordon Harper Harvard Medical School, Boston, United States

Matthew Hodes Imperial College London, London, United Kingdom; Central and North West London NHS Foundation Trust, London, United Kingdom

Xanthe Hunt Stellenbosch University, Stellenbosch, South Africa

Brian W. Jacobs King's College London, London, United Kingdom

Henrikje Klasen Leiden University, Leiden, The Netherlands

Selda Koydemir University of Roehampton, London, United Kingdom; University of Bamberg, Bamberg, Germany

Anusha Lachman Stellenbosch University, Cape Town, South Africa

Savita Malhotra Postgraduate Institute of Medical Education and Research, Chandigarh, India

Salma Malik Qatar Foundation, Doha, Qatar

Sasha Malik Miss Porter's School, Farmington, CT, United States

Angels Mayordomo-Aranda Enfield and Haringey Mental Health NHS Trust, London, United Kingdom

Marketa Mohaplova Charles University Second Faculty of Medicine, Prague, Czech Republic; Charles University First Faculty of Medicine, Prague, Czech Republic

Lisa Namerow Institute of Living/Hartford Hospital, Hartford, CT, United States

Tomas Novak National Institute of Mental Health, Klecany, Czech Republic; Charles University Third Faculty of Medicine, Prague, Czech Republic

Charlotte Ulrikka Rask Centre for Child and Adolescent Psychiatry, Aarhus University Hospital, Risskov, Denmark

Helmut Remschmidt Philipps-University, Marburg, Germany

Mary M. Robertson University College London, London, England

Paul Robertson University of Melbourne, Melbourne, Australia

Antonin Sebela National Institute of Mental Health, Klecany, Czech Republic; Charles University First Faculty of Medicine, Prague, Czech Republic

Ruchita Shah Postgraduate Institute of Medical Education and Research, Chandigarh, India

Susan Shur-Fen Gau National Taiwan University Hospital (NTUH) and College of Medicine, Taipei, Taiwan; National Taiwan University, Taipei, Taiwan

Eva Šnircová Instite Neuropsychiatrické Péče, Prague, Czech Republic

Ekin Sönmez Department of Psychiatry, Zonguldak Caycuma State Hospital, Caycuma, Turkey

Thorsten Sukale University of Ulm, Ulm, Germany

Mark Tomlinson Stellenbosch University, Stellenbosch, South Africa

Lucia Vašková INEP Institute of Neuropsychiatric Care, Prague, Czech Republic

Juané Voges Stellenbosch University, Cape Town, South Africa

Sophia A. Walker University of Connecticut School of Medicine, Farmington, CT, United States

Amelia Walter University of New South Wales, Sydney NSW, Australia; Liverpool Hospital & Ingham Institute, Liverpool NSW, Australia

Preface

Cultural and family background, developmental trajectories, gender, life events, and genes all contribute to the diversity and uniqueness of the children and adolescents with whom we work. This is the key lesson we can take from this monograph: uniqueness and diversity are integral to our work and we have to take them into account in diagnoses and treatments.

However, treatments also have to be evidence-based. In practice this usually means that they have to have been studied in randomized controlled trials. People often forget, though, that randomized controlled trials prove some kind of efficacy only for an "average" subject, a statistical abstraction at the opposite of the unique individual child and family we have in front of us every day. Is there a solution to this paradoxical situation? Perhaps a short historical perspective may help.

It is often considered that modern occidental or "Western" medicine really emerged at the beginning of the 19th century with some major breakthrough in pathophysiology. At that time, most clinical scientists did not consider evidence-based treatment to be statistically assessed. On the contrary, given the new biological way of considering humans, the paradigm of treatment development and evaluation was to find the mechanism of the disease and then to find a treatment that acted upon the mechanism. The evidence was biological, and the patient universal. No average subject. No diversity and uniqueness. Let us consider in more detail the position of Claude Bernard, a great physiologist of that time, in his *Introduction to the Study of Experimental Medicine* (1865):

> In the patient who succumbed, the cause of death was evidently something which was not found in the patient who recovered; this something we must determine, and then we can act on the phenomena or recognize or foresee them accurately; then only scientific determinism will be achieved. But not by statistics shall we succeed in this; never have statistics taught anything, and never can they teach anything about the nature of phenomena. I shall apply what I have just said to all the statistics compiled with the object of learning the efficacy of certain remedies in curing diseases.

Over the years it became clear that this ambitious and idealistic position was only partially helpful. Indeed, mechanisms of action are useful to determine whether a treatment, pharmacological or otherwise, is efficacious. But this usefulness is limited. In many situations treatment with promising mechanisms of action have not shown clinical utility (for instance, most new treatments in Alzheimer disease), whereas some products with unknown functioning are obviously improving patients (for instance, electroconvulsive therapy). To tackle this issue, as explained in Harry Marks' book *The Progress of Experiment: Science and Therapeutic Reform in the United States, 1900–1990*, a paradigm shift occurred toward the middle of the 20th century. What Claude Bernard feared most did happen: statistics and randomization were proposed to assess efficacy and the success of this approach has been considerable.

We are perhaps today at a new turning point. Given that randomized controlled trials deal only with an average subject and because, from oncology to child and adolescent psychiatry, there is a now the necessity to deal with diversity and uniqueness, we need some new basis for evidence-based practice. But how?

First, we have to come back to concepts. "Evidence" is not a magic word that allows us to reveal truth. According to the *Stanford Encyclopedia of Philosophy*, evidence is "that which justifies Belief." And because Belief is a complex phenomenon, there is no unique way to lead to evidence (Worrall, 2002). In child and adolescent mental health, the key word will likely be "triangulation": that is, a multiplicity of angles of attack, from different epistemologies. The range of evidence that will emerge from these different models and approaches should provide a comprehensive picture.

In practice, a precise description of the treatment under evaluation should first be systematically provided. For a medication, this corresponds classically to its biological or chemical formula. For a psychological treatment, it is just as important to know in detail the content of the therapeutic process.

The mechanism of action of a new treatment is also of major interest. This mechanism will be made explicit within an appropriate theoretical framework: neurobiology is relevant for pharmacological treatment, and psychological approaches will likely require different perspectives.

The effect of the treatment on the young person's experience and functioning will then have to be assessed. Here, qualitative studies will obviously be invaluable.

At some stage we will have to answer the question, "On average, is the new treatment better than a given alternative?" A randomized controlled trial or a nonrandomized cohort study will obviously be useful here.

The best recipe for evidence-based child and adolescent mental health practice in a context of diversity and uniqueness will probably be this: Take into account theories that deal with universal and abstract subjects combined with statistical inference that characterize efficacy on an average subject, as well as incorporate qualitative studies that focus on the individual experience.

Bruno Falissard
President of the International Association for Child
and Adolescent Psychiatry and Allied Professions

Reference

Worrall, J. (2002). *What evidence in evidence-based medicine?* Centre for Philosophy of Natural and Social Science. Causality: Metaphysics and Methods. Technical Report 01/03.

Introduction

Matthew Hodes[1,2], Susan Shur-Fen Gau[3,4], Petrus J. de Vries[5]

[1] Imperial College London, London, United Kingdom; [2] Central and North West London NHS Foundation Trust, London, United Kingdom; [3] National Taiwan University Hospital (NTUH) and College of Medicine, Taipei, Taiwan; [4] National Taiwan University, Taipei, Taiwan; [5] Division of Child & Adolescent Psychiatry, University of Cape Town, Cape Town, South Africa

INTRODUCTION

The International Association for Child and Adolescent Psychiatry and Allied Professions (IACAPAP) has a longstanding tradition of organizing a biennial congress, regular study groups, and ongoing support for the career development of child and adolescent mental health trainees. In addition, the association has for many years published and disseminated high-quality books in both paper and electronic form, including an IACAPAP Monograph published in conjunction with the biennial congresses. We are delighted to introduce the 2018 Monograph prepared for the 23rd IACAPAP World Congress to be held in Prague, Czech Republic, in July, 2018. The theme of the congress, "Understanding Diversity and Uniqueness," has influenced the title of this Monograph.

The IACAPAP Monographs have evolved and changed significantly over the decades. The first Monograph was published in 1970 with the title *The Child in His Family* (Anthony & Koupernik, 1970). This reflects the time, given the focus on one aspect of care and influences on a child's life, as well as the use of the masculine third person ("his"). Soon the Monograph titles broadened to, for instance, *Children at Psychiatric Risk* (Anthony, Chiland, & Koupernick, 1974). For 20 years, Colette Chiland was a coeditor of the Monograph, and during this time the Monographs covered a wide range of topics. Here we pay tribute to our colleague, Colette Chiland, a French child and adolescent psychiatrist and psychoanalyst who continued to be a staunch supporter of the Monograph even after she stepped down as editor. Sadly, Collette died in 2016, having made an immense contribution to the Monographs, IACAPAP, and the field of child and adolescent mental health (a fuller summary of her activities is given in the appendix to the chapter by Harper et al., in this volume).

A recent change for the Monographs, in keeping with IACAPAP's desire to be more Internet-based and to provide open access to materials, was the decision from the IACAPAP Board to make the Monograph freely available online 1 year after the congress, to be accessed via the IACAPAP website. We are delighted that Elsevier, now our established partner in publishing the Monographs, supports this free access, and so will contribute to IACAPAP's mission to disseminate high-quality information as widely as possible.

UNDERSTANDING UNIQUENESS IN DEVELOPMENT AND PSYCHOPATHOLOGY

The first section of the Monograph examines some of the consequences of abnormal development, as exemplified by five disorders that have been the subject of significant research. Childhood conduct disorders are among the most common presenting problems at the community level and are often associated with an impact on multiple agencies. Conduct disorders may have serious consequences and lead to adolescent antisocial behavior and offense, and are associated with high levels of distress and psychiatric comorbidity, especially attention-deficit hyperactivity disorder (ADHD) and substance misuse disorder. Acquaviva and colleagues summarize new ways of conceptualizing conduct problems, based on longitudinal studies, such as including the distinction between life course—persistent and adolescent-onset antisocial behavior. Further insights are provided by an account of callous unemotional traits in young people with conduct disorders, and discussions about the implications of subtyping and the underlying neuropsychological deficits. The interplay between genetic and environmental factors is included.

Developmental considerations in bipolar disorders are addressed next in the chapter by Goetz et al. Risk factors for bipolar disorder and the course of the disorder are described. Neuropsychological deficits are summarized and found to be heterogeneous, perhaps for methodological reasons. The chapter also summarizes the controversy regarding the US practice in which young children, who would now be regarded as having ADHD, were diagnosed with bipolar disorder instead, and outlines the way in which this controversy resulted in the creation of the *Diagnostic and Statistical Manual of Mental Disorders*, Fifth Edition category of disruptive mood dysregulation disorder (American Psychiatric Association, 2013).

Eapen and colleagues provide an illuminating account of heterogeneity of tics and tic disorders. They describe the clinical characteristics and heterogeneity of Gilles de la Tourette syndrome and review the genetics and epidemiology, which remind us of the high levels of psychiatric comorbidity especially with obsessive-compulsive disorder and ADHD. It is striking that these disorders, although phenomenologically different, seem to affect similar neuropathological processes involving the cortico-striato-thalamocortical pathways.

The theme of heterogeneity and diversity is continued in the chapter by Rask et al., which addresses functional somatic symptoms, ie, physical symptoms without a known medical explanation. These are prevalent among children and adolescents and in a minority of more severe cases they can be associated with surprisingly high levels of impairment. The chapter provides an elegant example of the need for a biopsychosocial approach and for sophisticated formulations to inform appropriate interventions.

The section is completed with a chapter on cross-cultural perspectives on anxiety and anxiety disorders. Koydemir and Essau show how anxiety can be related to culturally constructed conceptions of the self, and to the conceptualization of relationships. These may be the bedrock for the shaping of specific forms of anxiety disorders that are encountered in specific cultures. The authors show how cultural factors affect psychological treatment and need to be considered in treatment settings.

UNIQUENESS AND RISK IN MARGINALIZED GROUPS

The second section addresses the developmental and mental health implications of children and adolescents in high-risk contexts, and situations that may lead young people to become marginalized economically or socially. Hunt and Tomlinson provide a thoughtful account of crucial influences on child development including gene–environment interactions and epigenetic mechanisms and the way these may be associated with emerging psychiatric symptoms. They discuss contextual influences including socioeconomic adversity, maternal depression, violence exposure and HIV, and implications for intervention.

More specific insights into some of these processes are provided by Berg et al., who focus on the first 3 years of child development and discuss attachment and child-rearing in the African context, illustrated with some specific ethnographically-informed examples. An underlying theme of the chapter is the need to reflect on the extent to which child developmental processes and needs are universal, and to what extent they are culturally shaped and thus need be understood through local inquiry.

Refugees are exposed to risks and experiences that can be so extreme and overwhelming (such as being witness to high levels of organized violence or the need to flee persecution) that cultural and individual differences are relatively less powerful as explanatory variables. The chapter by Fegert et al. describes the plight of refugees fleeing the Middle

East, and especially the Syrian war, and their journey to central Europe. The authors summarize the high level of adversities experienced, but also outline some innovative intervention programs.

Another group that has experienced persecution, although under totally different circumstances, is people who are different with regard to their sexual identity or sexual preferences. The chapter by Harper et al. illustrates the shift in societal attitudes toward gender difference and youngsters with gender dysphoria. This has been associated with changes in classificatory systems that, in keeping with the broader cultural changes, also show more fluidity, such as in conceptualizing gender dysphoria as a continuum as well as a category. Greater acceptance of the problems has been associated with the expansion of specialist services for this group and has led to improved mental health outcomes for this unique group of children and adolescents.

SUPPORTING UNIQUENESS AND DIVERSITY THROUGH INTERVENTIONS AND SERVICES

One of the major developments in the clinical application of knowledge related to individual differences is the emergence of personalized or precision medicine, and this approach has been applied to mental health (Ng & Weisz, 2016; Perna, Grassi, Caldirola, & Nemeroff, 2017). A succinct account of the complex field of pharmacogenomics as applied to child and adolescent mental health is provided by Malik et al. Some of the basic concepts and applications are described. This is an area about which we will be hearing much more as the technology becomes more accessible and affordable.

A different application of technology is presented by Malhotra and Shah, who discuss the potential benefits of telepsychiatry. They outline how technology can be used in ways that go beyond simple remote communication with other mental professionals, and describe a pioneering technology-driven, medical knowledge-based, clinical decision support system for delivering mental health care in remote areas through nonspecialists in low-resource settings.

EUROPEAN PERSPECTIVES ON CHILD AND ADOLESCENT MENTAL HEALTH SERVICES AND TRAINING

The 2018 IACAPAP Congress in Prague represents the first time that the congress has been held in the former Eastern European Bloc. The emergence of a more united Europe has prompted chapters that address service and training issues in Europe. Remschmidt et al. provide accounts of the histories of child and adolescent mental health services in Germany, Czech Republic, and Switzerland, three diverse countries. Striking differences emerge regarding the resourcing and numbers of trained child and adolescent psychiatrists including academics in these countries. They also outline differences in the training.

Training across Europe is the topic of our final chapter. Here, Jacobs and colleagues present some of the striking differences in training across Europe and describe how they relate to the countries' psychiatric histories and recognition of child and adolescent psychiatry, or its lack, across European countries, and how such historical developments affect resourcing. It is hoped that the increasing dialogue across national borders and international organizations will facilitate an increase in training standards and lead to the convergence of training to facilitate the movement of child and adolescent psychiatrists, and comparable care delivery for families across the continent.

References

American Psychiatric Association. (2013). *Diagnostic and Statistical Manual of mental disorders*. Washington DC: American Psychiatric Association.

Anthony, E. J., Chiland, C., & Koupernick, C. (Eds.). (1974). *Children at psychiatric risk*. Wiley.

Anthony, E. J., & Koupernik, C. (Eds.). (1970). *The child in His family*. Wiley Masson.

Ng, M. Y., & Weisz, J. R. (2016). Annual Research Review: Building a science of personalized intervention for youth mental health. *J Child Psychol Psychiatry, 57*(3), 216–236. https://doi.org/10.1111/jcpp.12470.

Perna, G., Grassi, M., Caldirola, D., & Nemeroff, C. B. (2017). The revolution of personalized psychiatry: Will technology make it happen sooner? *Psychol Med*, 1–9. https://doi.org/10.1017/s0033291717002859.

UNDERSTANDING DIVERSITY IN DEVELOPMENT AND PSYCHOPATHOLOGY

1

Variations in Pathways Into and Out of Antisocial Behavior From the Perspective of Developmental Psychopathology

Eric Acquaviva[1], Pierre Ellul[1], Xavier Benarous[2,3]

[1] Hôpital Robert Debré, Paris, France; [2] Pitié-Salepêtrière Hospital, Sorbonne University, Paris, France; [3] INSERM Unit U1105 Research Group for Analysis of the Multimodal Cerebral Function, University of Picardy Jules Verne (UPJV), Amiens, France

INTRODUCTION

Antisocial behaviors refers to a heterogeneous set of actions outside the norms, rules, or laws of the social group in which the subject develops, such as physical aggression, theft, and violation of societal rules. Such behaviors may have a number of medical and social implications (Nau, 2005). For example, in France, a review ordered by the National Medical Research Institute in 2006 (Institut National de la Santé et de la Recherche Médicale, France, 2006) sparked an intense debate in the medical and scientific fields. The discussions focused on the use of early predictors for antisocial behaviors, which was interpreted by some to be a source of social stigma of at-risk populations as well as a determinist interpretation of disadvantaged populations (Ehrenberg, 2006; Lenoble, E., Malika, B.-B., Sandrine, C., & Forget, J.-M., 2006).

In daily practice, clinicians are often requested by families or institutions to be involved in caring for children and adolescents with antisocial or defiant behaviors when first-line educational interventions fail.

Understanding Uniqueness and Diversity in Child and Adolescent Mental Health
https://doi.org/10.1016/B978-0-12-815310-9.00001-0

3

It is important to take into account that exhibiting some antisocial behavior such as lying or theft is often considered the norm for children; however, such expressions are generally limited in time and number. For example, a peak in physical aggression is observed at age 3 in both boys and girls, with an expected decline following the emergence of the child's socioemotional skills (Tremblay, 2002). Antisocial behaviors can be seen in almost all contexts of psychopathology in children and adolescents, from a maladaptive reaction to stressful family situations to its episodic expression during an acute psychiatric episode (e.g., depressive episode, mania, or psychotic episode). Children who exhibit persistent and repetitive antisocial behaviors are defined in international classifications as having conduct disorders (CD).

The prevalence of CD in children and adolescents is high (2.7%– 5.2%) and both crises and life trajectories of these children and adolescents are difficult to manage for families, institutions, and themselves (Costello, Mustillo, Erkanli, Keeler, & Angold, 2003; Kessler et al., 2012).

The first study on the natural course of antisocial behaviors from childhood to adulthood was conducted by Robins (Robins, 1966). She examined at age 30 years 406 people who had been referred to a child guidance center at age 13 years. All subjects who had committed serious offenses in adulthood had shown antisocial behaviors in childhood. Among the outcomes in adulthood, 12% of youths with antisocial behavior had complete remission, 27% had partial improvement (more than three antisocial symptoms), and 61% remained unimproved in adulthood. Since this seminal work, a large amount of empirical data highlighted the assumption that the persistence of antisocial behaviors throughout the life span is a main risk for youths with CD. A systematic review reported that 40%–70% of youths with CD evolve into having an antisocial personality disorder in adulthood (R.J.R. Blair, 2015; National Collaborating Centre for Mental Health (UK) & Social Care Institute for Excellence (UK), 2013). When antisocial behaviors persist in adulthood, they are associated with dramatically elevated morbidity and mortality. For this group, the risk of premature death at age 40 is 33 times higher than that for the general population (Black, Baumgard, Bell, & Kao, 1996). Young adults with antisocial problems are at particular risk for trauma, sexually transmitted infections, and toxic-related infections (hepatitis C virus and HIV). Compliance with managing a medical problem (such as epilepsy) is often problematic and access to care services is chaotic (Black & Donald, 2015).

The need to develop effective interventions to reduce antisocial behaviors in childhood has become increasingly recognized by public health policy makers. In addition to preventive programs in the general population, the development of targeted prevention interventions for specific subgroups of youths is seen as an important approach. This requires a better understanding of the variety of pathways into and out of antisocial behaviors throughout the life span, and a definition of relevant subgroups of patients. In the early 1990s, Moffit (T.E. Moffitt, 1993) suggested that the onset of difficulties may differentiate groups of patients with distinct trajectories of antisocial behaviors, i.e., life course—persistent disorder (LCP) and adolescent-limited (AL) conduct problems. Another distinction was made with regard to the presence of prosocial emotions. Considering the vast number of studies addressing these questions, an updated review of this topic is needed.

This chapter synthesizes the studies on the variability of clinical expression and trajectories into and out of antisocial behaviors from a developmental point of view. First, we will describe how antisocial behaviors are categorized in the international classifications and how these classifications differentiate clinical subtypes and trajectories of antisocial behaviors. Second, we show how comorbidities are associated with different trajectories of antisocial behaviors. Then, we will consider the neuropsychological characteristics associated with specific pathways of antisocial behaviors. Finally, genetic and neurobiological factors involved in these trajectories are discussed.

SUBTYPES OF ANTISOCIAL BEHAVIORS IN INTERNATIONAL CLASSIFICATIONS

General Background

In the *Diagnostic and Statistical Manual of Mental Disorders*, Fifth Edition (DSM-5) (American Psychiatric Association, 2013), children and adolescents receive a diagnosis of CD according to the consideration of four domains: (1) aggression to people or animals, (2) destruction of property, (3) deceitfulness or theft, and (4) serious violation of rules. CD is diagnosed when there is a repetitive and persistent pattern of behavior in which the basic rights of others or major age-appropriate societal norms or rules are violated. The presence of at least 3 of 15 criteria in the past 12 months from any of these categories, with at least one criterion present in the past 6 months, is required. Moreover, "the disturbance in behaviour causes clinically significant impairment in social, academic, or occupational functioning." The International Classification of Disease, 10th Revision (ICD-10) (Organisation Mondiale de la Santé, 1993) includes the same items but insists that self-esteem be generally low, and an inability to develop social relationships and lack of concern for others may or may not be present.

To characterize the clinical heterogeneity of CD, subclassifications have been introduced. In the DSM-5 classification, subtypes of CD used two specifiers: on the one hand, the age of onset of antisocial behaviors, and on the other, the lack of prosocial emotions. Different clinical expressions and trajectories of antisocial behaviors are described through these different subtypes.

Age of Onset of Antisocial Behaviors

Two subcategories are specified: childhood onset, when at least one diagnostic criterion for CD occurred before 10 years old, and adolescent onset, when the first symptom occurred after 10 years old. Moffit proposed another distinction based on the persistence (or not) of CD symptoms after adolescence: LCP or AL antisocial behaviors (Moffitt, 1993).

Youths within LCP trajectories of antisocial behavior are more likely to have neurodevelopmental comorbidities (such as attention-deficit hyperactivity disorder [ADHD]), most of which present with a childhood-onset form of CD (Moffitt, 1993; Silberg, Moore, & Rutter, 2015). Some authors highlighted the importance of cognitive difficulties in the LCP form of CD compared with AL (Johnson, Kemp, Heard, Lennings, & Hickie, 2015). The contribution of genetic factors is postulated to be more important in the childhood-onset CD than in the adolescent-onset form. Youths with childhood-onset antisocial problems exhibit temperamental and cognitive problems (e.g., abnormal autonomic regularities, executive function deficits, and deficits in verbal intelligence) that constitute a vulnerability to early emotional and behavioral dysregulation (Dandreaux & Frick, 2009). Familial risk factors (low socioeconomic status, a lack of maternal closeness, and a history of harsh discipline) have also been identified for LCP (Moore, Silberg, Roberson-Nay, & Mezuk, 2017). Indeed, LCP antisocial CD is highly predictive of later problems in adults. The persistence of antisocial behaviors into adulthood is associated with a more severe form of antisocial behaviors. Adults with childhood-onset CD have more convictions, incarcerations, and criminal justice involvement. Moreover, adult outcomes of childhood-onset versus adolescent-onset antisocial behaviors are associated with an increased risk for substance use disorder (Goldstein, Grant, Ruan, Smith, & Saha, 2006; Moore et al., 2017). Most studies also found an elevated risk of poorer general mental health, unemployment, and impaired social relationships in the LCP group (Johnson et al., 2015).

Regarding the AL group, youth typically do not show early emerging oppositional behaviors, but rather a range of both oppositional and antisocial behaviors coinciding with the onset of puberty. They are generally encouraged by their peer group to engage in delinquent activities (Tremblay, Mâsse, Vitaro, & Dobkin, 1995), whereas the role of deviant peer group affiliation is less important in childhood-onset CD. The youth are less likely to show academic, occupational, social, or physical impairment in adulthood compared with the childhood-onset subtype.

It is noticeable that another subgroup has been identified, i.e., a childhood-limited (CL) form of CDs. CL begins in childhood but is limited in time. Predictors for LCP antisocial behavior versus CL are anxiety during pregnancy (32 weeks' gestation), partner cruelty to the mother (from age 0 to 4 years), harsh parenting, and higher levels of child's undercontrolled temperament (Barker & Maughan, 2009).

This distinction of CD according to the age of onset has also been discussed (Moore et al., 2017). Some authors argued that the severity of symptoms is a stronger predictor than the age of onset for the natural course of symptoms (Moore et al., 2017; Silberg et al., 2015).

Antisocial Behavior Outcomes and Prosocial Emotions

In the DSM-5, the diagnosis of CD can be specified with or without limited prosocial emotions (LPE). To be qualified as having LPE, an individual must have displayed at least two of the following characteristics persistently over at least 12 months and in multiple relationships and settings of the individual's typical pattern in interpersonal and emotional functioning over this period, not just upon occasional occurrences in some situation:

1. lack of remorse or guilt: does not feel bad or guilty when he or she does something wrong (exclude remorse when expressed only when caught and/or facing punishment). The individual shows a general lack of concern about the negative consequences of his or her actions. For example, the individual is not remorseful after hurting someone or does not care about the consequences of breaking rules;
2. callous (lack of empathy): disregards and is unconcerned about the feelings of others. The individual is described as cold and uncaring. The person appears more concerned about the effects of his or her actions on himself or herself, rather than their effects on others, even when they result in substantial harm to others;
3. unconcerned about performance: does not show concern about poor or problematic performance at school, at work, or in other important activities. The individual does not put forth the effort necessary to perform well, even when expectations are clear, and typically blames others for his or her poor performance; and

4. shallow or deficient affect: does not express feelings or show emotions to others, except in ways that seem shallow, insincere, or superficial (e.g., actions contradict the emotion displayed; can turn emotions "on" or "off" quickly) or when emotional expressions are used for gain (e.g., emotions displayed to manipulate or intimidate others).

Callous unemotional (CU) traits have been used to differentiate children who are capable of premediated antisocial behaviors and aggression from those whose antisocial behaviors are primarily impulsive and reactive to threat. Usually, children with conduct problems and who exhibit CU traits designate a group of youths who tap into the historical description of juvenile psychopathy (Christian, Frick, Hill, Tyler, & Frazer, 1997; Rowe, Maughan, et al., 2010). The presence of CU traits in youths with CD was later refined in the LPE category in the DSM-5. Not all youths with such temperamental features (i.e., CU or LPE) have conduct problems. A high level of LPE exists in 2.9% of the general pediatric population, only one-third of whom also meet criteria for CD (Rowe, Costello, Angold, Copeland, & Maughan, 2010). Around 25–30% of children with CD meet criteria for LPE.

The presence of LPE predicts a more severe and stable course of antisocial behaviors continuing into adulthood: conduct problems, delinquency, violence, and aggression (Frick & Morris, 2004; Pardini, Lochman, & Powell, 2007). Aggression is more likely to be premeditated and instrumental (i.e., in view of achieving a specific goal). On average, these children show a poorer response to many of the typical health interventions used for antisocial behavior. Youths with CD and LPE show higher rates of aggression and higher rates of cruelty (Kahn, Frick, Youngstrom, Findling, & Youngstrom, 2012). Moreover, a metaanalysis of 10 studies composed of 5731 participants was conducted to examine the relationship between CU traits and the severity of conduct problems before age 5 years. Overall, a significant positive relationship was found between LPE and the severity of conduct problems ($r = 0.39$; $p < .001$). Moderator analyses revealed that this relationship differed based on the use of the same versus different informants across measures, but was consistent across sex and sample type (at-risk/clinic referred or community) (Longman, Hawes, & Kohlhoff, 2016). Subjects with CD with LPE are more likely to have lower levels of academic achievement compared with those with other types of CD, and this was also largely accounted for by the callousness and uncaring dimensions (Ciucci & Baroncelli, 2014).

Reactive Versus Proactive Aggressive Behaviors

Although the distinction between reactive and proactive aggressions does not exist in international classifications such as the DSM and ICD, it has largely been used in studies employing developmental frameworks. Research has distinguished between reactive aggression, which occurs as an angry response to provocation or threat, and proactive aggression, which is typically unprovoked and often is used for instrumental gain or dominance over others (Dodge, Bates, & Pettit, 1990). Although these two types of behavior can be shown by the same subject, they are underpinned by different developmental trajectories (Hubbard, McAuliffe, Morrow, & Romano, 2010; Kempes, Matthys, de Vries, & van Engeland, 2005).

First, proactive aggression, but not reactive aggression, positively predicted delinquency 3 years later in two samples of French Canadians boys and girls (Vitaro, Gendreau, Tremblay, & Oligny, 1998; Vitaro, Brendgen, & Tremblay, 2002). Second, reactive but not proactive aggression predicted negative affect and suicidal behavior. Third, environmental influences differ between the two subtypes: physical abuse and lack of parental caregiving for reactive aggression, and parental substance abuse and a lack of parental monitoring for proactive aggression (Brendgen, Vitaro, Boivin, Dionne, & Pérusse, 2006). Finally, impairments in social information processing (e.g., hostile attributional bias) is associated with reactive but not proactive aggressive behaviors (Hubbard et al., 2010). Interestingly, symptoms of oppositional defiant disorder (ODD) reflecting irritability (loses one's temper and is angry and easily annoyed), a construct that is different but related to reactive aggressive behavior, uniquely predicted later emotional disorders after 3 years' follow-up, whereas symptoms reflecting headstrong behaviors (argumentative, noncompliant, and rule breaking) uniquely predicted later CD in a representative sample of British children and adolescents (N = 7912) (Stringaris & Goodman, 2009).

COMORBIDITIES AND DIFFERENT PATHWAYS OF CONDUCT DISORDERS

Comorbidities between CD and other psychiatric disorders are the norm rather than the exception, and occur in around 60% of children with CD. At least 30%–50% of children and adolescents with CD fulfill criteria for ADHD (Abram, Teplin, McClelland, & Dulcan, 2003; Costello et al., 2003; Jensen et al., 2001; Kim et al., 2017; Kuja-Halkola, Lichtenstein, D'Onofrio, & Larsson, 2015). CD in children is also considered a negative outcome of ADHD or ODD with a higher risk for developing antisocial behaviors in adolescence and psychopathic traits in adulthood (Caye, Spadini, et al., 2016; Caye, Swanson, et al., 2016). Rather than comorbidities, overlapping of ADHD, ODD, and CD has raised the hypothesis of the same developmental pattern with different clinical expressions (Kuja-Halkola et al., 2015; Tuvblad, Narusyte, Grann, Sarnecki, & Lichtenstein, 2011).

High rates of comorbidity are also found with internalizing disorders (anxiety and affective disorders). Around 35% of CD children fulfill criteria for these disorders. Around 23% of school-aged children with depression and 15%—18% of patients with anxiety also have the diagnosis of CD (Erskine, Norman, Ferrari, Chan, Copeland, et al., 2016; Loeber, 1994; Wolff & Ollendick, 2006).

In fact, CD subtypes are associated with different comorbidities patterns. Indeed, early-onset persistent (EOP) CD children have higher rates of comorbidities (ADHD, ODD, anxiety, and depression) and the trajectories of comorbidities and social adjustment follow the course of CD: in the CL group, adjustment problems decreased from middle to late childhood whereas prosocial behaviors increased around the same period. Furthermore, the CL group increased in adjustment problems (internalizing as well as externalizing) whereas it decreased in prosocial behaviors after about age 10 years (Barker, Oliver, & Maughan, 2010).

COGNITIVE DIFFICULTIES AND DIFFERENT PATHWAYS OF CONDUCT DISORDERS

The main cognitive functions implicated in CD are deficiencies in verbal learning, memory, and executive functions (Clark, Prior, & Kinsella, 2000; Johnson et al., 2015). These findings are similar to those with ADHD except for deficits in spatial planning, which is more pronounced in individuals with ADHD (Lin & Gau, 2017). One study showed that the childhood-onset group performed worse on the composite measure of auditory verbal learning and memory, whereas the composite measure of executive function, despite being in a low range function, does not seem to differ between ADHD and non-ADHD (Johnson et al., 2015). It is still unclear whether this difference is real or an artifact caused by more frequent association between ADHD and early-onset CD. Deficits in decision making were also noted in youths with CD, with a positive association between the level of impairment in decision making and the severity of antisocial behaviors in children with CD (Fanti, Kimonis, Hadjicharalambous, & Steinberg, 2016; Sonuga-Barke, Cortese, Fairchild, & Stringaris, 2016). Social cognition in CD was also explored. All trajectories of CD (EOP, CL, or adolescence-onset [AO]) have shown deficits in social cognitions in the domains of socioemotional and pragmatic language competences, but deficits were more marked in the EOP group. Despite differences in some cognitive domains, the different subtypes of

CD present similar deficits in cognitive functions that seem more impaired in the EOP type (Oliver, Barker, Mandy, Skuse, & Maughan, 2011).

NEUROPSYCHOLOGICAL, NEUROIMAGING, AND DIFFERENT PATHWAYS OF CONDUCT DISORDERS: SEARCHING FOR BIOMARKERS

Among youths who have CD, those with CU have poorer perfor-mances in neuropsychological tasks that involve an affective dimension of empathy compared with those without CU. Youths with CU have more difficulties in recognizing facial expressions of fear, sadness, or pain, as well as happiness, compared with other youths with CD (Dadds et al., 2006; Marsh & Blair, 2008). However, no difference was observed between youths with and without CU in terms of cognitive dimension of empathy (Blair, 2013). This impairment in recognizing others' emotions has been regarded as a possible reason why these youths are less concerned with victim suffering (Pardini & Byrd, 2012). Functional neuroimaging studies showed that youths with CD with CU have hypoactivation of the amygdala during these facial recognition tasks (Alegria, Radua, & Rubia, 2016). These abnormalities were statistically correlated with the severity of psychopathic traits (Marsh et al., 2013). Some authors proposed that dysfunction of the amygdala may be a possible marker of severity for CD underlying the CU trait.

Another group of patients with CD show a distinct pattern of neuro-psychological and neuroimaging findings. Some youths with CD without the CU trait did not exhibit a deficit in facial recognition but instead heightened sensitivity to an emotional cue related to fear and anger (that has been called a higher threat sensitivity) (Blair, Leibenluft, & Pine, 2014). These youths are more likely to interpret an ambiguous situation as hostile (called hostile attribution bias). It is assumed that these cognitive biases are responsible for reaction aggression in response to frustration or threat, in the same vein as the clinical reactive aggression profile described previously (Frick, Ray, Thornton, & Kahn, 2014). Interestingly, the clinical, psychological, and neuroimaging profiles of these youths were comparable to those of patients with posttraumatic stress disorder. Neuroimaging studies showed that these youths had increased threat-circuit responsiveness compared with others (Crowe & Blair, 2008; Dodge, Pettit, Bates, & Valente, 1995). The role of hyperactivation of the amygdala was hypothesized with regard to its adaptive role in graded responses to threats during development (Yates, 2015) and its putative role in neural substrates underlying the effects of stressful life events on the development of psychopathology (Quinlan et al., 2017).

Preliminary findings supported the possible role of the oxytocin, a neuropeptide with prosocial neurobehavioral effects (Meyer-Lindenberg, Domes, Kirsch, & Heinrichs, 2011), in the expression and natural course of CD. Looking at salivary oxytocin in youth with CD, lower levels were associated with a higher risk for CU traits (Levy et al., 2015). Several polymorphisms or a methylation state of the oxytocin gene was associated with a higher likelihood of exhibiting CU features in youths with CD (Beitchman et al., 2006; Dadds, Moul, Cauchi, Dobson-Stone, Hawes, Brennan, & Ebstein, 2014; Dadds, Moul, Cauchi, Dobson-Stone, Hawes, Brennan, Urwin, et al., 2014). Some genetic variations are associated with a lower circulating level of oxytocin (Dadds, Moul, Cauchi, Dobson-Stone, Hawes, Brennan, & Ebstein, 2014; Feldman et al., 2012). Studies are needed to understand the epigenetics process that could involve methylation of the oxytocin gene and affect the development of the child's affective empathy and risk for psychopathology (Cecil et al., 2014).

INTERPLAY BETWEEN GENETIC AND ENVIRONMENTAL FACTORS AND THE DIFFERENT PATHWAYS TO CONDUCT DISORDERS

Heritability and General Comments

The contribution of genetic factors to the heritability of CD in children and adolescence is estimated to be around 45% (Wesseldijk et al., 2017). However, three considerations should be remembered when considering this number.

First, the genetic contribution is explained by the presence of CU traits rather than the presence of CD *per se*. CU traits, with or without CD, are regarded as highly heritable (with h2g $= 0.67$, according to Hyde et al. (2016)).

Second, several well-replicated studies showed that genetic polymorphisms interact with environmental factors to determine the probabilistic vulnerability to CD (Blair, 2013). One can cite the effect of a polymorphism of the monoamine oxidase allele on the risk of developing CD during adolescence in children who had experienced abuse and emotional neglect (Caspi et al., 2002). Other candidate genes are the dopamine D2 receptor gene (DRD), the promoter of serotonin transporter (5-HTTLPR), and the catechol-O-methyltransferase gene (COMT) (Beitchman et al., 2006; Rujescu, Giegling, Gietl, Hartmann, & Möller, 2003; Zai et al., 2012).

Third, the heritability of antisocial behaviors involves interactive nongenetic factors (such as epigenetic, learned role models and cultural factors) interacting in a nonlinear way during the child's development. This model emphasizes the importance of bidirectional interplay among different levels of analysis (i.e., genetic, biological, behavioral, and environmental). For example, through such mechanisms, high-risk behaviors (e.g., harsh or inconsistent parenting or substance abuse) can amplify inherited vulnerability.

Role of Environmental Factors in Conduct Disorder Pathways

Considering the influences of environmental factors in CD, four sensitive periods can be distinguished: (1) the prenatal period and immediate postpartum period: sensitive for brain development (e.g., owing to abnormal fetal development or the maternal use of toxins); (2) infancy (age 0—2 years): mother—child interactions enable the development of social bonding and secure attachment that constitute the basis of socioemotional development; (3) early and late childhood (age 2—10 years): development and stabilization of an internalized model of socialization; and (4) early and middle adolescence (age 10—15 years): the "socializing" role of antisocial behavior among peers.

- Smoking during pregnancy is a robust risk factor for conduct problems in offspring. It causes poor neonatal health and may have indirect effects on antisocial behavior via effects on neurocognitive functioning, owing to low birth weight (Kramer, 2003) or reduced fetal head growth (Roza et al., 2007).
- Parenting: Harsh discipline (such as corporal punishment, shouting, swearing, and threatening) and inconsistent discipline of children's misbehavior are important risk factors (Kazdin, 2003). A metaanalysis found that the more corporal punishment children experienced, the more aggressive they were and the more they engaged in antisocial behavior in adulthood (Gershoff, 2002). A reciprocal effect of harsh discipline and children's antisocial behaviors was previously theorized by Patterson in the coercive model which provided the basis for most family interventions for antisocial problems (Smith et al., 2014). Lax supervision has a stronger role in late childhood and adolescence than in early childhood; poor parental supervision has an especially important role in AO antisocial behavior.

  Child maltreatment is a risk factor for antisocial behavior in childhood and adolescence (Dodge et al., 1990; Widom, 1989). In line with the bidirectional interplay noted earlier, one can cite the study of Sullivan and Knutson (2000), which found a strong association between maltreatment and disability including behavior disorders.

Decades of studies conducted in high-risk populations observed that children whose parents have a history of depression, antisocial behaviors, and substance use are at elevated risk for antisocial behaviors. There is evidence for a bidirectional relation between maternal depression and child problem behaviors (Kim-Cohen, Moffitt, Taylor, Pawlby, & Caspi, 2005) with a dose–effect relationship, although paternal depression does not have a specific effect. Based on data from the STAR*D trial Weissman et al., 2006 showed that treatment of maternal depression improves the level of children psychopathology after 3 months.

- Peers may also influence each other to engage in antisocial behavior (Keenan, Loeber, Zhang, Stouthamer-Loeber, & van Kammen, 1995). Affiliation with deviant peers has an important role in the development of AO antisocial behaviors (Moffitt, 2005b). However, initially the problem is not "association" with antisocial peers, but rather with "being rejected" by peers. Aggressive children who are rejected are more likely to exhibit diverse and severe conduct problems (Bierman, Smoot, & Aumiller, 1993). Rejection is evident as early as age 6 and predicts later negative outcomes.

- Regarding social factors, children living in disadvantaged neighborhoods experience more stress than do other children, which is associated with heightened aggression in children. Early onset of juvenile aggression occurs mostly in the worst neighborhoods (Sommers & Baskin, 1994). Precarious socioeconomic backgrounds also constitute a risk factor for the development of antisocial behavior. The effect of poverty and unemployment is partially, but not fully, mediated by parental stress that in turn impairs the quality of parenting. The impact of poverty is also related to other sociodemographic variables such as difficulties accessing the health care system and failure in school. Although less common, severe antisocial behaviors can emerge in wealthy families, where it is associated with severe emotional neglect (Stone, 1983).

CONCLUSIONS

Antisocial behaviors that occur in childhood usually cease or diminish; they persist into adulthood in only a minority of cases. Antisocial behaviors occurring in childhood and beginning in adolescence differ largely in term of their natural course. In an AO presentation, conduct problems result less from an enduring temperamental vulnerability than from maladaptive responses when faced with the developmental tasks of adolescence (e.g., to obtain a subjective sense of independence, maturity, and adult status). By contrast, childhood-onset antisocial behaviors reflect global difficulties in displaying efficient emotional and socialization strategies. CU traits are associated with the persistence of such behaviors; indeed, in these youths, socialization processes are severely disturbed whatever the reduction in risk factors or the enhancement of protective factors (e.g., educative intervention).

This chapter presents different criteria that have been used to define subgroups of youths with CD. Different subgroups with distinct pathways were proposed on the basis of clinical, cognitive, neuropsychological, and neuroimaging profiles. Interestingly, findings from these different streams of research converge regarding the importance of distinguishing between those with poor reactivity to emotional and social cues (callous and unemotional traits) and those with an excessive reactivity to emotional cues (i.e., higher threat sensitivity). It is likely that the former group of patients also fit the categories of "proactive aggressive behavior" or "youths with psychopathic traits," whereas the latter are more similar to children diagnosed with "reactive aggressive behavior," "temper tantrums," or "emotional dysregulation." However, this assumption would require further research, and much still needs to be done to understand the relation between these constructs developed by investigators with different perspectives (e.g., psychiatric, developmental psychology, and neurocognition).

In the future, the development of reliable biomarkers that can easily be used in large epidemiological samples would represent an opportunity to better understand the pathways to CD and the possible biological mechanisms involved. Studies of the epigenetic mechanisms in the embedding of childhood adverse effects (e.g., unsynchronized mother–child interaction, stressful life events) affecting the neural developmental basis of affective empathy seem to us to be one of the most exciting fields of child psychiatry.

It is useful to remind ourselves of a simple finding: that the evolution of antisocial behavior primarily depends on the exposure to risk and protective factors that contribute to the maintenance of this behavior (Loeber, Rolf, Burke, & Pardini, 2009). We worry that the efforts of research teams seeking to identify a "pure" subgroup of patients with a homogeneous and stable course of symptoms overshadow the critical role of identifying modifiable environmental risk factors (e.g., maternal depression, substance abuse) and the role of a treatable comorbid disorder. One also regrets the lack of data about protective factors in the research literature. The need for a better understanding of antisocial behavior pathways and the better management of patients with CD is crucial.

LIST OF ABBREVIATIONS

ADHD Attention-deficit hyperactivity disorder
AL Adolescent-limited
CD Conduct disorder
CL Childhood-limited
CU Callous unemotional
LCP Life course–persistent
LPE Limited prosocial emotions
ODD Oppositional defiant disorder

References

Abram, K. M., Teplin, L. A., McClelland, G. M., & Dulcan, M. K. (2003). Comorbid psychiatric disorders in youth in juvenile detention. *Archives of General Psychiatry, 60*(11), 1097–1108. https://doi.org/10.1001/archpsyc.60.11.1097.

Alegria, A. A., Radua, J., & Rubia, K. (2016). Meta-analysis of fMRI studies of disruptive behavior disorders. *American Journal of Psychiatry, 173*(11), 1119–1130. https://doi.org/10.1176/appi.ajp.2016.15081089.

Barker, E. D., & Maughan, B. (2009). Differentiating early-onset persistent versus childhood-limited conduct problem youth. *American Journal of Psychiatry, 166*(8), 900–908. https://doi.org/10.1176/appi.ajp.2009.08121770.

Barker, E. D., Oliver, B. R., & Maughan, B. (2010). Co-occurring problems of early onset persistent, childhood limited, and adolescent onset conduct problem youth: Co-developing adjustment problems. *Journal of Child Psychology and Psychiatry, 51*(11), 1217–1226. https://doi.org/10.1111/j.1469-7610.2010.02240.x.

Beitchman, J. H., Baldassarra, L., Mik, H., De Luca, V., King, N., Bender, D., et al. (2006). Serotonin transporter polymorphisms and persistent, pervasive childhood aggression. *American Journal of Psychiatry, 163*(6), 1103–1105. https://doi.org/10.1176/ajp.2006.163.6.1103.

Bierman, K. L., Smoot, D. L., & Aumiller, K. (1993). Characteristics of aggressive-rejected, aggressive (nonrejected), and rejected (nonaggressive) boys. *Child Development, 64*(1), 139–151.

Black, D. W. (2015). The natural history of antisocial personality disorder. *Canadian Journal of Psychiatry. Revue Canadienne De Psychiatrie, 60*(7), 309–314. https://doi.org/10.1177/070674371506000703.

Black, D. W., Baumgard, C. H., Bell, S. E., & Kao, C. (1996). Death rates in 71 men with antisocial personality disorder. A comparison with general population mortality. *Psychosomatics, 37*(2), 131–136. https://doi.org/10.1016/S0033-3182(96)71579-7.

Blair, R. J. R. (2013). The neurobiology of psychopathic traits in youths. *Nature Reviews Neuroscience, 14*(11), 786–799. https://doi.org/10.1038/nrn3577.

Blair, R. J. R. (2015). Psychopathic traits from an RDoC perspective. *Current Opinion in Neurobiology, 30*, 79–84. https://doi.org/10.1016/j.conb.2014.09.011.

Blair, R. J. R., Leibenluft, E., & Pine, D. S. (2014). Conduct disorder and callous-unemotional traits in youth. *New England Journal of Medicine, 371*(23), 2207–2216. https://doi.org/10.1056/NEJMra1315612.

Brendgen, M., Vitaro, F., Boivin, M., Dionne, G., & Pérusse, D. (2006). Examining genetic and environmental effects on reactive versus proactive aggression. *Developmental Psychology, 42*(6), 1299–1312. https://doi.org/10.1037/0012-1649.42.6.1299.

Caspi, A., McClay, J., Moffitt, T. E., Mill, J., Martin, J., Craig, I. W., et al. (2002). Role of genotype in the cycle of violence in maltreated children. *Science (New York, N.Y.), 297*(5582), 851–854. https://doi.org/10.1126/science.1072290.

Caye, A., Spadini, A. V., Karam, R. G., Grevet, E. H., Rovaris, D. L., Bau, C. H. D., et al. (2016). Predictors of persistence of ADHD into adulthood: A systematic review of the literature and meta-analysis. *European Child & Adolescent Psychiatry, 25*(11), 1151–1159. https://doi.org/10.1007/s00787-016-0831-8.

Caye, A., Swanson, J., Thapar, A., Sibley, M., Arseneault, L., Hechtman, L., & Rohde, L. A. (2016). Life span studies of ADHD-conceptual challenges and predictors of persistence and outcome. *Current Psychiatry Reports, 18*(12), 111. https://doi.org/10.1007/s11920-016-0750-x.

Cecil, C. A., Lysenko, L. J., Jaffee, S. R., Pingault, J.-B., Smith, R. G., Relton, C. L., et al. (2014). Environmental risk, oxytocin receptor gene (OXTR) methylation and youth callous-unemotional traits: A 13-year longitudinal study. *Molecular Psychiatry, 19*(10), 1071–1077. https://doi.org/10.1038/mp.2014.95.

Christian, R. E., Frick, P. J., Hill, N. L., Tyler, L., & Frazer, D. R. (1997). Psychopathy and conduct problems in children: II. Implications for subtyping children with conduct problems. *Journal of the American Academy of Child & Adolescent Psychiatry, 36*(2), 233–241. https://doi.org/10.1097/00004583-199702000-00014.

Ciucci, E., & Baroncelli, A. (2014). Emotion-related personality traits and peer social standing: Unique and interactive effects in cyberbullying behaviors. *Cyberpsychology, Behavior, and Social Networking, 17*(9), 584–590. https://doi.org/10.1089/cyber.2014.0020.

Clark, C., Prior, M., & Kinsella, G. J. (2000). Do executive function deficits differentiate between adolescents with ADHD and oppositional defiant/conduct disorder? A neuropsychological study using the six elements test and Hayling sentence completion test. *Journal of Abnormal Child Psychology, 28*(5), 403–414.

Costello, E. J., Mustillo, S., Erkanli, A., Keeler, G., & Angold, A. (2003). Prevalence and development of psychiatric disorders in childhood and adolescence. *Archives of General Psychiatry, 60*(8), 837. https://doi.org/10.1001/archpsyc.60.8.837.

Crowe, S. L., & Blair, R. J. R. (2008). The development of antisocial behavior: What can we learn from functional neuroimaging studies? *Development and Psychopathology, 20*(4), 1145–1159. https://doi.org/10.1017/S0954579408000540.

Dadds, M. R., Moul, C., Cauchi, A., Dobson-Stone, C., Hawes, D. J., Brennan, J., & Ebstein, R. E. (2014). Methylation of the oxytocin receptor gene and oxytocin blood levels in the development of psychopathy. *Development and Psychopathology, 26*(1), 33–40. https://doi.org/10.1017/S0954579413000497.

Dadds, M. R., Moul, C., Cauchi, A., Dobson-Stone, C., Hawes, D. J., Brennan, J., et al. (2014). Polymorphisms in the oxytocin receptor gene are associated with the development of psychopathy. *Development and Psychopathology, 26*(1), 21–31. https://doi.org/10.1017/S0954579413000485.

Dadds, M. R., Perry, Y., Hawes, D. J., Merz, S., Riddell, A. C., Haines, D. J., et al. (2006). Attention to the eyes and fear-recognition deficits in child psychopathy. *The British Journal of Psychiatry, 189*, 280–281. https://doi.org/10.1192/bjp.bp.105.018150.

Dandreaux, D. M., & Frick, P. J. (2009). Developmental pathways to conduct problems: A further test of the childhood and adolescent-onset distinction. *Journal of Abnormal Child Psychology, 37*(3), 375–385. https://doi.org/10.1007/s10802-008-9261-5.

Diagnostic and statistical manual of mental disorders (5th ed.). (2013). Paris: American Psychiatric Association. Elservier-Masson.

Dodge, K. A., Bates, J. E., & Pettit, G. S. (1990). Mechanisms in the cycle of violence. *Science (New York, N.Y.), 250*(4988), 1678–1683.

Dodge, K. A., Pettit, G. S., Bates, J. E., & Valente, E. (1995). Social information-processing patterns partially mediate the effect of early physical abuse on later conduct problems. *Journal of Abnormal Psychology, 104*(4), 632–643.

Ehrenberg, A. (2006). Malaise dans l'évaluation de la santé mentale. *Esprit, Mai, 89*(5). https://doi.org/10.3917/espri.0605.0089.

Erskine, H. E., Norman, R. E., Ferrari, A. J., Chan, G. C. K., Copeland, W. E., Whiteford, H. A., & Scott, J. G. (2016). Long-term outcomes of attention-Deficit/Hyperactivity disorder and conduct disorder: A systematic review and meta-analysis. *Journal of the American Academy of Child and Adolescent Psychiatry, 55*(10), 841–850. https://doi.org/10.1016/j.jaac.2016.06.016.

Fanti, K. A., Kimonis, E. R., Hadjicharalambous, M.-Z., & Steinberg, L. (2016). Do neurocognitive deficits in decision making differentiate conduct disorder subtypes? *European Child & Adolescent Psychiatry, 25*(9), 989–996. https://doi.org/10.1007/s00787-016-0822-9.

Feldman, R., Zagoory-Sharon, O., Weisman, O., Schneiderman, I., Gordon, I., Maoz, R., et al. (2012). Sensitive parenting is associated with plasma oxytocin and polymorphisms in the OXTR and CD38 genes. *Biological Psychiatry, 72*(3), 175–181. https://doi.org/10.1016/j.biopsych.2011.12.025.

Frick, P. J., & Morris, A. S. (2004). Temperament and developmental pathways to conduct problems. *Journal of Clinical Child and Adolescent Psychology, 33*(1), 54–68. https://doi.org/10.1207/S15374424JCCP3301_6.

Frick, P. J., Ray, J. V., Thornton, L. C., & Kahn, R. E. (2014). Can callous-unemotional traits enhance the understanding, diagnosis, and treatment of serious conduct problems in children and adolescents? A comprehensive review. *Psychological Bulletin, 140*(1), 1–57. https://doi.org/10.1037/a0033076.

Gershoff, E. T. (2002). Corporal punishment by parents and associated child behaviors and experiences: A meta-analytic and theoretical review. *Psychological Bulletin, 128*(4), 539–579.

Goldstein, R. B., Grant, B. F., Ruan, W. J., Smith, S. M., & Saha, T. D. (2006). Antisocial personality disorder with childhood- vs. adolescence-onset conduct disorder: Results from the National epidemiologic Survey on Alcohol and related Conditions. *The Journal of Nervous and Mental Disease, 194*(9), 667–675. https://doi.org/10.1097/01.nmd.0000235762.82264.a1.

Hubbard, J. A., McAuliffe, M. D., Morrow, M. T., & Romano, L. J. (2010). Reactive and proactive aggression in childhood and Adolescence: Precursors, outcomes, processes, experiences, and measurement. *Journal of Personality, 78*(1), 95–118. https://doi.org/10.1111/j.1467-6494.2009.00610.x.

Hyde, L. W., Waller, R., Trentacosta, C. J., Shaw, D. S., Neiderhiser, J. M., Ganiban, J. M., et al. (2016). Heritable and nonheritable pathways to early callous-unemotional behaviors. *American Journal of Psychiatry, 173*(9), 903–910. https://doi.org/10.1176/appi.ajp.2016.15111381.

Institut national de la santé et de la recherche médicale (France). (2006). *Troubles des conduites: chez l'enfant et l'adolescent.* Paris: INSERM.

Jensen, P. S., Hinshaw, S. P., Kraemer, H. C., Lenora, N., Newcorn, J. H., Abikoff, H. B., et al. (2001). ADHD comorbidity findings from the MTA study: Comparing comorbid subgroups. *Journal of the American Academy of Child & Adolescent Psychiatry, 40*(2), 147–158. https://doi.org/10.1097/00004583-200102000-00009.

Johnson, V. A., Kemp, A. H., Heard, R., Lennings, C. J., & Hickie, I. B. (2015). Childhood- versus adolescent-onset antisocial youth with conduct disorder: Psychiatric illness, neuropsychological and psychosocial function. *PLos One, 10*(4), e0121627. https://doi.org/10.1371/journal.pone.0121627.

Kahn, R. E., Frick, P. J., Youngstrom, E., Findling, R. L., & Youngstrom, J. K. (2012). The effects of including a callous-unemotional specifier for the diagnosis of conduct disorder. *Journal of Child Psychology and Psychiatry, and Allied Disciplines, 53*(3), 271–282. https://doi.org/10.1111/j.1469-7610.2011.02463.x.

Kazdin, A. E. (2003). Antisocial behavior in children and adolescents: A developmental analysis and model for intervention. *American Journal of Psychiatry, 160*(4), 805. https://doi.org/10.1176/appi.ajp.160.4.805.

Keenan, K., Loeber, R., Zhang, Q., Stouthamer-Loeber, M., & van Kammen, W. B. (1995). The influence of deviant peers on the development of boys' disruptive and delinquent behavior: A temporal analysis. *Development and Psychopathology, 7*(04), 715. https://doi.org/10.1017/S0954579400006805.

Kempes, M., Matthys, W., de Vries, H., & van Engeland, H. (2005). Reactive and proactive aggression in children—a review of theory, findings and the relevance for child and adolescent psychiatry. *European Child & Adolescent Psychiatry, 14*(1), 11—19. https://doi.org/10.1007/s00787-005-0432-4.

Kessler, R. C., Avenevoli, S., Costello, E. J., Georgiades, K., Green, J. G., Gruber, M. J., et al. (2012). Prevalence, persistence, and sociodemographic correlates of DSM-iv disorders in the National comorbidity survey replication adolescent supplement. *Archives of General Psychiatry, 69*(4), 372—380. https://doi.org/10.1001/archgenpsychiatry.2011.160.

Kim-Cohen, J., Moffitt, T. E., Taylor, A., Pawlby, S. J., & Caspi, A. (2005). Maternal depression and children's antisocial behavior: Nature and nurture effects. *Archives of General Psychiatry, 62*(2), 173—181. https://doi.org/10.1001/archpsyc.62.2.173.

Kim, J. I., Kim, B., Kim, B.-N., Hong, S.-B., Lee, D. W., Chung, J.-Y., et al. (2017). Prevalence of psychiatric disorders, comorbidity patterns, and repeat offending among male juvenile detainees in South Korea: A cross-sectional study. *Child and Adolescent Psychiatry and Mental Health, 11*(6). https://doi.org/10.1186/s13034-017-0143-x.

Kramer, M. S. (2003). The epidemiology of adverse pregnancy outcomes: An overview. *Journal of Nutrition, 133*(5 Suppl. 2), 1592S—1596S.

Kuja-Halkola, R., Lichtenstein, P., D'Onofrio, B. M., & Larsson, H. (2015). Codevelopment of ADHD and externalizing behavior from childhood to adulthood. *Journal of Child Psychology and Psychiatry, and Allied Disciplines, 56*(6), 640—647. https://doi.org/10.1111/jcpp.12340.

Lenoble, E., Malika, B.-B., Sandrine, C., & Forget, J.-M. (March 23, 2006). *L'Inserm sème le trouble. Le Monde.*

Levy, T., Bloch, Y., Bar-Maisels, M., Gat-Yablonski, G., Djalovski, A., Borodkin, K., & Apter, A. (2015). Salivary oxytocin in adolescents with conduct problems and callous-unemotional traits. *European Child & Adolescent Psychiatry, 24*(12), 1543—1551. https://doi.org/10.1007/s00787-015-0765-6.

Lin, Y.-J., & Gau, S. S.-F. (2017). Differential neuropsychological functioning between adolescents with attention-deficit/hyperactivity disorder with and without conduct disorder. *Journal of the Formosan Medical Association.* https://doi.org/10.1016/j.jfma.2017.02.009.

Loeber, R., Burke, J., & Pardini, D. A. (2009). Perspectives on oppositional defiant disorder, conduct disorder, and psychopathic features. *Journal of Child Psychology and Psychiatry, and Allied Disciplines, 50*(1—2), 133—142. https://doi.org/10.1111/j.1469-7610.2008.02011.x.

Loeber, R. (1994). Interaction between conduct disorder and its comorbid conditions: Effects of age and gender. *Clinical Psychology Review, 14*(6), 497—523. https://doi.org/10.1016/0272-7358(94)90015-9.

Longman, T., Hawes, D. J., & Kohlhoff, J. (2016). Callous-unemotional traits as markers for conduct problem severity in early childhood: A meta-analysis. *Child Psychiatry and Human Development, 47*(2), 326—334. https://doi.org/10.1007/s10578-015-0564-9.

Marsh, A. A., & Blair, R. J. R. (2008). Deficits in facial affect recognition among antisocial populations: A meta-analysis. *Neuroscience & Biobehavioral Reviews, 32*(3), 454—465. https://doi.org/10.1016/j.neubiorev.2007.08.003.

Marsh, A. A., Finger, E. C., Fowler, K. A., Adalio, C. J., Jurkowitz, I. T. N., Schechter, J. C., et al. (2013). Empathic responsiveness in amygdala and anterior cingulate cortex in youths with psychopathic traits. *Journal of Child Psychology and Psychiatry, and Allied Disciplines, 54*(8), 900—910. https://doi.org/10.1111/jcpp.12063.

Meyer-Lindenberg, A., Domes, G., Kirsch, P., & Heinrichs, M. (2011). Oxytocin and vasopressin in the human brain: Social neuropeptides for translational medicine. *Nature Reviews Neuroscience, 12*(9), 524–538. https://doi.org/10.1038/nrn3044.

Moffitt, T. E. (1993). Adolescence-limited and life-course-persistent antisocial behavior: A developmental taxonomy. *Psychological Review, 100*(4), 674–701.

Moffitt, T. E. (2005b). The new look of behavioral genetics in developmental psychopathology: Gene-environment interplay in antisocial behaviors. *Psychological Bulletin, 131*(4), 533–554. https://doi.org/10.1037/0033-2909.131.4.533.

Moore, A. A., Silberg, J. L., Roberson-Nay, R., & Mezuk, B. (2017). Life course persistent and adolescence limited conduct disorder in a nationally representative us sample: Prevalence, predictors, and outcomes. *Social Psychiatry and Psychiatric Epidemiology, 52*(4), 435–443. https://doi.org/10.1007/s00127-017-1337-5.

National Collaborating Centre for Mental Health (UK), & Social Care Institute for Excellence (UK). (2013). Antisocial behaviour and conduct disorders in children and young People: Recognition, intervention and management. *Leicester (UK): British Psychological Society.* Retrieved from http://www.ncbi.nlm.nih.gov/books/NBK299074/.

Nau, J.-Y. (2005). Conduct disorder in children and adolescents: what is the role of medicine? *Revue Medicale Suisse, 1*(35), 2296.

Oliver, B. R., Barker, E. D., Mandy, W. P. L., Skuse, D. H., & Maughan, B. (2011). Social cognition and conduct problems: A developmental approach. *Journal of the American Academy of Child and Adolescent Psychiatry, 50*(4), 385–394. https://doi.org/10.1016/j.jaac.2011.01.006.

Organisation Mondiale de la Santé. (1993). *Classification Internationale des Maladies, 10ème édition (CIM-10).* Paris: Masson.

Pardini, D. A., & Byrd, A. L. (2012). Perceptions of aggressive conflicts and others' distress in children with callous-unemotional traits: "I'll show you who's boss, even if you suffer and I get in trouble." *Journal of Child Psychology and Psychiatry, and Allied Disciplines, 53*(3), 283–291. https://doi.org/10.1111/j.1469-7610.2011.02487.x.

Pardini, D. A., Lochman, J. E., & Powell, N. (2007). The development of callous-unemotional traits and antisocial behavior in children: Are there shared and/or unique predictors? *Journal of Clinical Child and Adolescent Psychology, 36*(3), 319–333. https://doi.org/10.1080/15374410701444215.

Quinlan, E. B., Cattrell, A., Jia, T., Artiges, E., Banaschewski, T., Barker, G., et al. (2017). Psychosocial stress and brain function in adolescent psychopathology. *American Journal of Psychiatry.* https://doi.org/10.1176/appi.ajp.2017.16040464.

Robins, L. N. (1966). *Deviant children grown up.* Baltimore: Williams and Wilkins.

Rowe, R., Costello, E. J., Angold, A., Copeland, W. E., & Maughan, B. (2010). Developmental pathways in oppositional defiant disorder and conduct disorder. *Journal of Abnormal Psychology, 119*(4), 726–738. https://doi.org/10.1037/a0020798.

Rowe, R., Maughan, B., Moran, P., Ford, T., Briskman, J., & Goodman, R. (2010). The role of callous and unemotional traits in the diagnosis of conduct disorder. *Journal of Child Psychology and Psychiatry, and Allied Disciplines, 51*(6), 688–695. https://doi.org/10.1111/j.1469-7610.2009.02199.x.

Roza, S. J., Verburg, B. O., Jaddoe, V. W. V., Hofman, A., Mackenbach, J. P., Steegers, E. A. P., et al. (2007). Effects of maternal smoking in pregnancy on prenatal brain development. The generation R study. *European Journal of Neuroscience, 25*(3), 611–617. https://doi.org/10.1111/j.1460-9568.2007.05393.x.

Rujescu, D., Giegling, I., Gietl, A., Hartmann, A. M., & Möller, H.-J. (2003). A functional single nucleotide polymorphism (V158M) in the COMT gene is associated with aggressive personality traits. *Biological Psychiatry, 54*(1), 34–39.

Silberg, J., Moore, A. A., & Rutter, M. (2015). Age of onset and the subclassification of conduct/dissocial disorder. *Journal of Child Psychology and Psychiatry, and Allied Disciplines, 56*(7), 826–833. https://doi.org/10.1111/jcpp.12353.

Smith, J. D., Dishion, T. J., Shaw, D. S., Wilson, M. N., Winter, C. C., & Patterson, G. R. (2014). Coercive family process and early-onset conduct problems from age 2 to school entry. *Development and Psychopathology, 26*(4 Pt 1), 917–932. https://doi.org/10.1017/S0954579414000169.

Sommers, I., & Baskin, D. R. (1994). Factors related to female adolescent initiation into violent street crime. *Youth & Society, 25*(4), 468–489. https://doi.org/10.1177/0044118X94025004003.

Sonuga-Barke, E. J. S., Cortese, S., Fairchild, G., & Stringaris, A. (2016). Annual Research Review: Transdiagnostic neuroscience of child and adolescent mental disorders — differentiating decision making in attention-deficit/hyperactivity disorder, conduct disorder, depression, and anxiety. *Journal of Child Psychology and Psychiatry, 57*(3), 321–349. https://doi.org/10.1111/jcpp.12496.

Stone, M. H. (1983). Special problems in borderline adolescents from wealthy families. *Adolescent Psychiatry, 11*, 163–176.

Stringaris, A., & Goodman, R. (2009). Longitudinal outcome of youth oppositionality: Irritable, headstrong, and hurtful behaviors have distinctive predictions. *Journal of the American Academy of Child & Adolescent Psychiatry, 48*(4), 404–412. https://doi.org/10.1097/CHI.0b013e3181984f30.

Sullivan, P. M., & Knutson, J. F. (2000). Maltreatment and disabilities: A population-based epidemiological study. *Child Abuse & Neglect, 24*(10), 1257–1273.

Tremblay, R. E. (2002). Development of physical aggression from early childhood to adulthood. In R. E. Tremblay, R. G. Barr, & RdeV. Peters (Eds.), *Encyclopedia on Early Childhood Development*. Montreal, Quebec: Centre of Excellence for Early Childhood Development (pp. 1–6). Available at: www.excellence-earlychildhood.ca/documents/TremblayANGxp.pdf.

Tremblay, R. E., Mâsse, L. C., Vitaro, F., & Dobkin, P. L. (1995). The impact of friends' deviant behavior on early onset of delinquency: Longitudinal data from 6 to 13 years of age. *Development and Psychopathology, 7*(04), 649. https://doi.org/10.1017/S0954579400006763.

Tuvblad, C., Narusyte, J., Grann, M., Sarnecki, J., & Lichtenstein, P. (2011). The genetic and environmental etiology of antisocial behavior from childhood to emerging adulthood. *Behavior Genetics, 41*(5), 629–640. https://doi.org/10.1007/s10519-011-9463-4.

Vitaro, F., Brendgen, M., & Tremblay, R. E. (2002). Reactively and proactively aggressive children: Antecedent and subsequent characteristics. *Journal of Child Psychology and Psychiatry, and Allied Disciplines, 43*(4), 495–505.

Vitaro, F., Gendreau, P. L., Tremblay, R. E., & Oligny, P. (1998). Reactive and proactive aggression differentially predict later conduct problems. *Journal of Child Psychology and Psychiatry, and Allied Disciplines, 39*(3), 377–385.

Weissman, M. M., Pilowsky, D. J., Wickramaratne, P. J., Talati, A., Wisniewski, S. R., Fava, M., et al. (2006). Remissions in maternal depression and child psychopathology: A STAR*D-child report. *JAMA, 295*(12), 1389–1398. https://doi.org/10.1001/jama.295.12.1389.

Wesseldijk, L. W., Bartels, M., Vink, J. M., van Beijsterveldt, C. E. M., Ligthart, L., Boomsma, D. I., & Middeldorp, C. M. (2017). Genetic and environmental influences on conduct and antisocial personality problems in childhood, adolescence, and adulthood. *European Child & Adolescent Psychiatry.* https://doi.org/10.1007/s00787-017-1014-y.

Widom, C. S. (1989). The cycle of violence. *Science (New York, N.Y.), 244*(4901), 160–166.

Wolff, J. C., & Ollendick, T. H. (2006). The comorbidity of conduct problems and depression in childhood and adolescence. *Clinical Child and Family Psychology Review, 9*(3–4), 201–220. https://doi.org/10.1007/s10567-006-0011-3.

Yates, D. (2015). Neural circuits: A nucleus of fear. *Nature Reviews Neuroscience, 16*(3), 121. https://doi.org/10.1038/nrn3932.

Zai, C. C., Ehtesham, S., Choi, E., Nowrouzi, B., de Luca, V., Stankovich, L., et al. (2012). Dopaminergic system genes in childhood aggression: Possible role for DRD2. *World Journal of Biological Psychiatry, 13*(1), 65–74. https://doi.org/10.3109/15622975.2010.543431.

Further Reading

Amodio, D. M., & Frith, C. D. (2006). Meeting of minds: The medial frontal cortex and social cognition. *Nature Reviews Neuroscience, 7*(4), 268−277. https://doi.org/10.1038/nrn1884.

Blair, R. J. R. (2007). The amygdala and ventromedial prefrontal cortex in morality and psychopathy. *Trends in Cognitive Sciences, 11*(9), 387−392. https://doi.org/10.1016/j.tics.2007.07.003.

Classification Internationale des Maladies (CIM10) (10ème ed.). (1993). Paris: Masson.

Decety, J. (2011). The neuroevolution of empathy. *Annals of the New York Academy of Sciences, 1231*, 35−45. https://doi.org/10.1111/j.1749-6632.2011.06027.x.

Decety, J., & Cowell, J. M. (2014). Friends or Foes: Is empathy necessary for moral behavior? *Perspectives on Psychological Science, 9*(5), 525−537. https://doi.org/10.1177/1745691614545130.

Decety, J., Meidenbauer, K. L., & Cowell, J. M. (2017). The development of cognitive empathy and concern in preschool children: A behavioral neuroscience investigation. *Developmental Science*.

Imuta, K., Henry, J. D., Slaughter, V., Selcuk, B., & Ruffman, T. (2016). Theory of mind and prosocial behavior in childhood: A meta-analytic review. *Developmental Psychology, 52*(8), 1192−1205. https://doi.org/10.1037/dev0000140.

Jambroes, T., Jansen, L. M. C., Vermeiren, R. R. J. M., Doreleijers, T. A. H., Colins, O. F., & Popma, A. (2016). The clinical usefulness of the new LPE specifier for subtyping adolescents with conduct disorder in the DSM 5. *European Child & Adolescent Psychiatry, 25*(8), 891−902. https://doi.org/10.1007/s00787-015-0812-3.

Jeon, D., Kim, S., Chetana, M., Jo, D., Ruley, H. E., Lin, S.-Y., et al. (2010). Observational fear learning involves affective pain system and Cav1.2 Ca^{2+} channels in ACC. *Nature Neuroscience, 13*(4), 482−488. https://doi.org/10.1038/nn.2504.

Meaney, M. J. (2001). Maternal care, gene expression, and the transmission of individual differences in stress reactivity across generations. *Annual Review of Neuroscience, 24*, 1161−1192. https://doi.org/10.1146/annurev.neuro.24.1.1161.

Moffitt, T. E. (2005a). Genetic and environmental influences on antisocial behaviors: Evidence from behavioral-genetic research. *Advances in Genetics, 55*, 41−104. https://doi.org/10.1016/S0065-2660(05)55003-X.

Rogers, J. C., & De Brito, S. A. (2016). Cortical and subcortical gray matter volume in youths with conduct problems: A meta-analysis. *JAMA Psychiatry, 73*(1), 64−72. https://doi.org/10.1001/jamapsychiatry.2015.2423.

Silberg, J. L., Maes, H., & Eaves, L. J. (2010). Genetic and environmental influences on the transmission of parental depression to children's depression and conduct disturbance: An extended children of twins study: Genetic and environmental influences on the transmission of parental depression. *Journal of Child Psychology and Psychiatry, 51*(6), 734−744. https://doi.org/10.1111/j.1469-7610.2010.02205.x.

Stepp, S. D., Burke, J. D., Hipwell, A. E., & Loeber, R. (2012). Trajectories of attention deficit hyperactivity disorder and oppositional defiant disorder symptoms as precursors of borderline personality disorder symptoms in adolescent girls. *Journal of Abnormal Child Psychology, 40*(1), 7−20. https://doi.org/10.1007/s10802-011-9530-6.

Waschbusch, D. A., Carrey, N. J., Willoughby, M. T., King, S., & Andrade, B. F. (2007). Effects of methylphenidate and behavior modification on the social and academic behavior of children with disruptive behavior disorders: The moderating role of callous/unemotional traits. *Journal of Clinical Child and Adolescent Psychology, 36*(4), 629−644. https://doi.org/10.1080/15374410701662766.

Whittinger, N. S., Langley, K., Fowler, T. A., Thomas, H. V., & Thapar, A. (2007). Clinical precursors of adolescent conduct disorder in children with attention-deficit/hyperactivity disorder. *Journal of the American Academy of Child & Adolescent Psychiatry, 46*(2), 179−187. https://doi.org/10.1097/01.chi.0000246066.00825.53.

Wootton, J. M., Frick, P. J., Shelton, K. K., & Silverthorn, P. (1997). Ineffective parenting and childhood conduct problems: The moderating role of callous-unemotional traits. *Journal of Consulting and Clinical Psychology, 65*(2), 301−308.

2

Developmental Considerations in Bipolar Disorder

*Michal Goetz[1], Marketa Mohaplova[1,3],
Antonin Sebela[2,3], Tomas Novak[2,4]*

[1] Charles University Second Faculty of Medicine, Prague, Czech Republic;
[2] National Institute of Mental Health, Klecany, Czech Republic; [3] Charles
University First Faculty of Medicine, Prague, Czech Republic; [4] Charles
University Third Faculty of Medicine, Prague, Czech Republic

INTRODUCTION

Bipolar disorder (BP) is a common, clinically heterogeneous, lifelong illness that often clusters in families, and, as described by Carlson, its diagnosis has generated one of the greatest controversies in child psychiatry in the last two decades (Carlson & Klein, 2014; Parry, Allison, & Bastiampillai, 2014). A steep increase in the reported frequency of BP diagnosis in the USA pediatric population (Blader & Carlson, 2007; Moreno et al., 2007) caused by shifts in the conceptualization of mania has led to much needed research not only because its diagnosis has serious implications, and its treatment has numerous side effects but also because the European prevalence figures do not match this trend (James et al., 2014; Parry, Allison, & Bastiampillai, 2017).

In this chapter, we review current findings on the development of BP, as well as salient risk factors, prodromal conditions, and neuropsychological features associated with BP in youth, and different perspectives on the concept of BP.

*Understanding Uniqueness and Diversity in Child and
Adolescent Mental Health*
https://doi.org/10.1016/B978-0-12-815310-9.00002-2

25

DIAGNOSTIC CRITERIA: DIFFERENCES BETWEEN DIAGNOSTIC AND STATISTICAL MANUAL OF MENTAL DISORDERS AND INTERNATIONAL STATISTICAL CLASSIFICATION OF DISEASES AND RELATED HEALTH PROBLEMS

The two major diagnostic systems used, the International Statistical Classification of Diseases and Related Health Problems (ICD) and the *Diagnostic and Statistical Manual of Mental Disorders* (DSM), differ in several important respects regarding how they describe BP.

Whereas in the 10th revision of the ICD (ICD-10) (World Health Organization, 1992) BP is included in the group of affective disorders, it forms a separate chapter in the DSM, Fifth Edition (DSM-5) "Bipolar and Related Disorders," which is located between schizophrenia and depression. This change reflects overlap in genetics, symptoms, and risks among these three groups of disorders (Rasic, Hajek, Alda, & Uher, 2014). DSM-5 recognizes a spectrum of BPs composed of bipolar I and II disorders (BP I and II) and cyclothymia (American Psychiatric Association, 2013). The ICD-10 does not make such an explicit distinction among subtypes. Furthermore, bipolar syndrome appears in several chapters in the ICD-10 classification according to associated etiological factors (organic mood disorders and behavioral disorders resulting from the use of psychoactive substances), whereas the DSM "Bipolar and Related Disorders" category also includes BP caused by another medical condition, including manic symptoms resulting from medication. The switch from depression to hypomania associated with antidepressant therapy is no longer considered to be an exclusion criterion for bipolar II disorder in DSM-5 (Angst, 2013). On the contrary, it became an explicit criterion for this subtype of BP.

To qualify for the diagnosis of BP according to DSM-5, a single episode of mania or a single episode of hypomania plus a single episode of depression is required (Severus & Bauer, 2013); in ICD-10, on the other hand, a patient has to experience two discrete mood episodes, at least one of which must be manic (World Health Organization, 1992).

The shift from DSM-IV (American Psychiatric Association, 2000) to DSM-5 brought more strict criteria for a manic episode. The threshold for a diagnosis of mania is now higher in DSM-5 than in ICD-10. Whereas DSM-IV required for a diagnosis only the presence of a distinct period of abnormally and persistently elevated, expansive, or irritable mood, in DSM-5, the mood change must be accompanied by persistently increased (goal-directed) activity or energy. This change was criticized by some as not based on data (Angst, 2013), but it was welcomed by others because it might decrease the risk for a false-positive diagnosis, mainly in young people (Moreno et al., 2007; Severus & Bauer, 2013).

In the DSM-IV, the patient's clinically relevant BP symptoms that do not meet full criteria for any BP subtype are diagnosed as bipolar disorder not otherwise specified (BP-NOS) (a more detailed review is provided subsequently on BP-NOS). This category was replaced in DSM-5 with more concretely defined category: BP Other Specified (American Psychiatric Association, 2013). It is reserved for patients with a history of major depressive disorder (MDD) who experienced two or more fully symptomatic hypomanic episodes lasting only 2−3 days, or experienced 4-day episodes that do not meet fully symptomatic criteria; or patients without a history of MDD who experienced hypomanic episodes, and those who meet criteria for cyclothymia but less than 24 months.

AGE AT ONSET OF BIPOLAR DISORDER

Numerous studies agree that BP often begins in adolescence, typically between age 15 and 19 years (Larsson et al., 2010; Lewinsohn, Seeley, & Klein, 2003; Oedegaard, Syrstad, Morken, Akiskal, & Fasmer, 2009). The definition of the age at onset (AAO) of BP differs across studies (e.g., first treatment, first hospitalization, first mood episode, first mania) (Carlson & Pataki, 2016). In longitudinal high-risk offspring studies, because of the prospective observation of the cohort from childhood, the first mood episodes could be detected. However, although there is agreement across studies that depressive episodes may occur before puberty, the AAO of the first hypo/mania remains a matter of debate. In a Dutch study of 107 offspring of parents with BP who were observed for more than 12 years, the average AAO of the first mood episode was 14.6 years (range, 8.6−23.7 years) (Mesman, Nolen, Reichart, Wals, & Hillegers, 2013). A third of the offspring at risk experienced the first depressive episode before age 12 years, but the prepubertal onset of hypomanic or manic episodes was not observed. Average age at the time of the first manic episode was 19.4 years (Mesman et al., 2013). Similarly, in a Canadian study, hypomanic episodes did not occur before age 12.5 years (mean age of BP I onset was 19.9 years, and BP II was 20.4 years) (Goodday et al., 2017). Contrary to both of these studies, the AAO was much lower in a large study of 391 children and adolescents with risk for BP (aged 6−18 years) from Pittsburgh (Bipolar Offspring Study [BIOS]) (Birmaher, Axelson, Monk, et al., 2009; Birmaher et al., 2010). In the BIOS, the mean AAO was 13.4 years for mania/hypomania and 12.1 years for bipolar spectrum. In one-third of offspring, a full manic episode was diagnosed before age 10 years, and in more than half, before age 12 years; the earliest was at age 8 years. The average AAO of the first MDD episode was 13.7 and 12.5 years for any depressive episode

(Axelson et al., 2015). The BIOS cohort differed from the samples of studies cited previously, with a high comorbidity of nonaffective disorders (anxiety disorders, 40%; attention-deficit hyperactivity disorder (ADHD), 31%; disruptive disorders, 27%; oppositional defiant disorder (ODD), 25%); and higher psychiatric morbidity among other biological parents (coparents). Furthermore, unlike the Dutch and Canadian studies, which were scored by clinicians, symptoms during the clinical interviews were scored by trained raters (Duffy, Grof, Hajek, & Alda, 2010; Mesman et al., 2016).

DEVELOPMENT OF BIPOLAR DISORDER

Full development of BP may take several years, and the first mental difficulties preceding the onset of BP may not belong to the affective spectrum (Kim-Cohen et al., 2003). Instead, non-mood symptoms such as anxiety, sleep impairment, or a conduct problem may dominate the clinical picture. Mood symptoms may gradually emerge and increase in frequency and severity with age (Duffy et al., 2014). In most patients, the first mood episodes are depressive, and there may be several of these episodes before the first manic episode occurs. Longitudinal studies of offspring of bipolar parents have shown that the developmental path of the disorder may reflect the genetic background in the family (Duffy, Alda, Kutcher, Fusee, & Grof, 1998; Duffy et al., 2014). Psychiatrically ill children of lithium-responsive parents tended to have affective disorders that remitted and followed a recurrent course. In contrast, psychiatrically ill offspring of lithium-nonresponsive parents manifested a broad range of psychopathology, had high rates of comorbid illnesses, and experienced non-remitting affective diseases (Duffy et al., 1998).

Early hypomanic symptoms and episodes may not interfere with functioning and are usually not a reason to seek treatment; in adolescence, their distinction from developmentally normal mood changes can be difficult (Angst et al., 2003a). According to Thomsen, the clinical picture of BP with a very early onset is kaleidoscopic (Thomsen, Møller, Dehlholm, & Brask, 1992). Rapid cycling, mixed episodes, and frequent comorbidity are common, which makes a differential diagnosis more complicated than it is in adults (Holtzman et al., 2015). The correct diagnosis and appropriate treatment are not usually determined and initiated until years after the first mood episodes occur (Egeland, Blumenthal, Nee, Sharpe, & Endicott, 1987; Leverich et al., 2007). The consequences of not treating BP are more frequent and more severe episodes, rapid cycling, higher risk for substance abuse and suicide, and worse responses to treatment (Keck, Kessler, & Ross, 2008; Post et al., 2010).

CLINICAL COURSE OF BIPOLAR DISORDERS

Although Kraepelin postulated recurrence as the central aspect of manic-depressive illness, for a long time the clinical course was insufficiently studied and is not yet completely understood. In 2002, Judd et al. published the first longitudinal naturalistic observation of patients with BP I (n = 146; 14-year follow-up) and found that patients spent almost half of the time (47%) in morbid states despite treatment (Judd et al., 2002). Forte et al. (2015) reviewed 15 prospective studies composed of nearly 4000 patients with bipolar disorder (70% with BP I) who were observed for 8 years on average (range, 1—19 years), with similar findings. Even if they were treated, the overall time patients spent being ill, mainly depressed, was considerable (45%; range, 25%—64%) (Forte et al., 2015). Besides the time spent in a morbid state, the recurrence rate was also substantial. Vázquez, Holtzman, Lolich, Ketter, and Baldessarini (2015) compared the incidence of new episodes up to 2 years in different types of studies, and reported the recurrence rate of 26% per year in naturalistic studies, 22% in the treatment arm of randomized clinical trials (RCTs), and 31% in the placebo arm of RCTs (Vázquez et al., 2015). The last example might be used as a hint of the natural course of illness.

Addressing the developmental perspective, a younger AAO is considered to be a risk factor for both higher morbidity and a higher recurrence rate. However, not all studies support this assumption. For instance, although Baldessarini et al. (2012) found a poorer functional outcome in subgroup of patients with BP I with onset in adolescence, compared with those with adult onset, in a large pooled sample (n = 1665; 28% with adolescent onset; 15-year follow-up), symptomatic morbidity was comparable (episodes per year, percentage of months ill, comorbidity, hospitalization, and suicide attempts) (Baldessarini et al., 2012).

Generally speaking, the bipolar course is heterogeneous (Lader, 1968) as a result of the interplay of neurobiological and psychosocial factors and complex interactions. The resulting trajectory is variable, and the course may show episodic, chronic, or fluctuating forms, depending on the type of BP, the family history, comorbidities, and early development.

RISK FACTORS

A risk factor is a variable whose presence increases the probability of the person developing the disorder but is not part of its clinical features. The boundary between a risk factor and the clinical prodrome is not always clear. Behavioral disorders, for example, are a risk factor for BP, but they can also be labeled prodromal if they occur as part of the development of an abnormal mood.

We summarize some clinical manifestations and categories that are most commonly discussed as potential risk factors for BP in the following section, including anxiety, disruptive behaviors, and ADHD. In addition, we focus on a positive family history as the most important genetic and environmental risk factor, which also enhances the importance of clinical risk factors. Risk factors have a different impact depending on the individual's developmental period, the context of the prodromal manifestation, and the type of BP.

Family History

A positive family history is a major risk factor for the emergence of BP (Bienvenu, Davydow, & Kendler, 2011; Smoller & Finn, 2003). Heritability (the contribution to an observed phenotypic variability explained by genetic factors) is estimated in the classical manic-depressive form to be within the range 70–85%, and offspring of bipolar patients (OBP) have a 10-fold higher risk of developing BP than does the general population.

In addition to genetic factors, another source of familial risk is the exposure to parental illness and related consequences. Families with a bipolar parent have lower cohesiveness and organization and more conflicts (Chang, Blasey, Ketter, & Steiner, 2001; Ferreira et al., 2013). In the absence of appropriate support and intervention, this environment may lead to higher stress and anxiety, which can interact with genetic vulnerabilities and other undesirable events, potentially resulting in early-onset psychopathology. For example, in a cohort of offspring at risk for BP, maternal neglect increased the emotional sensitivity of neglected children; furthermore, it was a significant early predictor of mood disorder in offspring (Doucette et al., 2016).

The AAO of BP in a parent may influence the extent of risk for the offspring. A Swiss study of 145 OBP observed for 10 years identified an increased risk for BP only in offspring of parents with BP with an AAO of less than 21 years (hazard ratio = 7.9) but not for the offspring of parents with later onset of the disorder (Preisig et al., 2016). Furthermore, parental loading for BP may decrease the AAO of BP in the offspring (Post et al., 2013).

However, most OBP who develop psychiatric disorders do not develop BP. High-risk studies reported that the lifetime frequency of OBP having a mental disorder is 40%–80% (Birmaher et al., 2010; Birmaher, Axelson, Monk, et al., 2009; Chang, Steiner, & Ketter, 2000; Duffy et al., 1998, 2014; Goetz et al., 2017; Henin et al., 2005; Nurnberger et al., 2011; Sanchez-Gistau et al., 2015; Todd et al., 1996; Vandeleur et al., 2012; Wals et al., 2001).

The variability in study findings may be explained by differences in the psychopathology of parents with BP (classical BP versus bipolar spectrum, occurrence and severity of comorbid disorders, and presence of psychopathology in the second parent), socioeconomic status (SES) of the family (lower SES increases the risk of disorder in offspring), average age of offspring cohort (higher age means more frequent psychopathology), and method of examination of both offspring and parents (Duffy et al., 2011). The geographic location of the study may also have a role. A comparison of categorical and dimensional psychopathology among children and adolescents in the Pittsburgh BIOS and the Dutch BIOS showed that whereas the frequency of mood disorders was comparable between studies (although the diagnosis of BP-NOS was not used in the Dutch study), a significantly higher prevalence of non-mood disorders was reported by the US study (Mesman et al., 2016).

An extensive meta-analysis involving 33 studies with 3863 offspring of parents with severe mental disorders (schizophrenia, recurrent depression, and BP) and 3158 offspring in the control group showed a high rate of different mental disorders among OBP under age 20 years, a significant proportion of whom developed severe mental disorders. However, the frequency of hypomania and mania before age 20 years was only 4% (Rasic et al., 2014).

Anxiety

Anxiety disorders are among the most common comorbidities of BP both in youth and adults; it worsens in prognosis and response to treatment (Jolin, Weller, & Weller, 2008; Pavlova, Perlis, Alda, & Uher, 2015). Furthermore, anxiety disorders are a possible antecedent and risk factor for BP. Johnson and colleagues prospectively observed a cohort of 717 individuals from childhood to adulthood (Johnson, Cohen, & Brook, 2000) and found that an anxiety disorder in adolescence increased the risk for subsyndromal and fully expressed BP in early adulthood (odds ratio = 4.69) (Johnson et al., 2000). In a prospective 4-year study of adolescents and young adult cohorts (aged 14−24 years), Brückl et al. (2007) found that separation anxiety disorder increased the risk not only for a number of anxiety disorders and substance abuse but also for BP II (Brückl et al., 2007). In a Swedish study, the investigation of a community sample of adolescents (aged 16−17 years) positively screened for depression at baseline showed that both panic disorder and generalized anxiety predicted the development of BP in adulthood in adolescents who experienced an episode of the hypomanic spectrum during adolescence (Päären et al., 2014).

Evidence that anxiety disorders can be considered a risk factor for later mood disorders also came from prospective high-risk studies, although a direct relationship to BP was not found consistently. A Canadian study showed that mood disturbance occurred 2.6 times more frequently in OBP who had an anxiety disorder in childhood than in children at risk without previous anxiety (Duffy, Alda, Hajek, Sherry, & Grof, 2010). Specifically, generalized anxiety disorder was a predictor of a major mood disorder; furthermore, if any mood disorder had been determined as an outcome, social phobia also had predictive value (Duffy et al., 2013). Anxiety disorders occurred significantly earlier in development in high-risk than in control offspring (Duffy et al., 2013). During the study, no direct relationship was established between anxiety disorder and later BP, potentially because those in the cohort were younger than the probable peak for the first hypo/manic episode (Duffy et al., 2013). On the other hand, a direct relationship was found between anxiety and later BP I in the Children and Adolescent Research Evaluation high-risk study in an Amish population; however, only nine subjects in the sample developed BP during the study period, which made any link tentative (Egeland et al., 2012). Episodically occurring sensitivity, crying, hyperalertness, anxiety/worry and somatic reports were among the most common early (preschool age) symptoms that most identified offspring who developed BP I in adolescence and adulthood from well individuals (Egeland et al., 2012).

More studies are needed to determine whether anxiety is a specific predictor for bipolar illness, a nonspecific presentation of psychopathology risk in vulnerable children, or a general indicator of reactivity and sensitivity to stress, which itself may contribute to the risk for various disorders together with more disease-specific risk factors.

Attention-Deficit Hyperactivity Disorder

The debate about the role of ADHD as a risk factor for BP triggered some studies in the early 1990s that found an elevated incidence of mania in children with ADHD (Biederman et al., 1996; Wozniak et al., 1995). However, subsequent studies did not replicate this finding. For example, Hassan, Agha, Langley, and Thapar (2011) detected no occurrence of mania in a sample of 200 individuals with ADHD, and only one child was diagnosed with hypomania (Hassan et al., 2011). Similarly, Klein (2012) did not detect a higher frequency of BP in a group of 135 adults who received a diagnosis of ADHD in childhood than in controls (Klein, 2012). In a large study of more than 6000 Finnish adolescents, 6.7% of the sample received a diagnosis of ADHD and the prevalence of BP was 1% in the total sample; however, no adolescents with ADHD had comorbid BP (Smalley et al., 2007).

In cohort studies, the relationship between ADHD and the risk of BP in adulthood has not been confirmed (Johnson et al., 2000; Kim-Cohen et al., 2003). In the Dunedin cohort of 1037 individuals prospectively observed since childhood, ADHD at age 11−15 years did not predict mania in adulthood (Kim-Cohen et al., 2003). After 8 years of observation, the analysis of 705 adolescents from the Early Developmental Stages of Psychopathology study (EDSP) identified ADHD as a risk factor for the onset and persistence of depressive but not manic symptoms (Tijssen, van Os, Wittchen, Lieb, Beesdo, & Wichers, 2010).

Although two studies reported a more frequent occurrence of ADHD in OBP than in controls, most representative investigations using a stricter methodology have not found a positive link. A large Canadian study of 216 OBP did not detect a different frequency of ADHD between children at risk and controls (Duffy et al., 2014). Similarly, a Dutch study of 140 children at risk reported only a 5% prevalence of ADHD at baseline and 3% after a 12-year follow-up, which did not differ from controls (Mesman et al., 2013). Finally, in the Pittsburgh BIOS, the frequency of ADHD among high-risk children and controls was comparable when confounding factors such as SES, mental disorders in nonproband parents, and more children in one family were considered (Birmaher, Axelson, Monk, et al., 2009). In a follow-up of the BIOS sample, ADHD was significantly more frequent in OBP who developed hypo/mania; however, its predictive value disappeared when only prospective data were included in the analysis (Axelson et al., 2015) In contrast, in a Spanish study of 90 children at risk for BP, the rate of ADHD was higher than that of community controls (Sanchez-Gistau et al., 2015). Similarly, Henin et al. described a significantly higher frequency of ADHD in 117 pediatric OBP than in controls (Henin et al., 2005).

There are several explanations for these contradictory findings, including methodology issues, the heterogeneity of BP, and the low specificity of ADHD symptoms (Duffy, 2012).

Carlson and Klein (2014) suggested that the high comorbidity of ADHD and mania observed in some studies may result from ADHD symptoms being counted toward both mania and ADHD. This misattribution of symptoms may be true especially in cases for which assessments are not performed by child psychiatrists but rather by raters only. In addition to the core symptoms that are included in the diagnostic criteria, ADHD, sleep disorder, and emotional dysregulation often occur and contribute to the undulating course and variable functioning of patients over time (Cortese, Faraone, Konofal, & Lecendreux, 2009; Graziano & Garcia, 2016; Konofal, Lecendreux, & Cortese, 2010). These characteristics contribute to confusion with severe ADHD (especially if it is accompanied by ODD) and for its being mistaken for mania, especially in prepubescent children when hyperactivity symptoms may be significant.

Another explanation may lie in the heterogeneity of BP (Duffy, 2012). Duffy et al. compared the clinical and developmental characteristics of at-risk children of parents responding to lithium (LiR) and those not responding to lithium (LiNR). In children of LiNR parents, there was a higher frequency of ADHD, psychosis, specific learning disabilities, and paranoid and schizoid personality disorders than in children of LiR parents (Duffy et al., 1998). At the same time, a higher number of psychotic disorders was observed in the genealogy of LiNR children than in those who were LiR (Duffy et al., 2014), which suggested that ADHD is associated with affective disorders being accompanied by psychotic symptoms rather than with affective psychopathology. In other studies, ADHD was suggested to be a risk factor for psychotic disorders (Hamshere et al., 2013; Kim-Cohen et al., 2003; Shyu et al., 2015).

Therefore, ADHD is not a likely risk factor for BP itself, but perhaps for a particular subtype burdened with a higher rate of psychotic symptoms and lying on the spectrum closer to schizoaffective disorder. However, owing to the phenomenological similarity of some symptoms of mania and ADHD, diagnostic confusion could arise when broader diagnostic criteria are used.

Disruptive Symptoms and Disorders

Several studies suggested that children and adolescents with disruptive disorders are at a higher risk for BP; however, there is no universal agreement regarding this issue. In the Dunedin cohort, conduct disorders (CDs) in adolescence significantly increased the risk for BP at age 26 years as well as for other mental disorders (Kim-Cohen et al., 2003). In the previously mentioned community study by Johnson et al. (2000), disruptive disorders in adolescence were a predictor of BP in adulthood, but this relationship disappeared when the authors controlled for manic symptoms during adolescence (Johnson et al., 2000). Therefore, the disruptive symptoms were probably a manifestation of the previously undiagnosed bipolar spectrum and more of a prodrome. ODD was a significant risk factor for subsyndromal and fully expressed BP in the Oregon Adolescent Depression Project, a large cohort study of 1700 adolescents from age 16 to 24 years (Lewinsohn et al., 2003). A Swiss prospective study of 591 children and adolescents found that those who had symptoms of CDs, such as frequent escapes from home and physical conflicts, had a 2.6–3.5 times greater risk for developing BP II than did those who did not have a behavioral problem (Endrass et al., 2007). The occurrence of subthreshold behavioral disturbances in adolescents has been shown to be a risk factor for fully expressed bipolar syndrome over 15 years of follow-up (Shankman et al., 2009). In a prospective study of

287 adolescents (aged 16–17 years) with MDD, early disruptive disorders significantly predicted adult BP rather than continued MDD in adulthood (Päären et al., 2014).

A higher lifetime prevalence of disruptive disorders (or externalizing problems) in youth at risk for BP than in controls was also found in some (Birmaher et al., 2010; Birmaher, Axelson, Monk, et al., 2009; Henin et al., 2005; Wals et al., 2001) but not all offspring studies (Duffy et al., 2014; Goetz et al., 2017; Nurnberger et al., 2011; Sanchez-Gistau et al., 2015; Vandeleur et al., 2012).

PRODROMES

A prodrome is defined as a manifestation that is part of the spectrum of the disorder but is not its full expression and predicts its onset. In many patients with BP, the onset of the fully developed disorder is preceded by various prodromes (Faedda et al., 2015; Hauser & Correll, 2013; Skjelstad, Malt, & Holte, 2010; Van Meter, Burke, Youngstrom, Faedda, & Correll, 2016). The reported duration of the prodromal period varies considerably across studies. Egeland, Hostetter, Pauls, and Sussex (2000) found that the first affective symptoms may occur up to 9–12 years before the full onset of the mood disturbance (Egeland et al., 2000), which contrasts with the 1.8-year interval reported by Correll et al. (2014). The duration of the prodrome depends on factors such as how each study defines the onset of the disorder (first affective episode, first mania, or first hospitalization), the average age of the sample, and the methods used to detect the prodromes, among others (Carlson & Pataki, 2016). Rather than the occurrence of prodromes themselves, their clinical significance lies in their accumulation, recurrence, and duration.

Sleep Impairment

Sleep disturbances are often considered to be a prodrome of BP (Duffy et al., 2010). Impaired sleep and sleep–wake cycle disturbances are some of the main symptoms of affective disorders and a significant source of deterioration in functionality. In patients with BP, sleep disorders occur during both the mood disorder episodes and remission (Millar, Espie, & Scott, 2004; Murray & Harvey, 2010; Ng et al., 2015). A reduction in sleep is among the most significant predictors of manic episode recurrence; insomnia also precedes full depressive episodes (Jackson, Cavanagh, & Scott, 2003). Interestingly, stabilization of the circadian rhythm is considered to be one of the mechanisms of the prophylactic effect of lithium (Rybakowski, Dmitrzak-Weglarz, Kliwicki, & Hauser, 2013).

Some differences between controls and children at risk for BP have been found in their sleep and circadian rhythm, predominantly including changes in sleep latency, frequent night awakening, increased fatigue during awakening, and higher daytime sleepiness (Duffy et al., 2014; Jones, Tai, Evershed, Knowles, & Bentall, 2006; Levenson et al., 2015; Sebela, Novak, Kemlink, & Goetz, 2017; Shaw, Egeland, Endicott, Allen, & Hostetter, 2005). A meta-analysis showed that compared with controls, people at risk for BP had higher variability in sleep efficiency and a lower relative amplitude of the sleep–wake cycle (Ng et al., 2015). Because of the high frequency of psychopathology in these cohorts, whether these differences have a specific relation to the risk for BP has yet to be determined.

However, sleep disorders were confirmed to be close (up to 1 year) as well as distal prodromes of depression and anxiety in prospective community studies in adults and adolescents (Ritter, Marx, Bauer, Lepold, & Pfennig, 2011), which agrees with results from prospective studies within the Amish high-risk study (Egeland et al., 2012). Decreased sleep along with mood swings, feelings of low energy, and fearfulness (i.e., subsyndromal depressive symptoms) were among the signs that began to differentiate children who later developed BP I from healthy children (Egeland et al., 2012). In a Canadian study of children at risk for BP, Duffy et al. found that childhood sleep disorders, along with anxiety disorders, increased the risk of depression in adolescence (Duffy et al., 2014).

In a meta-analysis of studies focused on prodromes and both the first and recurrent episodes of mood disorders within BP, insomnia was among the most common prodromes before the first affective episode in general (Van Meter, Burke, Youngstrom, et al., 2016). Individual evaluation of studies that reported prodromes before the first manic episode demonstrated that one of the most commonly reported signs was a decreased need for sleep (Van Meter, Burke, Youngstrom, et al., 2016).

Progression From Unipolar Depression to Bipolar Disorder

Longitudinal, community and retrospective studies of youth at risk indicate that BP with early onset (before age 18 years) frequently begins with a depressive episode (Duffy et al., 2010a; Lewinsohn, Seeley, Buckley, & Klein, 2002; Mesman et al., 2013). Patients with a major depressive episode are therefore a risk group for the development of BP. The rate of change from unipolar depression to BP in studies of adults varies from 2% (Mattisson, Bogren, Horstmann, Munk-Jørgensen, & Nettelbladt, 2007) to 32% (Dudek, Siwek, Zielińska, Jaeschke, & Rybakowski, 2013). Similarly, there is a discrepancy as to whether the change from unipolar to bipolar declines with age or the number of episodes and what signs predict a higher conversion risk. In the literature, typical features include early onset, positive family history of BP, psychotic symptoms, rapid onset of depressive episodes, psychomotor retardation, and activation after antidepressants (Goodwin & Jamison, 2007; Strober & Carlson, 1982).

A meta-analysis (Kessing, Willer, Andersen, & Bukh, 2017) involving 77,600 adolescent and adult patients from 11 different studies showed that after 10 years of follow-up, 12.9% of depressed patients converted to BP, and the conversion rate was highest during the first 2 years (about 3%) with a decreasing frequency of 0.8%/year from years 5 to 10. Family history and early onset of depression were the factors most consistently associated with the change (Kessing et al., 2017).

Subsyndromal Hypomanic Manifestations

Hypomanic manifestations that do not meet diagnostic criteria for a full episode are reported to be a bipolar prodrome or predictor of conversion from unipolar depressive disorder to BP in various studies in adults (Faedda et al., 2015; Skjelstad et al., 2010). At the same time, large community studies showed that the experience of hypomanic symptoms in the youth population is common and temporary, and in most of the cases does not predict clinical outcomes (Määren et al., 2013; Tijssen et al., 2009).

In the analysis of a sample of 1902 adolescents from the EDSP cohort, Tijssen et al. (2010) found that 25% of participants displayed hypomanic and manic symptoms once over a 3-year follow-up period, whereas only 2.6% experienced symptoms twice (Tijssen, van Os, Wittchen, Lieb, Beesdo, Mengelers, et al., 2010). Adolescents who never experienced two or more hypo/manic symptoms had a 0.7% risk for developing DSM-IV hypo/manic episodes and a 9.4% risk for mental health care use owing to the affective symptoms in the 10-year follow-up. With greater levels of symptom loading, the risk for the development of hypo/manic episodes increased to 1.9%–3.3% (two to six symptoms) and the risk of mental health care use increased to 11.5%–12.8%. Similarly, with greater levels of persistence, the risk for the development of hypo/manic episodes increased from 0.7% to 2.0%–3.2% (symptoms were reported during one or two visits over a 3-year follow-up period), and the risk of mental health care use increased from 9.4% to 12.3%–14.1%. The dose–response association between persistence and clinical outcomes became stronger as the number of persistent symptoms increased (Tijssen, van Os, Wittchen, Lieb, Beesdo, Mengelers, et al., 2010). In a Swedish study of a community sample of 2300 adolescents (aged 16–17 years) screened for depression, the clinical interview was used to diagnose 197 participants with an MDD and 90 with a hypomania spectrum episode (most of them had also experienced an MDD). A hypomania spectrum episode was defined as having an "elevated mood," "grandiosity," or both, and at least one to three additional manic symptoms or irritability as the only core symptom and at least four additional manic symptoms. After reassessment 15 years later, mania was reported only by two participants and hypomania by an additional four, whereas depression appeared more stable because MDD was diagnosed in 38 participants. The frequency of mood episodes in adulthood did not differ across the adolescent hypomania spectrum subgroups (full syndromal, brief-episode, and subsyndromal) (Päären et al., 2013).

An elevated score of manic symptoms on the parental scale can also be found frequently in clinical populations of children across different behavioral and neurodevelopmental disorders, as demonstrated by the Longitudinal Assessment of Manic Symptoms (LAMS) study (Horwitz et al., 2010). Of 2622 children (aged 6−12 years) who visited outpatient mental health clinics, nearly half had an increased score of manic symptoms (≥12 points on the 10-item Parent−General Behavior Inventory [P-GBI]) (Youngstrom, Frazier, Demeter, Calabrese, & Findling, 2008). The average age of those in this group was 9.4 years, and almost half of those who screened positive were aged 6−8 years (Horwitz et al., 2010). Lifetime ADHD was diagnosed in 78% and disruptive disorders (mostly ODD) in 53%; only one-third of children lived with both biological parents and over half of the families received Medicaid (a social health care program for families and individuals with limited resources) (Findling et al., 2010). The P-GBI score fell below the risk threshold over 2 years in 85% of these children (Findling et al., 2013). This study suggested that mania-like symptoms may be related to the environment.

Arnold et al. (2011) compared groups of children from the LAMS with ADHD only, bipolar spectrum only, and those comorbid for both. The mania scores according to teachers did not differ between those with ADHD and those in the comorbid group (ADHD and bipolar spectrum), whereas parental scores were significantly higher in the comorbid group (Arnold et al., 2011).

Parental reports of manic symptoms, especially in younger children, can differ significantly from the assessment of a trained child psychiatrist. For example, in a study of 82 children aged 6−12 years who were admitted to an inpatient unit and assessed using the Child Mania Rating Scale−Parent version (CMRS-P) (Pavuluri, Henry, Devineni, Carbray, & Birmaher, 2006), manic symptoms exceeding the cutoff for "mania" (20 points and more) were reported by 57% of parents. However, upon clinical examination, BP was diagnosed in only three children (3.7%) whereas ADHD appeared in 63% and ODD in 69% of the total sample (Margulies, Weintraub, Basile, Grover, & Carlson, 2012). Similarly, a high correlation between parental assessment of manic symptoms using CMRSs (Pavuluri et al., 2006) and externalized disorders was found in a study of 911 outpatients aged 9–18 years, 7.3% of whom were diagnosed with BP by an expert panel of researchers from the study (BP I and II: 2.5%; BP-NOS: 4.7%) (Carlson & Blader, 2011). High scores of manic symptoms as assessed by the parents did not significantly predict the diagnosis of BP as assessed by a panel of investigators but predicted the use of a mood stabilizer in the period before the children were recommended to the study center.

Therefore, in most cases, mania-like symptoms in prepubertal children are unlikely to be part of the bipolar spectrum but represent an indicator of maladaptive behavior or nonspecific morbidity and less favorable clinical development related to social factors and family environment (Carlson & Youngstrom, 2003; Hazell, Carr, Lewin, & Sly, 2003). The most valid information on the predictive value of subthreshold hypomania for the future risk of BP development and the challenges in their assessment most likely comes from longitudinal studies of high-risk offspring.

In the long-term study of 238 OBP, Goodday et al. (2017) investigated whether the occurrence of hypomanic symptoms according to clinical assessment and a self-evaluation questionnaire (Hypomania Checklist-32, Revised) (Angst et al., 2005) differed between OBP and controls and whether their occurrence predicted the development of mood disorders. Interestingly, higher scores for manic symptoms in the self-assessment were not reported by the OBP but rather by the controls. In contrast, 14% of high-risk offspring and 0% of control offspring had clinically significant subthreshold hypomanic symptoms (CSHS) assessed using semistructured clinical interviews. High-risk offspring with CSHS had a fivefold higher risk of developing recurrent major depression compared with controls. The median onset of CSHS in the high-risk offspring was aged 16.4 years, which was before the onset of major mood episodes. Clinically evaluated hypomanic symptoms were evident in some high-risk offspring at age 6 years, but no hypomanic episodes meeting the diagnostic criteria occurred before age 12.5 years (Goodday et al., 2017).

Hypomanic symptoms were also predictors in the Dutch high-risk study (Hillegers et al., 2005). Symptoms such as elated mood, decreased the need for sleep, and racing thoughts as well as suicidal ideation and middle insomnia were found to be the most reliable predictors of BP development (Mesman, Nolen, Keijsers, & Hillegers, 2017). In a Pittsburgh BIOS (Birmaher et al., 2010; Birmaher, Axelson, Monk, et al., 2009), hypomanic symptoms were the most prominent predictors of the first manic episode. In contrast to previous studies in which the first affective episode was depression in the vast majority of cases, the BIOS study reported that only 50% of the first affective episodes were depression.

The association of hypomanic symptoms with a subsequent BP is the result of a complex interaction with other risk factors; furthermore, the meaning of hypomanic symptoms differs across age groups and cohorts. Finally, the assessment method is crucial, because the result of a manic symptom questionnaire does not always indicate the identification of manic manifestations when a thorough clinical assessment is performed.

Bipolar Disorder Not Otherwise Specified

Large prospective studies have suggested that the diagnostic criteria for BP are too narrow, and thus a number of individuals who have functionally significant hypomanic episodes are not detected (Merikangas et al., 2007). In adults, hypomanic episodes lasting 1–3 days have been shown to have the same clinical correlates as episodes lasting 4 or more days (Angst et al., 2003b). Finally, epidemiological studies demonstrated that DSM MDD is heterogeneous and includes approximately 40% of hidden bipolars (Angst, 2013).

According to DSM-IV, patients' clinically relevant BP symptoms that do not meet full criteria for any BP subtype were diagnosed with BP-NOS. Criteria for BP-NOS, including the required number of symptoms (one symptom to full hypomania syndrome) and their duration (1 hour to 3 days; consecutive days versus cumulative presence), vary across pediatric studies. This category was replaced in DSM-5 with the more solidly defined category of BP Other Specified (American Psychiatric Association, 2013).

The frequency of BP-NOS in the general population is relatively low. In a large population study involving 7977 British children and adolescents, Stringaris et al. (2010) found that seven individuals (0.1%) met definite or probable DSM-IV criteria for BP I or BP II, whereas the prevalence of BP-NOS was 10-fold higher. The average AAO of BP was 12.8 years according to parent information and 13.7 as assessed by youth (Stringaris et al., 2010). Only one from the group of 8- to 15-year-olds (N = 3618) fully met DSM-IV criteria for BP. BP-NOS showed strong associations with externalizing disorders but not with depression (Stringaris et al., 2010).

Pediatric studies in clinical samples that report prepubertal onset of BP showed a high frequency of BP-NOS, e.g., 52% by Donfrancesco et al. (2011) and 34% by Birmaher, Axelson, Goldstein, et al. (2009). Despite the different criteria used, the results of multiple studies agreed on the high comorbidity of BP-NOS with behavioral disorders (Findling et al. (2005): 64% for ADHD and 28% for ODD/CD (Findling et al., 2005); Birmaher et al. (2006): 60% for ADHD, 37% for ODD, and 14% for CD (Birmaher et al., 2006); and Fristad et al. (2016): 77% for ADHD and 53% for disruptive disorder (Fristad et al., 2016)). Therefore, unsurprisingly, Fristad et al. (2016) found that children diagnosed with BP-NOS have characteristics mostly similar to their peers with disruptive mood dysregulation disorder (DMDD) (Fristad et al., 2016).

In the Course and Outcome of Bipolar Youth (COBY) study of 413 youth (aged 7–17 years), 34% were diagnosed with BP-NOS and 66% and 7% with BP I and II, respectively (Birmaher, Axelson, Goldstein, et al., 2009). BP-NOS was defined as the presence of clinically relevant BP symptoms that did not fulfill DSM-IV criteria for BP I or BP II. Subjects were required to have a minimum of elated mood plus two associated DSM-IV symptoms or irritable mood plus three associated DSM-IV symptoms, along with a change in the level of functioning for a minimum of 4 h within a 24-h period and at least four cumulative lifetime days meeting the criteria. The retrospectively estimated AAO was 7.9 ± 3.4 years, which was significantly lower than that of other BP subtypes (BP I: 8.4 ± 4.0 years; BP II: 10.5 ± 3.9 years). In 84% of the BP-NOS individuals, the polarity of the index episode was not specified (Birmaher, Axelson, Goldstein, et al., 2009). Children with a diagnosis of BP-NOS had high comorbidity (87%), primarily with behavioral and anxiety disorders (62% ADHD, 40% ODD, and 37% anxiety) (Axelson et al., 2006). When the development of mood symptoms in the COBY study was analyzed over an average of 8 years' follow-up, Birmaher et al. (2014) distinguished four trajectories: Class 1, mostly euthymic; Class 2, moderately euthymic; Class 3, improving course; and Class 4, mostly ill (Birmaher et al., 2014). Surprisingly, the total frequency of drug treatment (93%, 96%, 94%, and 96%, respectively) did not differ across groups. The frequency of psychotropic drugs used across classes was 48%, 61%, 57%, and 64%, respectively, for antipsychotics; 48%, 61%, 57%, and 65% for antidepressants; 74%, 73%, 67%, and 76% for mood stabilizers; and 37%, 58%, 60%, and 67% for stimulants. Contrary to what one would expect in adults with clearly diagnosed BP, stimulants were used significantly more in the group with the most severe course (predominantly ill) than in the group of predominantly euthymic youth. During the 5-year average follow-up, 45% of youth with BP-NOS converted into BP I or BP II. A significant conversion predictor was a family history of BPs; however, a family history of hypo/mania was also present in 40% of children who did not convert to full-criteria BP (Axelson et al., 2011).

When correctly diagnosed, BP-NOS is rare in the community child population and correlates with externalizing disorders. In younger cohorts, a diagnosis of BP-NOS may capture children with chronic irritability, which does not represent a phenotype of BP. The predictive value of BP-NOS for fully expressed BP may differ across age groups, criteria used, and method of assessment. Although useful for research purposes, BP-NOS in regular clinical practice may lead to an overdiagnosis of BP in children. However, in specific subgroups, namely offspring of parents with BP, BP-NOS may represent a useful working diagnosis if other risk factors such as MDD are present and hypomania symptoms are observed in two settings.

NEUROPSYCHOLOGICAL FINDINGS RELATED TO BIPOLAR DISORDER AND ITS RISK IN YOUTH

Changes in cognitive function in many individuals with bipolar spectrum disorder have become apparent, even during intervals between mood episodes. Research studies have examined patients with the diagnosis of BP during various stages of the disease. These studies are discussed here to illuminate the individual's susceptibility to BP and implications for the course of the disorder.

Neuropsychological changes have been studied as a premorbid indicator of illness in OBP. A meta-analysis of 18 studies consisting of 786 first-degree relatives of patients with BP and 794 healthy controls (aged 10–25 years) suggested a worse performance of individuals at risk in general cognition, social cognition, visual memory, verbal memory, processing speed, and sustained attention, but groups did not differ in planning or working memory (Bora & Özerdem, 2017). As in previously mentioned metaanalyses, the subjects included in those studies were heterogeneous according to mood state, comorbidity, the course of the disorder, treatment, and other features.

Several studies attempted to identify neuropsychological traits that may distinguish between the risk for BP and schizophrenia. de la Serna et al. (2017) compared 90 OBP with 41 offspring of schizophrenic parents and 107 community controls. Visual memory deficits were found in both OBP and offspring of schizophrenic parents. In contrast, impaired verbal learning and a lower capacity of working memory were specific for offspring at risk for schizophrenia, and in another study, a lower processing speed was found only in OBP (de la Serna et al., 2017). Normal performance in spatial working memory also differentiated offspring with bipolar disorder from those with schizophrenia in the study by Diwadkar et al. (2011). When tested for sustained attention, OBP but not offspring with schizophrenia performed worse than controls (Diwadkar et al., 2011). In the Dunedin birth cohort study (Cannon et al., 2002), children who developed mania in adulthood experienced difficulties in social and emotional development but not in language or IQ test performance. On the other hand, children who progressed to schizophrenia showed impaired emotional development, language, cognitive functions, and motor abilities (Cannon et al., 2002).

Findings of studies on clinical samples of youth with BP are hard to integrate given the great heterogeneity of samples in terms of the age of included participants, the definition of BP, and the ratio of BP subtypes, as well as the inclusion of both patients with euthymic and mood episodes with different types of treatment. Frías, Palma, and Farriols (2014) reviewed 124 neuropsychological studies that compared youth diagnosed with BP I, BP II, or BP-NOS with healthy controls. The results suggested that verbal/visuospatial memory, processing speed, working memory, and social cognition may represent candidate domains for further research in well-defined samples. These deficits appeared greater in individuals with acute mood symptoms, BP I, and/or ADHD comorbidity (Frías et al., 2014).

In euthymic children and adolescents with BP, a metaanalysis by Elias et al. (2017) reported impaired verbal learning, verbal memory, working memory, visual learning, and visual memory compared with those parameters in healthy controls, with moderate to large effect sizes. Significant impairments were not observed for attention/vigilance, reasoning and problem solving, and/or processing speed. However, substantial heterogeneity was found in results across studies, the sources of which was identified as the varied definition of euthymia, comorbidity of ADHD and anxiety disorders, different medications, and the use of different neuropsychological tests across studies (Elias et al., 2017).

These findings reflect the heterogeneity of the bipolar spectrum and vary depending on different aspects and stages of the disease. The interpretation of available results in youth is more complicated than that in adults for several reasons. Given the broadened diagnostic criteria (Leibenluft, Charney, Towbin, Bhangoo, & Pine, 2003), some US studies included children and adolescents who, from a more conservative European point of view, would not be diagnosed with BP. Other complications are caused by a considerably high non-mood comorbidity in youth with BP (Van Meter, Burke, Kowatch, Findling, & Youngstrom, 2016). In addition, the diagnosis of BP in children seems less stable than in adults (Birmaher et al., 2014). The developmental aspects of cognition, as well as psychosocial and educational factors, also have a role in younger patients. However, BP may be presumed to be associated with worse neuropsychological outcomes that may be detectable before the onset of mood episodes. Longitudinal neuropsychological research using complex batteries of tests in well-defined samples of high-risk offspring observed from early childhood may elucidate the remaining controversies.

IRRITABILITY CONTROVERSY AND DISRUPTIVE MOOD DYSREGULATION DISORDER

Interest in irritability in child psychiatry had grown considerably since the mid-1990s when several publications suggested that chronic irritability accompanied by rage and aggression may represent a pediatric phenotype of mania that may be unrecognized (Biederman et al., 1996; Wozniak et al., 1995). Although this view has not been universally accepted by other researchers, it had a large impact on routine clinical practice as well as research criteria in some studies. Thus, although the onset of mania in prepubertal children was considered possible but rare until that time, a number of articles, mostly by US research groups, examined samples of early school-aged children or even preschoolers with the diagnosis of bipolar disorder from clinical, neuroscience, pharmacological, and many other aspects.

Irritability is defined as an increased tendency to feel anger in response to frustration (Brotman, Kircanski, & Leibenluft, 2017). This anger can manifest outwardly in different ways, and in extreme cases even by physical aggression. From a developmental perspective, irritability has two intensity peaks: the culmination of irritability in preschool-aged children decreases but then increases slightly during adolescence (Leibenluft & Stoddard, 2013).

Increased irritability occurs in a wide range of mental disorders in childhood and adolescence and can be observed in individuals with internalized disorders such as anxiety disorders, depression, and post-traumatic disorder; externalized disorders such as ODD, CD, and mania; or neurodevelopmental disorders including ADHD, mental retardation, and autism spectrum disorders.

To shed light on the relationship between irritability and BP, Leibenluft et al. (2003) defined several potential phenotypes of juvenile mania (classical to narrow, intermediate phenotypes) and a broad phenotype for research purposes (Leibenluft et al., 2003). The broad phenotype included at least 12 months of chronically present and obvious pathological mood (anger or sadness), irritability characterized by exaggerated reactions to negative emotional stimuli, and at least three hyperarousal manifestations such as insomnia, racing thoughts, pressured speech, distractibility, and intrusiveness (Leibenluft et al., 2003). Because of uncertainty regarding whether this phenotype was a manifestation of BP, this syndrome was termed severe mood dysregulation (SMD) (Brotman et al., 2006).

SMD in the youth population has proven to be relatively common but not stable. In an analysis of a cohort of 1420 children and adolescents (aged 9—19 years) from the longitudinal Great Smoky Mountains Study (Costello et al., 1996), the lifetime prevalence of SMD was 3.3% (Brotman et al., 2006). Most SMD youth met the criteria in just one of four waves of assessments (Brotman et al., 2006). SMD in childhood did not progress to BP, but rather progressed to depression and anxiety disorders. Those who met SMD criteria in the first wave (mean age, 10.6 years) had a sevenfold higher risk of being diagnosed with depression in young adulthood (mean age, 18.3 years) than those who never met SMD criteria; this association remained significant regardless of covariates (ADHD, ODD, or CD). In contrast, BP occurred in only one child in this group, even when the more liberal criteria for BP-NOS (Birmaher et al., 2006) was used.

Another remarkable finding from this study was the low stability of BP diagnosis in children from the non-SMD group. Of the six children with the diagnosis of bipolar disorder, none met the criteria in young adulthood (Brotman et al., 2006).

In addition, the progression of SMD to BP was not shown in a clinical sample of 84 patients with SMD (mean age, 11.6 years) prospectively observed for 2 years (Stringaris, Baroni, et al., 2010). A hypomanic episode occurred in only one individual with SMD. However, of the 93 subjects with BP, 62% developed at least one episode of mania, hypomania, or a mixed state over follow-up. Other occurrences of elevated mood episodes were not detected in the SMD group even during a 6-year follow-on extension, i.e., during late adolescence when BP often emerges (Stringaris, Baroni, et al., 2010).

The predictive value of chronic versus episodic irritability was studied in a community sample of 776 adolescents (Leibenluft, Cohen, Gorrindo, Brook, & Pine, 2006). Chronic irritability at study entry (mean age, 13.5 years) predicted ADHD in a further assessment (mean age, 16.2 years) and major depression in adulthood (mean age, 22.1 years). Episodic irritability at the first assessment was significantly associated with mood and anxiety disorders at the second assessment and mania in adulthood (Leibenluft et al., 2006). Similarly, in a large longitudinal Swedish twin study of child and adolescent development (1348 twin pairs) starting in childhood (aged 8–9 years) and ending in young adulthood (aged 19–20 years), childhood irritability predicted anxious/depressed symptoms at older ages (Savage et al., 2015). Further evidence that the SMD phenotype characterized by chronic irritability does not belong to the bipolar spectrum was demonstrated by the rare occurrence of BP in parents of children with SMD, compared with frequent occurrence in the parents of youth with the classical bipolar phenotype (Brotman et al., 2007). These findings led to the creation of a new category of DMDD in DSM-5 with a common primary criterion for chronic irritable mood accompanied by frequent and developmentally disproportionate explosions of anger, in which symptoms of hyperarousal were eliminated. One of the aims of defining DMDD was to identify a concept that would reduce the tendency in US clinical practice to mark children with frequent and severe rages of anger as "bipolar" (Margulies et al., 2012), thus reducing the exposure of these children to a polypharmacy of stimulants, mood stabilizers, antipsychotics, and antidepressants that would rarely be seen in adults with BP.

This new diagnostic unit has been classified as a mood disorder rather than a behavioral disorder, but unsurprisingly, they frequently overlap. For example, 31% of individuals in the 597 children and adolescents (aged 6–18 years) who were admitted to community mental health centers met DMDD criteria. Of these, 96% had ODD, and 81% ADHD

(Freeman, Youngstrom, Youngstrom, & Findling, 2016). Therefore, the diagnosis of DMDD in most cases is likely to capture children with more severe ODD symptoms and its comorbidity with ADHD.

Further research will determine whether the diagnosis of DMDD serves its original intention as a refuge for children at risk for being classified "bipolar." Margulies et al. (2012) found that children whose parent-reported score of manic symptoms on the CMRS (Pavuluri et al., 2006) exceeded the cutoff for mania were in fact chronically irritable and explosive and that 71% had ADHD and 76% had ODD. The diagnosis of BP was established only by a careful clinical examination in one patient. However, 37% of these children were not diagnosed with DMDD because they had exclusionary diagnoses; 46% of the children would have been given the diagnosis of DMDD. In other words, DMDD would have protected only half of these children with chronically explosive, irritable behavior and other emotion dysregulation symptoms from a presumably erroneous bipolar diagnosis (Margulies et al., 2012).

The differences in findings from two BP child studies suggest that a DMDD diagnosis will depend highly on the assessment methodology. In a cohort of OBP aged 6–17 years, Sparks et al. (2014) found that the risk for DMDD was eight times higher for OBP than for controls (6.7% versus 0.8%, respectively), and children at risk also had a higher frequency of chronic irritability compared with community controls (12.5% vs. 2.5%) (Sparks et al., 2014). In contrast, Propper et al. (2017) detected no case of DMDD in OBP (in the same age range as in the previous study) but diagnosed DMDD in 7% of children of parents with MDD (Propper et al., 2017), which agreed with data on the relationship between chronic irritability and depression previously mentioned (Brotman et al., 2007; Savage et al., 2015; Stringaris, Baroni et al., 2010).

CONCLUSION

BP in young people has become one of the most often discussed diagnoses in child and adolescent psychiatry and the subject of intense research. The controversy generated by the diagnosis of pediatric BP in US clinical practice highlighted methodological problems in research in the field, such as the overemphasis on narrow diagnostic instruments, and apparent pressure to publish new results in prestigious psychiatric journals. Fortunately, this trend has passed, and we have reestablished the importance of high-quality longitudinal research, the significance of clinical expertise that cannot easily be substituted, and the relevance of international collaboration. Although it remains clear that BP in childhood is rare, it appears to have a neurodevelopmental basis. Nevertheless, when diagnosing psychopathology, it is essential to consider the developmental trajectories and related genetic and environmental factors. It seems that our research paradigm would benefit from considering the tried and tested clinical question:

"Why does a child growing in this particular family manifest these particular symptoms at this particular time?"

Acknowledgments

The authors would like to thank Paul Grof for very helpful comments on the preparation of this manuscript, and Martina Vnukova for her assistance in language editing. Manuscript preparation was funded by the Ministry of Health of the Czech Republic, Grant Number 17-32478A.

References

American Psychiatric Association. (2000). *Diagnostic and statistical manual of mental disorders* (4th ed.). Washington, DC: Author.

American Psychiatric Association. (2013). *Diagnostic and statistical manual of mental disorders* (5th ed.). American Psychiatric Association http://doi.org/10.1176/appi. books.9780890425596.

Angst, J. (2013). Bipolar disorders in DSM-5: Strengths, problems and perspectives. *International Journal of Bipolar Disorders, 1*(1), 1. http://doi.org/10.1186/2194-7511-1-12.

Angst, J., Adolfsson, R., Benazzi, F., Gamma, A., Hantouche, E., Meyer, T. D., et al. (2005). The HCL-32: Towards a self-assessment tool for hypomanic symptoms in outpatients. *Journal of Affective Disorders, 88*(2), 217–233. http://doi.org/10.1016/j.jad.2005.05.011.

Angst, J., Gamma, A., Benazzi, F., Ajdacic, V., Eich, D., & Rössler, W. (2003a). Diagnostic issues in bipolar disorder. *European Neuropsychopharmacology, 13*, 43–50. http://doi.org/10.1016/S0924-977X(03)00077-4.

Angst, J., Gamma, A., Benazzi, F., Ajdacic, V., Eich, D., & Rössler, W. (2003b). Toward a re-definition of subthreshold bipolarity: Epidemiology and proposed criteria for bipolar-II, minor bipolar disorders and hypomania. *Journal of Affective Disorders, 73*(1–2), 133–146.

Arnold, L. E., Demeter, C., Mount, K., Frazier, T. W., Youngstrom, E. A., Fristad, M., et al. (2011). Pediatric bipolar spectrum disorder and ADHD: Comparison and comorbidity in the LAMS clinical sample. *Bipolar Disorders, 13*(5–6), 509–521. http://doi.org/10.1111/j.1399-5618.2011.00948.x.

Axelson, D., Birmaher, B., Strober, M., Gill, M. K., Valeri, S., Chiappetta, L., et al. (2006). Phenomenology of children and adolescents with bipolar spectrum disorders. *Archives of General Psychiatry, 63*(10), 1139–1148. http://doi.org/10.1001/archpsyc.63.10.1139.

Axelson, D. A., Birmaher, B., Strober, M. A., Goldstein, B. I., Ha, W., Gill, M. K., et al. (2011). Course of subthreshold bipolar disorder in youth: Diagnostic progression from bipolar disorder not otherwise specified. *Journal of the American Academy of Child and Adolescent Psychiatry, 50*(10), 1001–1016.e3. http://doi.org/10.1016/j.jaac.2011.07.005.

Axelson, D., Goldstein, B., Goldstein, T., Monk, K., Yu, H., Hickey, M. B., et al. (2015). Diagnostic precursors to bipolar disorder in offspring of parents with bipolar disorder: A longitudinal study. *American Journal of Psychiatry, 172*(7), 638–646. http://doi.org/10.1176/appi.ajp.2014.14010035.

Baldessarini, R. J., Tondo, L., Vázquez, G. H., Undurraga, J., Bolzani, L., Yildiz, A., et al. (2012). Age at onset versus family history and clinical outcomes in 1,665 international bipolar-I disorder patients. *World Psychiatry, 11*(1), 40–46. https://doi.org/10.1016/j.wpsyc.2012.01.006.

Biederman, J., Faraone, S., Mick, E., Wozniak, J., Chen, L., Ouellette, C., et al. (1996). Attention-deficit hyperactivity disorder and juvenile mania: An overlooked comorbidity? *Journal of the American Academy of Child and Adolescent Psychiatry, 35*(8), 997–1008. http://doi.org/10.1097/00004583-199608000-00010.

Bienvenu, O. J., Davydow, D. S., & Kendler, K. S. (2011). Psychiatric "diseases" versus behavioral disorders and degree of genetic influence. *Psychological Medicine, 41*(1), 33–40. http://doi.org/10.1017/S003329171000084X.

Birmaher, B., Axelson, D., Goldstein, B., Monk, K., Kalas, C., Obreja, M., et al. (2010). Psychiatric disorders in preschool offspring of parents with bipolar disorder: The Pittsburgh bipolar offspring study (BIOS). *American Journal of Psychiatry, 167*(3), 321–330. http://doi.org/10.1176/appi.ajp.2009.09070977.

Birmaher, B., Axelson, D., Goldstein, B., Strober, M., Gill, M. K., Hunt, J., et al. (2009). Four-year longitudinal course of children and adolescents with bipolar spectrum disorders: The course and outcome of bipolar youth (COBY) study. *American Journal of Psychiatry, 166*(7), 795–804. http://doi.org/10.1176/appi.ajp.2009.08101569.

Birmaher, B., Axelson, D., Monk, K., Kalas, C., Goldstein, B., Hickey, M. B., et al. (2009). Lifetime psychiatric disorders in school-aged offspring of parents with bipolar disorder: The Pittsburgh bipolar offspring study. *Archives of General Psychiatry, 66*(3), 287–296. http://doi.org/10.1001/archgenpsychiatry.2008.546.

Birmaher, B., Axelson, D., Strober, M., Gill, M. K., Valeri, S., Chiappetta, L., et al. (2006). Clinical course of children and adolescents with bipolar spectrum disorders. *Archives of General Psychiatry, 63*(2), 175–183. http://doi.org/10.1001/archpsyc.63.2.175.

Birmaher, B., Gill, M. K., Axelson, D. A., Goldstein, B. I., Goldstein, T. R., Yu, H., et al. (2014). Longitudinal trajectories and associated baseline predictors in youths with bipolar spectrum disorders. *American Journal of Psychiatry, 171*(9), 990–999. http://doi.org/10.1176/appi.ajp.2014.13121577.

Blader, J. C., & Carlson, G. A. (2007). Increased rates of bipolar disorder diagnoses among U.S. Child, adolescent, and adult inpatients, 1996–2004. *Biological Psychiatry, 62*(2), 107–114. http://doi.org/10.1016/j.biopsych.2006.11.006.

Bora, E., & Özerdem, A. (2017). A meta-analysis of neurocognition in youth with familial high risk for bipolar disorder. *European Psychiatry, 44*, 1–7. http://doi.org/10.1016/j.eurpsy.2017.02.483.

Brotman, M. A., Kassem, L., Reising, M. M., Guyer, A. E., Dickstein, D. P., Rich, B. A., et al. (2007). Parental diagnoses in youth with narrow phenotype bipolar disorder or severe mood dysregulation. *American Journal of Psychiatry, 164*(8), 1238–1241. http://doi.org/10.1176/appi.ajp.2007.06101619.

Brotman, M. A., Kircanski, K., & Leibenluft, E. (2017). Irritability in children and adolescents. *Annual Review of Clinical Psychology, 13*(1), 317–341. http://doi.org/10.1146/annurev-clinpsy-032816-044941.

Brotman, M. A., Schmajuk, M., Rich, B. A., Dickstein, D. P., Guyer, A. E., Costello, E. J., et al. (2006). Prevalence, clinical correlates, and longitudinal course of severe mood dysregulation in children. *Biological Psychiatry, 60*(9), 991–997. http://doi.org/10.1016/j.biopsych.2006.08.042.

Brückl, T. M., Wittchen, H.-U., Höfler, M., Pfister, H., Schneider, S., & Lieb, R. (2007). Childhood separation anxiety and the risk of subsequent psychopathology: Results from a community study. *Psychotherapy and Psychosomatics, 76*(1), 47–56. http://doi.org/10.1159/000096364.

Cannon, M., Caspi, A., Moffitt, T. E., Harrington, H., Taylor, A., Murray, R. M., et al. (2002). Evidence for early-childhood, pan-developmental impairment specific to schizophreniform disorder: Results from a longitudinal birth cohort. *Archives of General Psychiatry, 59*(5), 449–456.

Carlson, G. A., & Blader, J. C. (2011). Diagnostic implications of informant disagreement for manic symptoms. *Journal of Child and Adolescent Psychopharmacology, 21*(5), 399–405. http://doi.org/10.1089/cap.2011.0007.

Carlson, G. A., & Klein, D. N. (2014). How to understand divergent views on bipolar disorder in youth. *Annual Review of Clinical Psychology, 10*(1), 529–551. http://doi.org/10.1146/annurev-clinpsy-032813-153702.

Carlson, G. A., & Pataki, C. (2016). Understanding early age of onset: A review of the last 5 years. *Current Psychiatry Reports, 18*(12), 1–11. http://doi.org/10.1007/s11920-016-0744-8.

Carlson, G. A., & Youngstrom, E. A. (2003). Clinical implications of pervasive manic symptoms in children. *Biological Psychiatry, 53*(11), 1050–1058. http://doi.org/10.1016/S0006-3223(03)00068-4.

Chang, K. D., Blasey, C., Ketter, T. A., & Steiner, H. (2001). Family environment of children and adolescents with bipolar parents. *Bipolar Disorders, 3*(2), 73–78.

Chang, K. D., Steiner, H., & Ketter, T. A. (2000). Psychiatric phenomenology of child and adolescent bipolar offspring. *Journal of the American Academy of Child and Adolescent Psychiatry, 39*(4), 453–460. http://doi.org/10.1097/00004583-200004000-00014.

Correll, C. U., Hauser, M., Penzner, J. B., Auther, A. M., Kafantaris, V., Saito, E., et al. (2014). Type and duration of subsyndromal symptoms in youth with bipolar I disorder prior to their first manic episode. *Bipolar Disorders, 16*(5), 478–492. http://doi.org/10.1111/bdi.12194.

Cortese, S., Faraone, S. V., Konofal, E., & Lecendreux, M. (2009). Sleep in children with attention-deficit/hyperactivity disorder: meta-analysis of subjective and objective studies. *Journal of the American Academy of Child and Adolescent Psychiatry, 48*(9), 894–908. http://doi.org/10.1097/CHI.0b013e3181ac09c9.

Costello, E. J., Angold, A., Burns, B. J., Stangl, D. K., Tweed, D. L., Erkanli, A., et al. (1996). The great Smoky Mountains study of youth. Goals, design, methods, and the prevalence of DSM-III-R disorders. *Archives of General Psychiatry, 53*(12), 1129–1136.

Diwadkar, V. A., Goradia, D., Hosanagar, A., Mermon, D., Montrose, D. M., Birmaher, B., et al. (2011). Working memory and attention deficits in adolescent offspring of schizophrenia or bipolar patients: Comparing vulnerability markers. *Progress in Neuropsychopharmacology and Biological Psychiatry, 35*(5), 1349–1354. http://doi.org/10.1016/j.pnpbp.2011.04.009.

Donfrancesco, R., Miano, S., Martines, F., Ferrante, L., Melegari, M. G., & Masi, G. (2011). Bipolar disorder co-morbidity in children with attention deficit hyperactivity disorder. *Psychiatry Research, 186*(2–3), 333–337. http://doi.org/10.1016/j.psychres.2010.07.008.

Doucette, S., Levy, A., Flowerdew, G., Horrocks, J., Grof, P., Ellenbogen, M., et al. (2016). Early parent-child relationships and risk of mood disorder in a Canadian sample of offspring of a parent with bipolar disorder: Findings from a 16-year prospective cohort study. *Early Intervention in Psychiatry, 10*(5), 381–389. http://doi.org/10.1111/eip.12195.

Dudek, D., Siwek, M., Zielińska, D., Jaeschke, R., & Rybakowski, J. (2013). Diagnostic conversions from major depressive disorder into bipolar disorder in an outpatient setting: Results of a retrospective chart review. *Journal of Affective Disorders, 144*(1–2), 112–115. http://doi.org/10.1016/j.jad.2012.06.014.

Duffy, A. (2012). The nature of the association between childhood ADHD and the development of bipolar disorder: A review of prospective high-risk studies. *American Journal of Psychiatry, 169*(12), 1247–1255. http://doi.org/10.1176/appi.ajp.2012.11111725.

Duffy, A., Alda, M., Hajek, T., Sherry, S. B., & Grof, P. (2010). Early stages in the development of bipolar disorder. *Journal of Affective Disorders, 121*(1–2), 127–135. http://doi.org/10.1016/j.jad.2009.05.022.

Duffy, A., Alda, M., Kutcher, S., Fusee, C., & Grof, P. (1998). Psychiatric symptoms and syndromes among adolescent children of parents with lithium-responsive or lithium-nonresponsive bipolar disorder. *American Journal of Psychiatry, 155*(3), 431–433. http://doi.org/10.1176/ajp.155.3.431.

Duffy, A., Doucette, S., Lewitzka, U., Alda, M., Hajek, T., & Grof, P. (2011). Findings from bipolar offspring studies: Methodology matters. *Early Intervention in Psychiatry, 5*(3), 181–191. http://doi.org/10.1111/j.1751-7893.2011.00276.x.

Duffy, A., Grof, P., Hajek, T., & Alda, M. (2010). Resolving the discrepancy in childhood bipolar high-risk study findings. *American Journal of Psychiatry, 167*(6), 716. http://doi.org/10.1176/appi.ajp.2010.10020170.

Duffy, A., Horrocks, J., Doucette, S., Keown-Stoneman, C., McCloskey, S., & Grof, P. (2013). Childhood anxiety: An early predictor of mood disorders in offspring of bipolar parents. *Journal of Affective Disorders, 150*(2), 363–369. http://doi.org/10.1016/j.jad.2013.04.021.

Duffy, A., Horrocks, J., Doucette, S., Keown-Stoneman, C., McCloskey, S., & Grof, P. (2014). The developmental trajectory of bipolar disorder. *The British Journal of Psychiatry, 204*(2), 122–128. http://doi.org/10.1192/bjp.bp.113.126706.

Egeland, J. A., Blumenthal, R. L., Nee, J., Sharpe, L., & Endicott, J. (1987). Reliability and relationship of various ages of onset criteria for major affective disorder. *Journal of Affective Disorders, 12*(2), 159–165.

Egeland, J. A., Endicott, J., Hostetter, A. M., Allen, C. R., Pauls, D. L., & Shaw, J. A. (2012). Journal of affective disorders. *Journal of Affective Disorders, 142*(1–3), 186–192. http://doi.org/10.1016/j.jad.2012.04.023.

Egeland, J. A., Hostetter, A. M., Pauls, D. L., & Sussex, J. N. (2000). Prodromal symptoms before onset of manic-depressive disorder suggested by first hospital admission histories. *Journal of the American Academy of Child and Adolescent Psychiatry, 39*(10), 1245–1252. http://doi.org/10.1097/00004583-200010000-00011.

Elias, L. R., Miskowiak, K. W., Vale, A. M. O., Köhler, C. A., Kjærstad, H. L., Stubbs, B., et al. (2017). Cognitive impairment in euthymic pediatric bipolar disorder: A systematic review and meta-analysis. *Journal of the American Academy of Child and Adolescent Psychiatry, 56*(4), 286–296. http://doi.org/10.1016/j.jaac.2017.01.008.

Endrass, J., Vetter, S., Gamma, A., Gallo, W. T., Rossegger, A., Urbaniok, F., et al. (2007). Are behavioral problems in childhood and adolescence associated with bipolar disorder in early adulthood? *European Archives of Psychiatry and Clinical Neuroscience, 257*(4), 217–221. http://doi.org/10.1007/s00406-006-0710-2.

Faedda, G. L., Marangoni, C., Serra, G., Salvatore, P., Sani, G., Vázquez, G. H., et al. (2015). Precursors of bipolar disorders: A systematic literature review of prospective studies. *The Journal of Clinical Psychiatry, 76*(5), 614–624. http://doi.org/10.4088/JCP.13r08900.

Ferreira, G. S., Moreira, C. R., Kleinman, A., Nader, E. C., Gomes, B. C., Teixeira, A. M. A., et al. (2013). Dysfunctional family environment in affected versus unaffected offspring of parents with bipolar disorder. *Australian & New Zealand Journal of Psychiatry, 47*(11), 1051–1057. http://doi.org/10.1177/0004867413506754.

Findling, R. L., Jo, B., Frazier, T. W., Youngstrom, E. A., Demeter, C. A., Fristad, M. A., et al. (2013). The 24-month course of manic symptoms in children. *Bipolar Disorders, 15*(6), 669–679. http://doi.org/10.1111/bdi.12100.

Findling, R. L., Youngstrom, E. A., Fristad, M. A., Birmaher, B., Kowatch, R. A., Arnold, L. E., et al. (2010). Characteristics of children with elevated symptoms of mania: The longitudinal assessment of manic symptoms (LAMS) study. *The Journal of Clinical Psychiatry, 71*(12), 1664–1672. http://doi.org/10.4088/JCP.09m05859yel.

Findling, R. L., Youngstrom, E. A., McNamara, N. K., Stansbrey, R. J., Demeter, C. A., Bedoya, D., et al. (2005). Early symptoms of mania and the role of parental risk. *Bipolar Disorders, 7*(6), 623–634. http://doi.org/10.1111/j.1399-5618.2005.00260.x.

Forte, A., Baldessarini, R. J., Tondo, L., Vázquez, G. H., Pompili, M., & Girardi, P. (2015). Long-term morbidity in bipolar-I, bipolar-II, and unipolar major depressive disorders. *Journal of Affective Disorders, 178*, 71–78. https://doi.org/10.1016/j.jad.2015.02.011.

Freeman, A. J., Youngstrom, E. A., Youngstrom, J. K., & Findling, R. L. (2016). Disruptive mood dysregulation disorder in a community mental health Clinic: Prevalence, comorbidity and correlates. *Journal of Child and Adolescent Psychopharmacology, 26*(2), 123–130. http://doi.org/10.1089/cap.2015.0061.

Frías, Á., Palma, C., & Farriols, N. (2014). Neurocognitive impairments among youth with pediatric bipolar disorder: A systematic review of neuropsychological research. *Journal of Affective Disorders, 166*, 297–306. http://doi.org/10.1016/j.jad.2014.05.025.

Fristad, M. A., Wolfson, H., Algorta, G. P., Youngstrom, E. A., Arnold, L. E., Birmaher, B., et al. (2016). Disruptive mood dysregulation disorder and bipolar disorder not otherwise specified: Fraternal or identical twins? *Journal of Child and Adolescent Psychopharmacology, 26*(2), 138–146. http://doi.org/10.1089/cap.2015.0062.

Goetz, M., Sebela, A., Mohaplova, M., Ceresnakova, S., Ptacek, R., & Novak, T. (2017). Psychiatric disorders and quality of life in the offspring of parents with bipolar disorder. *Journal of Child and Adolescent Psychopharmacology.* http://doi.org/10.1089/cap.2016.0056.

Goodday, S. M., Preisig, M., Gholamrezaee, M., Grof, P., Angst, J., & Duffy, A. (2017). The association between self-reported and clinically determined hypomanic symptoms and the onset of major mood disorders. *BJPsych Open, 3*(2), 71–77. http://doi.org/10.1192/bjpo.bp.116.004234.

Goodwin, F. K., & Jamison, K. R. (2007). Manic-depressive illness: Bipolar disorders and recurrent depression. *The British Journal of Psychiatry, 193*(1), 86–87. http://doi.org/10.1192/bjp.bp.107.042242.

Graziano, P. A., & Garcia, A. (2016). Attention-deficit hyperactivity disorder and children's emotion dysregulation: A meta-analysis. *Clinical Psychology Review, 46*, 106–123. http://doi.org/10.1016/j.cpr.2016.04.011.

Hamshere, M. L., Langley, K., Martin, J., Agha, S. S., Stergiakouli, E., Anney, R. J. L., et al. (2013). High loading of polygenic risk for ADHD in children with comorbid aggression. *American Journal of Psychiatry, 170*(8), 909–916. http://doi.org/10.1176/appi.ajp.2013.12081129.

Hassan, A., Agha, S. S., Langley, K., & Thapar, A. (2011). Prevalence of bipolar disorder in children and adolescents with attention-deficit hyperactivity disorder. *The British Journal of Psychiatry, 198*(3), 195–198. http://doi.org/10.1192/bjp.bp.110.078741.

Hauser, M., & Correll, C. U. (2013). The significance of at-risk or prodromal symptoms for bipolar I disorder in children and adolescents. *Canadian Journal of Psychiatry. Revue Canadienne De Psychiatrie, 58*(1), 22–31. http://doi.org/10.1177/070674371305800106.

Hazell, P. L., Carr, V., Lewin, T. J., & Sly, K. (2003). Manic symptoms in young males with ADHD predict functioning but not diagnosis after 6 years. *Journal of the American Academy of Child and Adolescent Psychiatry, 42*(5), 552–560. http://doi.org/10.1097/01.CHI.0000046830.95464.33.

Henin, A., Biederman, J., Mick, E., Sachs, G. S., Hirshfeld-Becker, D. R., Siegel, R. S., et al. (2005). Psychopathology in the offspring of parents with bipolar disorder: A controlled study. *Biological Psychiatry, 58*(7), 554–561. http://doi.org/10.1016/j.biopsych.2005.06.010.

Hillegers, M. H., Reichart, C. G., Wals, M., Verhulst, F. C., Ormel, J., & Nolen, W. A. (2005). Five-year prospective outcome of psychopathology in the adolescent offspring of bipolar parents. *Bipolar Disorders, 7*(4), 344–350. http://doi.org/10.1111/j.1399-5618.2005.00215.x.

Holtzman, J. N., Miller, S., Hooshmand, F., Wang, P. W., Chang, K. D., Hill, S. J., et al. (2015). Childhood-compared to adolescent-onset bipolar disorder has more statistically significant clinical correlates. *Journal of Affective Disorders, 179*, 114–120. http://doi.org/10.1016/j.jad.2015.03.019.

Horwitz, S. M., Demeter, C. A., Pagano, M. E., Youngstrom, E. A., Fristad, M. A., Arnold, L. E., et al. (2010). Longitudinal assessment of manic symptoms (LAMS) study. *The Journal of Clinical Psychiatry, 71*(11), 1511–1517. http://doi.org/10.4088/JCP.09m05835yel.

Jackson, A., Cavanagh, J., & Scott, J. (2003). A systematic review of manic and depressive prodromes. *Journal of Affective Disorders, 74*(3), 209–217. http://doi.org/10.1016/S0165-0327(02)00266-5.

James, A., Hoang, U., Seagroatt, V., Clacey, J., Goldacre, M., & Leibenluft, E. (2014). A comparison of American and English hospital discharge rates for pediatric bipolar disorder, 2000 to 2010. *Journal of the American Academy of Child and Adolescent Psychiatry, 53*(6), 614–624. http://doi.org/10.1016/j.jaac.2014.02.008.

Johnson, J. G., Cohen, P., & Brook, J. S. (2000). Associations between bipolar disorder and other psychiatric disorders during adolescence and early adulthood: A community-based longitudinal investigation. *American Journal of Psychiatry, 157*(10), 1679–1681. http://doi.org/10.1176/appi.ajp.157.10.1679.

Jolin, E. M., Weller, E. B., & Weller, R. A. (2008). Anxiety symptoms and syndromes in bipolar children and adolescents. *Current Psychiatry Reports, 10*(2), 123–129.

Jones, S. H., Tai, S., Evershed, K., Knowles, R., & Bentall, R. (2006). Early detection of bipolar disorder: A pilot familial high-risk study of parents with bipolar disorder and their adolescent children. *Bipolar Disorders, 8*(4), 362–372. http://doi.org/10.1111/j.1399-5618.2006.00329.x.

Judd, L. L., Akiskal, H. S., Schettler, P. J., Endicott, J., Maser, J., Solomon, D. A., et al. (2002). The long-term natural history of the weekly symptomatic status of bipolar I disorder. *Archives of General Psychiatry, 59*(6), 530. https://doi.org/10.1001/archpsyc.59.6.530.

Keck, P. E., Kessler, R. C., & Ross, R. (2008). Clinical and economic effects of unrecognized or inadequately treated bipolar disorder. *Journal of Psychiatric Practice, 14*(Suppl. 2), 31–38. http://doi.org/10.1097/01.pra.0000320124.91799.2a.

Kessing, L. V., Willer, I., Andersen, P. K., & Bukh, J. D. (2017). Rate and predictors of conversion from unipolar to bipolar disorder: A systematic review and meta-analysis. *Bipolar Disorders, 19*(5), 324–335. http://doi.org/10.1111/bdi.12513.

Kim-Cohen, J., Caspi, A., Moffitt, T. E., Harrington, H., Milne, B. J., & Poulton, R. (2003). Prior juvenile diagnoses in adults with mental disorder - developmental follow-back of a prospective-longitudinal cohort. *Archives of General Psychiatry, 60*(7), 709–717. http://doi.org/10.1001/archpsyc.60.7.709.

Klein, R. G. (2012). Clinical and functional outcome of childhood attention-deficit/hyperactivity disorder 33 years later outcome of childhood ADHD 33 years later. *Archives of General Psychiatry, 69*(12), 1295. http://doi.org/10.1001/archgenpsychiatry.2012.271.

Konofal, E., Lecendreux, M., & Cortese, S. (2010). Sleep and ADHD. *Sleep Medicine, 11*(7), 652–658. http://doi.org/10.1016/j.sleep.2010.02.012.

Lader, M. H. (1968). Prophylactic lithium? *Lancet, 2,* 103.

Larsson, S., Lorentzen, S., Mork, E., Barrett, E. A., Steen, N. E., Lagerberg, T. V., et al. (2010). Age at onset of bipolar disorder in a Norwegian catchment area sample. *Journal of Affective Disorders, 124*(1–2), 174–177. http://doi.org/10.1016/j.jad.2009.10.031.

Leibenluft, E., Charney, D. S., Towbin, K. E., Bhangoo, R. K., & Pine, D. S. (2003). Defining clinical phenotypes of juvenile mania. *American Journal of Psychiatry, 160*(3), 430–437. http://doi.org/10.1176/appi.ajp.160.3.430.

Leibenluft, E., Cohen, P., Gorrindo, T., Brook, J. S., & Pine, D. S. (2006). Chronic versus episodic irritability in youth: A community-based, longitudinal study of clinical and diagnostic associations. *Journal of Child and Adolescent Psychopharmacology, 16*(4), 456–466. http://doi.org/10.1089/cap.2006.16.456.

Leibenluft, E., & Stoddard, J. (2013). The developmental psychopathology of irritability. *Development and Psychopathology, 25*(4 Pt 2), 1473–1487. http://doi.org/10.1017/S0954579413000722.

Levenson, J. C., Axelson, D. A., Merranko, J., Angulo, M., Goldstein, T. R., Mullin, B. C., et al. (2015). Differences in sleep disturbances among offspring of parents with and without bipolar disorder: Association with conversion to bipolar disorder. *Bipolar Disorders, 17*(8), 836–848. http://doi.org/10.1111/bdi.12345.

Leverich, G. S., Post, R. M., Keck, P. E., Jr., Altshuler, L. L., Frye, M. A., Kupka, R. W., et al. (2007). The poor prognosis of childhood-onset bipolar disorder. *The Journal of Pediatrics, 150*(5), 485–490. http://doi.org/10.1016/j.jpeds.2006.10.070.

Lewinsohn, P. M., Seeley, J. R., Buckley, M. E., & Klein, D. N. (2002). Bipolar disorder in adolescence and young adulthood. *Child and Adolescent Psychiatric Clinics of North America, 11*(3), 461–475.

Lewinsohn, P. M., Seeley, J. R., & Klein, D. N. (2003). Bipolar disorders during adolescence. *Acta Psychiatrica Scandinavica. Supplementum,* (418), 47–50.

Margulies, D. M., Weintraub, S., Basile, J., Grover, P. J., & Carlson, G. A. (2012). Will disruptive mood dysregulation disorder reduce false diagnosis of bipolar disorder in children? *Bipolar Disorders, 14*(5), 488–496. http://doi.org/10.1111/j.1399-5618.2012.01029.x.

Mattisson, C., Bogren, M., Horstmann, V., Munk-Jørgensen, P., & Nettelbladt, P. (2007). The long-term course of depressive disorders in the Lundby Study. *Psychological Medicine, 37*(6), 883–891. http://doi.org/10.1017/S0033291707000074.

Merikangas, K. R., Akiskal, H. S., Angst, J., Greenberg, P. E., Hirschfeld, R. M. A., Petukhova, M., et al. (2007). Lifetime and 12-month prevalence of bipolar spectrum disorder in the National Comorbidity Survey replication. *Archives of General Psychiatry, 64*(5), 543–552. http://doi.org/10.1001/archpsyc.64.5.543.

Mesman, E., Birmaher, B. B., Goldstein, B. I., Goldstein, T., Derks, E. M., Vleeschouwer, M., et al. (2016). Categorical and dimensional psychopathology in Dutch and US offspring of parents with bipolar disorder: A preliminary cross-national comparison. *Journal of Affective Disorders, 205*(C), 95–102. http://doi.org/10.1016/j.jad.2016.06.011.

Mesman, E., Nolen, W. A., Keijsers, L., & Hillegers, M. H. J. (2017). Baseline dimensional psychopathology and future mood disorder onset: Findings from the Dutch bipolar offspring study. *Acta Psychiatrica Scandinavica, 136*(2), 201–209. http://doi.org/10.1111/acps.12739.

Mesman, E., Nolen, W. A., Reichart, C. G., Wals, M., & Hillegers, M. H. J. (2013). The Dutch bipolar offspring study: 12-year follow-up. *American Journal of Psychiatry, 170*(5), 542–549. http://doi.org/10.1176/appi.ajp.2012.12030401.

Millar, A., Espie, C. A., & Scott, J. (2004). The sleep of remitted bipolar outpatients: A controlled naturalistic study using actigraphy. *Journal of Affective Disorders, 80*(2–3), 145–153. http://doi.org/10.1016/S0165-0327(03)00055-7.

Moreno, C., Laje, G., Blanco, C., Jiang, H., Schmidt, A. B., & Olfson, M. (2007). National trends in the outpatient diagnosis and treatment of bipolar disorder in youth. *Archives of General Psychiatry, 64*(9), 1032–1039. http://doi.org/10.1001/archpsyc.64.9.1032.

Murray, G., & Harvey, A. (2010). Circadian rhythms and sleep in bipolar disorder. *Bipolar Disorders, 12*(5), 459–472. http://doi.org/10.1111/j.1399-5618.2010.00843.x.

Ng, T. H., Chung, K.-F., Ho, F. Y.-Y., Yeung, W.-F., Yung, K.-P., & Lam, T.-H. (2015). Sleep-wake disturbance in interepisode bipolar disorder and high-risk individuals: A systematic review and meta-analysis. *Sleep Medicine Reviews, 20*, 46–58. http://doi.org/10.1016/j.smrv.2014.06.006.

Nurnberger, J. I., McInnis, M., Reich, W., Kastelic, E., Wilcox, H. C., Glowinski, A., et al. (2011). A high-risk study of bipolar disorder. Childhood clinical phenotypes as precursors of major mood disorders. *Archives of General Psychiatry, 68*(10), 1012–1020. http://doi.org/10.1001/archgenpsychiatry.2011.126.

Oedegaard, K. J., Syrstad, V. E. G., Morken, G., Akiskal, H. S., & Fasmer, O. B. (2009). A study of age at onset and affective temperaments in a Norwegian sample of patients with mood disorders. *Journal of Affective Disorders, 118*(1–3), 229–233. http://doi.org/10.1016/j.jad.2009.01.030.

Päären, A., Bohman, H., von Knorring, L., Olsson, G., von Knorring, A.-L., & Jonsson, U. (2014). Early risk factors for adult bipolar disorder in adolescents with mood disorders: A 15-year follow-up of a community sample. *BMC Psychiatry, 14*, 363. http://doi.org/10.1186/s12888-014-0363-z.

Päären, A., von Knorring, A.-L., Olsson, G., von Knorring, L., Bohman, H., & Jonsson, U. (2013). Hypomania spectrum disorders from adolescence to adulthood: A 15-year follow-up of a community sample. *Journal of Affective Disorders, 145*(2), 190–199. http://doi.org/10.1016/j.jad.2012.07.031.

Parry, P. I., Allison, S., & Bastiampillai, T. (2014). Reification of the paediatric bipolar hypothesis in the USA. *The Lancet Psychiatry, 2*(1), 14–16. http://doi.org/10.1016/S2215-0366(14)00075-3.

Parry, P., Allison, S., & Bastiampillai, T. (2017). Measurement issues: "Paediatric bipolar disorder" rates are lower than claimed - a reexamination of the epidemiological surveys used by a meta-analysis. *Child and Adolescent Mental Health, 45*(3p2), 26–29. http://doi.org/10.1111/camh.12231.

Pavlova, B., Perlis, R. H., Alda, M., & Uher, R. (2015). Lifetime prevalence of anxiety disorders in people with bipolar disorder: A systematic review and meta-analysis. *The Lancet Psychiatry, 2*(8), 710–717. http://doi.org/10.1016/S2215-0366(15)00112-1.

Pavuluri, M. N., Henry, D. B., Devineni, B., Carbray, J. A., & Birmaher, B. (2006). Child mania rating scale: Development, reliability, and validity. *Journal of the American Academy of Child and Adolescent Psychiatry, 45*(5), 550–560. http://doi.org/10.1097/01.chi.0000205700.40700.50.

Post, R. M., Leverich, G. S., Kupka, R., Keck, P., Jr., McElroy, S., Altshuler, L., et al. (2013). Increased parental history of bipolar disorder in the United States: Association with early age of onset. *Acta Psychiatrica Scandinavica, 129*(5), 375–382. http://doi.org/10.1111/acps.12208.

Post, R. M., Leverich, G. S., Kupka, R. W., Keck, P. E., McElroy, S. L., Altshuler, L. L., et al. (2010). Early-onset bipolar disorder and treatment delay are risk factors for poor outcome in adulthood. *The Journal of Clinical Psychiatry, 71*(7), 864–872. http://doi.org/10.4088/JCP.08m04994yel.

Preisig, M., Strippoli, M.-P. F., Castelao, E., Merikangas, K. R., Gholam-Rezaee, M., Marquet, P., et al. (2016). The specificity of the familial aggregation of early-onset bipolar disorder: A controlled 10-year follow-up study of offspring of parents with mood disorders. *Journal of Affective Disorders, 190*(C), 26–33. http://doi.org/10.1016/j.jad.2015.10.005.

Propper, L., Cumby, J., Patterson, V. C., Drobinin, V., Glover, J. M., MacKenzie, L. E., et al. (2017). Disruptive mood dysregulation disorder in offspring of parents with depression and bipolar disorder. *The British Journal of Psychiatry, 210*(6), 408–412. http://doi.org/10.1192/bjp.bp.117.198754.

Rasic, D., Hajek, T., Alda, M., & Uher, R. (2014). Risk of mental illness in offspring of parents with schizophrenia, bipolar disorder, and major depressive disorder: A meta-analysis of family high-risk studies. *Schizophrenia Bulletin, 40*(1), 28–38. http://doi.org/10.1093/schbul/sbt114.

Ritter, P. S., Marx, C., Bauer, M., Lepold, K., & Pfennig, A. (2011). The role of disturbed sleep in the early recognition of bipolar disorder: A systematic review. *Bipolar Disorders, 13*(3), 227–237. http://doi.org/10.1111/j.1399-5618.2011.00917.x.

Rybakowski, J. K., Dmitrzak-Weglarz, M., Kliwicki, S., & Hauser, J. (2013). Polymorphism of circadian clock genes and prophylactic lithium response. *Bipolar Disorders, 16*(2), 151–158. http://doi.org/10.1111/bdi.12136.

Sanchez-Gistau, V., Romero, S., Moreno, D., de la Serna, E., Baeza, I., Sugranyes, G., et al. (2015). Psychiatric disorders in child and adolescent offspring of patients with schizophrenia and bipolar disorder: A controlled study. *Schizophrenia Research, 168*(1–2), 197–203. http://doi.org/10.1016/j.schres.2015.08.034.

Savage, J., Verhulst, B., Copeland, W., Althoff, R. R., Lichtenstein, P., & Roberson-Nay, R. (2015). A genetically informed study of the longitudinal relation between irritability and anxious/depressed symptoms. *Journal of the American Academy of Child and Adolescent Psychiatry, 54*(5), 377–384. http://doi.org/10.1016/j.jaac.2015.02.010.

Sebela, A., Novak, T., Kemlink, D., & Goetz, M. (2017). Sleep characteristics in child and adolescent offspring of parents with bipolar disorder: A case control study. *BMC Psychiatry, 17*(1), 199. http://doi.org/10.1186/s12888-017-1361-8.

de la Serna, E., Sugranyes, G., Sanchez-Gistau, V., Rodriguez-Toscano, E., Baeza, I., Vila, M., et al. (2017). Neuropsychological characteristics of child and adolescent offspring of patients with schizophrenia or bipolar disorder. *Schizophrenia Research, 183*, 110–115. http://doi.org/10.1016/j.schres.2016.11.007.

Severus, E., & Bauer, M. (2013). Diagnosing bipolar disorders in DSM-5. *International Journal of Bipolar Disorders, 23*(1), 14. https://doi.org/10.1186/2194-7511-1-14.

Shankman, S. A., Lewinsohn, P. M., Klein, D. N., Small, J. W., Seeley, J. R., & Altman, S. E. (2009). Subthreshold conditions as precursors for full syndrome disorders: A 15-year longitudinal study of multiple diagnostic classes. *Journal of Child Psychology and Psychiatry, 50*(12), 1485–1494. http://doi.org/10.1111/j.1469-7610.2009.02117.x.

Shaw, J. A., Egeland, J. A., Endicott, J., Allen, C. R., & Hostetter, A. M. (2005). A 10-year prospective study of prodromal patterns for bipolar disorder among amish youth. *Journal of the American Academy of Child and Adolescent Psychiatry, 44*(11), 1104–1111. http://doi.org/10.1097/01.chi.0000177052.26476.e5.

Shyu, Y.-C., Yuan, S.-S., Lee, S.-Y., Yang, C.-J., Yang, K.-C., Lee, T.-L., et al. (2015). Attention-deficit/hyperactivity disorder, methylphenidate use and the risk of developing schizophrenia spectrum disorders: A nationwide population-based study in Taiwan. *Schizophrenia Research, 168*(1–2), 1–7. http://doi.org/10.1016/j.schres.2015.08.033.

Skjelstad, D. V., Malt, U. F., & Holte, A. (2010). Symptoms and signs of the initial prodrome of bipolar disorder: A systematic review. *Journal of Affective Disorders, 126*(1–2), 1–13. http://doi.org/10.1016/j.jad.2009.10.003.

Smalley, S. L., McGough, J. J., Moilanen, I. K., Loo, S. K., Taanila, A., Ebeling, H., et al. (2007). Prevalence and psychiatric comorbidity of attention-deficit/hyperactivity disorder in an adolescent Finnish population. *Journal of the American Academy of Child and Adolescent Psychiatry, 46*(12), 1575–1583. http://doi.org/10.1097/chi.0b013e3181573137.

Smoller, J. W., & Finn, C. T. (2003). Family, twin, and adoption studies of bipolar disorder. *American Journal of Medical Genetics, 123C*(1), 48–58. http://doi.org/10.1002/ajmg.c.20013.

Sparks, G. M., Axelson, D. A., Yu, H., Ha, W., Ballester, J., Diler, R. S., et al. (2014). Disruptive mood dysregulation disorder and chronic irritability in youth at familial risk for bipolar disorder. *Journal of the American Academy of Child and Adolescent Psychiatry, 53*(4), 408–416. http://doi.org/10.1016/j.jaac.2013.12.026.

Stringaris, A., Baroni, A., Haimm, C., Brotman, M., Lowe, C. H., Myers, F., et al. (2010). Pediatric bipolar disorder versus severe mood dysregulation: Risk for manic episodes on follow-up. *Journal of the American Academy of Child and Adolescent Psychiatry, 49*(4), 397–405.

Stringaris, A., Santosh, P., Leibenluft, E., & Goodman, R. (2010). Youth meeting symptom and impairment criteria for mania-like episodes lasting less than four days: An epidemiological enquiry. *Journal of Child Psychology and Psychiatry, 51*(1), 31–38. http://doi.org/10.1111/j.1469-7610.2009.02129.x.

Strober, M., & Carlson, G. (1982). Bipolar illness in adolescents with major depression: Clinical, genetic, and psychopharmacologic predictors in a three- to four-year prospective follow-up investigation. *Archives of General Psychiatry, 39*(5), 549–555.

Thomsen, P. H., Møller, L. L., Dehlholm, B., & Brask, B. H. (1992). Manic-depressive psychosis in children younger than 15 years: A register-based investigation of 39 cases in Denmark. *Acta Psychiatrica Scandinavica, 85*(5), 401–406.

Tijssen, M. J. A., van Os, J., Wittchen, H. U., Lieb, R., Beesdo, K., Mengelers, R., et al. (2009). Evidence that bipolar disorder is the poor outcome fraction of a common developmental phenotype: An 8-year cohort study in young people. *Psychological Medicine, 40*(02), 289–299. http://doi.org/10.1017/S0033291709006138.

Tijssen, M. J. A., van Os, J., Wittchen, H. U., Lieb, R., Beesdo, K., Mengelers, R., et al. (2010). Prediction of transition from common adolescent bipolar experiences to bipolar disorder: 10-year study. *The British Journal of Psychiatry, 196*(2), 102–108. http://doi.org/10.1192/bjp.bp.109.065763.

Tijssen, M. J. A., van Os, J., Wittchen, H. U., Lieb, R., Beesdo, K., & Wichers, M. (2010). Risk factors predicting onset and persistence of subthreshold expression of bipolar psychopathology among youth from the community. *Acta Psychiatrica Scandinavica, 122*(3), 255–266. http://doi.org/10.1111/j.1600-0447.2010.01539.x.

Todd, R. D., Reich, W., Petti, T. A., Joshi, P., DePaulo, J. R. J., Nurnberger, J. J., et al. (1996). Psychiatric diagnoses in the child and adolescent members of extended families identified through adult bipolar affective disorder probands. *Journal of the American Academy of Child and Adolescent Psychiatry, 35*(5), 664–671. http://doi.org/10.1097/00004583-199605000-00022.

Van Meter, A. R., Burke, C., Kowatch, R. A., Findling, R. L., & Youngstrom, E. A. (2016). Ten-year updated meta-analysis of the clinical characteristics of pediatric mania and hypomania. *Bipolar Disorders, 18*(1), 19–32. http://doi.org/10.1111/bdi.12358.

Van Meter, A. R., Burke, C., Youngstrom, E. A., Faedda, G. L., & Correll, C. U. (2016). The bipolar prodrome: Meta-analysis of symptom prevalence prior to initial or recurrent mood episodes. *Journal of the American Academy of Child and Adolescent Psychiatry, 55*(7), 543–555. http://doi.org/10.1016/j.jaac.2016.04.017.

Vandeleur, C., Rothen, S., Gholam-Rezaee, M., Castelao, E., Vidal, S., Favre, S., et al. (2012). Mental disorders in offspring of parents with bipolar and major depressive disorders. *Bipolar Disorders, 14*(6), 641–653. http://doi.org/10.1111/j.1399-5618.2012.01048.x.

Vázquez, G. H., Holtzman, J. N., Lolich, M., Ketter, T. A., & Baldessarini, R. J. (2015). Recurrence rates in bipolar disorder: Systematic comparison of long-term prospective, naturalistic studies versus randomized controlled trials. *European Neuropsychopharmacology, 25*(10), 1501–1512. https://doi.org/10.1016/j.euroneuro.2015.07.013.

Wals, M., Hillegers, M. H. J., Reichart, C. G., Ormel, J., Nolen, W. A., & Verhulst, F. C. (2001). Prevalence of psychopathology in children of a bipolar parent. *Journal of the American Academy of Child and Adolescent Psychiatry, 40*(9), 1094–1102. http://doi.org/10.1097/00004583-200109000-00019.

World Health Organization. (1992). *The ICD-10 classification of mental and behavioural disorders: Clinical descriptions and diagnostic guidelines.* Geneva: World Health Organization.

Wozniak, J., Biederman, J., Kiely, K., Ablon, J. S., Faraone, S. V., Mundy, E., et al. (1995). Mania-like symptoms suggestive of childhood-onset bipolar disorder in clinically referred children. *Journal of the American Academy of Child and Adolescent Psychiatry, 34*(7), 867–876. http://doi.org/10.1097/00004583-199507000-00010.

Youngstrom, E. A., Frazier, T. W., Demeter, C., Calabrese, J. R., & Findling, R. L. (2008). Developing a 10-item mania scale from the parent general behavior inventory for children and adolescents. *The Journal of Clinical Psychiatry, 69*(5), 831–839.

Heterogeneity in Tics and Gilles de la Tourette Syndrome

Valsamma Eapen[1,2], *Amelia Walter*[1,2], *Mary M. Robertson*[3]

[1] University of New South Wales, Sydney NSW, Australia;
[2] Liverpool Hospital & Ingham Institute, Liverpool NSW, Australia;
[3] University College London, London, England

INTRODUCTION

Gilles de la Tourette syndrome (GTS), a common disorder affecting about 1% of the population in most parts of the world (apart from Sub-Saharan Africa), affects males three to four times more commonly than females, and has had a long albeit controversial history. First described in the 19th century (Tourette, 1885; Itard, 1825), the main features of GTS have remained constant. The core diagnostic features are multiple motor and one or more vocal (phonic) tics lasting for over a year. The most common motor tics include repetitive blinking, eyebrow raising, and nasal twitching, whereas the most common phonic tics are sniffing, coughing, and throat clearing. In addition, almost pathognomonic but not necessary features described in early documentations include coprolalia (involuntary, inappropriate swearing, found in about 10% of patients) and echophenomena (copying behaviors), as well as many comorbidities and psychopathologies (Robertson, 2015; Robertson et al., 2017), many of which we will discuss in this chapter.

CLINICAL HETEROGENEITY

There is considerable clinical heterogeneity among patients with GTS with regard to the type and complexity of tics, as well as associated comorbidities and coexistent psychopathologies. Based on the associated

Understanding Uniqueness and Diversity in Child and
Adolescent Mental Health
https://doi.org/10.1016/B978-0-12-815310-9.00003-4

clinical features, GTS can be classified into three subgroups: one with motor and vocal tics only ("pure" GTS); one with associated features such as coprophenomena and echophenomena ("full-blown" GTS), and one with associated comorbidities such as obsessive-compulsive disorder (OCD), attention-deficit hyperactivity disorder (ADHD), and coexistent psychopathologies including anxiety, depression, and personality disorder (GTS "plus").

Because clinical heterogeneity is often linked to genetic heterogeneity, and this has significant implications for the management of GTS as well as its course and prognosis, research is critical to identify homogeneous symptom clusters and subphenotypes. In this chapter, we review the literature based on different approaches that may be helpful in this regard: factor, cluster, and latent class analysis (LCA) studies; epidemiological studies; and genetic studies with a focus on comorbidities. In turn, this may prove useful in the search for putative genes implicated in GTS, organizing assessment and treatment procedures more effectively regarding symptom groups, and in explaining differential treatment response and overall outcomes.

FACTOR, CLUSTER, AND LATENT CLASS ANALYSIS STUDIES

Twelve studies to date have used factor analysis, cluster analysis, or LCA to examine symptom clusters or profiles among individuals with GTS, 11 of which are discussed subsequently. Four of those studies used cluster and factor analytic techniques (Alsobrook & Pauls, 2002; Mathews et al., 2007; Robertson & Cavanna, 2007; Robertson, Althoff, Hafez, & Pauls, 2008), two cluster analysis alone (Kircanski, Woods, Chang, Ricketts, & Piacentini, 2010; McGuire et al., 2013), three factor analysis alone (Cavanna et al., 2011; Eapen, Fox-Hiley, Banerjee, & Robertson, 2004; Huisman-van Dijk, van de Schoot, Rijkeboer, Mathews, & Cath, 2016), and two LCA (Grados, Mathews, & Tourette Syndrome Association International Consortium for Genetics, 2008; Rodgers et al., 2014). The study by Storch et al. (2004) is not included because the primary aim was to examine the factor structure of an established scale, and also less than a quarter of the sample had a primary diagnosis of GTS.

In the first of these, Alsobrook and Pauls (2002) collected lifetime data for 29 motor and phonic tic symptoms from 85 adult patients with GTS using the Schedule for Tourette and Other Behavioral Syndromes (Pauls & Hurst, 1981). Because the original variables were binary in nature (the absence or presence of tics) and thus were not ideal for standard principal component factor analysis (PCFA), hierarchical agglomerative cluster analysis (HACA) was applied to the 29 tic symptoms to generate 12 symptom clusters from which continuous variables could be created. PCFA was then undertaken on these 12 symptom clusters. Four factors were identified that accounted for 61% of the symptomatic variance. The first factor, "aggressive phenomena," accounted for 20% of the variance, and was composed of symptoms including argumentativeness, temper fits, coprolalia (involuntary swearing), kicking, self-injurious behavior (SIB), imitation of actions, blocking, and hopping. This factor was significantly associated with the occurrence of ADHD. The second factor included "purely motor and phonic tic symptoms" and accounted for 16.8% of symptomatic variance. Males had significantly higher scores on this factor than did females, which was consistent with the higher prevalence rate of GTS among males. The third factor, accounting for 14% of variance, was classified as "compulsive phenomena" and included the symptoms of throat clearing, coughing, touching (of others, objects, or body), picking at things, and utterance or repetition of words (random words, palilalia, and echolalia). This factor was significantly associated with an earlier age of onset of GTS and the occurrence of ADHD, but not OCD, among the patients with GTS themselves. However, it was significantly related to the occurrence of both ADHD and OCD in the patients' relatives. The fourth and final factor, which the authors acknowledged remained difficult to explain, accounted for 10% of variance, and included tapping and the absence of grunting.

Similar methodology was used by Robertson and Cavanna (2007) in their study of 69 individuals from a multigenerational kindred, who had symptoms related to the GTS spectrum. A list of 106 endorsed symptoms, encompassing tics and other symptoms related to GTS, was generated from data obtained through two diagnostic interviews (the National Hospital Interview Schedule for Gilles de la Tourette Syndrome [NHIS-GTS] [Robertson & Eapen, 1996] and the Schedule for Affective Disorders and Schizophrenia [Spitzer & Endicott, 1978]) and two questionnaires (the Middlesex Hospital Questionnaire [Crown & Crisp, 1966] and the Leyton Obsessional Inventory [Snowdon, 1980]). The authors grouped tics according to muscle districts and based psychopathological features on diagnostic categories. Similar to the work of Alsobrook and Pauls (2002), HACA was then performed on the resulting 27 variables, generating 18 symptom clusters; these were used in PCFA. Three significant factors emerged from this analysis, accounting for 41.9% of symptomatic variance. The first factor, "pure tics," accounted for 22.9% of variance. This factor was composed predominantly of pure motor and vocal tics, similar to the second factor of Alsobrook and Pauls (purely motor and phonic tic symptoms), but it included symptoms that loaded on Alsobrook and Pauls' third factor (compulsive phenomena), including forced touching of objects, throat clearing, coughing, vocalizations, and echophenomena. Robertson and Cavanna's (2007) second factor, "ADHD-aggressive behaviors," accounted for 10.8% of variance and included symptoms of hyperactivity, inattention, sleep disturbance, aggressive behavior, and some tics involving the mouth area and limbs, plus the absence of paliphenomena and symptoms of mood and anxiety disorders. Unlike Alsobrook and Pauls' first factor (aggressive phenomena), it did not include SIB, which instead loaded on a third factor, "depression-anxiety-obsessive compulsive symptoms (OCS)-SIB." This third factor accounted for 8.3% of total variance and was characterized by specific fears and phobias, anxiety, depression, obsessive-compulsive symptoms, stuttering, and SIB, with the inclusion of some tics such as facial grimaces and abdominal contractions.

Robertson et al. (2008) also used HACA and PCFA with a larger sample of 410 unrelated child and adult patients with GTS. Detailed information on motor and phonic tics was collected from 402 patients using the NHIS-GTS (Robertson & Eapen, 1996) and Yale Global Tic Severity Scale (YGTSS) (Leckman et al., 1989). Data were also coded for the presence or absence of obsessive-compulsive behaviors, SIB, and aggression, along with the presence of absence of a family history of GTS or chronic tics, ADHD, and OCD. HACA was conducted on the 32 tic symptoms, generating seven clusters of symptoms and 13 symptoms that did not cluster with others but were treated as separate clusters in subsequent PCFA. Five factors emerged from PCFA, accounting for 46.6% of total variance. The first factor, which the authors argued could be considered a "socially inappropriate factor," accounted for 22.9% of variance and included coprophenomena, echophenomena, paliphenomena, aggressive behavior (eg, hitting, spitting, and kicking), and SIB. This factor was significantly associated with comorbid ADHD, OCD, self-injury, and aggression. Robertson et al. (2008) suggested that this factor may relate to Alsobrook and Pauls' (2002) first factor (aggressive phenomena), although echophenomena and paliphenomena loaded instead on the third factor (compulsive phenomena) in their study. Similarly, whereas there may be overlap with Robertson and Cavanna's (2007) second factor (ADHD-aggressive) behaviors, there are important differences, most notably with paliphenomena, which was significantly and negatively associated with the ADHD-aggressive behaviors factor in their study. Unlike earlier studies by Alsobrook and Pauls (2002) and Robertson and Cavanna (2007), which suggested a single factor composed of purely tics, Robertson et al. (2008) found evidence of two factors composed of tics alone, which they labeled "complex motor tics" (Factor 2, accounting for 7.4% of variance) and "simple tics," which included both motor and phonic tics (Factor 3, accounting for 5.8% of variance). The fourth and fifth factors, characterized by "compulsive behaviors" and "touching self" (including simple motor and phonic tics), accounted for 5.4% and 5.1% of variance, respectively. Consistent with Alsobrook and Pauls' (2002) findings and the prevalence rates for GTS, males had significantly higher scores than did females on Factors 2, 3, and 5, all of which included what could be seen as "typical" tic symptoms.

Mathews et al. (2007) also conducted HACA in a sample of child and adult patients with GTS from two genetically isolated populations. The study sample consisted of 121 individuals from the Central Valley of Costa Rica and 133 individuals of Ashkenazi Jewish descent from the United States. Lifetime data were collected retrospectively using the Yale Self-Report Form (YSRF), a diagnostic instrument designed by the Tourette Syndrome Association International Consortium for Genetics (TSAICG, 1999). In addition to tic symptoms, the YSRF contains questions about obsessions and compulsions, as well as inattention, impulsivity, and hyperactivity. In each of the two populations, although there were differences in cluster membership, the researchers found evidence for two major symptom clusters: "simple body tics" and "complex tics." These also resembled factors that emerged during exploratory PCFA. Membership of the complex tic cluster was associated with increased tic severity, medication treatment, greater global impairment, comorbid OCD and ADHD symptoms, and an earlier age of onset for GTS. Mathews et al. (2007) noted the limitation in their study of having collected participant retrospective self-report data.

In the first study restricted to children and adolescents (88 with GTS and 11 with chronic motor tic disorder in an outpatient setting), Kircanski et al. (2010) used HACA to identify symptom clusters based on the 46 tic symptoms on the YGTSS (Leckman et al., 1989), and examined relationships among tic symptom clusters, symptom severity, and demographic variables. Four overlapping symptom clusters emerged from their analysis. The first, "predominantly complex tics," was positively associated with the experience of premonitory urges on the Premonitory Urge for Tics Scale (PUTS) (Woods, Piacentini, Himle, & Chang, 2005), internalizing and externalizing behavior scores on the Child Behavior Checklist (Achenbach, 1991), and overall impairment on the YGTSS. It was also associated with participants' OCD scores on the Child Yale-Brown Obsessive-Compulsive Scale (Scahill et al., 1997) as well as a concurrent diagnosis of OCD based on diagnostic interview. The second cluster, "simple head/face tics," included four tic symptoms; it was also associated with impairment on the YGTSS and was uniquely and negatively associated with school functioning and academic performance. The authors posited that these types of tics (eg, eye movements, head jerks) may be particularly disruptive in classroom sittings where visual concentration on material is critical. Similar to Cluster 1, the third cluster, "simple body tics," which included one complex motor tic (tic-related compulsive behaviors), was associated with patients' YGTSS impairment and OCD scores. The final cluster, "simple vocal/facial tics," included facial grimaces, breath-related sounds, sniffing, grunting, throat clearing, and nose movements. Cluster scores were significantly intercorrelated, with the exception of Clusters 2 and 4, which is surprising given the proximity of involved areas: simple face tics (Cluster 2) and simple facial tics (Cluster 4). Furthermore, most participants (52.5%) endorsed at least one tic on all four clusters. Unlike previous studies, there was no relationship between gender and any of the clusters.

Whereas several studies examined relationships between cluster membership and tic symptom severity, comorbidities, and overall impairment, only one study explored associations between cluster membership and response to treatment (McGuire et al., 2013). In a study of 239 child and adult patients with chronic tic disorders from two multicenter randomized, controlled trials, McGuire et al. (2013) applied HACA to identify symptom clusters based on the 40 tic types on the YGTSS (Leckman et al., 1989); four tic symptom clusters emerged. The first, "impulse control and complex phonic tics," consisted primarily of complex phonic tics (eg, disinhibited speech, complex words, speech atypicalities) and impulse control tics (e.g., coprophenomena, SIB, disinhibited behavior). Membership of this cluster was positively associated with the use of tic medication in children and the presence of premonitory urges in adults based on the PUTS (Woods et al., 2005), which suggested greater tic complexity. The second cluster, "complex motor tics," included nine complex motor tics affecting the face, head, and body. The third cluster, "simple head motor/vocal tics," included three tics (head jerk movements, eye blinking, and any simple phonic tic). The final cluster, "predominantly simple motor tics," was composed of nine simple motor tics affecting the face, head, and body, in addition to two complex motor tics. This factor was positively associated with ADHD severity ratings in adults, as measured by the Attention-Deficit Hyperactivity Disorder Rating Scale (DuPaul, Power, McGoey, Ikeda, & Anastopoulos, 1998). Only 8% of participants endorsed tics in only one cluster; 30% reported at least one tic on all four clusters (McGuire et al., 2013). McGuire et al. (2013) noted similarities between three of their tic symptom clusters and those found by Kircanski et al. (2010). Both studies described clusters of complex tics ("complex motor tics" and "predominantly complex tics"), simple tics affecting the head and face ("simple head motor/vocal tics" and "simple head/face tics"), and simple motor or body tics ("predominantly simple motor tics" and "simple body tics"). There were disparities between the remaining tic cluster in each study ("impulse control and complex phonic tics" and "simple vocal/facial tics"), although there was some overlap between the findings of Kircanski et al. (2010) "simple vocal/facial tics" and McGuire et al. (2013) "predominantly simple motor tics," with facial grimaces and nose movements loading on both. McGuire et al. (2013) found no significant associations, positive or negative, between cluster membership and patients' response to a behavioral treatment, Comprehensive Behavioral Intervention for Tics (CBIT) (Woods et al., 2008); CBIT was equally effective across a range of tic types. The authors noted that the degree of heterogeneity within tic clusters may have obscured their ability to detect an association between tic cluster and treatment outcome (McGuire et al., 2013).

In a large factor analytic study of patients with GTS, Cavanna et al. (2011) reviewed the clinical files of 639 patients with GTS recruited from two tertiary referral centers between 1980 and 2008, and used PCFA to analyze tic symptomology based on the NHIS-GTS (Robertson & Eapen, 1996) or its preliminary versions. Only 10.6% of subjects who were interviewed presented with GTS only, 36.4% of patients who had a diagnosis of comorbid OCD, and 66.6% who had a diagnosis of comorbid ADHD, and 36.1% who fulfilled diagnostic criteria for affective disorders. Three significant factors resulted from PCFA, accounting for 48.5% of symptomatic variance. The first factor, "complex motor tics and echopaliphenomena," consisted primarily of tics involving more than one muscular group, including whole-body movements, complex tics involving mimicking and repeating, as well as echolalia, echopraxia, and palilalia. There were some overlapping tics between this factor and Alsobrook and Pauls' (2002) "compulsive phenomena" factor (palilalia and echolalia). Factor 2, "ADHD symptoms and aggressive behaviors," was characterized by symptoms of inattention, hyperactivity/impulsivity, and disinhibited behavior including aggression and SIB. This factor appears similar to Alsobrook and Pauls' (2002) "aggressive phenomena" factor. Interestingly, OCD symptoms (eg, checking, touching, counting, and concerns about symmetry), loaded significantly on both the first and second factors. The third and final factor, "complex vocal tics and coprophenomena," was characterized by coprolalia and copropraxia, as well as other complex vocal tics, including talking to oneself and barely audible muttering.

Four studies used grouping analysis methods among patients with GTS with a specific focus on associated psychopathology or comorbidities, rather than tic symptoms themselves (Eapen et al., 2004; Grados et al., 2008; Huisman-van Dijk et al., 2016; Rodgers et al., 2014). Eapen et al. (2004) used PCFA in a sample of 91 adult patients with GTS recruited from a tertiary specialist clinic. Patients were interviewed using the NHIS (Robertson & Eapen, 1996), and a range of self-report scales were administered to assess psychopathology, including depression, anxiety, obsessionality, personality traits, and hostility. PCFA was performed on scores derived from these rating scales, yielding two components that accounted for 72% of variance. The first component, "obsessionality," accounted for 46.6% of variance in psychopathology scores and included symptoms of obsessionality, neuroticism, anxiety, and depression. The second component, a separate "anxiety/depression" factor, was composed of several measures of anxiety and depression, as well as the absence of extroversion. Because psychopathology scores alone, and not tic symptoms, were entered into the PCFA, no specific tic symptom factor emerged from the analysis.

Grados et al. (2008) undertook the first of two LCAs among individuals affected by GTS in a large sample of 952 individuals (sibling pairs and parents) from 222 families with GTS recruited for genetic studies. Their focus was on GTS and its most common comorbid diagnoses, obsessive-compulsive symptoms and behaviors (OCS/OCB), OCD, and ADHD. All participants were interviewed using a battery of structured interviews assessing tics, OCS, and ADHD symptoms, and final diagnoses for all disorders were assigned by two or more independent clinicians. LCA identified a best-fit model for combinations of the diagnoses of GTS, OCD, OCS/OCB, and ADHD (predominantly inattentive, predominantly hyperactive-impulsive, and combined type) in a random sample of one sibling from each family, a replication sample randomly chosen from the remaining siblings, and in the entire sample including all siblings and parents. In both of the sibling samples, three GTS-affected groups were identified: "GTS + OCS/OCB," "GTS + OCD," and "GTS + OCD + ADHD combined." Analysis of the entire sample of 952 participants (596 individuals with GTS, 72 with chronic tics, and 284 nonaffected individuals) produced a best-fit, five-class solution, which included these three groups, as well as a "minimal disorder" group and a numerically smaller "chronic tics + OCD" group. The five-class solution was graded from least to most severe: 30% of the entire sample was categorized into the "minimal disorder" group (Class 1), 4% as "chronic tics + OCD" (Class 2), 11% as "GTS only" but with OCS/OCB (Class 3), 31% as "GTS + OCD" (Class 4), and 23% as "GTS + OCD + ADHD combined" (Class 5). A higher proportion of males and an earlier age of onset for motor and phonic tics were evident as the tic severity and number of comorbid diagnoses increased. Grados et al. (2008) also discussed previous PCFA findings and suggested that patients with GTS can be divided into those with a simple form of GTS, which they likened to Class 3, and those with a more complex form, which they observed to be consistent with Classes 4 and 5.

The second LCA was undertaken by Rodgers et al. (2014) using data from the PsyCoLaus study (n = 3691), a population-based study of psychiatric syndromes conducted in Lausanne, Switzerland. The sample for the LCA was composed of 80 adult participants who had reported motor or phonic tics before age 18 years. Data were drawn from the semistructured Diagnostic Interview for Genetic Studies (DIGS) (Preisig, Fenton, Matthey, Berney, & Ferrero, 1999) as well as self-report questionnaires assessing anxiety, temperament, and personality traits. The six selected LCA indicators, based on yes/no responses to screening items on the DIGS, were OCD, inattentive ADHD, impulsive ADHD, depression, phobias, and panic attacks. A best-fit, four-class solution was found, with all classes characterized by a high probability for depression. The first class, "ADHD + depression," was associated with pronounced inattentive and impulsive symptoms in addition to depression, but zero probability for anxiety (OCD, phobias, and panic attacks). The second class, comprising over half the sample, endorsed "depression only." The first two classes included a higher proportion of males than females. Class 3, "OCD excluding ADHD," appeared to be largely converse to Class 1 with the exception of both classes having a high likelihood of depression, and was associated with a high probability for OCD, phobias, and panic attacks, and zero and low probabilities for ADHD impulsivity and inattention, respectively. Class 3 was composed of significantly more females than the other classes (in fact, it was made up solely of females), in line with higher prevalence rates of anxiety disorders among females (McLean, Asnaani, Litz, & Hofmann, 2011). High levels of psychosocial impairment were found in this class. Finally, participants in Class 4, "anxiety and depression," had a high probability for depression, phobias, and panic attacks, but zero or low probability for OCD and ADHD inattention and impulsivity.

Huisman-van Dijk et al. (2016) used factor analysis on data from 225 patients with GTS who were recruited from mental health outpatient clinics in The Netherlands and the Dutch Tourette Syndrome Association, as well as 371 of their family members. A range of self-report questionnaires were administered, including the YGTSS (Leckman et al., 1989), the Yale-Brown Obsessive Compulsive Symptom Scale (Y-BOCS) (Goodman et al., 1989), the Conners Adult ADHD Rating Scale (CAARS) (Conners, Erhardt, & Sparrow, 1999), and the autism-spectrum quotient (AQ) (Baron-Cohen, Wheelwright, Skinner, Martin, & Clubley, 2001). Confirmatory factor analysis was performed to establish the most optimal factor solution for each questionnaire separately. Best-fit models were composed of three factors on the YTGSS (complex tics, body tics, and head and neck tics), four factors on the Y-BOCS (aggression, symmetry, contamination, and hoarding), three factors on the CAARS (inattention, hyperactivity, and impulsivity), and five factors on the AQ (social skills, routines, attention switching, imagination, numbers, and patterns). Exploratory factor analysis was then used to examine the underlying factor structure across these symptom groups. A five-factor structure emerged from this analysis. When examining loadings of

0.40, or more there were several interrelationships across categories. The first factor, "tics/aggression/symmetry/hyperactivity," included the three dimensions of the YGTSS in addition to "aggression" and "symmetry" from the Y-BOCS and "hyperactivity" from the CAARS. The second factor, "obsessive-compulsive symptoms/compulsive tics/numbers and patterns" included the four dimensions of the Y-BOCS in addition to "body tics" from the YGTSS and "numbers and patterns" from the AQ. The third factor, "ADHD symptoms," included the three dimensions of the CAARS alone. Similarly, the fourth factor, "autism symptoms," included all symptoms of the AQ, with the exception of "numbers and patterns," which loaded on the second factor. Finally, the fifth factor, "hoarding/inattention," was composed of the "hoarding" dimension of the Y-BOCS and the "inattention" dimension of the CAARS.

Despite the fact that all the above studies used grouping analysis methods in samples of patients affected by GTS, there are several methodological differences across these 11 studies. These include differences in the study samples (eg, size, age, included diagnoses, recruitment method), analytic methods (HACA, PCFA, and LCA), and the focus of the study (eg, clusters of tic symptoms themselves versus comorbidities). These differences make it more difficult to synthesize the research and draw overall conclusions; however, several findings appear to be consistent across multiple studies and deserve particular mention.

Across all studies, there is evidence of multiple clusters and factors, which highlights the heterogeneity of GTS. Although distinct groups invariably emerge, there is significant overlap between clusters, with large proportions of patients showing symptoms across all identified clusters (Kircanski et al., 2010; McGuire et al., 2013). In all studies that included tic symptoms in the analysis (9 of the 11 studies), there was at least one cluster or factor composed of "pure tics," including when primary factor loadings were examined (Huisman-van Dijk et al., 2016). Consistent with the higher prevalence rate of GTS among males, they often have higher scores on the "pure tics" groups than do females (Alsobrook & Pauls, 2002; Robertson et al., 2008). Across several studies, tic symptoms appear to cluster by complexity, with evidence of simple and complex tic clusters (Kircanski et al., 2010; Mathews et al., 2007; McGuire et al., 2013; Robertson et al., 2008). Complex tic clusters are associated with clinical features including an earlier age of onset for GTS, increased tic severity, higher levels of impairment, and the presence of comorbid symptoms or diagnoses (Kircanski et al., 2010; Mathews et al., 2007). In addition to complexity, tic symptoms also seem to cluster by type (motor versus phonic) or location (Cavanna et al., 2011; Huisman-van Dijk et al., 2016; Kircanski et al., 2010; McGuire et al., 2013). Despite some differences in included symptoms, two additional factors emerge across multiple studies. One of these could be broadly described as "aggressive behaviors or impulse control difficulties/ ADHD" (Alsobrook & Pauls, 2002; Cavanna et al., 2011; Robertson & Cavanna, 2007; Robertson et al., 2008; Rodgers et al., 2014) and the other as "obsessive-compulsive behaviors" (Alsobrook & Pauls, 2002; Cavanna et al., 2011; Eapen et al., 2004; Huisman-van Dijk et al., 2016; Robertson et al., 2008; Rodgers et al., 2014). Furthermore, three studies found evidence for an "anxiety or depression" factor (Eapen et al., 2004; Robertson & Cavanna, 2007; Rodgers et al., 2014).

To the reader who is unfamiliar with either the GTS or factor/cluster analytic literature, this may appear overwhelming. A broad synthesis of these articles is difficult, but one might be tempted to suggest that despite significant heterogeneity the following groups may be proposed, although in a simplified way: (1) "pure" (only) tics (simple or complex); (2) aggressive behaviors and ADHD; (3) compulsive behaviors; (4) touching self; (5) depression anxiety—OCS—SIB; (6) socially inappropriate behaviors (including coprophenomena); (7) autism; and (8) hoarding and inattention. Furthermore, there may be gender differences in these clusters.

What is intriguing and important is that, when clinical heterogeneity is examined from a different perspective, via a review of epidemiological and genetic studies, many group differences are again highlighted, as can be seen in the subsequent discussion and analysis.

EPIDEMIOLOGICAL AND GENETIC STUDIES

Available evidence from epidemiological and genetic studies points to significant phenotypic heterogeneity in GTS, with considerable variability in both the type and complexity of patients' tics, as well as associated comorbidities. In particular, high rates of comorbid OCD and ADHD have been well-documented (for a review, see Table 3 in Robertson, 2015). In a multisite international study of 3500 patients with GTS, it was noted that the most commonly encountered comorbidity was that of ADHD, followed by OCB/OCD (Freeman et al., 2000). There is converging evidence from population and family studies that OCS/OCB frequently co-occur with GTS and that they are integrally linked, which has been acknowledged in the inclusion of the new category of OCD with and without tics in the Diagnostic and Statistical Manual of Mental Disorders, Fifth Edition (American Psychiatric Association, 2013).

Significant shared heritability has been found between GTS and OCD ($r = 0.41$; standard error $= 0.15$), although there is also evidence to suggest distinct genetic risk in the two disorders (Davis et al., 2013). Using polygenic risk scores, Yu et al. (2014) examined the polygenic risk burden of OCD in relation to GTS and chronic tic disorder and found that whereas OCD polygenic risk scores predicted OCD case status in the absence of comorbid GTS/tics, these risk scores were less strongly associated with case status among individuals with OCD plus comorbid tic disorders. Furthermore, phenomenological and family studies showed that some OCS are characteristic of comorbid GTS compared with other symptoms that are associated with primary OCD without comorbid GTS/tics (Cath et al., 2001; Eapen, Robertson, Alsobrook, & Pauls, 1997). Across studies, patients with OCD report more contamination fears and washing or cleaning compulsions, whereas patients with GTS experience more sexual and violent/aggressive obsessions, the need for symmetry and doing things "just right," forced touching, counting, and SIB (Cath et al., 2001; Eapen et al., 1997; George, Trimble, Ring, Sallee, & Robertson, 1993). Moreover, compulsions appear to arise spontaneously in patients with both GTS and OCD, but are often preceded by cognitions in patients with OCD alone (George et al., 1993). These findings are consistent with the results of a study by Leckman et al. (2003) that examined OCS in sibling pairs diagnosed with GTS. Two factors (one associated with aggressive, sexual, and religious obsessions and checking compulsions, and another associated with symmetry and ordering obsessions and compulsions) were associated with increased familial risk for OCD and both factors were observed to be significantly correlated in sibling pairs concordant for GTS.

It has also been suggested that there may be gender-dependent differences in the phenotypic expression of the putative GTS gene(s), and that male members of the family exhibit tics whereas female members more often present with OCS/OCB/OCD (Eapen, Pauls, & Robertson, 1993). When OCD occurs in the context of tics in males, a prepubertal age of onset and higher comorbidity with disruptive behavior disorders, as well as a subjective perception of the OCD symptoms as egosyntonic, has been reported (Tanidir et al., 2015).

Neuroimaging studies also suggested distinct profiles, in that patients with GTS and related OCB often show hypoperfusion involving frontal, striatal, and temporal areas of the brain, whereas those with OCB in the context of primary OCD show hyperperfusion of frontal areas (Moriarty et al., 1997; Swedo et al., 1989). This difference has been attributed to the lack of accompanying anxiety symptoms in patients with GTS and comorbid OCB compared with primary OCD. In this regard, Cath et al. (2001) reported that specific nonanxiety-related impulsions seem to discriminate between individuals with GTS and OCD-tic disorder.

Several studies examined the genetic relationship between GTS and associated comorbidities including OCD and ADHD, and psychopathologies such as mood symptoms (Robertson et al., 2017). A study of

3500 patients with GTS and their relatives observed that the most heritable form of the disorder was associated with having socially inappropriate tics (including coprophenomena) and having a combination of GTS with OCD and ADHD (Darrow et al., 2016). Furthermore, GTS has been shown to be associated with an increased risk for anxiety and mood disorders; the latter was accounted for by OCD whereas mood, anxiety, and disruptive behaviors was accounted for by ADHD (Hirschtritt et al., 2015).

Another clinical feature that has attracted attention is non-obscene socially inappropriate behaviors (NOSIs), originally described by Kurlan et al. (1996), which have been found to occur at higher frequency in those with GTS and comorbid ADHD or OCD. NOSIs have also been linked to ADHD and conduct disorder, with the suggestion that the common link between these coexisting clinical symptoms may be the lack of impulse control (Kurlan et al., 1996). This is in keeping with the exciting finding that social disinhibition is a heritable subphenotype of tic disorders (Hirschtritt et al., 2016). However, there is a suggestion that ADHD and the associated impulse dyscontrol behaviors may segregate independently in families with risk for both of the disorders, with the presence of ADHD being the link to the other psychopathologies. In this regard, similar observations were made about conduct disorder in the context of GTS, with the finding that it is associated with the presence of ADHD in the proband as well as a family history of aggressive and violent behavior and forensic encounters (Robertson, Cavanna, & Eapen, 2015). ADHD in the context of GTS has also been found to be associated with greater substance abuse, more depression and anxiety, more severe aggression toward property or people, and more encounters with the justice system; individuals with both disorders reported significantly more relatives with a history of ADHD than did patients with GTS without ADHD (Haddad, Umoh, Bhatia, & Robertson, 2009). Similarly, a study examining GTS with and without comorbidity found that the pure form of GTS with no comorbidity was not associated with a family history of OCD, which suggested independent segregation of the two disorders. This may also suggest that additional genes specific to the comorbid condition such as ADHD or OCD and or other environmental factors might have a part when GTS is associated with comorbidities (Eapen & Robertson, 2015). This is further compounded by the possibility of bilineal (from maternal and paternal sides) transmission of GTS. One study showed rates of 33% for tics and 41% for tics or OCB in high-density pedigrees with GTS; the probands in those situations had greater severity of symptoms (Kurlan, Eapen, Stern, McDermott, & Robertson, 1994).

There is also emerging evidence suggesting the co-occurrence of GTS with autism spectrum disorder (Eapen, Crnčec, McPherson, & Snedden,

2013), based on epidemiological studies (Baron-Cohen, Scahill, Izaguirre, Hornsey, & Robertson, 1999; Burd, Li, Kerbeshian, Klug, & Freeman, 2009; Freeman et al., 2000; Kadesjö & Gillberg, 2000), as well as at the clinical and phenomenological level; symptoms such as obsessions, compulsive behaviors, ordering, arranging and lining up behaviors, echolalia, palilalia, abnormal speech patterns, and repetitive stereotypic behaviors are common in both conditions. This symptomatic convergence suggests that some genetic variants may be common to both disorders, which is supported by genetic epidemiology studies (State, 2010) and pathogenetic models (Clarke, Lee, & Eapen, 2012).

Other coexistent psychopathologies encountered in GTS include anxiety, separation anxiety, depression, and personality disorders, as well as sleep difficulties, learning problems, and SIB. Coexistent anxiety and depression in the context of GTS have been suggested to be multifactorial (Robertson, 2006), with a potential link to the presence of OCD (Hirschtritt et al., 2015) but not involving a genetic link (Khalifa & Von Knorring, 2006). Studies that examined personality characteristics in GTS found evidence for the increased occurrence of a number of personality traits and disorders (Robertson, Banerjee, Hiley, & Tannock, 1997; Trillini & Müller-Vahl, 2015), but by and large, evidence is lacking for a genetic relationship between the two (Robertson, 2015). Although some studies pointed to the presence of several psychiatric comorbidities and psychopathologies in those with personality disorders, other studies showed no association of specific symptoms with associated psychiatric conditions or treatment outcomes (McGuire et al., 2013), which suggests a multifactorial origin including environmental and cultural factors (Robertson, 2008).

The only study to compare patients with GTS from two cultures directly using the same diagnostic and assessment instruments was done by Eapen and Robertson (2008) using patients with GTS who were of Arab descent in the United Arab Emirates (UAE) and age- and gender-matched Caucasian patients from the United Kingdom (UK). The occurrence of OCD and ADHD were similar across the two cohorts, with consistent GTS features including male preponderance, mean age of onset at approximately 6 years, and location of the initial tic in the facial area. This is in keeping with available evidence from the literature suggesting that across varying cultures, core symptoms of GTS are similar, which may reflect the underlying biological basis of the disorder (Robertson, Eapen, & Cavanna, 2009). Although the rate of coprolalia was higher in the UK cohort, the association found between coprolalia and severity of GTS in the study suggests that the differences in the rate of coprolalia reported between different cultures in earlier studies may be at least partly attributable to differences in the severity of the condition and the source or setting of data collection. However, there were also distinct differences between the two groups, with increased rates of behavioral problems including aggression and oppositional behavior noted in the UK cohort (54.5% and 20%, respectively) compared with the UAE cohort (11.4% and 5.7%, respectively). Unlike coprolalia, which was linked to severity, co-occurrence of these behaviors was not linked to any other clinical features of GTS, which suggests that there may be other explanations. Although the UK cohort was ascertained from a tertiary referral specialist clinic for GTS and as a group had higher severity scores, the lack of association between severity and these behaviors suggests that severity alone cannot explain these differences, and that other factors may be involved, such as family stability, disciplining and parenting factors, and societal expectations.

Thus, it appears that GTS is both clinically and genetically heterogeneous and that GTS and related neurodevelopmental disorders such as OCD and ADHD may share overlapping genetic underpinnings, neuropathological processes, as well as neurochemical and circuitry involvement (Eapen, 2012). In this regard, anatomical substrates and neuronal circuitry involvement in the form of cortico-striato-thalamo-cortical pathways lend themselves to the notion that overlap or delineations in symptom clusters may be the product of the nature and type of neurodevelopmental gene involvement as well as the consequent impact on the site and extent of the circuitry involvement. For example, those with only striatal circuitry involvement may present with "pure" GTS, whereas those with more extensive involvement may present with "full-blown" GTS in which tic-related behaviors such as coprophenomena and echophenomena are also present. Involvement of striatal connections with the frontocortical networks may be associated with ADHD and impulse dyscontrol behaviors, whereas basal ganglia limbic circuitry involvement may present as comorbid OCS, resulting in what is described as GTS "plus" (GTS in addition to comorbidity). Such differential involvement of the different circuitry may have treatment implications in that tic symptoms linked to striatal circuitry and dopamine pathways may respond to dopamine blocking agents, whereas those with OCS may indicate more extensive involvement of circuitry mediated by the serotonin system as well. In this regard, it has been shown that when OCD is comorbid with tic disorder, the usual treatment method of using selective serotonin reuptake inhibitors alone may not be effective, and that this may require augmentation with a neuroleptic for successful symptom resolution (McDougle et al., 1994). Furthermore, it has been reported that individuals with pure tics have a better prognosis whereas the presence of comorbidities such as ADHD and OCD suggests worse prognosis, which in turn may be caused by the more extensive neuronal circuitry involvement resulting in multiple neurochemical pathways being disrupted.

The comorbidities and severity of involvement may also be a function of the penetrance as well as gender-dependent differences in the expression of the putative gene(s), as well as epigenetic, perinatal, and postnatal biological, immunological, and environmental factors, to name just a few. Advances in genetic technology coupled with the availability of statistical programs that allow cross-disorder transdiagnostic analysis of risk, further facilitated by neuroimaging studies and animal models, are expected to advance the field and elucidate the genetic and clinical phenotypic heterogeneity encountered in GTS. A better understanding of such subphenotypes has significant clinical implications in terms of management including the choice of medications as well as the course and prognosis.

CONCLUSIONS

It has been consistently shown that GTS is not a unitary condition and that the presence of comorbidity predicts worse outcomes including chronicity, adverse social impact, and poor quality of life (Eapen, Cavanna, & Robertson, 2016). Furthermore, although the association with comorbidities and psychopathologies is multifactorial, as described earlier, it has a consistent negative impact on the overall outcomes; suicidal thoughts and behaviors reported in the context of GTS are also attributed to the presence and severity of OCD, ADHD, depression, and anxiety (Storch et al., 2015). It is therefore critical that clinicians involved in assessing and managing GTS consider the issue of heterogeneity and ascertain and address not only tic symptoms but also the nature, extent, and impact of associated comorbidities and psychopathologies, to achieve better outcomes.

References

Achenbach, T. M. (1991). *Manual for the child behavior checklist/4-18 and 1991 child profile*. Burlington: University of Vermont Department of Psychiatry.

Alsobrook, J. P., & Pauls, D. L. (2002). A factor analysis of tic symptoms in Gilles de la Tourette's syndrome. *American Journal of Psychiatry, 159*(2), 291–296.

American Psychiatric Association. (2013). *Diagnostic and statistical manual of mental disorders - fifth edition (DSM-5)*. Washington, DC: American Psychiatric Publishing.

Baron-Cohen, S., Scahill, V. L., Izaguirre, J., Hornsey, H., & Robertson, M. (1999). The prevalence of Gilles de la Tourette syndrome in children and adolescents with autism: A large scale study. *Psychological Medicine, 29*(5), 1151–1159.

Baron-Cohen, S., Wheelwright, S., Skinner, R., Martin, J., & Clubley, E. (2001). The autism-spectrum quotient (AQ): Evidence from asperger syndrome/high-functioning autism, malesand females, scientists and mathematicians. *Journal of Autism and Developmental Disorders, 31*(1), 5—17.

Burd, L., Li, Q., Kerbeshian, J., Klug, M. G., & Freeman, R. D. (2009). Tourette syndrome and comorbid pervasive developmental disorders. *Journal of Child Neurology, 24*(2), 170—175.

Cath, D. C., Spinhoven, P., Van Woerkom, T. C., Van De Wetering, B. J., Hoogduin, C. A., Landman, A. D., et al. (2001). Gilles de la Tourette's syndrome with and without obsessive-compulsive disorder compared with obsessive-compulsive disorder without tics: Which symptoms discriminate? *The Journal of Nervous and Mental Disease, 189*(4), 219—228.

Cavanna, A. E., Critchley, H. D., Orth, M., Stern, J. S., Young, M.-B., & Robertson, M. M. (2011). Dissecting the Gilles de la Tourette spectrum: A factor analytic study on 639 patients. *Journal of Neurology, Neurosurgery, and Psychiatry, 82*(12), 1320—1323.

Clarke, R. A., Lee, S., & Eapen, V. (2012). Pathogenetic model for Tourette syndrome delineates overlap with related neurodevelopmental disorders including Autism. *Translational Psychiatry, 2*(9), e158.

Conners, C. K., Erhardt, D., & Sparrow, E. P. (1999). *Conners' adult ADHD rating scales (CAARS): Technical manual.* North Tonawanda: MHS.

Crown, S., & Crisp, A. H. (1966). A short clinical diagnostic self-rating scale for psychoneurotic patients: The Middlesex Hospital Questionnaire (MHQ). *The British Journal of Psychiatry, 112,* 917—923.

Darrow, S. M., Hirschtritt, M. E., Davis, L. K., Illmann, C., Osiecki, L., Grados, M., et al. (2016). Identification of two heritable cross-disorder endophenotypes for Tourette syndrome. *American Journal of Psychiatry, 174*(4), 387—396.

Davis, L. K., Yu, D., Keenan, C. L., Gamazon, E. R., Konkashbaev, A. I., Derks, E. M., et al. (2013). Partitioning the heritability of Tourette syndrome and obsessive compulsive disorder reveals differences in genetic architecture. *PLoS Genetics, 9*(10), e1003864.

DuPaul, G. J., Power, T. J., McGoey, K. E., Ikeda, M. J., & Anastopoulos, A. D. (1998). Reliability and validity of parent and teacher ratings of attention-deficit/hyperactivity disorder symptoms. *Journal of Psychoeducational Assessment, 16*(1), 55—68.

Eapen, V. (2012). Neurodevelopmental disorders haven't read the DSM. Or have they? *Frontiers in Psychiatry, 3,* 75.

Eapen, V., Cavanna, A. E., & Robertson, M. M. (2016). Comorbidities, social impact, and quality of life in Tourette syndrome. *Frontiers in Psychiatry, 7.*

Eapen, V., Črnčec, R., McPherson, S., & Snedden, C. (2013). Tic disorders and learning disability: Clinical characteristics, cognitive performance and comorbidity. *Australasian Journal of Special Education, 37*(2), 162—172.

Eapen, V., Fox-Hiley, P., Banerjee, S., & Robertson, M. (2004). Clinical features and associated psychopathology in a Tourette syndrome cohort. *Acta Neurologica Scandinavica, 109*(4), 255—260.

Eapen, V., Pauls, D. L., & Robertson, M. M. (1993). Evidence for autosomal dominant transmission in Tourette's syndrome. United Kingdom cohort study. *The British Journal of Psychiatry, 162*(5), 593—596.

Eapen, V., & Robertson, M. M. (2008). Clinical correlates of Tourette's disorder across cultures: A comparative study between the United Arab Emirates and the United Kingdom. *Primary Care Companion to the Journal of Clinical Psychiatry, 10*(2), 103.

Eapen, V., & Robertson, M. M. (2015). Are there distinct subtypes in Tourette syndrome? Pure-Tourette syndrome versus Tourette syndrome-plus, and simple versus complex tics. *Neuropsychiatric Disease and Treatment, 11,* 1431.

Eapen, V., Robertson, M. M., Alsobrook, J. P., & Pauls, D. L. (1997). Obsessive compulsive symptoms in Gilles de la Tourette syndrome and obsessive compulsive disorder. *American Journal of Medical Genetics, Part A, 74*(4), 432–438.

Freeman, R. D., Fast, D. K., Burd, L., Kerbeshian, J., Robertson, M. M., & Sandor, P. (2000). An international perspective on Tourette syndrome: Selected findings from 3500 individuals in 22 countries. *Developmental Medicine and Child Neurology, 42*(7), 436–447.

George, M. S., Trimble, M. R., Ring, H. A., Sallee, F., & Robertson, M. M. (1993). Obsessions in obsessive-compulsive disorder with and without Gilles de la Tourette's disorder. *The American Journal of Psychiatry, 150*(1), 93.

Goodman, W. K., Price, L. H., Rasmussen, S. A., Mazure, C., Fleischmann, R. L., Hill, C. L., et al. (1989). The Yale-Brown obsessive compulsive scale: I. Development, use, and reliability. *Archives of General Psychiatry, 46*(11), 1006–1011.

Grados, M. A., Mathews, C. A., & Tourette Syndrome Association International Consortium for Genetics. (2008). Latent class analysis of Gilles de la Tourette syndrome using comorbidities: Clinical and genetic implications. *Biological Psychiatry, 64*(3), 219–225.

Haddad, A., Umoh, G., Bhatia, V., & Robertson, M. (2009). Adults with Tourette's syndrome with and without attention deficit hyperactivity disorder. *Acta Psychiatrica Scandinavica, 120*(4), 299–307.

Hirschtritt, M. E., Darrow, S. M., Illmann, C., Osiecki, L., Grados, M., Sandor, P., et al. (2016). Social disinhibition is a heritable subphenotype of tics in Tourette syndrome. *Neurology, 87*(5), 497–504.

Hirschtritt, M. E., Lee, P. C., Pauls, D. L., Dion, Y., Grados, M. A., Illmann, C., et al. (2015). Lifetime prevalence, age of risk, and genetic relationships of comorbid psychiatric disorders in Tourette syndrome. *JAMA Psychiatry, 72*(4), 325–333.

Huisman-van Dijk, H. M., van de Schoot, R., Rijkeboer, M. M., Mathews, C. A., & Cath, D. C. (2016). The relationship between tics, OC, ADHD and autism symptoms: A cross-disorder symptom analysis in Gilles de la Tourette syndrome patients and family-members. *Psychiatry Research, 237*, 138–146.

Itard, J. M. G. (1825). Mémoire sur quelques fonctions involontaires des appareils de la locomotion, de la préhension et de la voix. *Arch Gen Med, 8*, 385–407.

Kadesjö, B., & Gillberg, C. (2000). Tourette's disorder: Epidemiology and comorbidity in primary school children. *Journal of the American Academy of Child and Adolescent Psychiatry, 39*(5), 548–555.

Khalifa, N., & Von Knorring, A.-L. (2006). Psychopathology in a Swedish population of school children with tic disorders. *Journal of the American Academy of Child and Adolescent Psychiatry, 45*(11), 1346–1353.

Kircanski, K., Woods, D. W., Chang, S. W., Ricketts, E. J., & Piacentini, J. C. (2010). Cluster analysis of the Yale Global Tic Severity Scale (YGTSS): Symptom dimensions and clinical correlates in an outpatient youth sample. *Journal of Abnormal Child Psychology, 38*(6), 777–788.

Kurlan, R., Daragjati, C., Como, P. G., McDermott, M. P., Trinidad, K. S., Roddy, S., et al. (1996). Non-obscene complex socially inappropriate behavior in Tourette's syndrome. *Journal of Neuropsychiatry and Clinical Neurosciences, 8*(3), 311–317.

Kurlan, R., Eapen, V., Stern, J., McDermott, M., & Robertson, M. (1994). Bilineal transmission in Tourette's syndrome families. *Neurology, 44*(12), 2336.

Leckman, J. F., Pauls, D. L., Zhang, H., Rosario-Campos, M. C., Katsovich, L., Kidd, K. K., et al. (2003). Obsessive-compulsive symptom dimensions in affected sibling pairs diagnosed with Gilles de la Tourette syndrome. *American Journal of Medical Genetics Part B: Neuropsychiatric Genetics, 116*(1), 60–68.

Leckman, J. F., Riddle, M. A., Hardin, M. T., Ort, S. I., Swartz, K. L., Stevenson, J., et al. (1989). The Yale global tic severity scale: Initial testing of a clinician-rated scale of tic severity. *Journal of the American Academy of Child and Adolescent Psychiatry, 28*(4), 566−573.

Mathews, C. A., Jang, K. L., Herrera, L. D., Lowe, T. L., Budman, C. L., Erenberg, G., et al. (2007). Tic symptom profiles in subjects with Tourette Syndrome from two genetically isolated populations. *Biological Psychiatry, 61*(3), 292−300.

McDougle, C. J., Goodman, W. K., Leckman, J. F., Lee, N. C., Heninger, G. R., & Price, L. H. (1994). Haloperidol addition in fluvoxamine-refractory obsessive-compulsive disorder: A double-blind, placebo-controlled study in patients with and without tics. *Archives of General Psychiatry, 51*(4), 302−308.

McGuire, J. F., Nyirabahizi, E., Kircanski, K., Piacentini, J., Peterson, A. L., Woods, D. W., et al. (2013). A cluster analysis of tic symptoms in children and adults with Tourette syndrome: Clinical correlates and treatment outcome. *Psychiatry Research, 210*(3), 1198−1204.

McLean, C. P., Asnaani, A., Litz, B. T., & Hofmann, S. G. (2011). Gender differences in anxiety disorders: Prevalence, course of illness, comorbidity and burden of illness. *Journal of Psychiatric Research, 45*(8), 1027−1035.

Moriarty, J., Eapen, V., Costa, D., Gacinovic, S., Trimble, M., Ell, P., et al. (1997). HMPAO SPET does not distinguish obsessive−compulsive and tic syndromes in families multiply affected with Gilles de la Tourette's syndrome. *Psychological Medicine, 27*(3), 737−740.

Pauls, D. L., & Hurst, C. (1981). *Schedule for Tourette and other behavioral syndromes*. New Haven, Conn: Yale University School of Medicine, Child Study Center.

Preisig, M., Fenton, B. T., Matthey, M.-L., Berney, A., & Ferrero, F. (1999). Diagnostic interview for genetic studies (DIGS): Inter-rater and test-retest reliability of the French version. *European Archives of Psychiatry and Clinical Neuroscience, 249*(4), 174−179.

Robertson, M. M. (2006). Mood disorders and Gilles de la Tourette's syndrome: An update on prevalence, etiology, comorbidity, clinical associations, and implications. *Journal of Psychosomatic Research, 61*(3), 349−358.

Robertson, M. M. (2008). The international prevalence, epidemiology, and clinical phenomenology of Tourette syndrome: Part 1-the epidemiological and prevalence studies. *Journal of Psychosomatic Research, 65*, 461−472.

Robertson, M. M. (2015). A personal 35 year perspective on Gilles de la Tourette syndrome: Prevalence, phenomenology, comorbidities, and coexistent psychopathologies. *The Lancet Psychiatry, 2*(1), 68−87.

Robertson, M. M., Althoff, R. R., Hafez, A., & Pauls, D. L. (2008). Principal components analysis of a large cohort with Tourette syndrome. *The British Journal of Psychiatry, 193*(1), 31−36.

Robertson, M. M., Banerjee, S., Hiley, P., & Tannock, C. (1997). Personality disorder and psychopathology in Tourette's syndrome: A controlled study. *The British Journal of Psychiatry, 171*(3), 283−286.

Robertson, M. M., & Cavanna, A. E. (2007). The Gilles de la Tourette syndrome: A principal component factor analytic study of a large pedigree. *Psychiatric Genetics, 17*(3), 143−152.

Robertson, M. M., Cavanna, A. E., & Eapen, V. (2015). Gilles de la Tourette syndrome and disruptive behavior disorders: Prevalence, associations, and explanation of the relationships. *The Journal of Neuropsychiatry and Clinical Neurosciences, 27*(1), 33−41.

Robertson, M. M., & Eapen, V. (1996). The National Hospital Interview Schedule for the assessment of Gilles de la Tourette syndrome. *International Journal of Methods in Psychiatric Research, 6*(4), 203−226.

Robertson, M. M., Eapen, V., & Cavanna, A. E. (2009). The international prevalence, epidemiology, and clinical phenomenology of Tourette syndrome: A cross-cultural perspective. *Journal of Psychosomatic Research, 67*(6), 475−483.

Robertson, M. M., Eapen, V., Singer, H. S., Martino, D., Scharf, J. M., Paschou, P., et al. (2017). Gilles de la Tourette syndrome. *Nature Reviews Disease Primers, 3,* 16097.

Rodgers, S., Müller, M., Kawohl, W., Knöpfli, D., Rössler, W., Castelao, E., et al. (2014). Sex-related and non-sex-related comorbidity subtypes of tic disorders: A latent class approach. *European Journal of Neurology, 21*(5), 700.

Scahill, L., Riddle, M. A., McSwiggin-Hardin, M., Ort, S. I., King, R. A., Goodman, W. K., et al. (1997). Children's Yale-Brown obsessive compulsive scale: Reliability and validity. *Journal of the American Academy of Child and Adolescent Psychiatry, 36*(6), 844–852.

Snowdon, J. (1980). A comparison of written and postbox forms of the Leyton Obsessional Inventory. *Psychological Medicine, 10*(1), 165–170.

Spitzer, R., & Endicott, J. (1978). *Schedule for affective disorders and schizophrenia - lifetime version* (3rd ed.). New York: New York State Psychiatric Institute.

State, M. W. (2010). The genetics of child psychiatric disorders: Focus on autism and Tourette syndrome. *Neuron, 68*(2), 254–269.

Storch, E. A., Hanks, C. E., Mink, J. W., McGuire, J. F., Adams, H. R., Augustine, E. F., et al. (2015). Suicidal thoughts and behaviors in children and adolescents with chronic tic disorders. *Depression and Anxiety, 32*(10), 744–753.

Storch, E. A., Murphy, T. K., Geffken, G. R., Soto, O., Sajid, M., Allen, P., et al. (2004). Further psychometric properties of the Tourette's disorder scale-parent rated version (TODS-PR). *Child Psychiatry and Human Development, 35*(2), 107–120.

Swedo, S. E., Schapiro, M. B., Grady, C. L., Cheslow, D. L., Leonard, H. L., Kumar, A., et al. (1989). Cerebral glucose metabolism in childhood-onset obsessive-compulsive disorder. *Archives of General Psychiatry, 46*(6), 518–523.

Tanidir, C., Adaletli, H., Gunes, H., Kilicoglu, A. G., Mutlu, C., Bahali, M. K., et al. (2015). Impact of gender, age at onset, and lifetime tic disorders on the clinical presentation and comorbidity pattern of obsessive-compulsive disorder in children and adolescents. *Journal of Child and Adolescent Psychopharmacology, 25*(5), 425–431.

Tourette, G. G. (1885). Étude sur une affection nerveuse caractérisée par de l'incoordination motrice accompagnée d'écholalie et de coprolalie (jumping, latah, and myriachit). *Arch Neurol, 9,* 19–42, 158–200.

Trillini, M. O., & Müller-Vahl, K. R. (2015). Patients with Gilles de la Tourette syndrome have widespread personality differences. *Psychiatry Research, 228*(3), 765–773.

TSAICG. (1999). A complete genome screen in sib pairs affected by Gilles de la Tourette syndrome. The Tourette Syndrome Association International Consortium for Genetics. *The American Journal of Human Genetics, 65,* 1428–1436.

Woods, D. W., Piacentini, J., Chang, S., Deckersbach, T., Ginsburg, G., Peterson, A., et al. (2008). *Managing Tourette syndrome: A behavioral intervention for children and adults therapist guide.* Oxford University Press.

Woods, D. W., Piacentini, J., Himle, M. B., & Chang, S. (2005). Premonitory urge for tics scale (PUTS): Initial psychometric results and examination of the premonitory urge phenomenon in youths with tic disorders. *Journal of Developmental and Behavioral Pediatrics, 26*(6), 397–403.

Yu, D., Mathews, C. A., Scharf, J. M., Neale, B. M., Davis, L. K., Gamazon, E. R., et al. (2014). Cross-disorder genome-wide analyses suggest a complex genetic relationship between Tourette's syndrome and OCD. *American Journal of Psychiatry, 172*(1), 82–93.

Risk and Protective Factors and Course of Functional Somatic Symptoms in Young People

Charlotte Ulrikka Rask[1], Irma J. Bonvanie[2], Elena M. Garralda[3]

[1] Centre for Child and Adolescent Psychiatry, Aarhus University Hospital, Risskov, Denmark; [2] Paediatric Department Martini Hospital, Groningen, The Netherlands; [3] Imperial College London, London, United Kingdom

Understanding Uniqueness and Diversity in Child and Adolescent Mental Health
https://doi.org/10.1016/B978-0-12-815310-9.00004-6

PREVALENCE AND GENERAL OUTCOMES OF FUNCTIONAL SOMATIC SYMPTOMS

Functional somatic symptoms (FSS) are common in the general population. Around 25%—30% of all children and adolescents experience these symptoms to some degree, girls more often than boys (Berntsson, Kohler, & Gustafsson, 2001; Domènech-Llaberia et al., 2004; Eminson, 2007; Janssens, Klis, Kingma, Oldehinkel, & Rosmalen, 2014). FSS can be related to any bodily system. Abdominal pain is the most typical symptom in young children, whereas headache, fatigue, and musculoskeletal pains are more frequently seen in adolescents (King et al., 2011; Lievesley, Rimes, & Chalder, 2014). Pseudoneurological symptoms such as gait disturbances, sensory loss, or nonepileptic seizures are more rare symptom presentations across the age span (Ani, Reading, Lynn, Forlee, & Garralda, 2013; Kozlowska, 2007). FSS may be multisymptomatic, but young children usually present with a single prominent symptom (Domènech-Llaberia et al., 2004; Rask et al., 2009). Symptoms of health anxiety, another condition among the somatic symptom disorders (SSDs), are also commonly prevalent in children and adolescents. Around 8% —9% of the preadolescent general population, girls and boys to a similar extent, report high levels of health anxiety (Rask et al., 2016).

The severity of FSS ranges from everyday bodily sensations that reflect temporary and self-limiting physiological changes to conditions with severe chronic and disabling symptoms. Only one-third of children with FSS visits primary care for these problems, and 50% will be symptom-free within 6 months (Rask et al., 2009). However, 4—10% of the general child and adolescent population experiences daily or high levels of FSS persisting for months or years, and around the same percentage reports related impairments in daily functioning (Hoftun, Romundstad, Zwart, & Rygg, 2011; Janssens, Klis, et al., 2014; Rask et al., 2009). In some individuals, FSS can become disabling with long-lasting school absenteeism and impairment in physical and social activities (Hoftun et al., 2011; Janssens, Oldehinkel, Dijkstra, Veenstra, & Rosmalen, 2011). In addition, the symptoms are commonly associated with anxiety and depressive symptoms and disorders (Campo et al., 2004; Campo, Jansen-Mcwilliams, Comer, & Kelleher, 1999). Consequently, health care use in this subgroup is high (Græsholt-Knudsen, Skovgaard, Jensen, & Rask, 2017; Rask, Ørnbøl, Fink, & Skovgaard, 2013), representing those most in need for professional help. Overall, levels of distress, functional disability, comorbid psychopathology, and health resource use and costs are likely to increase from one end of the FSS severity continuum to the other (Fig. 4.1).

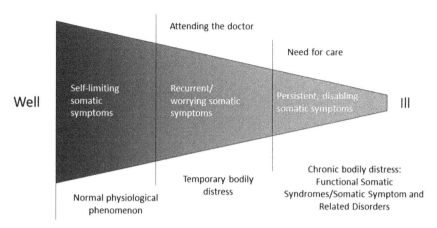

FIGURE 4.1   Somatic symptoms on a continuum from normal physiological response to chronic states.

The long-term prognosis of severe FSS in childhood varies from complete recovery to persistent symptoms into adulthood; the latter group has poorer physical and emotional functioning, lower educational qualifications, and more medical visits than do individuals who recover from these symptoms (Kashikar-Zuck et al., 2014; Westendorp et al., 2016). Chronicity, severity, and multiplicity of symptoms are all predictors of poor prognosis, and with increasing age, recovery of severe FSS seems to become increasingly unlikely (Joyce, Hotopf, & Wessely, 1997; Rosendal et al., 2017). For example, whereas around 75% of all fatigued children recovered during childhood or adolescence, less than 10% of adults eventually returned to premorbid levels of functioning (Joyce et al., 1997; Norris et al., 2017). Therefore, timely treatment of young people with severe FSS is central to improving the long-term physical, psychosocial, and financial consequences of experiencing FSS.

DIAGNOSTIC CLASSIFICATION

Children with significant FSS usually present to pediatric medical services first. In somatic health care, underlying mental health problems are often unexplored and unrecognized, and based on the prominent symptom and the medical specialty consulted, one of the various "functional somatic syndromes" may be diagnosed. Examples of these diagnoses are irritable bowel syndrome, fibromyalgia, and chronic fatigue syndrome. However, research suggests that despite the different names, these syndromes may not be different clinical phenotypes but different permutations of the same underlying phenotype or related phenotypes (Fink & Schroder, 2010; Wessely, Nimnuan, & Sharpe, 1999). Furthermore, psychiatric assessment of the most severe cases may identify a somatic symptom or somatoform disorder. Thus, parallel to somatic health care, mental health care has its own diagnostic labels for the same group of patients with chronic and impairing FSS. Severe FSS were formerly categorized under somatoform and related disorders in both the *Diagnostic and Statistical Manual of Mental Disorders*, Fourth Edition (DSM-IV) and the 10th revision of the International Statistical Classification of Diseases and Related Health Problems (ICD-10). However, these classification systems have come under criticism with regard to their utility in daily practice. One important criticism is that children rarely present with symptoms sufficiently varied or severe or disabling enough to qualify for the somatoform and related disorders diagnoses (Schulte & Petermann, 2011). In addition, many clinicians regard the terms "somatoform" and "somatization" to be pejorative and to overemphasize a mind—body dualism for disorders that are now mainly understood within an integrated biopsychosocial framework (Beck, 2008; Dimsdale, Sharma, & Sharpe, 2011; Henningsen, Zipfel, & Herzog, 2007).

Responding to these criticisms, somatoform and related disorders have been renamed and grouped as somatic symptom and related disorders in the recent DSM-5. The disorders in this category are characterized by the prominence of somatic symptoms associated with significant distress and impairment. In children, this often means substantial school absence. The major diagnosis, somatic symptom disorder (SSD), is designed to lump together different DSM-IV somatoform diagnoses. It covers not only the DSM-IV diagnosis of somatization disorder but also chronic pain disorder, undifferentiated somatoform disorder, and to some extent, hypochondriasis. Key features are positive symptoms and signs, i.e., distressing somatic symptoms plus maladaptive thoughts, feelings, and behaviors such as repeated medical help seeking and avoidance of physical activity in response to these symptoms, rather than the absence of a medical explanation for somatic symptoms.

Besides SSD, this new category includes illness anxiety disorder to diagnose individuals with primarily high levels of anxiety about the possibility of having an illness rather than distress about the experience of somatic symptoms themselves, conversion disorder (functional neurological symptom disorder), characterized by sensory or motor symptoms not explained by neurological disease, psychological factors affecting other medical conditions, and factitious disorder.

In ICD-11, the plan is to substitute many of the somatoform disorders and presentations dominated by fatigue, diagnosed as neurasthenia, with bodily distress disorder (BDD), which is broadly similar to the DSM-5's SSD. As opposed to the DSM-5, ICD-11 is planning to place hypochondriasis within the grouping of obsessive-compulsive and related disorders, supported by some evidence that hypochondriasis may respond to the same treatments as these disorders (Gureje & Reed, 2016). The ICD-11 will have functional neurological disorders within the neurology section for the first time. However, these disorders will also remain in the psychiatry section as the separate category of dissociative disorders.

Specific criteria for the three DSM-5 diagnoses of most relevance for younger persons, namely SSD, illness anxiety disorder, and conversion disorder, and the corresponding ICD-10/ICD-11 diagnoses are shown in Table 4.1.

MAIN CLINICAL PRESENTATIONS

Based on a clinical approach and supported by the revised classification systems described above, severe FSS in children and adolescents can be grouped into three main categories of conditions dominated by: (1) persistent somatic symptoms, (2) dissociative or "pseudoneurological" symptoms, and (3) illness worries or health anxiety. Although these conditions overlap in their clinical presentations and are often comorbid, the primary problem and concerns and thus targets for treatment can be different. It is therefore important to differentiate among these three main categories.

Conditions Dominated by Persistent Somatic Symptoms

This is by far the most common presentation of severe FSS in children and adolescents. The young person's thriving and ability to function are affected by various somatic symptoms not attributable to any known medical condition. Although symptoms of anxiety, illness, worry, and depression may be present as well, the main limitation and problems stem from the somatic symptoms. Typical presentations are pain, such as recurrent episodes of severe abdominal pain or headaches, or severe and incapacitating fatigue. Because these children usually first present to pediatric and specialist medical services, they may often also have received diagnoses of various FSS.

Developmental Aspects

Young preschool children with recurrent FSS seldom manifest a multisymptomatic presentation, nor are the key features of the psychiatric diagnoses associated with symptom preoccupation and medical help seeking, because these reside in their parents (Rask et al., 2009; Schulte & Petermann, 2011). These aspects have been incorporated in the DSM-5, which specifies that in children, a single prominent symptom is more

TABLE 4.1   DSM-5 Diagnostic Criteria for Most Common Conditions With Marked/Severe Functional Somatic Symptoms in Children and Adolescents

Somatic Symptom Disorder (Formally Known as Most of the Somatoform Disorders in DSM-IV) *Corresponds to most F45.x in ICD-10/bodily distress disorder in ICD-11*	Conversion Disorder 300.11/Functional Neurological Symptom Disorder (Formerly Known Only as Conversion Disorder in DSM-IV *Corresponds to dissociative disorders F44.X in ICD-10/dissociative neurological symptom disorder in ICD-11*	Illness Anxiety Disorder 300.7 (Formerly Known as Hypochondriasis in DSM-IV) *Corresponds to hypochondriasis in ICD-10/hypochondriasis or health anxiety disorder in ICD-11*
A: One or more somatic symptoms that are distressing and/or result in significant disruption in daily life. **B:** Excessive thoughts, feelings and behaviors related to these somatic symptoms or associated health concerns: at least one of the following must be present. 1. Disproportionate and persistent thoughts about the seriousness of one's symptoms. 2. Persistently high levels of anxiety about health or symptoms 3. Excessive time and energy devoted to these symptoms or health concerns **C:** Although the symptoms may not be continuously present, the state of being symptomatic is persistent for >6 months.	**A:** One or more symptoms of attached voluntary motor or sensory function. **B:** Clinical findings demonstrate incompatibility between the symptoms and recognized neurologic or general medical condition (e.g., Hoover's sign of functional limb weakness) **C:** The deficit or symptoms are not better explained by another medical or mental disorder. **D:** The symptom or deficit causes significant distress or psychosocial impairment, or warrants medical evaluation.	**A:** A preoccupation with and fear of having or acquiring a serious medical illness. **B:** Persists for >6 months despite appropriate medical evaluation that excludes a medical disorder and despite reassurance. **C:** It is not better accounted for by depression or another mental disorder.

DSM, Diagnostic and Statistical Manual of Mental Disorders; ICD, International Statistical Classification of Diseases and Related Health Problems.

common than in adults. It also notes that whereas young children may have physical problems, they rarely worry about "illness" before adolescence. Instead the parents' response to the symptoms is crucial, because this may determine levels of associated distress. Thus, it is the parents who may interpret the symptoms and determine the associated time off from school and medical help seeking.

Clinical Case: Anne is a 12-year-old girl who worries that she will not be able to fulfil her dream of obtaining a higher education because daily distressing symptoms have led to a high degree of school absence of over 60%, and to concentration difficulties during classes. Besides colic in infancy and a tendency to episodes of stomachache when she started school, she has not had health problems until 2 years ago, when she had acute tonsillitis. Subsequently, she continued to feel unwell and started to develop many different and fluctuating somatic symptoms. She is now especially impaired by constant pain in the muscles and joints but also headache, nausea, and dizziness. In addition, the stomachache has recurred. She and her parents are preoccupied with and attentive to the symptoms. Often, she sleeps badly at night owing to the pain and feels fatigued during daytime.

Anne has been examined several times by different medical experts, with no organic explanation for the symptoms. Also, a psychiatric evaluation has shown no indications that the symptoms are an expression of anxiety or depressive problems. She and her mother have the feeling that the doctors view her as hysterical and attention seeking. She has tried physiotherapy, various pain killers, and different types of alternative treatments with only short-term effect.

Before Anne became ill, she was engaged in horse riding and saw many friends in her spare time. Now she has given up the sport and has lost contact with several friends because, as a result of the symptoms, she often declines social gatherings.

Diagnosis: DSM-5: SSD, ICD-10: somatoform disorder/ICD-11: BDD.

Conditions Dominated by Dissociative Symptoms

This is a group of disorders with dramatic symptoms that involve voluntary motor or sensory function such as seizures, loss of sensation, visual disturbances, or total blindness, paralysis, and aphonia. The symptoms are also called pseudoneurological because they look like a neurological disorder. However, after closer assessment, they are found not to be compatible with known neuropathology. This is demonstrated when physical signs are inconsistent with neuroanatomy, e.g., muscle weakness, tactile disturbances, and sensory disturbances that do not follow nerve pathways (Stone & Carson, 2015). Because of the dramatic presentation and serious differential diagnoses, such as epilepsy or intracerebral vascular lesions, these young persons are typically seen in emergency departments and neuropediatric units. The onset is often sudden and may be related to psychological stress or difficult personal circumstances (Kozlowska, 2007), although a clear psychological stressor is not always identifiable at symptom onset. The symptoms may also change from time to time and be related to attention from others. The child or adolescent may appear remarkably emotionally unaffected by his or her illness despite the severe symptom presentation. However, this so-called *belle indifference* is not specific, and thus lack of concern about the nature or implications of the symptoms should not be used to establish the diagnosis of a dissociative or conversion disorder. One of the most important clinical expressions in this category is functional seizures, which in the literature often are referred to as (psychogenic) nonepileptic seizures (Patel et al., 2011).

Developmental Aspects

Dissociative symptoms are rarely identified in children below age 7 years; the incidence increases with age and has a female preponderance (Ani et al., 2013). In children, disturbance of motor function, sensory symptoms, or convulsions/seizures are the most common symptom presentations (Kozlowska, 2007). More complex and mixed symptoms may become prominent during adolescence. The semiology of the seizures is reported to differ between young children and adolescents. In younger children, seizures often manifest as subtle motor activity such as prolonged staring with unresponsiveness, isolated head shaking, eye fluttering, generalized limpness, and behavioral changes or combativeness. In children aged 13 years and older, clinical features more resemble those described in adults, with prominent motor activity with generalized arrhythmic jerking or flailing of extremities, side-to-side head movements, and forward pelvic thrusting (Patel, Scott, Dunn, & Garg, 2007).

Clinical Case: Ten-year-old Simon is brought to the emergency room with persistent spasms in the arms and legs which started suddenly during a lesson in school. The spasms resemble an epileptic seizure, and therefore he has been given large doses of antiepileptic medication in the ambulance, but that has only briefly stopped the spasms. In the emergency room, Simon manifests new spasms which are so violent that it takes two adults to hold him down. A young doctor attends to Simon and wants him transferred to the neuropediatric department on suspicion of new-onset epilepsy. At the neuropediatric evaluation, it appears that Simon is conscious during the attacks, that he can speak, and that he can briefly be distracted from the violent spasms. After a video electroencephalo-gram confirming no epileptic activity during the attacks, the neuropediatricians judge that Simon's symptoms are incompatible with epileptic seizures or other neurological disorders. From a detailed history taking with his mother, it appears that the parents are in the middle of conflict-ridden divorce in which Simon is going to move to another town with his mother. He is thus to be separated from his half-brother with whom he is close. He is described as a friendly boy who is good at adapting to new situations. He has learning problems in school and has always had difficulties getting new friends.

Diagnosis: DSM-5: conversion disorder/functional neurological symptom disorder, ICD-10: dissociative and conversion disorder (conversion disorder with seizures and convulsions)/ICD-11: dissociative neurological symptom disorder.

Condition Dominated by Health Anxiety

This condition may best be understood as an underlying anxiety problem, but the strong focus on somatic concerns often leads these young persons to attend medical settings. At first glance, their clinical presentation can be similar to that of persisting somatic symptoms, but the key feature is worry about the symptoms being an expression of illness or hypersensitivity to bodily sensations believed to be signs of a serious illness (Asmundson, Abramowitz, Richter, & Whedon, 2010). For example, a bruise or irritated skin can induce worries that it may be a sign of a serious undetected illness. The young person may also keep a close eye on bodily functions, such as taking his or her own pulse or checking urine and stool for blood. If the young person hears or reads about a disease or someone close becomes ill, he or she will become inclined to fear having that disease. When the young person with health anxiety first starts to think of a disease, he or she will not stop thinking about this. All thoughts are centered on a suspected, often life-threatening disease. The body and (online) medical information are checked frequently, with the result that the young person finds increasing "evidence" for the worries. The growing anxiety spiral ultimately leads the young person to seek reassurance either from his or her parents or by persuading the parents to take him or her to a doctor.

Developmental Aspects

Only a few children and adolescents meet the ICD-10 or former DSM-IV diagnostic criteria for hypochondriasis (Bisht, Sankhyan, Kaushal,

Sharma, & Grover, 2008; Essau, Conradt, & Petermann, 1999; Lieb, Pfister, Mastaler, & Wittchen, 2000). This low prevalence may mainly be explained by the lack of specific, developmentally appropriate diagnostic criteria targeting children and adolescents (Fritz, Fritsch, & Hagino, 1997). Retrospective studies on adults with hypochondriasis indicate that health anxiety precursors already exist during childhood (Fink et al., 2004; Noyes et al., 2002), and studies exploring symptoms rather than the full hypochondriasis disorder suggest that excessive expressions of health anxiety can be present in younger age groups with fears, beliefs, and attitudes similar to cognitive and behavioral features of severe health anxiety in adults (Eminson, Benjamin, Shortall, Woods, & Faragher, 1996; Rask, Elberling, Skovgaard, Thomsen, & Fink, 2012; Rask et al., 2016; van Geelen, Rydelius, & Hagquist, 2015; Wright & Asmundson, 2003). Clinical use of the new DSM-5 diagnosis of illness anxiety disorder, in which the differentiation from SSD depends on having anxiety about illness in the absence of distressing physical symptoms, has yet to be validated for younger age groups.

Clinical Case: Fifteen-year-old Peter is growing increasingly worried that he is seriously ill. He is especially worried that he has cancer and fears that it will not be detected in time. During the past year, he has persuaded his mother to visit his general practitioner several times owing to concerns about various physical symptoms, most recently headaches and visual disturbances. He has been referred to specialist doctors for further medical assessments, all of which have come back without positive results. Still, he has a hard time being reassured that the bodily sensations he experiences are benign.

Since he was little, he has had a tendency to be afraid of illness, but it has become much worse since his grandfather died of a brain tumor 1 year ago. He seeks information online and experiences severe symptoms when he reads but also when he accidentally hears about various types of cancer. He has begun to withdraw from social interactions with friends and family because he does not feel that they take him seriously. Sometimes he is so anxious that he is about to die from cancer that he has said goodbye to his family and been afraid of falling asleep in case he does not wake up again.

His parents feel powerless; they have tried unsuccessfully to calm him down and talk him out of further medical visits, which they find only make him focus even more on his bodily sensations and symptoms. There are neither compulsive symptoms nor indications of depression or psychotic symptomatology.

Diagnosis: DSM-5: illness anxiety disorder; ICD-10: hypochondriasis/ICD-11 hypochondriasis/health anxiety disorder.

OTHER CLINICAL PRESENTATIONS

In some instances, severe FSS in children and adolescents can become extreme and even life-threatening in states of severe withdrawal, sometimes referred to as "pervasive refusal" (Lee, Duff, Martin, & Barrett, 2013). Profound withdrawal in these young persons may include failure to eat, drink, talk, walk, and engage in self-care and is usually accompanied by comorbid psychiatric disorders such as anxiety or depressive disorders.

Occasionally, excessive and seemingly unreasonable parental concern about children's symptoms, which has been conceptualized as health anxiety by proxy (Lockhart, 2016; Thorgaard, Frostholm, Walker, Jensen, et al., 2017), can lead to unnecessary medical assessments and treatments, risk of iatrogenic harm, as well as compromise the child's physical and mental health. This is not to be confused with the more rare cases in which the concerns are rather an expression of parental problems within the spectrum of factitious illness or Munchhausen by proxy, in which a caregiver falsifies illness in a child by fabricating or producing symptoms (Bass & Glaser, 2014; Eminson & Postlethwaite, 1992).

DIFFERENTIAL DIAGNOSIS AND PSYCHIATRIC COMORBIDITY

Disorders with severe FSS differ from malingering or factitious disorder in that, in the latter case, there is an intentional production of either grossly exaggerated or falsely produced symptoms to achieve privileges or attention. However, a spectrum of intentionality can be present and indeed is to be expected in cases with severe FSS, and should be duly evaluated.

Somatic symptoms and health concerns are often a feature of anxiety and depressive disorders but usually not the main focus of concern. A depressive disorder should be considered the primary diagnosis if the young person presents with core depressive symptoms such as low mood and lack of interest and the somatic symptoms, such as tiredness, are not regarded as key or central to the distress and impairment. In obsessive-compulsive disorder, a child or adolescent may display distressing illness-related thoughts and behaviors, but the obsessive nature of the thoughts and the associated compulsions take the center stage. Likewise, in generalized anxiety, the predominant anxieties and fears are not linked specifically to persistent worries about harboring a serious disease. Nevertheless, anxiety and mood disorders are often comorbid with severe FSS and these disorders are reported to be present in one-third to one-half and even higher numbers of children and adolescents with different clinical presentations of severe FSS (Campo et al., 2004; Garralda, 1999; Pehlivantürk & Unal, 2000).

In rare cases, and mainly in older children and adolescents, the physical problems and illness worries can be a manifestation of a psychotic disorder. In such cases, the health concerns and bodily symptoms are often bizarre and held with extreme rigidity.

CAUSES AND EXPLANATORY MODEL

The development and maintenance of severe FSS in children and young people are best understood within a *generic biopsychosocial explanatory model.*

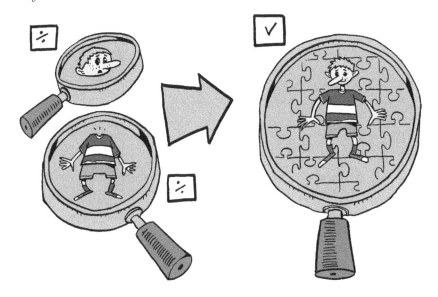

Within this model, a combination of biological, psychological, and social processes in the child, family, and broader environment are thought to interact to bring on individual, severe FSS. The overriding assumption is that environmental factors act in synergy with the individual's genetic and acquired susceptibility. Clinically, it is helpful to subdivide biopsychosocial risk factors further into predisposing, precipitating, perpetuating, and protective factors to identify *vulnerability* (the person's susceptibility to developing the disorder), *triggers* (factors that are directly involved in the onset of the disorder), and *maintaining* factors aggravating the pathological processes (Fig. 4.2).

This generic disease model may mainly be applicable to the most common clinical presentation of severe FSS in young persons, that is conditions dominated by persisting somatic symptoms. It has been suggested that the precipitating or triggering factors influence which somatic

Predisposing factors:
Biological, psychological and social:
Genes, parental illness, previous disease, abuse, etc.

Precipitating factors:
Infection or other physical disease
Physical trauma, e.g. accident
Emotional trauma, e.g. death of parent
Longstanding stress and strains, e.g. bullying, family conflicts, undetected intellectual disabilities
Iatrogenic, e.g. misinterpretation of nonsignificant clinical findings

Symptom onset
Early/acute phase

Perpetuating factors
Dysfunctional thoughts and behaviors related to the symptoms
(child, family, school/other environment)
Repeated unnecessary medical examinations (iatrogenicity)
Many ineffective treatment attempts
CNS sensitization and dysregulation in stress system

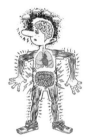

The body becomes 'noisy'
and hypersensitive with
persisting and distressing
symptoms

Fully developed disorder
with severe
Functional Somatic Symptoms

FIGURE 4.2 General explanatory model. The factors shown are examples and do not represent an exhaustive description of suggested involved factors. *CNS*, central nervous system.

symptoms develop. For example, acute gastroenteritis may trigger recurrent abdominal pains, a bone fracture can lead to loss of function of a limb or abnormal gait, and chronic headache can follow a minor head trauma. Whereas vulnerability and maintaining factors have a central etiological role and often overlap, maintaining factors are most likely to be susceptible to change and tend to be addressed in treatment. However, one should keep in mind that many risk factors can be predisposing as well as precipitating and perpetuating factors. Psychological stressors such as early childhood abuse can be a trigger for FSS but may also influence the vulnerability of a person to develop FSS later in life. In addition, many psychosocial stressors such as living in poverty or family conflicts are chronic and act insidiously as predisposing and perpetuating factors without the need for additional symptom triggers. Thus, in clinical practice it is not always possible to trace one obvious trigger for the development of FSS. Also, triggers can be psychosocial but also biological in nature. Moreover, some factors may act as both biological and psychosocial influences. For example, family transmission may be indicative of both genetic susceptibility and sociocultural learning. In addition, although many potential risk factors have been identified in children with severe FSS in cross-sectional studies, a number have not been confirmed by prospective research. This means that these identified factors could also (partly) be consequences of severe childhood FSS rather than the cause.

RISK FACTORS

In the following paragraphs, we have divided potential risk factors for FSS into biological versus psychological and social risk factors. Other explanatory factors that are thought to be specifically related to conversion/dissociative disorders and health anxiety will be discussed briefly in separate sections.

Biological Risk Factors

Familial Clustering

Familial clustering is well-established in a number of conditions dominated by FSS, such as irritable bowel syndrome and chronic fatigue (Craig, Cox, & Klein, 2002; Crawley & Smith, 2007; Farmer, Scourfield, Martin, Cardno, & Mcguffin, 1999; Garralda, 2000; Levy et al., 2004; Schulte & Petermann, 2011). Together with evidence arising from twin studies, this is thought to reflect genetic influences. Studies in adult patients have identified genetic influences interacting with environmental hazards in irritable bowel syndrome (Bengtson, Rønning, Vatn, & Harris, 2006), and generally a joint action of genes and environment is assumed, although there is still insufficient clarity on the actual genes and environmental factors involved.

Inherited Susceptibility

Biological susceptibilities may be expected to influence the clinical expression of severe FSS. For example, children and young people with recurrent abdominal pains report significantly greater symptom increase to a water load symptom provocation test than controls suggesting gastrointestinal sensitivity (Walker et al., 2006), and in infancy, hypersensitivity to sensory and tactile stimulation has been found to predict the development of recurrent somatic and impairing symptoms in later childhood (Ramchandani, Stein, Hotopf, & Wiles, 2006; Rask, Ørnbøl, Olsen, Fink, & Skovgaard, 2013).

Dysregulation of the Stress System

The case has been made for FSS reflecting dysregulation of the stress system in its various forms, including hypothalamic—pituitary—adrenal function, imbalances in vagal-sympathetic tone, and upregulation of immune inflammatory function. For example, overtiredness and musculoskeletal pains have been associated with low cortisol after awakening, and gastrointestinal and headache symptoms with low cortisol levels during psychosocial stress (Janssens et al., 2012). Cortisol has an important role in pain modulation by suppressing peripheral inflammatory signals and other nociceptive stimuli (Boakye et al., 2015), and low cortisol may thus be responsible for experiencing more bodily symptoms. High blood pressure and heart rate at rest and orthostatic anomalies have been noted in pediatric chronic fatigue syndrome (Wyller, Barbieri, Thaulow, & Saul, 2008; Wyller, Saul, Amlie, & Thaulow, 2007), and children with functional abdominal pains fail to report the expected higher pain threshold in the presence of elevated blood pressure, which possibly reflects autonomic dysregulation or its interplay with overlapping systems modulating pain (Bruehl, Dengler-Crish, Smith, & Walker, 2010). These anomalies, together with cognitive, emotional, and behavioral responses, would amplify reactivity to threatening stimuli, thus contributing to the subjective experience of somatic symptoms (Kozlowska, 2013).

Central Sensitization

Deserving further exploration is the possibility that both trauma and experience of illness induce central symptom hypersensibility in some children. When severe, pain disorders usually involve different bodily sites and could reflect central pain sensitization as a result of elevated responsiveness to nociceptive stimuli from increased spinal cord neuron excitability (Al-Chaer, Kawasaki, & Pasricha, 2000; Mayer & Collins, 2002; Walker, Sherman, Bruehl, Garber, & Smith, 2012).

Sleep and Physical Activity

Lack of sleep or other sleep problems have been shown to influence pain levels in both the short-term and long-term in adolescents (Bonvanie, Oldehinkel, Rosmalen, & Janssens, 2016; Law et al., 2014). Suggested mechanisms are altered pain thresholds owing to dysregulation of stress systems or the central sensitization discussed earlier, emotional disturbances such as depressive symptoms, which are related to both sleep problems and pain reports, and behavioral changes such as lack of activities because of fatigue (Smith & Haythornthwaite, 2004). Lack of physical exercise and high sedentary behavior are also associated with FSS in adolescents (Janssens, Oldhinkel, et al., 2014). Although poorer physical fitness seems to explain part of this association, it is possible that other additional factors are responsible, such as emotional disturbances, both as a potential result of withdrawal from activities and as a potential risk factor for FSS (Janssens, Klis, et al., 2014).

Psychological Risk Factors

Child Personality and Temperament

Earlier descriptions of children with recurrent functional abdominal pains noted certain characteristics in their personalities, such as conformism and obvious attempts to please adults and obtain approval, sensitivity to distress and insecurity, and anticipation of dangers and failures for themselves and their families (Garralda, 1992). These children have also been described as displaying irregular temperamental styles and to have a tendency to withdraw in new situations (Davison, Faull, & Nicol, 1986); in infancy, difficulty in self-regulation has been found to predict the development of recurrent somatic and impairing symptoms in later childhood (Ramchandani et al., 2006; Rask, Ørnbøl, Olsen, et al., 2013).

Childhood FSS has been further articulated in terms of superficially compliant children who tend to avoid overt expressions of vulnerability or distress but who find themselves in intolerable "predicaments" they cannot escape or communicate without threatening their feeling of safety. Physical illness would serve to elicit parental care and protection and safeguard the child from parental expectations and anger, displeasure, or rejection in the face of failure to perform (Kozlowska, 2001). Work on young people with fatigue syndromes identified high rates of personality disorder and difficulty characterized by conscientiousness, vulnerability, worthlessness, and emotional liability (Rangel, Garralda, & Levin, 2000), and a study in the general population of older adolescents found positive links between perfectionism and levels of somatic symptoms experienced (Bonvanie, Rosmalen, van Rhede van der Kloot, Oldehinkel, & Janssens, 2015).

Increased Stress Sensitivity and Coping Style

Stress sensitivity in children with FSS is supported by research in children with recurrent abdominal pains, because they report more daily hassles and stressors, both at home and at school, than well children and a stronger association between daily stressors and somatic symptoms (Walker, Garber, Smith, Van Slyke, & Claar, 2001). They also appear to be less confident in their ability to change or adapt to stress and less likely to use accommodative coping strategies (Walker, Smith, Garber, & Claar, 2007). Moreover, children with high levels of somatic symptoms tend to use comparatively poor coping strategies to deal with stress characterized by negative affect and avoidance (Walker et al., 2012), by being particularly distressed about their condition (more so than children with other pediatric disorders) and by less use of active problem-solving techniques when dealing with illness and impairment (Garralda & Rangel, 2004).

Emotional Disturbances

As mentioned earlier, anxiety and mood disorders can be comorbid with severe FSS (Campo et al., 2004; Garralda, 1999; Pehlivantürk & Unal, 2000). More important, symptoms of anxiety and depression seem to increase the level of FSS over time, and vice versa, which makes emotional disturbances an important potential perpetuating risk factor (Janssens, Rosmalen, Ormel, Van Oort, & Oldehinkel, 2010).

Social/Environmental Risk Factors

Stressful Events

Epidemiological studies have found associations between childhood FSS and broad psychosocial stressors such as broken families, negative life stresses, or events including loss of a close family member, parental divorce, and school events such as being bullied (Aro, 1987; Boey & Goh, 2001; Bonvanie, Janssens, Rosmalen, & Oldehinkel, 2016; Vila, Kramer, Obiols, & Garralda, 2012). Also, pressure on the child to perform (whether self- or externally induced) is thought to be a risk factor for FSS. Especially in children with low intelligence, high parental expectations increase the level of experienced somatic symptoms (Kingma et al., 2011). Studies in adults with somatoform disorders tended to highlight earlier experiences of family disruption and of sexual abuse (Chen et al., 2010), but although abuse may be expected to be linked with somatic symptoms in affected children, it does not present as a factor in most children with severe presentations of FSS (Bonvanie et al., 2015).

Parental Health

Mothers of children with FSS have an excess of histories of anxiety and depression (Campo et al., 2007), and parental anxiety and psychiatric disorder during the child's first year of life actually predict later somatic symptoms in the child (Ramchandani et al., 2006; Rask, Ørnbøl, Olsen, et al., 2013). Children of parents diagnosed with somatoform and related disorders have been found to have an excess of somatic symptoms and school absence (Craig et al., 2002). It has also been suggested that personal experience of physical illness or having parents with severe physical illnesses predisposes development of FSS, but evidence remains scarce (Bonvanie, Janssens, et al., 2016).

Parental Coping

Parental emotional overinvolvement with the children's symptoms may also be at the root of some of these conditions (Rangel, Garralda, Jeffs, & Rose, 2005). Whereas parental behaviors that involve giving attention to the somatic symptoms can result in an increase in child functional complaints, distraction helps to reduce them. It is reported that children with FSS view distraction as making the symptoms better, whereas parents rate this as more likely than attention to have a negative impact on them (Walker et al., 2006). Parents may thus unwittingly contribute to continuing their children's symptoms.

Parenting Styles

Specific parenting styles are also likely to have a part. Intense affect and preoccupation with the child and overprotectiveness have been reported in children with severe FSS, more so than in parents of children with other chronic physical disorders or with emotional disorders (Rangel et al., 2005). This might be compounded by parental "disease conviction" or overemphasis on possible medical causes for the symptoms, and it may impede children and adolescents in developing active coping mechanisms. Thus, longitudinal population research has also shown that overprotective parenting increases the level of somatic symptoms experienced by adolescents (Janssens, Oldehinkel, & Rosmalen, 2009).

Iatrogenic Factors

Often pediatric and medical services are not well-attuned to identify conditions dominated by FSS in children and adolescents, and this can result in physicians pursuing organic explanations and medical investigations excessively. This in itself can amplify children and families' illness worry and behavior (Ani et al., 2013; Rangel, Garralda, Levin, & Roberts, 2000). Whereas there is a danger of underinvestigating and missing underlying treatable medical disorders, it is also important to be aware of the dangers of overinvestigation and the possibility of making a positive diagnosis of an SSD or BDD (Cottrell, 2016).

Based on these risk factors, an overall formulation of the developmental course of severe FSS in children and young people would include:

- joint biological and psychological vulnerabilities resulting in an enhanced tendency to respond to environmental (physical and psychosocial) stressors through a combination of somatic and psychological symptoms; and
- somatic symptoms tending to attract more interest than psychological ones; their prominence would be reinforced by:
  - the development of high levels of concern and focus by parents on the symptoms and on the symptomatic child, which may override other family stressors;
  - illness-related school avoidance, which reduces any existing and underlying school and peer relationship stressors; and
  - repeated medical investigations, which increase the focus on, and might increase anxiety about, the somatic symptoms.

SPECIFIC FACTORS RELATED TO CONVERSION DISORDERS AND HEALTH ANXIETY

Conversion Disorder

We know comparatively little about etiological factors of relevance for childhood conversion disorders in general except that stressful events, which are often centered on school and relationships, are noted to be illness precipitants in most studies of children with conversion disorder (Ani et al., 2013). More information is available on nonepileptic seizures. Compared with sibling controls, these children have been found to have higher rates of lifetime adversities and comorbid medical illness (Plioplys et al., 2014). An excess of psychopathology including posttraumatic stress disorder and anxiety disorders and poor stress coping techniques have also been noted alongside a tendency toward fearful misinterpretations of physical sensations and passive, deficient emotion regulation and problem-solving and coping skills (Plioplys et al., 2014). In addition, brain neuroimaging studies in adults, although not yet conclusive, have suggested altered functional brain connectivity in areas involved with motor function, emotion regulation, and cognitive control (Baslet, Seshadri, Bermeo-Ovalle, Willment, & Myers, 2016; Perez et al., 2015), and the physiological changes of anxiety-related hyperventilation are likely to have a part in some children (Chandra et al., 2017).

Heath Anxiety

Health anxiety has been little studied in children. It has been shown that mothers with health anxiety perceive their children to be more ill and to present them more to health services compared with mothers with a chronic physical illness (Thorgaard, Frostholm, Walker, Stengaard-Pedersen, et al., 2017). However, evidence for intergenerational transmission of maladaptive illness perceptions remains scarce (Thorgaard, Frostholm, & Rask, 2018). Future work could help clarify whether familial transactional cycles of maladaptive illness beliefs and behaviors in combination with early insecure relations with caregivers may prove to be specific early risk factors for this condition, and also explore to what extent health anxiety existing in childhood constitutes a distinct disorder.

PROTECTIVE FACTORS

Given the established links between FSS and both stressors and psychopathology, factors which reduce the former and protect from the latter may also be expected to be protective for the development of severe FSS (Vanderbilt-Adriance & Shaw, 2008). On an individual level, good intelligence levels provide children with a broader range of coping mechanisms, the potential for academic success and high related self-efficacy and social standing. An easy temperamental and good personality function reduces stressors, facilitates the use of appropriate emotional regulation techniques, and helps elicit social supports in the face of adversity. Acute as opposed to insidious onsets also tend to have better prognosis. The presence of intact and/or well-functioning families with good parenting skills and of good school and peer supports will similarly decrease stress and facilitate coping, as will a favorable socioeconomic background.

The child displaying positive and active coping mechanisms in preference to distress, withdrawal and acceptance of impairment will be facilitive to reduce the FSS. Families that encourage positive coping with somatic symptoms once their benign nature has been established, that discourage dwelling on symptoms and continuing to worry about their medical significance, and accept that somatic symptoms can be strongly influenced by psychological factors will be protective, as will parents who appreciate and are able to guide and support the child sensitively in dealing with any existing psychological vulnerability. Thus, parental acceptance of a multifactorial illness model that acknowledges the contribution of not just medical but also psychological and social factors to illness has been associated with better outcomes (Crushell et al., 2003). Medical services able to make psychosocial assessments and positive referrals to psychological treatment and the existence of pediatric liaison teams with experience in the field are also thought to be protective factors (Garralda & Slaveska-Hollis, 2016).

ASSESSMENT

Most children with recurrent somatic problems will be known to their general practitioners or family doctors and referred by them in the first instance to their local pediatric clinic. For many children, a pediatric assessment will be sufficient to clarify the nature of the problem and lead to a resolution (Cottrell, 2016).

It is important that an appropriate physical examination is conducted to exclude a treatable medical disorder. However, there is also a danger, especially in more severe cases, of medical overinvestigation, which is likely to be unproductive and potentially harmful as well as cost-ineffective (Dhroove, Chogle, & Saps, 2010; Lindley, Glaser, & Milla, 2005). Furthermore, this can delay addressing the potential underlying psychosocial aspects.

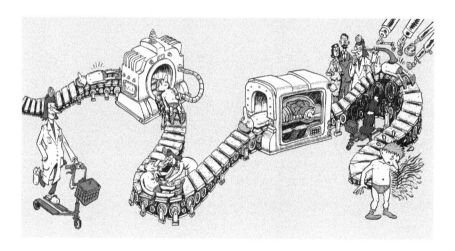

A psychiatric assessment is important in patients with severe FSS for differential diagnosis to confirm or exclude the presence of a somatic symptom or a related disorder and the potential presence of comorbid psychiatric disorders amenable to psychiatric intervention. Core elements of the assessment are outlined in Table 4.2.

For young children, the assessment depends primarily on parental information and child—parent interactions, whereas in older children more emphasis will be put on their own reporting. Furthermore, contact with schools and especially documentation of school absence and of other potential educational and social problems is important. Standardized questionnaires that may be helpful in the assessment are outlined in Table 4.3. In addition, various measures of levels of comorbid anxiety and depression will be helpful.

TABLE 4.2   Psychiatric Assessment of Children and Adolescents With Severe Functional Somatic Symptoms (FSS)

1. Review medical records/illness history with emphasis on the following:
   a. Negative findings despite thorough medical investigations
   b. Inconsistent findings at clinical assessments
   c. Potential time coincidence with psychosocial stressors
2. Biopsychosocial history taking with focus on the following:
   a. Family history of FSS and somatic symptom and related disorders
   b. Elaboration on details of the symptoms and their development
   c. Potential psychiatric comorbidity
   d. Potential strain and stressors
   e. Degree of associated impairment including school absence
   f. The child's and the family's illness perceptions and expectations from the assessment and treatment
   g. Potential reinforcing environmental responses/behaviors (e.g., in the family and/or school)
3. Focused clinical assessment on and judgment of whether further medical evaluation is needed

TABLE 4.3   Selected Questionnaires for Assessment

Clinical Presentation	Questionnaire	Age Group	Number of Items
Multiple somatic symptoms	Symptom Checklist Revised—90 (SCL) somatisation subscale (Derogatis & Cleary, 1977) Bodily Distress Check list (Budtz-Lilly et al., 2015)	Adolescents Adolescents	12 25
	Children's Somatization Inventory[a] (Walker, Garber, & Greene, 1991)	Children and adolescents	35
Health anxiety	Whiteley Index (Fink et al., 1999)	Adolescents	7
	Childhood Illness Attitude Scale (Wright & Asmundson, 2003)	Children and adolescents	35
Physical and mental fatigue	Chalder Fatigue Scale (Cella & Chalder, 2010)	Children and adolescents	11
Symptom-related interference	Functional Disability Inventory (Walker & Greene, 1991)	Children and adolescents	15
	Limitation index (Holmstrom, Kemani, Kanstrup, & Wicksell, 2015)	Children and adolescents	6
Anxiety and depression	SCL depression and anxiety subscales) (Derogatis & Cleary, 1977)	Adolescents	10
	Hospital Anxiety and Depression Questionnaire (White, Leach, Sims, Atkinson, & Cottrell, 1999)	Adolescents	14
Depression	Moods and Feelings Questionnaire (Angold et al., 1995)	Children and adolescents	33
Anxiety	The Spence Children's Anxiety Scale (Spence, 1998)	Children and adolescents	44

[a]Includes pseudoneurological symptoms.

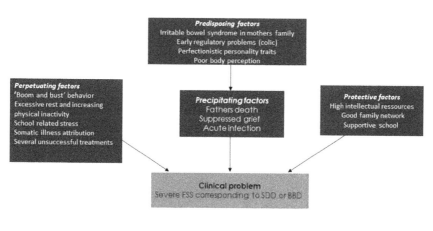

FSS: Functional Somatic Symptoms
SSD: Somatic Symptom Disorder
BDD: Bodily Distress Disorder

FIGURE 4.3 Case formulation for Anne, based on a biopsychosocial framework.

Drawing a timeline with a chronological recording of symptom development, medical evaluations, and treatments on one side and psychosocial events and stressors on the other can be a useful tool to obtain an overview of the often complex illness history. This systematic approach can constitute the basis for a case formulation that takes into account biological, psychological, and social risk and maintaining factors as well as protective factors which will be central to the further rehabilitation process. An example of a case formulation, based on these principles, of the clinical case with Anne is given below (Fig. 4.3).

CLINICAL CASE OF "ANNE," CONTINUED

Anne is a bright girl who is generally well-liked among her peers. However, her mother also describes her as a conscientious and perfectionistic girl who has high demands for herself. She tends to live according to the rule that one should always do one's best. Before she became ill after an infectious illness 2 years previously, she seldom noticed bodily symptoms and could sometimes "collapse" after a period with high level of activities. Even now, Anne suppresses pain and fatigue on some days, which results in days when she finds it impossible to get out of bed owing to worsening of the symptoms.

Anne's father died in a car accident when she was 9 years old. She now lives with her mother, stepfather, and younger brother. She has a good relationship with the stepfather but often misses her father and finds it difficult to talk about him in her new family context.

Schoolwork has become a vicious circle for Anne. She would like to achieve good grades, but her high school absence and lack of energy make it difficult to perform her best, and she is stressed by it.

Anne's mother is supportive but uncertain about how best to help her. She is afraid that something was damaged in Anne's body as a result of the infection 2 years ago, and she often encourages Anne to rest. Also, she has taken Anne to several alternative practitioners who suggested various forms of herbal medicine to "restore the physiological balance" in Anne's body.

The family has a good social network with a close relationship with grandparents on both sides. The school is supportive and has offered that Anne attend school under special conditions until she gets better.

Several family members on the mother's side have symptoms of irritable bowel syndrome.

It follows that the psychiatric assessment requires specific skills in medical/psychiatric differential diagnoses, liaison with pediatric services, prioritizing family engagement in assessment and treatment, and helping families move from a purely physical to a biopsychosocial framework, crucially at a pace that is appropriate and acceptable to them. General communicative principles for engagement and motivation for treatment that may be helpful in this process are provided in Table 4.4.

TABLE 4.4 General Communicative Principles for Engagement and Motivation for Treatment

Feedback on Results of the Examination

Reframe the problems in a biopsychosocial model: link physical, psychological, and social factors using the following:
1. Give a simple explanation
   a. How anxiety causes physical symptoms
   b. How depression lowers the pain threshold
2. Demonstrate
   a. Practical (e.g., how pain results from tense muscles)
   b. Link to life events (e.g., how pain can be made worse by stressors)
   c. "Here and now" (e.g., how the pain is at the moment, and ask about feelings)
3. Project or identify (ask if anyone else in the family or among friends has experienced similar symptoms)

MANAGEMENT AND TREATMENT SETTING

Similar basic treatment strategies are effective in managing various somatic symptoms regardless of the symptom type or the specific diagnoses the child or adolescent may have received. This perspective is based on comprehensive reviews covering the whole field of somatic symptoms (Bonvanie et al., 2017) as well as systematic reviews focused on specific syndrome diagnoses (Brent, Lobato, & LeLeiko, 2009; Eccleston, Palermo, Williams, Lewandowski, & Morley, 2009). In practice, many experts propose a stepped-care model in which management is not based on the diagnostic label or predominant symptomatology, but rather on illness severity and complexity (Schroder & Fink, 2011) (Fig. 4.4). Evidence is strongest for the specific treatments (step 3), whereas the recommended general principles and models for management (steps 1 and 2) are based primarily on clinical experience and consensus on best practice.

Step 1 covers mild or transient FSS. Most children with FSS are seen by primary health care practitioners and pediatricians and improve after these medical consultations with clarification of the lack of underlying pathology and possibly also with coping advice. The

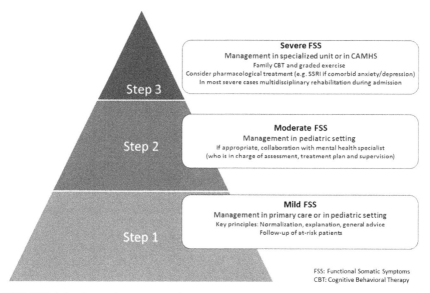

FIGURE 4.4   Stepped-care approach to the management of functional somatic symptoms (FSS) in children and adolescents. *CAMHS,* Child and Adolescent Mental Health Services; *SSRI,* selective serotonin reuptake inhibitor. *Modified after Garralda, M.E., & Rask, C.U. (2015). Somatoform and related disorders (Chapter 72). In A. Thapar, D. S. Pine, J. F. Leckman, S. Scott, M. J. Snowling, & E. A. Taylor (Eds.), Rutter's Child and Adolescent Psychiatry, 6th edition. Wiley-Blackwell.*

majority will receive a diagnosis of unspecific symptoms or adjustment reactions if the symptoms follow closely on the experience of a marked and universally stressful event. Parents with high anxiety levels related to their child's somatic symptoms give more positive feedback to biopsychosocial than to purely biomedical pediatric consultations (Williams, Smith, Bruehl, Gigante, & Walker, 2009). This accords with the fact that many mothers of children consulting for abdominal pains as well as with conversion disorder acknowledge a contribution of psychosocial factors to their children's symptoms (Ani et al., 2013; Claar & Walker, 1999).

Step 2 concerns children and adolescents with moderate FSS and involves management approaches that may be provided mostly in pediatric settings. This group primarily consists of young persons diagnosed in pediatric care with the syndromal diagnoses used in medical specialties for adult patients with moderate to severe FSS such as fibromyalgia, irritable bowel syndrome, and chronic fatigue syndrome. The cornerstone of successful management is the pediatric clinicians' ability to take a proper biopsychosocial history, carry out the necessary investigations, and emphatically discuss with the young person and the parents that organic disease has been excluded, as well as reveal potential stressful aspects in the child's environment and help modify them (Garralda, 1999). Sharing information about the general prevalence of FSS, existing knowledge about risk factors, as well as guidance about adaptive coping strategies can be helpful in "normalizing" the problem and "empowering" families in management.

More specific approaches may involve: (1) pain management with the use of, e.g., relaxation (especially for headaches) and distraction techniques or self-exercises with gut-directed hypnotherapy in the case of functional abdominal pain (Rutten et al., 2014) and, if applicable, with a graded increase in physical activity and school attendance; (2) addressing perpetuating factors such as stressors related to schoolwork or peer interactions; (3) encouraging a balance between activity and rest and the reestablishment of a normal sleep pattern (Cottrell, 2016); and (4) helping parents decrease concerns related to the symptoms while increasing attention and encouragement of more adaptive pain-related behavior and shared enjoyable activities.

Step 3 covers specialized mental health treatment in units or by pediatric liaison teams specialized in the care of young patients with SSD and related illnesses (Garralda & Slaveska-Hollis, 2016). However, in general, the minority of children with highly persistent and disabling symptoms are referred to mental health care (Tot-Strate, Dehlholm-Lambertsen, Lassen, & Rask, 2016) even though most will fulfil the criteria of psychiatric diagnoses for severe FSS. This is probably because the referral from pediatrics to child psychiatry settings requires a sensitive appreciation by all concerned of the "somatic focus" and reluctance by a number of children and families to accept a mental health approach (Garralda & Rangel, 2001).

Currently, the best evidence for treatment of severe FSS in children and adolescents is based on specialized psychological interventions with active child and parental involvement such as graded exercise and cognitive behavioral therapy (CBT) (Eccleston et al., 2009; Knight, Scheinberg, & Harvey, 2013) and other psychological treatment such as hypnotherapy (Rutten, Reitsma, Vlieger, & Benninga, 2013). Internet-delivered CBT has also shown promising results for chronic or recurrent pain as well as chronic fatigue in children and adolescents (Fisher et al., 2014; Nijhof, Bleijenberg, Uiterwaal, Kimpen, & van de Putte, 2012). Psychological treatment approaches typically involve psychoeducation and exploration of concerns and illness beliefs followed by symptomatic treatment with an emphasis on rehabilitation and learning of adaptive symptom coping alongside the exploration and management of contributory stressors and/or psychiatric disorders. Because of the importance of parental influences, family work is often of the essence, especially in younger age groups (Hulgaard, Dehlholm-Lambertsen, & Rask, 2017).

Specific classical CBT techniques may involve self-monitoring of the main symptoms through diaries, teaching children to observe symptom fluctuation with changes in intensity and severity, limiting attention given to the symptom by others, relaxation when appropriate, and encouraging participation in routine activities through gradual exposure, while confirming that the child is not feigning the symptom. Third-wave behavior therapy, such as acceptance and commitment therapy (ACT), which integrates mindfulness and acceptance training with behavior-change processes, has shown promising results in children and adolescents with functional chronic pain (Wicksell, Melin, Lekander, & Olsson, 2009). ACT is currently being tested in a trial of adolescents with various types of severe FSS (Kallesøe, Schröder, Wicksell, & Rask, 2016). Therapeutically, acceptance and mindfulness are promoted through the use of patient-specific exercises, metaphors, and behavioral tasks which in many ways make this treatment form well-suited for young persons.

Psychopharmacologic interventions such as the use of selective serotonin reuptake inhibitors, serotonin—norepinephrine reuptake inhibitors, and tricyclic antidepressants appear to be helpful in adults with diagnoses of somatoform disorders or with functional pain syndromes such as fibromyalgia or irritable bowel syndrome (Agger et al., 2017; Ford, Talley, Schoenfeld, Quigley, & Moayyedi, 2009). However, there are no similar trials to support the evidence of the effect of psychotropic medications in treating children and adolescents with severe FSS (Martin et al., 2017).

Comorbid mood disorders will require specific and coordinated treatment, including recommendation of pharmacotherapy when indicated. Also comorbid medical disorders may require additional treatment. Severe cases, such as children with pervasive withdrawal and complex regional pain syndrome or young persons who have failed to respond to outpatient treatment, may call for day-hospital or inpatient interdisciplinary rehabilitation (composed of physical therapy, occupational therapy, and CBT alongside medical and nursing services) combined with school involvement (Logan et al., 2012).

CONCLUSION

This chapter outlines current knowledge on the risk and protective factors as well as course of FSS and corresponding main clinical presentations in young people. The care of this group of children and adolescents bridges the borders of health care sectors as well as psychosocial and somatic disciplines, and therefore requires close collaboration between pediatric or general practice and liaison child and adolescent psychiatrists or mental health services. The special skills required from general practitioners and pediatricians include recognition and management of child and adolescent psychopathology, exploration of potential environmental stresses, and child vulnerability within the context of the family's disease convictions, mental distress, and emotional involvement with the child's symptoms. The skills required from the mental health services involve the ability to appraise the medical relevance of the somatic symptoms and possible subtle anomalies from physical investigations, the family's medical beliefs, and sometimes distress and reluctance to consider a psychiatric or psychosocial contribution. For a number of cases, this will call for a joint pediatric/mental health approach. However, there are few pediatric liaison psychiatry services able to work in this joint fashion. Therefore, the development of interventions appropriate for the primary care setting and hospital pediatric liaison psychiatry services should be a main area for future research. Epidemiological studies mapping the extent of clinically significant FSS and the dissemination of existing evidence on the rationale for interface work should further inform service development and clinical practice in this area.

The consequence of the lacking implementation of systematic models for shared care in many places is that most young patients with severe FSS are offered no or limited specialized assessment and treatment. Existing knowledge and clinical experience provide evidence for the implementation of unified or integrated treatment programs. An important rationale is that psychological-behavioral interventions have proven effective, regardless of the diagnostic label and the young person's symptom profile, although on occasions organ-specific treatments may have an additional role in the management. An integrated approach therefore seems to be preferable to separate specialized treatment approaches for various subtypes of severe FSS. Unfortunately, it remains largely unclear who benefits most from psychological treatment. So far, little attention has been paid to identifying child characteristics and other key clinical issues of importance for outcome: for example, the management of family disease beliefs, parental distress and emotional involvement with the child, the process of referral for therapeutic help, and therapeutic engagement. Nor is there much literature on the role of psychopharmacological treatment for emotional comorbidity. Increased knowledge regarding these factors may make treatments more tailored to the individual child or adolescent and therefore more effective.

Several clinical guidelines have emerged to improve the diagnosis and management of adult patients with persistent somatic symptoms or severe FSS. Unfortunately, these do not always consider the developmental aspect by including younger age groups. It may be expected that future guidelines in this area will also improve the quality of care for younger age groups with FSS.

References

Agger, J. L., Schröder, A., Gormsen, L. K., Jensen, J. S., Jensen, T. S., & Fink, P. K. (2017). Imipramine versus placebo for multiple functional somatic syndromes (STreSS-3): A double-blind, randomised study. *The Lancet Psychiatry*, *4*(5), 378–388. https://doi.org/10.1016/S2215-0366(17)30126-8.

Al-Chaer, E. D., Kawasaki, M., & Pasricha, P. J. (2000). A new model of chronic visceral hypersensitivity in adult rats induced by colon irritation during postnatal development. *Gastroenterology*, *119*(5), 1276–1285. S0016508500924892 [pii].

Angold, A., Costello, E. J., Messer, S. C., Pickles, A., Winder, F., & Silver, D. (1995). The development of a short questionnaire for use in epidemiological studies of depression in children and adolescents. *International Journal of Methods in Psychiatric Research*. doi: 1049-8931/95/040251-12.

Ani, C., Reading, R., Lynn, R., Forlee, S., & Garralda, E. (2013). Incidence and 12-month outcome of non-transient childhood conversion disorder in the UK and Ireland. *British Journal of Psychiatry*, *202*(6), 413–418. https://doi.org/10.1192/bjp.bp.112.116707.

Aro, H. (1987). Life stress and psychosomatic symptoms among 14 to 16-year old Finnish adolescents. *Psychological Medicine*, *17*(1), 191–201. https://doi.org/10.1017/S0033291700013088.

Asmundson, G. J. G., Abramowitz, J. S., Richter, A. A., & Whedon, M. (2010). Health anxiety: Current perspectives and future directions. *Current Psychiatry Reports*, *12*(4). https://doi.org/10.1007/s11920-010-0123-9.

Baslet, G., Seshadri, A., Bermeo-Ovalle, A., Willment, K., & Myers, L. (2016). Psychogenic non-epileptic Seizures: An updated primer. *Psychosomatics*. https://doi.org/10.1016/j.psym.2015.10.004.

Bass, C., & Glaser, D. (2014). Early recognition and management of fabricated or induced illness in children. *Lancet*, *383*(9926), 1412–1421. https://doi.org/10.1016/S0140-6736(13)62183-2.

Beck, J. E. (2008). A developmental perspective on functional somatic symptoms. *Journal of Pediatric Psychology, 33*(5), 547−562. https://doi.org/10.1093/jpepsy/jsm113.

Bengtson, M.-B., Rønning, T., Vatn, M. H., & Harris, J. R. (2006). Irritable bowel syndrome in twins: Genes and environment. *Gut, 55*(12), 1754−1759. https://doi.org/10.1136/gut.2006.097287.

Berntsson, L. T., Kohler, L., & Gustafsson, J. E. (2001). Psychosomatic complaints in school-children: A nordic comparison. *Scandinavian Journal of Public Health, 29*(1), 44−54.

Bisht, J., Sankhyan, N., Kaushal, R. K., Sharma, R. C., & Grover, N. (2008). Clinical profile of pediatric somatoform disorders. *Indian Pediatrics, 45*(2), 111−115.

Boakye, P. A., Olechowski, C., Rashiq, S., Verrier, M. J., Kerr, B., Witmans, M., et al. (2015). A critical review of neurobiological factors involved in the interactions between chronic pain, depression, and sleep disruption. *The Clinical Journal of Pain.* https://doi.org/10.1097/AJP.0000000000000260.

Boey, C. C. M., & Goh, K. L. (2001). The significance of life-events as contributing factors in childhood recurrent abdominal pain in an urban community in Malaysia. *Journal of Psychosomatic Research, 51*(4), 559−562. https://doi.org/10.1016/S0022-3999(01)00232-X.

Bonvanie, I. J., Janssens, K. A. M., Rosmalen, J. G. M., & Oldehinkel, A. J. (2016). Life events and functional somatic symptoms: A population study in older adolescents. *British Journal of Psychology.* https://doi.org/10.1111/bjop.12198.

Bonvanie, I., Kallesøe, K., Janssens, K., Schröder, A., Rosmalen, J., & Rask, C. (2017). Psychological interventions for children with functional somatic symptoms: A systematic review and meta-analysis. *The Journal of Pediatrics.* pii: S0022.

Bonvanie, I. J., Oldehinkel, A. J., Rosmalen, J. G. M., & Janssens, K. A. M. (2016). Sleep problems and pain: A longitudinal cohort study in emerging adults. *Pain, 157*(4). https://doi.org/10.1097/j.pain.0000000000000466.

Bonvanie, I. J., Rosmalen, J. G. M., van Rhede van der Kloot, C. M., Oldehinkel, A. J., & Janssens, K. A. M. (2015). Short report: Functional somatic symptoms are associated with perfectionism in adolescents. *Journal of Psychosomatic Research, 79*(4). https://doi.org/10.1016/j.jpsychores.2015.07.009.

Bonvanie, I. J., van Gils, A., Janssens, K. A. M., & Rosmalen, J. G. M. (2015). Sexual abuse predicts functional somatic symptoms: An adolescent population study. *Child Abuse & Neglect, 46.* https://doi.org/10.1016/j.chiabu.2015.06.001.

Brent, M., Lobato, D., & LeLeiko, N. (2009). Psychological treatments for pediatric functional gastrointestinal disorders. *Journal of Pediatric Gastroenterology and Nutrition, 48*(1), 13−21. https://doi.org/10.1097/MPG.0b013e3181761516.

Bruehl, S., Dengler-Crish, C. M., Smith, C. A., & Walker, L. S. (2010). Hypoalgesia related to elevated resting blood pressure is absent in adolescents and young adults with a history of functional abdominal pain. *Pain, 149*(1), 57−63. https://doi.org/10.1016/j.pain.2010.01.009.

Budtz-Lilly, A., Fink, P., Ørnbøl, E., Vestergaard, M., Moth, G., Christensen, K. S., et al. (2015). A new questionnaire to identify bodily distress in primary care: The "BDS checklist". *Journal of Psychosomatic Research, 78*(6), 536−545. https://doi.org/10.1016/j.jpsychores.2015.03.006.

Campo, J. V., Bridge, J., Ehmann, M., Altman, S., Lucas, A., Birmaher, B., et al. (2004). Recurrent abdominal pain, anxiety, and depression in primary care. *Pediatrics, 113*(4). https://doi.org/10.1542/peds.113.4.817.

Campo, J. V., Bridge, J., Lucas, A., Savorelli, S., Walker, L., Di Lorenzo, C., et al. (2007). Physical and emotional health of mothers of youth with functional abdominal pain. *Archives of Pediatrics and Adolescent Medicine, 161*(2), 131. https://doi.org/10.1001/archpedi.161.2.131.

Campo, J. V., Jansen-Mcwilliams, L., Comer, D. M., & Kelleher, K. J. (1999). Somatization in pediatric primary care: Association with psychopathology, functional impairment, and use of services. *Journal of the American Academy of Child and Adolescent Psychiatry, 38*(9), 1093–1101. https://doi.org/10.1097/00004583-199909000-00012.

Cella, M., & Chalder, T. (2010). Measuring fatigue in clinical and community settings. *Journal of Psychosomatic Research, 69*(1), 17–22. https://doi.org/10.1016/j.jpsychores.2009.10.007.

Chandra, P., Kozlowska, K., Cruz, C., Baslet, G., Perez, D., & Garralda, M. (2017). Hyperventilation-induced non-epileptic seizures in an adolescent boy with pediatric medical traumatic stress. *Harvard Review of Psychiatry, 11*(1).

Chen, L. P., Murad, M. H., Paras, M. L., Colbenson, K. M., Sattler, A. L., Goranson, E. N., et al. (2010). Sexual abuse and lifetime diagnosis of psychiatric disorders: Systematic review and meta-analysis. *Mayo Clinic Proceedings, 85*(7), 618–629. https://doi.org/10.4065/mcp.2009.0583.

Claar, R. L., & Walker, L. S. (1999). Maternal attributions for the causes and remedies of their children's abdominal pain. *Journal of Pediatric Psychology, 24*(4), 345–354. https://doi.org/10.1093/jpepsy/24.4.345.

Cottrell, D. J. (2016). Fifteen-minute consultation: Medically unexplained symptoms. *Archives of Disease in Childhood. Education & Practice Edition, 101*(3), 114–118. https://doi.org/10.1136/archdischild-2015-309344.

Craig, T. K. J., Cox, A. D., & Klein, K. (2002). Intergenerational transmission of somatization behaviour: A study of chronic somatizers and their children. *Psychological Medicine, 32*(5). https://doi.org/10.1017/S0033291702005846.

Crawley, E., & Smith, G. D. (2007). Is chronic fatigue syndrome (CFS/ME) heritable in children, and if so, why does it matter? *Archives of Disease in Childhood, 92*, 1058–1061. https://doi.org/10.1136/adc.2006.110502.

Crushell, E., Rowland, M., Doherty, M., Gormally, S., Harty, S., Bourke, B., et al. (2003). Importance of parental conceptual model of illness in severe recurrent abdominal pain. *Pediatrics, 112*(6 Pt 1), 1368–1372. https://doi.org/10.1542/peds.112.6.1368.

Davison, I. S., Faull, C., & Nicol, A. R. (1986). Research note: Temperament and behaviour in six-year-olds with recurrent abdominal pain: A follow up. *Journal of Child Psychology and Psychiatry, 27*(4), 539–544. https://doi.org/10.1111/j.1469-7610.1986.tb00640.x.

Derogatis, L. R., & Cleary, P. A. (1977). Confirmation of the dimensional structure of the scl-90: A study in construct validation. *Journal of Clinical Psychology, 33*(4), 981–989. https://doi.org/10.1002/1097-4679(197710)33:4<981::AID-JCLP2270330412>3.0.CO;2–0.

Dhroove, G., Chogle, A., & Saps, M. (2010). A million-dollar work-up for abdominal Pain: Is it worth it? *Journal of Pediatric Gastroenterology and Nutrition, 51*(5), 579–583. https://doi.org/10.1097/MPG.0b013e3181de0639.

Dimsdale, J., Sharma, N., & Sharpe, M. (2011). What do physicians think of somatoform disorders? *Psychosomatics, 52*(2), 154–159. https://doi.org/10.1016/j.psym.2010.12.011.

Domènech-Llaberia, E., Jané, C., Canals, J., Ballespí, S., Esparó, G., & Garralda, E. (2004). Parental reports of somatic symptoms in preschool children: Prevalence and associations in a Spanish sample. *Journal of the American Academy of Child and Adolescent Psychiatry, 43*(5), 598–604. https://doi.org/10.1097/00004583-200405000-00013.

Eccleston, C., Palermo, T. M., Williams, A. C., Lewandowski, A., & Morley, S. (2009). Psychological therapies for the management of chronic and recurrent pain in children and adolescents. *Cochrane Database of Systematic Reviews*, CD003968. https://doi.org/10.1002/14651858.CD003968.pub2.

Eminson, D. M. (2007). Medically unexplained symptoms in children and adolescents. *Clinical Psychology Review, 27*(7), 855–871. S0272-7358(07)00128-6 [pii].

Eminson, M., Benjamin, S., Shortall, A., Woods, T., & Faragher, B. (1996). Physical symptoms and illness attitudes in adolescents: An epidemiological study. *The Journal of Child Psychology and Psychiatry and Allied Disciplines, 37*(5), 519–528. https://doi.org/10.1111/j.1469-7610.1996.tb01438.x.

Eminson, D. M., & Postlethwaite, R. J. (1992). Factitious illness: Recognition and management. *Archives of Disease in Childhood, 67*(12), 1510–1516. https://doi.org/10.1136/adc.67.12.1510.

Essau, C. A., Conradt, J., & Petermann, F. (1999). Prevalence, comorbidity and psychosocial impairment of somatoform disorders in adolescents. *Psychology Health & Medicine, 4*(2), 169–180. https://doi.org/10.1080/135485099106306.

Farmer, A., Scourfield, J., Martin, N., Cardno, A., & Mcguffin, P. (1999). Is disabling fatigue in childhood influenced by genes? *Psychological Medicine, 29*(2). https://doi.org/10.1017/S0033291798008095. S0033291798008095.

Fink, P., Ewald, H., Jensen, J., Sørensen, L., Engberg, M., Holm, M., et al. (1999). Screening for somatization and hypochondriasis in primary care and neurological in-patients: A seven-item scale for hypochondriasis and somatization. *Journal of Psychosomatic Research, 46*(3), 261–273. https://doi.org/10.1016/S0022-3999(98)00092-0.

Fink, P., Ørnbøl, E., Toft, T., Sparle, K. C., Frostholm, L., & Olesen, F. (2004). A new, empirically established hypochondriasis diagnosis. *American Journal of Psychiatry, 161*(9), 1680–1691. https://doi.org/10.1176/appi.ajp.161.9.1680.

Fink, P., & Schroder, A. (2010). One single diagnosis, bodily distress syndrome, succeeded to capture 10 diagnostic categories of functional somatic syndromes and somatoform disorders. *Journal of Psychosomatic Research, 68*(5), 415–426. https://doi.org/10.1016/j.jpsychores.2010.02.004.

Fisher, E., Heathcote, L., Palermo, T. M., de C Williams, A. C., Lau, J., & Eccleston, C. (2014). Systematic review and meta-analysis of psychological therapies for children with chronic pain. *Journal of Pediatric Psychology, 39*(8), 763–782. https://doi.org/10.1093/jpepsy/jsu008.

Ford, A. C., Talley, N. J., Schoenfeld, P. S., Quigley, E. M. M., & Moayyedi, P. (2009). Efficacy of antidepressants and psychological therapies in irritable bowel syndrome: Systematic review and meta-analysis. *Gut, 58*(3), 367–378. https://doi.org/10.1136/gut.2008.163162.

Fritz, G. K., Fritsch, S., & Hagino, O. (1997). Somatoform disorders in children and adolescents: A review of the past 10 years. *Journal of the American Academy of Child & Adolescent Psychiatry, 36*(10), 1329–1338. https://doi.org/10.1097/00004583-199710000-00014.

Garralda, M. E. (1992). A selective review of child psychiatric syndromes with a somatic presentation. *British Journal of Psychiatry.* https://doi.org/10.1192/bjp.161.6.759.

Garralda, M. E. (1999). Practitioner review: Assessment and management of somatisation in childhood and adolescence: A practical perspective. *Journal of Child Psychology and Psychiatry, and Allied Disciplines, 40*(8), 1159–1167. https://doi.org/10.1111/1469-7610.00533.

Garralda, M. E. (2000). The links between somatisation in children and adults. In P. Reder, M. McClure, & P. Jolley (Eds.), *Family Matters: Interfaces between child and adult mental health.* London and Philadelphia: Routledge.

Garralda, E., & Rangel, L. (2001). Childhood chronic fatigue syndrome. *American Journal of Psychiatry, 158*(7), 1161.

Garralda, M. E., & Rangel, L. (2004). Impairment and coping in children and adolescents with chronic fatigue syndrome: A comparative study with other paediatric disorders. *The Journal of Child Psychology and Psychiatry and Allied Disciplines, 45*(3), 543–552. https://doi.org/10.1111/j.1469-7610.2004.00244.x.

Garralda, M. E., & Slaveska-Hollis, K. (2016). What is special about a paediatric liaison child and adolescent mental health service? *Child and Adolescent Mental Health, 21*(2), 96–101. https://doi.org/10.1111/camh.12146.

Græsholt-Knudsen, T., Skovgaard, A. M., Jensen, J. S., & Rask, C. U. (2017 Jul). Impact of functional somatic symptoms on 5-7-year-olds' healthcare use and costs. *Arch Dis Child, 102*(7), 617–623. https://doi.org/10.1136/archdischild-2016-311808. Epub 2017 Jan 30.

Gureje, O., & Reed, G. M. (2016). Bodily distress disorder in ICD-11: Problems and prospects. *World Psychiatry.* https://doi.org/10.1002/wps.20353.

Henningsen, P., Zipfel, S., & Herzog, W. (2007). Management of functional somatic syndromes. *Lancet (London, England), 369*(9565), 946−955. S0140-6736(07)60159-7 [pii].

Hoftun, G. B., Romundstad, P. R., Zwart, J. A., & Rygg, M. (2011). Chronic idiopathic pain in adolescence−high prevalence and disability: The young HUNT study 2008. *Pain, 152*(10), 2259−2266. https://doi.org/10.1016/j.pain.2011.05.007.

Holmstrom, L., Kemani, M. K., Kanstrup, M., & Wicksell, R. K. (2015). Evaluating the statistical properties of the pain interference index in children and adolescents with chronic pain. *Journal of Developmental and Behavioral Pediatrics: Journal of Developmental and Behavioral Pediatrics, 36*(6), 450−454. https://doi.org/10.1097/DBP.0000000000000191.

Hulgaard, D., Dehlholm-Lambertsen, G., & Rask, C. (2017). Family based treatment for children with functional somatic symptoms. A systematic Review. *Journal of Family Therapy.* https://doi.org/10.1111/1467-6427.12199.

Janssens, K. A., Klis, S., Kingma, E. M., Oldehinkel, A. J., & Rosmalen, J. G. (2014). Predictors for persistence of functional somatic symptoms in adolescents. *The Journal of Pediatrics, 164*(4), 900−905.e2. https://doi.org/10.1016/j.jpeds.2013.12.003.

Janssens, K. A. M., Oldehinkel, A. J., Bonvanie, I. J., & Rosmalen, J. G. M. (2014). An inactive lifestyle and low physical fitness are associated with functional somatic symptoms in adolescents. The TRAILS study. *Journal of Psychosomatic Research, 76*(6). https://doi.org/10.1016/j.jpsychores.2014.03.008.

Janssens, K. A., Oldehinkel, A. J., Dijkstra, J. K., Veenstra, R., & Rosmalen, J. G. (2011). School absenteeism as a perpetuating factor of functional somatic symptoms in adolescents: The TRAILS study. *The Journal of Pediatrics, 159*(6), 988−993.e1. https://doi.org/10.1016/j.jpeds.2011.06.008.

Janssens, K. A., Oldehinkel, A. J., & Rosmalen, J. G. (2009). Parental overprotection predicts the development of functional somatic symptoms in young adolescents. *The Journal of Pediatrics, 154*(6), 918−923.e1. https://doi.org/10.1016/j.jpeds.2008.12.023.

Janssens, K. A. M., Oldehinkel, A. J., Verhulst, F. C., Hunfeld, J. A. M., Ormel, J., & Rosmalen, J. G. M. (2012). Symptom-specific associations between low cortisol responses and functional somatic symptoms: The TRAILS study. *Psychoneuroendocrinology, 37*(3), 332−340. https://doi.org/10.1016/j.psyneuen.2011.06.016.

Janssens, K. A. M., Rosmalen, J. G. M., Ormel, J., Van Oort, F. V. A., & Oldehinkel, A. J. (2010). Anxiety and depression are risk factors rather than consequences of functional somatic symptoms in a general population of adolescents: The TRAILS study. *The Journal of Child Psychology and Psychiatry and Allied Disciplines, 51*(3), 304−312. https://doi.org/10.1111/j.1469-7610.2009.02174.x.

Joyce, J., Hotopf, M., & Wessely, S. (1997). The prognosis of chronic fatigue and chronic fatigue syndrome: A systematic review. *QJM: Monthly Journal of the Association of Physicians, 90*, 223−233. https://doi.org/10.1093/qjmed/90.3.223.

Kallesøe, K., Schröder, A., Wicksell, R., & Rask, C. (2016). Acceptance and Commitment Therapy for adolescents with functional syndromes: Study protocol for a randomized controlled trial. *BMJ Open, 6*(9), 485−492.

Kashikar-Zuck, S., Cunningham, N., Sil, S., Bromberg, M. H., Lynch-Jordan, A. M., Strotman, D., et al. (2014). Long-term outcomes of adolescents with juvenile-onset fibromyalgia in early adulthood. *Pediatrics, 133*(3), e592−e600. https://doi.org/10.1542/peds.2013-2220.

King, S., Chambers, C. T., Huguet, A., MacNevin, R. C., McGrath, P. J., Parker, L., et al. (2011). The epidemiology of chronic pain in children and adolescents revisited: A systematic review. *Pain, 152*(12), 2729−2738. https://doi.org/10.1016/j.pain.2011.07.016.

Kingma, E. M., Janssens, K. A., Venema, M., Ormel, J., de Jonge, P., & Rosmalen, J. G. (2011). Adolescents with low intelligence are at risk of functional somatic symptoms: The TRAILS study. *The Journal of Adolescent Health: Official Publication of the Society for Adolescent Medicine, 49*(6), 621−626. https://doi.org/10.1016/j.jadohealth.2011.04.022.

Knight, S. J., Scheinberg, A., & Harvey, A. R. (2013). Interventions in pediatric chronic fatigue syndrome/myalgic encephalomyelitis: A systematic review. *Journal of Adolescent Health*. https://doi.org/10.1016/j.jadohealth.2013.03.009.

Kozlowska, K. (2001). Good children presenting with conversion disorder. *Clinical Child Psychology and Psychiatry*, 6(4), 575–591. https://doi.org/10.1177/1359104501006004011.

Kozlowska, K. (2007). The developmental origins of conversion disorders. *Clinical Child Psychology and Psychiatry*, 12(4), 487–510. https://doi.org/10.1177/1359104507080977.

Kozlowska, K. (2013). Functional somatic symptoms in childhood and adolescence. *Current Opinion in Psychiatry*, 26(5), 485–492. https://doi.org/10.1097/YCO.0b013e3283642ca0.

Law, E., Palermo, T., Logan, D., Tai, G., Lewandowski Holley, A., & Zhou, C. (2014). Pain and function: Understanding temporal changes during behavioral treatment for youth with chronic pain. *The Journal of Pain*, 15(4), S107. https://doi.org/10.1016/j.jpain.2014.01.439.

Lee, T. W. R., Duff, A. J. A., Martin, T., & Barrett, J. M. (2013). Enuresis and more. *Archives of Disease in Childhood. Education and Practice Edition*, 98(5), 162–170. https://doi.org/10.1136/archdischild-2012-303489.

Levy, R. L., Whitehead, W. E., Walker, L. S., Von Korff, M., Feld, A. D., Garner, M., et al. (2004). Increased somatic complaints and health-care utilization in children: Effects of parent IBS status and parent response to gastrointestinal symptoms. *American Journal of Gastroenterology*, 99(12), 2442–2451. https://doi.org/10.1111/j.1572-0241.2004.40478.x.

Lieb, R., Pfister, H., Mastaler, M., & Wittchen, H. U. (2000). Somatoform syndromes and disorders in a representative population sample of adolescents and young adults: Prevalence, comorbidity and impairments. *Acta Psychiatrica Scandinavica*, 101(3), 194–208. https://doi.org/10.1034/j.1600-0447.2000.101003194.x.

Lievesley, K., Rimes, K. A., & Chalder, T. (2014). A review of the predisposing, precipitating and perpetuating factors in Chronic Fatigue Syndrome in children and adolescents. *Clinical Psychology Review*, 34(3), 233–248. https://doi.org/10.1016/j.cpr.2014.02.002.

Lindley, K. J., Glaser, D., & Milla, P. J. (2005). Consumerism in healthcare can be detrimental to child health: Lessons from children with functional abdominal pain. *Archives of Disease in Childhood*, 90(4), 335–337. https://doi.org/10.1136/adc.2003.032524.

Lockhart, E. (2016). Health anxiety in children and parents. *BMJ British Medical Journal*, (353), 2891.

Logan, D. E., Carpino, E. A., Chiang, G., Condon, M., Firn, E., Gaughan, V. J., et al. (2012). A day-hospital approach to treatment of pediatric complex regional pain syndrome: Initial functional outcomes. *The Clinical Journal of Pain*, 28(9), 766–774. https://doi.org/10.1097/AJP.0b013e3182457619.

Martin, A. E., Newlove-Delgado, T. V., Abbott, R. A., Bethel, A., Thompson-Coon, J., Whear, R., et al. (2017). Pharmacological interventions for recurrent abdominal pain in childhood. *Cochrane Database of Systematic Reviews*. https://doi.org/10.1002/14651858.CD010973.pub2.

Mayer, E. A., & Collins, S. M. (2002). Evolving pathophysiologic models of functional gastrointestinal disorders. *Gastroenterology*, 122(7), 2032–2048. https://doi.org/10.1053/gast.2002.33584.

Nijhof, S. L., Bleijenberg, G., Uiterwaal, C. S., Kimpen, J. L., & van de Putte, E. M. (2012). Effectiveness of internet-based cognitive behavioural treatment for adolescents with chronic fatigue syndrome (FITNET): A randomised controlled trial. *Lancet (London, England)*, 379(9824), 1412–1418. https://doi.org/10.1016/S0140-6736(12)60025-7.

Norris, T., Collin, S. M., Tilling, K., Nuevo, R., Stansfeld, S. A., Sterne, J. A., et al. (2017). Natural course of chronic fatigue syndrome/myalgic encephalomyelitis in adolescents. *Archives of Disease in Childhood*. https://doi.org/10.1136/archdischild-2016-311198.

Noyes, R., Stuart, S., Langbehn, D. R., Happel, R. L., Longley, S. L., & Yagla, S. J. (2002). Childhood antecedents of hypochondriasis. *Psychosomatics*, 43(4), 282–289. https://doi.org/10.1176/appi.psy.43.4.282.

Patel, H., Dunn, D. W., Austin, J. K., Doss, J. L., LaFrance, W. C., Plioplys, S., et al. (2011). Psychogenic nonepileptic seizures (pseudoseizures). *Pediatrics in Review/American Academy of Pediatrics, 32*(6), e66—e72. https://doi.org/10.1542/pir.32-6-e66.

Patel, H., Scott, E., Dunn, D., & Garg, B. (2007). Nonepileptic seizures in children. *Epilepsia, 48*(11), 2086—2092. https://doi.org/10.1111/j.1528-1167.2007.01200.x.

Pehlivantürk, B., & Unal, F. (2000). Conversion disorder in children and adolescents: Clinical features and comorbidity with depressive and anxiety disorders. *Turkish Journal of Pediatrics, 42*(2), 132—137. Retrieved from http://www.ncbi.nlm.nih.gov/pubmed/10936979.

Perez, D. L., Dworetzky, B. A., Dickerson, B. C., Leung, L., Cohn, R., Baslet, G., et al. (2015). An integrative neurocircuit perspective on psychogenic nonepileptic seizures and functional movement disorders: Neural functional unawareness. *Clinical EEG and Neuroscience, 46*(1), 4—15. https://doi.org/10.1177/1550059414555905.

Plioplys, S., Doss, J., Siddarth, P., Bursch, B., Falcone, T., Forgey, M., et al. (2014). A multisite controlled study of risk factors in pediatric psychogenic nonepileptic seizures. *Epilepsia, 55*(11), 1739—1747. https://doi.org/10.1111/epi.12773.

Ramchandani, P. G., Stein, A., Hotopf, M., & Wiles, N. J. (2006). Early parental and child predictors of recurrent abdominal pain at school age: Results of a large population-based study. *Journal of the American Academy of Child & Adolescent Psychiatry, 45*(June), 729—736. https://doi.org/10.1097/01.chi.0000215329.35928.e0.

Rangel, L., Garralda, M. E., Jeffs, J., & Rose, G. (2005). Family health and characteristics in chronic fatigue syndrome, juvenile rheumatoid arthritis, and emotional disorders of childhood. *Journal of the American Academy of Child & Adolescent Psychiatry, 44*(2), 150—158. https://dx.doi.org/10.1097/00004583-200502000-00007.

Rangel, L., Garralda, E., & Levin, M. (2000). Personality in adolescents with chronic fatigue syndrome. *Eur Child Adolesc Psychiatry, 9*(1), 39—45.

Rangel, L., Garralda, M. E., Levin, M., & Roberts, H. (2000). The course of severe chronic fatigue syndrome in childhood. *Journal of the Royal Society of Medicine, 93*(3), 129—134. Retrieved from http://jrs.sagepub.com/content/93/3/129.abstract.

Rask, C. U., Elberling, H., Skovgaard, A. M., Thomsen, P. H., & Fink, P. (2012). Parental-reported health anxiety symptoms in 5- to 7-year-old children: The Copenhagen Child Cohort CCC 2000. *Psychosomatics, 53*(1), 58—67. https://doi.org/10.1016/j.psym.2011.05.006.

Rask, C. U., Munkholm, A., Clemmensen, L., Rimvall, M. K., Ørnbøl, E., Jeppesen, P., et al. (2016). Health anxiety in preadolescence - associated health problems, healthcare expenditure, and continuity in childhood. *Journal of Abnormal Child Psychology, 44*(4), 823—832. https://doi.org/10.1007/s10802-015-0071-2.

Rask, C. U., Olsen, E. M., Elberling, H., Christensen, M. F., Ørnbøl, E., Fink, P., et al. (2009). Functional somatic symptoms and associated impairment in 5-7-year-old children: The Copenhagen Child Cohort 2000. *European Journal of Epidemiology, 24*(10), 625—634. https://doi.org/10.1007/s10654-009-9366-3.

Rask, C. U., Ørnbøl, E., Fink, P. K., & Skovgaard, A. M. (2013). Functional somatic symptoms and consultation patterns in 5- to 7-year-olds. *Pediatrics, 132*(2), e459—e467. https://doi.org/10.1542/peds.2013-0159.

Rask, C. U., Ørnbøl, E., Olsen, E. M., Fink, P., & Skovgaard, A. M. (2013). Infant behaviors are predictive of functional somatic symptoms at ages 5-7 years: Results from the Copenhagen Child Cohort CCC2000. *The Journal of Pediatrics, 162*(2), 335—342. https://doi.org/10.1016/j.jpeds.2012.08.001.

Rosendal, M., Olde Hartman, T. C., Aamland, A., van der Horst, H., Lucassen, P., Budtz-Lilly, A., et al. (2017). "Medically unexplained" symptoms and symptom disorders in primary care: Prognosis-based recognition and classification. *BMC Family Practice, 18*(1), 18. https://doi.org/10.1186/s12875-017-0592-6.

Rutten, J. M., Reitsma, J. B., Vlieger, A. M., & Benninga, M. A. (2013). Gut-directed hypno-therapy for functional abdominal pain or irritable bowel syndrome in children: A systematic review. *Archives of Disease in Childhood, 98*(4), 252–257. https://doi.org/10.1136/archdischild-2012-302906.

Rutten, J. M., Vlieger, A. M., Frankenhuis, C., George, E. K., Groeneweg, M., Norbruis, O. F., et al. (2014). Gut-directed hypnotherapy in children with irritable bowel syndrome or functional abdominal pain (syndrome): A randomized controlled trial on self exercises at home using CD versus individual therapy by qualified therapists. *BMC Pediatrics, 14*(140). https://doi.org/10.1186/1471-2431-14-140.

Schroder, A., & Fink, P. (2011). Functional somatic syndromes and somatoform disorders in special psychosomatic units: Organizational aspects and evidence-based treatment. *Psychiatric Clinics of North America.* https://doi.org/10.1016/j.psc.2011.05.008.

Schulte, I. E., & Petermann, F. (2011). Somatoform disorders: 30 years of debate about criteria! What about children and adolescents? *Journal of Psychosomatic Research, 70*(3), 218–228. https://doi.org/10.1016/j.jpsychores.2010.08.005.

Smith, M. T., & Haythornthwaite, J. A. (2004). How do sleep disturbance and chronic pain inter-relate? Insights from the longitudinal and cognitive-behavioral clinical trials literature. *Sleep Medicine Reviews, 8*(2), 119–132. https://doi.org/10.1016/S1087-0792(03)00044-3.

Spence, S. H. (1998). A measure of anxiety symptoms among children. *Behaviour Research and Therapy, 36*(5), 545–566. https://doi.org/10.1016/S0005-7967(98)00034-5.

Stone, J., & Carson, A. (2015). Functional neurologic disorders. *Continuum, 21*(3 Behavioral Neurology and Neuropsychiatry), 818–837. https://doi.org/10.1212/01.CON.0000466669.02477.45.

Thorgaard, M., Frostholm, L., & Rask, C. (2018). Childhood and family factors in the development of health anxiety: A systematic review. *Children's Health Care, 47*(2), 198–238.

Thorgaard, M. V., Frostholm, L., Walker, L. S., Jensen, J. S., Morina, B., Lindegaard, H., et al. (2017). Health anxiety by proxy in women with severe health anxiety: A case control study. *Journal of Anxiety Disorders, 52*, 8–14. https://doi.org/10.1016/j.janxdis.2017.09.001.

Thorgaard, M. V., Frostholm, L., Walker, L. S., Stengaard-Pedersen, K., Karlsson, M. M., Jensen, J. S., et al. (2017). Effects of maternal health anxiety on children's health complaints, emotional symptoms, and quality of life. *European Child & Adolescent Psychiatry, 26*(5), 591–601. https://doi.org/10.1007/s00787-016-0927-1. Epub 2016 Dec 1.

Tot-Strate, S., Dehlholm-Lambertsen, G., Lassen, K., & Rask, C. U. (2016). Clinical features of functional somatic symptoms in children and referral patterns to child and adolescent mental health services. *Acta Paediatrica, 105*(5), 514–521. https://doi.org/10.1111/apa.13310.

van Geelen, S. M., Rydelius, P. A., & Hagquist, C. (2015). Somatic symptoms and psychological concerns in a general adolescent population: Exploring the relevance of DSM-5 somatic symptom disorder. *Journal of Psychosomatic Research, 79*(4), 251–258. https://doi.org/10.1016/j.jpsychores.2015.07.012.

Vanderbilt-Adriance, E., & Shaw, D. S. (2008). Protective factors and the development of resilience in the context of neighborhood disadvantage. *Journal of Abnormal Child Psychology, 36*(6), 887–901. https://doi.org/10.1007/s10802-008-9220-1.

Vila, M., Kramer, T., Obiols, J. E., & Garralda, M. E. (2012). Abdominal pain in British young people: Associations, impairment and health care use. *Journal of Psychosomatic Research, 73*(6), 437–442. https://doi.org/10.1016/j.jpsychores.2012.09.009.

Walker, L. S., Garber, J., & Greene, J. W. (1991). Somatization symptoms in pediatric abdominal pain patients: Relation to chronicity of abdominal pain and parent somatization. *Journal of Abnormal Child Psychology, 19*(4), 379–394. https://doi.org/10.1007/BF00919084.

Walker, L. S., Garber, J., Smith, C. A., Van Slyke, D. A., & Claar, R. L. (2001). The relation of daily stressors to somatic and emotional symptoms in children with and without recurrent abdominal pain. *Journal of Consulting and Clinical Psychology, 69*(1), 85—91. https://doi.org/10.1037/0022-006X.69.1.85.

Walker, L. S., & Greene, J. W. (1991). The functional disability inventory: Measuring a neglected dimension of child health status. *Journal of Pediatric Psychology, 16*(1), 39—58. https://doi.org/10.1093/jpepsy/16.1.39.

Walker, L. S., Sherman, A. L., Bruehl, S., Garber, J., & Smith, C. A. (2012). Functional abdominal pain patient subtypes in childhood predict functional gastrointestinal disorders with chronic pain and psychiatric comorbidities in adolescence and adulthood. *Pain, 153*(9), 1798—1806. https://doi.org/10.1016/j.pain.2012.03.026.

Walker, L. S., Smith, C. A., Garber, J., & Claar, R. L. (2007). Appraisal and coping with daily stressors by pediatric patients with chronic abdominal pain. *Journal of Pediatric Psychology, 32*(2), 206—216. https://doi.org/10.1093/jpepsy/jsj124.

Walker, L. S., Williams, S. E., Smith, C. A., Garber, J., Slyke, D. A., & Lipani, T. A. (2006). Parent attention versus distraction: Impact on symptom complaints by children with and without chronic functional abdominal pain. *Pain, 122*(1—2), 43—52. https://doi.org/10.1016/j.pain.2005.12.020.

Wessely, S., Nimnuan, C., & Sharpe, M. (1999). Functional somatic syndromes: One or many? *Lancet (London, England), 354*(9182), 936—939. S0140-6736(98)08320-2 [pii].

Westendorp, T., Verbunt, J. A., Remerie, S. C., de Blécourt, A. C., van Baalen, B., & Smeets, R. J. E. M. (2016). Social functioning in adulthood: Understanding long-term outcomes of adolescents with chronic pain/fatigue treated at inpatient rehabilitation programs. *European Journal of Pain, 20*(7), 1121—1130. https://doi.org/10.1002/ejp.836.

White, D., Leach, C., Sims, R., Atkinson, M., & Cottrell, D. (1999). Validation of the hospital anxiety and depression scale for use with adolescents. *The British Journal of Psychiatry, 175*(5), 452—454. https://doi.org/10.1192/bjp.175.5.452.

Wicksell, R. K., Melin, L., Lekander, M., & Olsson, G. L. (2009). Evaluating the effectiveness of exposure and acceptance strategies to improve functioning and quality of life in long-standing pediatric pain—a randomized controlled trial. *Pain, 141*(3), 248—257. https://doi.org/10.1016/j.pain.2008.11.006.

Williams, S. E., Smith, C. A., Bruehl, S. P., Gigante, J., & Walker, L. S. (2009). Medical evaluation of children with chronic abdominal pain: Impact of diagnosis, physician practice orientation, and maternal trait anxiety on mothers responses to the evaluation. *Pain, 146*(3), 283—292. https://doi.org/10.1016/j.pain.2009.07.039.

Wright, K. D., & Asmundson, G. J. G. (2003). Health anxiety in Children: Development and psychometric properties of the childhood illness attitude scales. *Cognitive Behaviour Therapy, 32*(4), 194—202. https://doi.org/10.1080/16506070310014691.

Wyller, V. B., Barbieri, R., Thaulow, E., & Saul, J. P. (2008). Enhanced vagal withdrawal during mild orthostatic stress in adolescents with chronic fatigue. *Annals of Noninvasive Electrocardiology, 13*(1), 67—73. https://doi.org/10.1111/j.1542-474X.2007.00202.x.

Wyller, V. B., Saul, J. P., Amlie, J. P., & Thaulow, E. (2007). Sympathetic predominance of cardiovascular regulation during mild orthostatic stress in adolescents with chronic fatigue. *Clinical Physiology and Functional Imaging, 27*(4), 231—238. https://doi.org/10.1111/j.1475-097X.2007.00743.x.

Anxiety and Anxiety Disorders in Young People: A Cross-Cultural Perspective

Selda Koydemir[1,2], *Cecilia A. Essau*[1]

[1] University of Roehampton, London, United Kingdom; [2] University of Bamberg, Bamberg, Germany

INTRODUCTION: ANXIETY AND ANXIETY DISORDERS

All children and adolescents experience anxieties and fears as a normal part of growing up (Essau, Sasagawa, Anastassiou-Hadjicharalambous, Guzmán, & Ollendick, 2011). However, the types of these anxieties and fears change with age, which is related to changes in cognitive and social competencies. Anxiety is classed as a disorder when (Essau, 2007): (1) the duration and intensity do not correspond to the real danger of the situation; (2) it occurs in a "harmless" situation; (3) it is chronic; (4) it causes impairment in various life domains. Finally, in older children, they have no possibility of explaining, reducing, and coping with the situation.

Our current classification systems (the *Diagnostic and Statistical Manual of Mental Disorders*, Fifth Edition [DSM-5] [APA, 2013] and the International Classification of Diseases, 10th Revision [WHO, 1992]) differentiate between "normal" and "pathological" anxiety based on the number, severity, persistence, and impairment of symptoms. In addition, the symptoms cannot be better accounted for by another mental disorder or a general medical condition, or result from substance use (APA, 2000). DSM-5 (APA, 2013) differentiates among various types of anxiety disorders:

- *Separation anxiety disorder* is defined as an excessive fear of separation from a caregiver that is developmentally inappropriate.

Understanding Uniqueness and Diversity in Child and Adolescent Mental Health
https://doi.org/10.1016/B978-0-12-815310-9.00005-8

- *Specific phobia* is characterized by persistent fear and anxiety about or avoidance of circumscribed objects or situations. Confrontation with the feared objects or situations provokes an immediate anxiety response that is out of proportion to the actual risk posed. Common types of specific phobias include animals, the natural environment, blood injection injury, and situational phobias.
- *Social anxiety disorder* is characterized by fear or anxiety about or avoidance of social interactions and situations involving the possibility of being scrutinized.
- *Generalized anxiety disorder* is characterized by a persistent and excessive anxiety and worry about several areas of life functioning. Anxiety and worry are frequently accompanied by somatic problems such as irritability, fatigue, muscle tension, and sleep disturbance.
- *Panic disorder* is characterized by the presence of repeated unexpected panic attack and a persistent concern about having more panic attacks, or it may be related to changes in maladaptive ways as a consequence of the panic attacks (eg, avoidance of unfamiliar locations). A panic attack is a period of intense fear or discomfort that usually develops abruptly and reaches a peak within minutes, and which is accompanied by physical and/or cognitive symptoms.
- *Agoraphobia* is characterized by fear and anxiety about two or more of the following situations: using public transportation, being in open spaces, being in enclosed places, standing in line or being in a crowd, or being outside the home alone in other situations.
- *Selective mutism* is a consistent failure to speak in social situations in which there is an expectation to speak, although the individual speaks in other situations.

Other types of anxiety disorders do not occur commonly in children and adolescents: (1) Substance/medication-induced anxiety disorder involves anxiety as a result of substance intoxication or withdrawal or of treatment with medication; (2) anxiety disorder may result from another medical condition such as endocrine disease (e.g., hyperthyroidism, hypoglycemia), cardiovascular disorders (e.g., congestive heart failure, arrhythmia), respiratory illness (e.g., asthma), metabolic disturbances (eg, porphyria), and neurological illnesses (e.g., seizure disorder).

Anxiety disorders are among the most common psychiatric disorders affecting children and adolescents in the general population (Cohen, Tyrrell, Russell, Jarvis, & Smith, 1993; Essau, Conradt, & Petermann, 2000; Lewinsohn, Hops, Roberts, Seeley, & Andrews, 1993; Wittchen, Nelson, & Lachner, 1998). It is estimated that up to 10% of children and up to 20% of adolescents meet the criteria for an anxiety disorder.

CROSS-CULTURAL RESEARCH IN ANXIETY

For many years, studies on anxiety disorders in children and adolescents were conducted with Western samples. However, culture has a considerable influence on the way in which individuals think, feel, and behave (Cross, Hardin, & Gercek-Swing, 2011; Heine, 2008; Markus & Kitayama, 1991), in organizing people's everyday lives and how they interact with others (Kitayama & Markus, 1995), how emotions are felt and expressed in a particular cultural context, and how people should feel in a given situation (Turner & Stets, 2005).

Definition of Culture

Over the past three decades, the importance of culture on various psychological processes has been discussed and empirically examined, and a number of frameworks have been proposed to explain the effect of culture (Kagitcibasi, 2005; Kashima et al., 1995; Markus & Kitayama, 1991; Triandis, 1989). Although culture has been used to refer to many different things (Kroeber & Kluckhohn, 1952), many scholars and researchers agree on certain common characteristics of culture. A comprehensive definition was suggested by Triandis (1993), who defined culture as "shared attitudes, beliefs, categorizations, expectations, norms, roles, self-definitions, values, and other such elements of subjective culture found among individuals whose interactions were facilitated by shared language, historical period, and geographic region" (p. 156). Matsumoto (2007), in his definition, emphasized that culture is a "meaning and information system," and that it is "transmitted across generations" (p. 1293).

Culture is an effective tool in guiding our behavior, attention, and emotion, and in determining the ways in which we form and maintain relationships with others (D'Andrade & Strauss, 1992; Markus & Kitayama, 1991). Culture has an important role in the formation and expression of the self and identity (Morf & Mischel, 2012; Suh, 2000) and in understanding and making sense of the world (Matsumoto, 2007). Besides, it affects the experience and expression of mental illness (López & Guarnaccia, 2008; Marsella & Yamada, 2007), given that people in different cultural contexts tend to express symptoms in culturally acceptable ways (Kleinman, 1988).

Dimensions of Culture: Individualism and Collectivism

One of the most commonly applied frameworks for explaining and predicting cultural differences is individualism and collectivism (Hofstede, 2001; Triandis, 2001). Individualism and collectivism pertain to the ways in which people perceive themselves, their relationships with others, the goals they pursue, and their behavioral motives (Triandis, 2001). This construct has contributed significantly to the understanding of individual behaviors.

In general, individualistic cultures are known to emphasize the differentiation of self from others and the social context, and thus consider the individual to be independent and autonomous (Ho & Chiu, 1994; Triandis, 2001). Freedom of choice, personal goals, and self-reliance are some important aspects that are emphasized in individualistic cultures. In contrast, collectivistic cultures tend to value group goals, harmony in groups, maintaining the relationships and order, and duties and obligations (Hofstede, 2001; Oyserman & Lee, 2007). Collectivist cultures prioritise the group over the individual and perceive personal achievement to be a means to benefit the group (Triandis, 1994). Given the emphases attached to different values in individualistic and collectivistic cultures, the norms are influenced accordingly. For instance, in individualistic cultures, social standards of behavior require individuals to be assertive and not to show signs of weakness. On the other hand, collectivistic cultures are more attuned to the social appropriateness of behaviors and are expected to obey the authority (Argyle, 1986; Triandis, 1989).

It is well-known that compared with Westerners, East Asian people are more collectivist in the sense that their needs and feelings are more closely related to others', and perceive the self as an extension of significant others (Bochner, 1994; Hofstede, 1980; Triandis, 1994). However, a number of issues have been raised in relation to this conceptualization. For example, individualism and collectivism are not opposites, nor do the relevant values conflict with each other (Watson & Morris, 2002; Yamaguchi et al., 1992). Besides, comparing mean differences between individuals in Western and Eastern cultures means that any observed differences result from differences in individualism and collectivism, which does not provide sufficient information to understand the cultural differences (Matsumoto, 1999; Oyserman, Coon, & Kemmelmeier, 2002). Furthermore, treating cultures as nations and categorizing people into one national culture is too simplistic because most nations include diverse cultures (Fiske, 2002). In fact, it has been argued that the scores of Western and Eastern samples on the individualism and collectivism scales differed only slightly, and that generalizability of the findings across populations or regions is questionable (Fiske, 2002; Oyserman et al., 2002). Considering these issues, a number of propositions have been made. For instance, measuring individual-level data and not inferring individualism and collectivism based on nationality is essential to demonstrate that the variable is actually affecting the cultural differences (Bond, 2002; Singelis & Brown, 1995; Triandis et al., 1986). Nevertheless, individualism and collectivism are accepted as reliable dimensions of cultural differences and provide a useful framework for understanding such differences (Oyserman et al., 2002).

Self-Construals

More contemporary models of cultural views of selfexamined cultural differences at the individual level (Kashima et al., 1995; Markus & Kitayama, 1991; Singelis, 1994). The model of self-construals proposed by Markus and Kitayama (1991) has become a fundamental concept in cross-cultural research and has been widely used to examine cultural differences. Self-construals are cultural views of self (a cultural schema) to explain the ways in which individuals perceive themselves in relation to others and the social context (Markus & Kitayama, 1991). According to the model of self-construals, people differ in the extent to which they perceive themselves from others versus related with others. In this respect, Markus and Kitayama (1991) identified two types of self-construals: independent and interdependent.

The fundamental characteristic of independent self-construal is conceiving the self as an independent entity and as distinct from context (Kashima et al., 1995; Matsumoto, 1999). People with high independent self-construal emphasize internal traits, preferences, attributes, and individual goals. Cross and Madson (1997) described independent self-construal as the self separate from others. As such, people with well-developed independent self-construal think about themselves based on their abilities and goals (Singelis, 1994). On the other hand, someone with interdependent self-construal perceives the self in relation to others and the social context (Kitayama & Markus, 1995). Individuals with high interdependent self-construal attach great importance to relationships with others and maintaining harmony in groups. Accordingly, when thinking about themselves, individuals who have high levels of interdependent self-construal focus on others and important relationships (Markus & Kitayama, 1991). These cultural views of the self have been extensively studied in relation to many psychological processes since the model was introduced (Cross & Madson, 1997; Kim, Sharkey, & Singelis, 1994; Lee, Aaker, & Gardner, 2000; Lun, Kesebir, & Oishi, 2008; Matsumoto, 1999; Singelis, 1994).

In the development of cultural views of the self, individual differences may predispose a person to possess certain preferences in social interactions and perceptions (Rubin et al., 2006). However, cultural environment and the social context also affect the construction of the self and how the self in turn affects psychological processes (Kagitcibasi, 1990; Okazaki, Liu, Longworth, & Minn, 2002). People tend to construe the self differently depending on their relationships and interactions with others and the social environment, and the cultural scripts that are transmitted through child-rearing patterns and socialization (Cross & Madson, 1997; Neff & Harter, 2003; Stryker & Burke, 2000).

In general, Western cultural contexts are more likely to foster independent self-construal, whereas Eastern cultural contexts tend to encourage interdependent self-construal (Chao, 1995; Kim & Sherman, 2007). It is known that in Western cultural contexts, identifying one's internal attributes and expressing them to oneself and others is an important element of self. On the other hand, in East Asian cultural contexts, a fundamental aspect of self-concept involves identifying the needs of significant others and adjusting one's behavior accordingly. In line with these, in Western societies, children are raised to be independent and self-reliant, whereas in Eastern societies, children are socialized in a way that supports interconnectedness and attendance to the needs of others and the social groups (Chao & Tseng, 2002; Kao & Sinha, 2000; Oyserman & Markus, 1998). Therefore, within different cultures, the two types of self-construal are valued differently, resulting in the differential development of independent and interdependent self-construals (Singelis, 1994).

However, as in the case of individualism and collectivism, independence and interdependence do not form a singular bipolar dimension, nor they are mutually exclusive. Rather, they should be perceived as existing on a continuum. An individual can develop both sense of selves simultaneously, and equally or to similar degrees (Singelis, 1994; Yamada & Singelis, 1999). Although variability exists across individuals of a given culture in terms of the way people define the self in different cultural contexts, there are also similarities across cultures (Fiske, Kitayama, Markus, & Nisbett, 1998). For example, East Asian people do not differ from Americans in terms of independent self-construal although East Asian people score higher on interdependent self-construal (Cross, 1995). Thus, the autonomous self is not restricted to Western cultures (Chirkov, Ryan, Kim, & Kaplan, 2003; Cross et al., 2011). In a similar way, Western cultural contexts are not free from interdependence. In North America, autonomy is valued along with relatedness to significant others (Chen, Boucher, & Tapias, 2006; Cross, Bacon, & Morris, 2000). Besides, there is research evidence that contextual cues can make a particular self-construal temporarily accessible (Kühnen, 2009; Oyserman & Lee, 2007). An individual possessing chronically independent self-construal can be primed to take an interdependent view of the self (Oyserman & Lee, 2007; Trafimow, Triandis, & Goto, 1991). Oyserman et al. (Oyserman, 2011; Oyserman & Lee, 2007) introduced the concept of situated cognition to explain the idea that culture is not uniformly endorsed by all members of a given cultural group. Thus, the self is not stable; rather, it is malleable and should be understood with reference to contextual cues of everyday life (Oyserman, Elmore, & Smith, 2012). In fact, there is evidence that individuals with a strong independent as well as interdependent self-construal adjust better to a new environment (Shim, Freund, Stopsack, Kammerer, & Barnow, 2014).

CULTURAL SYNDROMES

The term "culture-bound syndrome" has been used to describe behavioral, affective, and cognitive manifestations which are unique to specific cultures. However, this term was replaced in DSM-5 by three newer terms: cultural syndromes (i.e., clusters of symptoms that are commonly found among individuals in specific cultures), cultural idioms of distress (i.e., the ways in which distress are expressed by individuals in a particular culture), and cultural explanations of distress or perceived causes (APA, 2013).

The next sections present some examples of common anxiety-related cultural syndromes among young people.

Taijin Kyofusho

Taijin kyofusho (TKS) is characterized by an intense fear that one's body parts or functions displease, embarrass, or are offensive to others (APA, 2000). Individuals with TKS are hypersensitive to certain body parts in that they fear that they will offend or embarrass others with their "inappropriate" behavior, which may offend others and therefore bring shame upon their social or familial group (Maeda & Nathan, 1999).

Common symptoms of TKS include (1) fear of offending others by blushing, emitting offensive odors, or staring inappropriately; (2) fear of offending others by presenting an improper facial expression; (3) being convinced of offending others; and (4) being obsessed with feelings of shame (Kirmayer, 1991; Maeda & Nathan, 1999). These fears often lead to social avoidance because individuals with this condition are concerned that their behavior will bring shame upon their ingroup or they fear disrupting group cohesiveness by making others feel uncomfortable. TKS is experienced when individuals have face-to-face contact with other people; it tends to become most exacerbated in social situations with acquaintances (Kirmayer, 1991; Maeda & Nathan, 1999).

Hikikomori

Hikikomori is a severe syndrome of social withdrawal first identified in Japan. Individuals with this condition avoid social situations (e.g., having social interactions outside the home) and engagement (e.g., education, friendships) with persistent withdrawal into one's residence for at least six months (Saito, 2010). According to the Japanese Ministry of Health, Labor, and Welfare (2003), criteria for *hikikomori* are: (1) a lifestyle centered on the home; (2) no interest in or willingness to attend school or work; (3) symptom duration of at least six months; (4) the exclusion of schizophrenia, mental retardation, and other mental disorders; (5) among those with no interest in or willingness to attend school or work, those who maintain personal relationships (eg, friendships) have been excluded.

Ataque de Nervios

Ataque de nervios (ADN), literally translated as an attack of the nerves, is characterized primarily by a range of symptoms such as trembling, convulsions, uncontrollable screaming, shouting or crying, feelings of impending loss of control, shortness of breath, chest tightness, palpitations, feelings of heat in the chest that rise to the head, shaking arms and legs, and physical and/or verbal aggression. ADN is classified in DSM-5 (American Psychiatric Association, 2013) as a culture-bound syndrome or a recurrent, locally specific pattern of aberrant behavior that may or may not relate to any standard DSM diagnostic category. It has also been described as an idiom of distress that is common among individuals of Hispanic-Latino heritage from the Caribbean region and throughout the Americas.

CULTURAL FACTORS IN THE DEVELOPMENT OF ANXIETY

Culture has a substantial effect on the development and treatment of anxiety and in shaping the manner in which children and adolescents express psychopathological symptoms. Many studies documented that the prevalence of anxiety (Essau, Ishikawa, & Sasagawa, 2011; Ishikawa, Sato, & Sasagawa, 2009; Kessler, Petukhova, Sampson, Zaslavsky, & Wittchen, 2012), its expression and contexts in which it is elicited (Kleinknecht, Dinnel, Kleinknecht, Hiruma, & Harada, 1997; Hinton, 2012), its onset, course, and outcome (Hinton, 2012), and how individuals respond to its treatment (Yeh, Hough, McCabe, Lau, & Garland, 2004) are affected by various cultural factors. Among these factors are beliefs concerning the disorder, norms with which individuals are confronted in a given culture, the way individuals pursue their selves, and traditions associated with socialization practices (Hinton, 2012; Hofmann, Asnaani, & Hinton, 2010; Lewis-Fernandez et al., 2010).

Psychopathological symptoms occur commonly in both Western and non-Western cultures (Essau et al., 2000). However, their correlates may vary across cultures as well as between different generations of a given culture. Cross-cultural studies on the prevalence and correlates of anxiety problems are important in the sense that they can enable researchers and practitioners to understand the universality of the concept, and the extent to which culture and socialization practices influence anxiety in children and adolescents.

In an early cross-cultural study, it was found that among Thai and American children who were referred to mental health clinics, Thai children reported more internalizing problems such as anxiety and depression than did American children, whereas American children reported more externalizing problems such as aggression (Weisz et al., 1987). In a similar vein, Embu children were reported by parents to have heightened problems such as fears and feeling guilty more so than Caucasian American children (Weisz, Sigman, Weiss, & Mosk, 1993).

Studies investigating fears among children and adolescents in different cultures reported some cultural differences as well. For instance, Dong, Yang, and Ollendick (1994) examined fears in children and adolescents among Chinese children and adolescents, and found that among 11- to 13-year-olds, Chinese children reported higher levels of social-evaluative fears than did Australian and US children, as shown in other studies (Ollendick, King, & Frary, 1989), whereas self-reported levels of anxiety in Chinese children were lower. Besides, Ollendick, King, and Frary (1989) reported that Nigerian children endorsed higher levels of fears than did Australian and American children. It has been argued that differences in the content of fears across cultures are influenced by cultural differences in child-rearing practices of parents and exposure to specific fear-provoking stimuli (such as the use of threat of religious punishment) (Dong et al., 1994; Ollendick, Yule, & Ollier, 1991). A similar argument was put forth by Muris, Schmidt, Engelbrecht, and Perold (2002), who found that South African children had higher levels of anxiety symptoms than did Dutch children. Essau, Sakano, Ishikawa, and Sasagawa (2004), on the other hand, found no significant differences between Japanese and German children in terms of anxiety symptoms.

Cross-cultural differences in correlates of anxiety symptoms are also important in understanding the effect of culture on these symptoms. Muris et al. (2006) studied the link between perceived parental rearing behavior and anxiety disorder symptoms among children and adolescents in South Africa. It was found that colored and black South African children and adolescents reported higher levels of anxiety than did their white counterparts. Essau, Leung, Conradt, Cheng, and Wong (2008) studied general anxiety symptoms among adolescents in Germany and Hong Kong. Their findings indicated that in Germany, anxiety symptoms of adolescents were associated with reinforcement received for anxiety-related symptoms and with parental transmission about the danger of learning, i.e., growing-up experiences in the family. In contrast, the anxiety symptoms of adolescents in Hong Kong were correlated with goals concerned with being extrinsically rewarded for performance and learning. However, in comparing adolescents and their parents in Japan and England, Essau, Ishikawa, Sasagawa, Sato et al. (2011) found that the two samples did not differ in terms of the relationship between self-construal and psychopathology symptoms of adolescents. On the other hand, it was found that English participants with low independent and high interdependent self-construal reported more psychopathology when perceived social support was low. Thus, social support showed a buffering effect.

The most commonly studied anxiety problems in cross-cultural research are social anxiety and social phobia. There is considerable evidence that young people score higher on social anxiety than do their counterparts in relatively individualistic cultures (Essau, Leung, et al., 2011, Essau et al., 2012; Heinrichs et al., 2006; Kleinknecht et al., 1997; Okazaki, 1997). This has been attributed to child-rearing practices in collectivist cultures, because families in these cultures are more inclined to foster interdependence and obedience to authority. Socialization processes in collectivist cultures include encouragement of self-control, being concerned with others' evaluations, and restrictiveness (Dong et al., 1994), which may increase the prevalence of anxiety problems among children and young people.

A study by Kleinknecht et al. (1997) examined TKS symptoms and showed that self-construals were differentially related to forms of social anxiety between Japanese citizens and US citizens. Independent self-construal was negatively related to social anxiety for both cultures; however, it predicted TKS for Japanese participants, whereas in the US sample, independent self-construal did not contribute significant independent variance when predicting social anxiety. Interdependent self-construal did not significantly correlate with social anxiety in the Japanese sample. Similarly, another study comparing the frequency and correlates of TKS in Japanese adolescents and their parents or guardians found that independent self-construal was correlated with lower TKS among adolescents (Essau et al., 2012). Similar findings were reported by Essau, Leung, et al. (2011), who used samples from Hong Kong and the United Kingdom. They demonstrated that independent self-construal was negatively correlated with social anxiety symptoms in both cultures. Interdependent self-construal, on the other hand, was not associated with social anxiety in either Hong Kong or the United Kingdom. They also found that in the Hong Kong sample only, the more accepting the perceived culture was toward attention-avoidant social behavior, the higher the social anxiety was. Finally, Moscovitch, Hofman, and Litz (2005) reported that among males, a higher level of interdependent self-construal was associated with higher social anxiety, whereas independent self-construal was associated with lower social anxiety. The opposite pattern was observed among females.

Despite the cross-cultural differences reported in these studies, it should be noted that self-report questions for anxiety symptoms may contain measurement bias for ethnic minority and for those in non-Western cultures (Ho & Lau, 2011). Lewis-Fernandez et al. (2010) argued that cultural differences may arise because of a lack of measurement equivalence, applicability of diagnostic criteria, and differences in prevalence. Cross-cultural studies should consider several factors in comparing different cultures, including measurement equivalence and linguistic equivalence of instruments (for a review, see Koydemir & Essau, 2016). Additionally, in some cultures, because of social stigma, children tend to internalize anxiety, which may lead to overreported somatic symptoms. For example, even in anxiety-provoking contexts, Latino children are encouraged to be pleasant so that they do not disturb their parents (Varela & Hensley-Maloney, 2009). Thus, the findings of cross-cultural studies related to the level of anxiety symptoms should be interpreted with such considerations in mind, and researchers need to ensure that what is being measured is not different in different cultures.

Not only the prevalence and correlates, but also assessment and treatment of anxiety disorders are influenced by culture (Agarastos, Haasen, & Huber, 2012). It is known that depending on cultural values, beliefs as to the etiology and origin of children's anxiety may be different in each family. For example, in Japanese culture, social problems are regarded as the explanation of most anxiety problems (Narikiyo & Kameoka, 1992). Furthermore, in African American, Asian Pacific Islander, and Latino families, parents are less likely than non-Hispanic white parents to attribute their children's mental health problems to a combination of biological, psychological, and sociological factors (Yeh et al., 2004). These findings are important in the sense that if parents' beliefs about children's mental health problems do not match bio-psychosocial causes consistently, they may be less willing to comply with the dominant treatments. Thus, in assessing adolescents referred with an anxiety disorder, it is recommended that professionals obtain information about child-rearing practices of parents, which may have a considerable effect on the development and maintenance of anxiety symptoms (Essau, Ederer, O'Callaghan, & Aschemann, 2008).

CULTURAL FACTORS IN THE TREATMENT OF ANXIETY

Culture-specific values and norms have a large influence on the course of psychotherapeutic treatment (Draguns & Tanaka-Matsumi, 2003). For instance, social and cultural norms in many non-Western cultures such as China emphasize refraining from explicitly discussing personal emotions (Kirmayer, 2001; Kitanaka, 2008). As such, assessment and treatments for mental health should be in line with the cultural values and contexts of the clients (Castro & Alarcon, 2002; Griner & Smith, 2006).

Culture also affects the tendency to seek help and treatment-seeking delay (Hsu & Alden, 2008; Lin & Cheung, 1999). Ethnic minority groups, for example, may be more willing to delay treatment for mental health problems. Hsu and Alden (2008) showed that first-generation Chinese participants in the United States were less inclined to seek treatment for social anxiety compared with European-heritage students. This reluctance to seek help was associated with acculturation. In fact, high acculturation is associated with more positive help-seeking attitudes and behaviors in other studies as well (Tata & Leong, 1994; Ying & Miller, 1992). Zhang, Ginzburg, McNaughton, and Sejnowski (1998) argued that Asian cultural values are incompatible with positive help-seeking attitudes for mental health problems. In collectivist cultures, individuals are more concerned with bringing shame on the family, and thus they are less willing to seek professional help. It has been argued that psychological interventions reflect a bias toward individualism, which may be a factor accounting for the underuse of mental health services by certain cultural groups (Griner & Smith, 2006).

In terms of the treatment of anxiety disorders among children and adolescents, cognitive behavioral therapy (CBT) is the treatment of choice; 50–70% of young people with an anxiety disorder responded positively to CBT (Barrett, Dadds, & Rapee, 1996; Barrett & Tuner, 2001; Essau et al., 2012; Kendall et al., 1997; Seligman & Ollendick, 2011; Stallard, Simpson, Anderson, Hibbert, & Osborn, 2007). The basic principle of CBT is that thought influences feelings and behavior. Thus, the aim of CBT is to help young people identify, evaluate, and change maladaptive cognitive and behavioral patterns. CBT is a solution-focused, directive approach and is goal-oriented. However, randomized controlled trials of CBT among young people with anxiety disorders in collectivistic cultures are lacking, and to our knowledge no studies have compared "regular" CBT versus "culturally sensitive CBT." Some reasons for this lack of research include: (1) the lack of guidelines to inform treatment development in non-Western countries; and (2) differences in values and worldviews between Asian and Western cultures that present challenges in adapting and implementing CBT in Asian/collectivistic cultures, such as in the way emotions are expressed and interpreted. On the other hand, there are some components of CBT that make it appropriate for implementation in collectivistic cultures. For example, because therapists are regarded as professional and knowledgeable, and as being directive in their approach, CBT could facilitate the development of trust and a therapeutic relationship (Chen & Davenport, 2005). Furthermore, because collectivistic culture places a high value on tangible and practical matters, it is likely that young people would comply with the tasks they need to carry out as part of CBT.

CONCLUSION

Studies reviewed in this chapter show the importance of cultural values in manifesting, developing, assessing, and treating anxiety disorders among young people. Based on our review, several recommendations are offered for future research. First, all of the self-report questionnaires that were used to examine anxiety symptoms and their correlates in different cultures were developed in Western countries. Future studies need to examine the equivalence of the constructs (anxiety, worry, and fear) in different cultural groups. As argued by Varela and Hensley-Maloney (2009), for cross-cultural comparisons and generalizations of processes involved in the development of anxiety to be meaningful, it is important for the constructs to be equivalent across cultures. Secondly, to provide evidence-based information for prevention and treatment, more studies are needed to examine factors which increase young people's risk for developing anxiety disorders. This would include the use of culturally sensitive approaches to examine individual (e.g., temperament, cognitive functioning), interpersonal (e.g., family), and ecological factors (e.g., school system). Research in anxiety disorders in young people is an exciting area of research; however, much more needs to be done in helping us understand anxiety from a cross-cultural perspective.

References

Agarastos, A., Haasen, C., & Huber, C. G. (2012). Anxiety disorders through a transcultural perspective: Implications for migrants. *Psychopathology, 45*(2), 67–77.

American Psychiatric Association. (2000). *Diagnostic and statistical manual of mental disorders* (4th ed.). Washington, DC: American Psychiatric Association.

American Psychiatric Association. (2013). *Diagnostic and statistical manual of mental disorders* (5th ed.). Arlington, VA: American Psychiatric Association.

Argyle, M. (1986). Rules for social relationships in four cultures. *Australian Journal of Psychology, 38*, 309–318.

Barrett, P. M., Dadds, M. R., & Rapee, R. M. (1996). Family treatment of childhood anxiety: A controlled trial. *Journal of Consulting and Clinical Psychology, 64*, 333–342.

Barrett, P. M., & Turner, C. (2001). Prevention of anxiety symptoms in primary school children: Preliminary results from a universal school-based trial. *British Journal of Clinical Psychology, 40*, 399–410.

Bochner, S. (1994). Cross-cultural differences in self concept: A test of Hofstede's individualism/collectivism distinction. *Journal of Cross-Cultural Psychology, 25*, 273–283.

Bond, M. H. (2002). Reclaiming the individual from Hofstede's ecological analysis — a 20-year odyssey: Comment on Oyserman et al. (2002). *Psychological Bulletin, 128*, 73—77.

Castro, F. G., & Alarcon, E. H. (2002). Integrating cultural variables into drug abuse prevention and treatment with racial/ethnic minorities. *The Journal of Drug Culturally Adapted Mental Health Interventions, 32*, 783—810.

Chao, R. K. (1995). Chinese and European American cultural models of the self reflected in mothers' childrearing beliefs. *Ethos, 23*, 328—354.

Chao, R., & Tseng, V. (2002). Parenting of Asians. In M. H. Bornstein (Ed.), *Handbook of parenting: Vol. 4. Social conditions and applied parenting* (pp. 59—93). Mahwah, NJ: Erlbaum.

Chen, S., Boucher, H. C., & Tapias, M. P. (2006). The relational self revealed: Integrative conceptualization and implications for interpersonal life. *Psychological Bulletin, 132*, 151—179.

Chen, S. W.-H., & Davenport, D. S. (2005). Cognitive-behavioral therapy with Chinese American clients: Cautions and modifications. *Psychotherapy: Theory, Research, Practice, Training, 42*(1), 101—110.

Chirkov, V. I., Ryan, R. M., Kim, Y., & Kaplan, U. (2003). Differentiating autonomy from individualism and independence: A self-determination theory perspective on internalization of cultural orientations and well-being. *Journal of Personality and Social Psychology, 84*, 97—110.

Cohen, S., Tyrrell, D. A. J., Russell, M. A. H., Jarvis, M. J., & Smith, A. P. (1993). Smoking, alcohol consumption and susceptibility to the common cold. *American Journal of Public Health, 83*, 1277—1283.

Cross, S. E. (1995). Self-construals, coping, and stress in cross-cultural adaptation. *Journal of Cross-Cultural Psychology, 26*, 673—697.

Cross, S. E., Bacon, P. L., & Morris, M. L. (2000). The relational-interdependent self-construal and relationships. *Journal of Personality and Social Psychology, 78*, 791—808.

Cross, S. E., Hardin, E. E., & Gercek-Swing, B. (2011). The what, how, why, and where of self-construal. *Personality and Sociological Psychology Review, 15*, 142—179.

Cross, S., & Madson, L. (1997). Models of the self: Self-construals and gender. *Psychological Bulletin, 122*, 5—37.

D'Andrade, R., & Strauss, C. (1992). Review: Human motives and cultural models. *The Journal of Mind and Behavior, 14*, 89—93.

Dong, Q., Yang, B., & Ollendick, T. H. (1994). Fears in Chinese children and adolescents and their relations to anxiety and depression. *Journal of Child Psychology and Psychiatry, 35*(2), 351—363.

Draguns, J. G., & Tanaka-Matsumi, J. (2003). Assessment of psychopathology across and within cultures: Issues and findings. *Behavior Research and Therapy, 41*, 755—776.

Essau, C. A. (2007). Anxiety in children: When is it classed as a disorder that should be treated. *Expert Review of Neurotherapeutics, 7*(8), 909—911.

Essau, C. A., Conradt, J., & Petermann, F. (2000). Frequency, comorbidity, and psychosocial impairment of anxiety disorders in German adolescents. *Journal of Anxiety Disorders, 14*(3), 263—279.

Essau, C. A., Ederer, E. M., O'Callaghan, J., & Aschemann, B. (2008). Doing it now or later? Correlates, predictors and prevention of academic, decisional and general procrastination among students in Austria. In *A poster presentation at the 8th Alps-Adria psychology conference, October 2—4, Ljubljana, Slovenia.*

Essau, C. A., Ishikawa, S., & Sasagawa, S. (2011). Early learning experience and adolescent anxiety: A cross-cultural comparison between Japan and England. *Journal of Children Family Studies, 20*, 196—204.

Essau, C. A., Ishikawa, S., Sasagawa, S., Sato, H., Okajima, I., Otsui, K., et al. (2011). Anxiety symptoms among adolescents in Japan and England: Their relationship with self-construals and social support. *Depression and Anxiety, 28*, 509—518.

Essau, C. A., Leung, P. W. L., Conradt, J., Cheng, H., & Wong, T. (2008). Anxiety symptoms in Chinese and German adolescents: Their relationship with early learning experiences, perfectionism and learning motivation. *Depression and Anxiety, 25,* 801–810.

Essau, C. A., Leung, P. W. L., Koydemir, S., Sasagawa, S., O'Callaghan, J., & Bray, D. (2011). The impact of self-construals and perceived social norms on social anxiety in young adults: A cross-cultural comparison. *International Journal of Culture and Mental Health, 2,* 109–120.

Essau, C. A., Sakano, Y., Ishikawa, S., & Sasagawa, S. (2004). Anxiety symptoms in Japanese and in German children. *Behavior Research and Therapy, 42*(5), 601–612.

Essau, C. A., Sasagawa, S., Anastassiou-Hadjicharalambous, X., Guzmán, B. O., & Ollendick, T. H. (2011). Psychometric properties of the spence child anxiety scale with adolescents from five European countries. *Journal of Anxiety Disorders, 25,* 19–27.

Essau, C. A., Sasagawa, S., Ishikawa, S., Okajima, I., O'Callaghan, J., & Bray, D. (2012). A Japanese form of social anxiety (taijin kyofusho): Frequency and correlates in two generations of the same family in Japan. *International Journal of Social Psychiatry, 58*(6), 635–642.

Fiske, A. P. (2002). Using individualism and collectivism to compare cultures—A critique of the validity and measurement of the constructs: Comment on Oyserman et al. (2002). *Psychological Bulletin, 128,* 78–88.

Fiske, A., Kitayama, S., Markus, H. R., & Nisbett, R. E. (1998). The cultural matrix of social psychology. In D. Gilbert, S. Fiske, & G. Lindzey (Eds.), *The handbook of social psychology* (4th ed., Vol. 2, pp. 915–981). San Francisco: McGraw-Hill.

Griner, D., & Smith, T. B. (2006). Culturally adapted mental health interventions: A metaanalytic review. *Psychotherapy: Theory, Research, Practice, Training, 43,* 531–548.

Heine, S. J. (2008). *Cultural psychology.* New York: Norton.

Heinrichs, N., Rapee, R. M., Alden, L. A., Bogels, S., Hofmann, S. G., Oh, K. J., et al. (2006). Cultural differences in perceived social norms and social anxiety. *Behaviour Research and Therapy, 44,* 1187–1197.

Hinton, D. E. (2012). Multicultural in the delivery of anxiety treatment. *Depression and Anxiety, 29,* 1–3.

Ho, D. Y., & Chiu, C. (1994). Component ideas of individualism, collectivism, and social organization: An application in the study of Chinese culture. In U. Kim, H. C. Triandis, C. Kagitcibasi, S. C. Choi, & G. Yoon (Eds.), *Individualism and collectivism: Theory, method, and applications* (pp. 123–136). Thousand Oaks, CA: Sage.

Hofmann, S. G., Asnaani, A., & Hinton, D. E. (2010). Cultural aspects in social anxiety and social anxiety disorder. *Depression and Anxiety, 27,* 1117–1127.

Hofstede, G. (1980). *Culture's consequences.* Beverly Hills, CA: Sage.

Hofstede, G. (2001). *Culture's consequences: Comparing values, behaviors, institutions and organizations across nations* (2nd ed.). Thousand Oaks, CA: Sage Publications.

Ho, L. Y., & Lau, A. S. (2011). Do self-report measures of social anxiety reflect cultural bias or real difficulties for Asian American college students? *Cultural Diversity & Ethnic Minority Psychology, 17,* 52–58.

Hsu, L., & Alden, L. E. (2008). Cultural influences on willingness to seek treatment for social anxiety in Chinese- and European-heritage students. *Cultural Diversity & Ethnic Minority Psychology, 14*(3), 215–223.

Ishikawa, S., Sato, H., & Sasagawa, S. (2009). Anxiety disorder symptoms in Japanese children and adolescents. *Journal of Anxiety Disorders, 23,* 104–111.

Japanese Ministry of Health Labor and Welfare. (2003). *Community mental health intervention guidelines aimed at socially withdrawn teenagers and young adults.* National Center of Neurology and Psychiatry.

Kagitcibasi, C. (1990). Family and socialisation in cross-cultural perspective: A model of change. In J. Berman (Ed.), *Nebraska symposium on motivation: Cross-cultural perspectives* (pp. 135–200). Lincoln, NE: University of Nebraska Press.

Kagitcibasi, C. (2005). Autonomy and relatedness in cultural context: Implications for self and family. *Journal of Cross-Cultural Psychology, 36*, 403—422.

Kao, H. S. R., & Sinha, D. (Eds.). (2000). *Asian perspectives on psychology* (2nd ed.) New Delhi.

Kashima, Y., Yamaguchi, S., Kim, U., Choi, S. C., Gelfand, M., & Yuki, M. (1995). Culture, gender, and self: A perspective from individualism-collectivism research. *Journal of Personality and Social Psychology, 69*, 925—937.

Kendall, P. C., Flannery-Schroeder, E., Panichelli-Mindel, S. M., Southam-Gerow, M., Henin, A., & Warman, M. (1997). Therapy for youths with anxiety disorders: A second randomized clinical trial. *Journal of Consulting and Clinical Psychology, 65*, 366—380.

Kessler, R. C., Petukhova, M., Sampson, N. A., Zaslavsky, A. M., & Wittchen, H. U. (2012). Twelve month and lifetime prevalence and livetime morbid risk of anxiety and mood disorders in the United States. *International Journal of Methods in Psychiatric Research, 21*, 169—174.

Kim, H. S., & Sherman, D. K. (2007). "Express yourself": Culture and the effect of self-expression on choice. *Journal of Personality and Social Psychology, 92*, 1—11.

Kim, M. S., Sharkey, W. F., & Singelis, T. M. (1994). The relationships between individuals' self-construals and perceived importance of interactive constraints. *International Journal of Intercultural Relations, 18*, 117—140.

Kirmayer, L. J. (1991). The place of culture in psychiatric nosology: Taijin Kyofusho and DSM-III-R. *Journal of Nervous and Mental Disorder, 179*, 19—28.

Kirmayer, L. J. (2001). Cultural variations in the clinical presentation of depression and anxiety: Implications for diagnosis and treatment. *Journal of Clinical Psychiatry, 62*(Suppl. 13), 22—30.

Kitanaka, J. (2008). Questioning the suicide of resolve: Medico-legal disputes regarding overwork suicide in twentieth-century Japan. In *Histories of suicide: international perspectives on self-destruction in the modern world* (pp. 257—280). University of Toronto Press.

Kitayama, S., & Markus, H. R. (1995). Culture and self: Implications for internationalizing psychology. In N. R. Goldberger, & J. B. Veroff (Eds.), *The culture and psychology reader.* New York: New York University Press.

Kleinknecht, R. A., Dinnel, D. L., Kleinknecht, E. E., Hiruma, N., & Harada, N. (1997). Cultural factors in social anxiety: A comparison of social phobia symptoms and taijin kyofusho. *Journal of Anxiety Disorders, 11*, 157—177.

Kleinman, A. (1988). *Rethinking psychiatry: From cultural category to personal experience.* New York Free Press.

Koydemir, S., & Essau, C. A. (2016). Cross-cultural research. In R. Cautin, & S. Lilienfeld (Eds.), *The encyclopedia of clinical psychology.* Wiley-Blackwell.

Kroeber, A. L., & Kluckhohn, C. (1952). *Culture: A critical review of concepts and definitions.* New York: Vintage Books.

Kühnen, U. (2009). Culture, self-construal and social cognition: Evidence from cross-cultural and priming studies. In A. Gari, K. Mylonas, & A. Gari (Eds.), *Q.E.D. from Herodotus: Ethnographic journeys to cross-cultural research* (pp. 303—310). Athens: Atrapos Editions.

Lee, A. Y., Aaker, J. L., & Gardner, W. K. (2000). The pleasures and pains of distinct self-construals: The role of interdependence in regulatory focus. *Journal of Personality and Social Psychology, 78*, 1122—1134.

Lewinsohn, P. M., Hops, H., Roberts, R. E., Seeley, J. R., & Andrews, J. A. (1993). Adolescent psychopathology: Prevalence and incidence of depression and other DSM-III R disorders in high school students. *Journal of Abnormal Psychology, 102*, 133—144.

Lewis-Fernandez, R., Hinton, D. E., Laria, A. J., Patterson, E. H., Hofmann, S. G., & Craske, M. G. (2010). Culture and the anxiety disorders: Recommendations for DSM-V. *Depression and Anxiety, 27*, 212—229.

Lin, K., & Cheung, F. (1999). Mental health issues for Asian Americans. *Psychiatric Services, 50*, 774—780.

López, S. R., & Guarnaccia, P. J. (2008). Cultural dimensions of psychopathology: The social world's impact on mental disorders. In J. Maddux, & B. Winstead (Eds.), *Psychopathology: Foundations for a contemporary understanding* (2nd ed., pp. 19–38). New York: Routledge/Taylor & Francis Group.

Lun, J., Kesebir, S., & Oishi, S. (2008). On feeling understood and feeling well: The role of interdependence. *Journal of Research in Personality, 42,* 1623–1628.

Maeda, F., & Nathan, J. H. (1999). Understanding taijin kyofusho through its treatment, Morita therapy. *Journal of Psychosomatic Research, 46,* 525–530.

Markus, H. R., & Kitayama, S. (1991). Culture and the self: Implications for cognition, emotion, and motivation. *Psychological Review, 98*(2), 224–253.

Marsella, A. J., & Yamada, A. M. (2007). Culture and psychopathology: Foundations, issues, directions. In S. Kitayama, & D. Cohen (Eds.), *Handbook of cultural psychology* (pp. 797–818). New York: Guilford Press.

Matsumoto, D. (1999). Culture and self: An empirical assessment of Markus and Kitayama's theory of independent and interdependent self-construals. *Asian Journal of Social Psychology, 2,* 289–310.

Matsumoto, D. (2007). Culture, context, and behavior. *Personality, 75,* 1285–1320.

Morf, C., & Mischel, W. (2012). The self as a psycho-social dynamic processing system: Towards a converging science of selfhood. In M. Leary, & J. Tangney (Eds.), *Handbook of self and identity* (2nd ed., pp. 21–49). New York, NY: The Guilford Press.

Moscovitch, D., Hofmann, S., & Litz, B. (2005). The impact of self-construals on social anxiety: A gender-specific interaction. *Personality and Individual Difference, 38,* 659–672.

Muris, P., Loxton, H., Neumann, A., Plessis, M., King, N. J., & Ollendick, T. H. (2006). DSM-defined anxiety disorders symptoms in South African youths: Their assessment and relationship with perceived parental rearing behaviors. *Behaviour Research and Therapy, 44*(6), 883–896.

Muris, P., Schmidt, H., Engelbrecht, P., & Preold, M. (2002). DSM-IV-defined anxiety disorder symptoms in South African children. *Journal of American Academy of Children Adolescence Psychiatry, 41*(11), 1360–1368.

Narikiyo, T. A., & Kameoka, V. A. (1992). Attributions of mental illness and judgments about help seeking among Japanese-American and White-American students. *Journal of Counseling Psychology, 39,* 363–369.

Neff, K. D., & Harter, S. (2003). Relationship styles of self-focused autonomy, other-focused connectedness, and mutuality across multiple relationship contexts. *Journal of Social and Personal Relationships, 20,* 81–99.

Okazaki, S. (1997). Sources of ethnic differences between Asian American and White American college students on measures of depression and social anxiety. *Journal of Abnormal Psychology, 106,* 52–60.

Okazaki, S., Liu, J. F., Longworth, S. L., & Minn, J. Y. (2002). Asian American-white American differences in expressions of social anxiety: A replication and extension. *Cultural Diversity & Ethnic Minority Psychology, 8,* 234–247.

Ollendick, T. H., King, N. J., & Frary, R. B. (1989). Fears in children and adolescents: Reliability and generalizability across gender, age and nationality. *Behaviour Research and Therapy, 27,* 19–26.

Ollendick, T. H., Yule, W., & Ollier, K. (1991). Fears in British children and their relationship to manifest anxiety and depression. *Journal of Child Psychology and Psychiatry, 32,* 321–331.

Oyserman, D. (2011). Culture as situated cognition: Cultural mindsets, cultural fluency, and meaning making. *European Review of Social Psychology, 22*(1), 164–214.

Oyserman, D., Coon, M. H., & Kemmelmeier, M. (2002). Rethinking individualism and collectivism: Evaluation of theoretical assumptions and meta-analyses. *Psychological Bulletin, 128,* 3–72.

Oyserman, D., Elmore, K., & Smith, G. (2012). Self, self-concept, and identity. In M. Leary, & J. Tangney (Eds.), *Handbook of self and identity* (2nd ed., pp. 69–104). NY: Guilford.

Oyserman, D., & Lee, S. W. S. (2007). Priming "culture": Culture as situated cognition. In S. Kitayama, & D. Cohen (Eds.), *Handbook of cultural psychology* (pp. 255–279). New York, NY: Guilford Press.

Oyserman, D., & Markus, H. R. (1998). Self as social representation. In U. Flick (Ed.), *The psychology of the social* (pp. 107–125). New York, NY: Cambridge University Press.

Rubin, K. H., Hemphill, S. A., Chen, X., Hastings, P., Sanson, A., Coco, A. L., Zappulla, C., et al. (2006). Cross-cultural study of behavioral inhibition in toddlers: East–West–North–South. *International Journal of Behavioral Development, 30*(3), 219–226.

Saito, K. (2010). *Guideline of hikikomori for their evaluations and supports.* Tokyo: Ministry of Health, Labour and Welfare.

Seligman, L. D., & Ollendick, T. H. (2011). .Cognitive behavior therapy for anxiety disorders in children and adolescents. *Psychiatric Clinics of North America, 20,* 217–238.

Shim, G., Freund, H., Stopsack, M., Kämmerer, A., & Barnow, S. (2014). Acculturation, self-construal, mental and physical health: An explorative study of East Asian students in Germany. *International Journal of Psychology, 49,* 295–303.

Singelis, T. M. (1994). The measurement of independent and interdependent self-construals. *Personality & Social Psychology Bulletin, 20,* 580–591.

Singelis, T. M., & Brown, J. W. (1995). Culture, self, and collectivist communication linking culture to individual behavior. *Human Communication Research, 21,* 354–389.

Stallard, P., Simpson, N., Anderson, S., Hibbert, S., & Osborn, C. (2007). The FRIENDS emotional health programme: Initial findings from a school-based project. *Child and Adolescent Mental Health, 12,* 32–37.

Stryker, S., & Burke, P. J. (2000). The past, present, and future of an identity theory. *Social Psychology Quarterly, 63,* 284–297.

Suh, E. M. (2000). Self, the hyphen between culture and subjective well-being. In E. Diener, & E. M. Suh (Eds.), *Culture and subjective well-being* (pp. 63–86). Cambridge, MA: MIT Press.

Tata, S. P., & Leong, F. T. L. (1994). Individualism-collectivism, social-network orientation, and acculturation as predictors of attitudes toward seeking professional psychological help among Chinese-Americans. *Journal of Counseling Psychology, 41*(3), 280–287.

Trafimow, D., Triandis, H. C., & Goto, G. S. (1991). Some tests of the distinction between the private self and the collective self. *Journal of Personality and Social Psychology, 60*(5), 649.

Triandis, H. C. (1989). The self and social behavior in differing cultural contexts. *Psychological Review, 96,* 506–520.

Triandis, H. C. (1993). The contingency model in cross-cultural perspective. In M. M. Chemers, & R. Ayman (Eds.), *Leadership theory and research: Perspectives and directions* (pp. 167–188). San Diego, CA: Academic Press.

Triandis, H. C. (1994). Theoretical and methodological approaches to the study of collectivism and individualism. In U. Kim, H. C. Triandis, C. Kagitcibasi, S. C. Choi, & G. Yoon (Eds.), *Individualism and collectivism: Theory, method, and applications* (pp. 41–51). Thousand Oaks, CA: Sage.

Triandis, H. C. (2001). Individualism-collectivism and personality. *Journal of Personality, 69,* 907–924.

Triandis, H. C., Bontempo, R., Betancourt, H., Bond, M., Leung, K., Brenes, A., et al. (1986). The measurement of ethic aspects of individualism and collectivism across cultures. *Australian Journal of Psychology, 38,* 257–267.

Turner, J. H., & Stets, J. E. (2005). *The sociology of emotions.* Cambridge: Cambridge University Press.

Varela, R. E., & Hensley-Maloney, L. (2009). The Influence of culture on anxiety in Latino youth: A review. *Clinical Child and Family Psychology Review, 12,* 217–233.

Watson, P., & Morris, R. (2002). Individualist and collectivist values: Hypotheses suggested by Alexis de Tocqueville. *The Journal of Psychology: Interdisciplinary and Applied, 136,* 263–271.

Weisz, J. R., Sigman, M., Weiss, B., & Mosk, J. (1993). Parent reports of behavioral and emotional problems among children in Kenya, Thailand, and the United States. *Child Development, 64,* 98–109.

Weisz, J. R., Suwanlert, S., Chaiyasit, W., Weiss, B., Achenbach, T. M., & Walter, B. A. (1987). Epidemiology of behavioral and emotional problems among Thai and American children: Parent reports for ages 6–11. *Journal of Child Psychological and Psychiatry, 26,* 890–898.

Wittchen, H.-U., Nelson, C. B., & Lachner, G. (1998). Prevalence of mental disorders and psychosocial impairments in adolescents and young adults. *Psychological Medicine, 28,* 109–126.

World Health Organization. (1992). *The ICD-10 classification of mental and behavioural disorders: Clinical descriptions and diagnostic guidelines.* Geneva: World Health Organization.

Yamada, A. M., & Singelis, T. M. (1999). Biculturalism and self-construal. *International Journal of Intercultural Relations, 23,* 697–709.

Yamaguchi, S., Kashima, Y., Kim, U., Choi, S., Gelfand, M. J., & Yuki, M. (1992). Culture, gender and self: A perspective from individualism-collectivism research. *Journal of Personality and Social Psychology, 69,* 925–937.

Yeh, M., Hough, R. L., McCabe, K., Lau, A., & Garland, A. (2004). Parental beliefs about the causes of child problems: Exploring racial/ethnic patterns. *Journal of the American Academy of Child and Adolescent Psychiatry, 43,* 605–612.

Ying, Y. W., & Miller, L. S. (1992). Help-seeking behavior and attitude of Chinese Americans regarding psycho-logical problems. *American Journal of Community Psychology, 20,* 549–556.

Zhang, K., Ginzburg, I., McNaughton, B. L., & Sejnowski, T. J. (1998). Interpreting neuronal population activity by reconstruction: Unified framework with application to hippocampal place cells. *Journal of Neurophysiology, 79,* 1017–1044.

Further Reading

Dinnel, D. L., Kleinknecht, R. A., & Tanaka-Matsumi, J. (2002). A cross-cultural comparison of social phobia symptoms. *Journal of Psychopathology and Behavioral Assessment, 24,* 75–84.

Essau, C. A., Sasagawa, S., Chen, J., & Sakano, Y. (2010). Taijin kyofusho and social phobia symptoms in young adults in England and in Japan. *Journal of Cross-Cultural Psychology, 43,* 219–232.

Gerull, F. C., & Rapee, R. M. (2002). Mother knows best: Effects of maternal modelling on the acquisition of fear and avoidance behaviour in toddlers. *Behaviour Research and Therapy, 40*(3), 279–287.

Ginsburg, G. S., & Silverman, W. K. (1996). Phobic and anxiety disorders in Hispanic and Caucasian youth. *Journal of Anxiety Disorders, 10*(6), 517–528.

Kagitcibasi, C. (1996). The autonomous-relational self: A new synthesis. *European Psychologist, 1,* 180–186.

Lowry-Webster, H. M., Barrett, P. M., & Dadds, M. R. (2001). A universal prevention trial of anxiety and depressive symptomatology in childhood: Preliminary data from an Australian study. *Behaviour Change, 18,* 36–50.

Mostert, J., & Loxton, H. (2008). Exploring the effectiveness of the FRIENDS program in reducing anxiety symptoms among South African children. *Behaviour Change, 25,* 85–96.

Mullen, M. K., & Soonhyung, Y. (1995). The cultural context of talk about the past: Implications for the development of autobiographical memory. *Cognitive Development, 10,* 407–419.

Saito, T. (1998). *Social withdrawal; never ending adolescent period.* Tokyo, Japan: PHP.

Singelis, T. M., & Sharkey, W. F. (1995). Culture, self-construal, and embarrassability. *Journal of Cross-Cultural Psychology, 26,* 622–644.

PART II

UNIQUENESS AND RISK IN MARGINALIZED GROUPS

6

Child Developmental Trajectories in Adversity: Environmental Embedding and Developmental Cascades in Contexts of Risk

Xanthe Hunt, Mark Tomlinson
Stellenbosch University, Stellenbosch, South Africa

INTRODUCTION

Development is continuous and normatively progresses in a predictable manner, although the rate and nature of this progression may differ greatly. Development is usually also conceived of as occurring in a sequence as the child ages. Age-related development periods include the prenatal and neonatal periods, infancy and early childhood, school age, and adolescence. A cornerstone of the developmental literature is the idea that development is most malleable (individuals are most changeable, vulnerable to risk, and open to positive development) in the earliest years of life. The effects of the environment on human characteristics are enormous during the earliest and most rapid periods of development (Bloom, 1964).

Developmental changes are influenced by the individual child's genetics, environment (including prenatal environment), and exposure to risk and supportive factors. We can conceive of development as occurring in two realms primarily: biological development, controlled largely by genetics (maturation); and cognitive and socioemotional development, which occurs because of learning and experience. Both processes are interdependent and influenced by the context in which the child is developing.

When environments are adverse (or toxic), normative developmental processes may be interrupted. Here, adversity is defined in terms of cumulative stressors, primarily poverty, toxic stress, and the common precipitants of toxic stress, such as abuse or neglect, parental substance abuse or mental illness, and exposure to violence (Felitti et al., 1998; Shonkoff et al., 2012). Being born into and growing up in the context of adversity, extreme or otherwise, can have a myriad of impacts on child development.

However, adversity is not a static phenomenon with linear consequences. Developmental neuroscience has shown that early biological and psychosocial experiences affect brain development and therefore subsequent functioning (Walker et al., 2007). Thus, negative outcomes endure even if exposure to adversity ends, for instance, when an individual moves to a less adverse environment. The effects of exposure to adversity early in life are also intergenerationally transmitted. Caregiver socioeconomic status (SES), for instance, is predicted by his or her exposure to negative environments in childhood, and SES will influence the likelihood of negative outcomes (such as depression) and the likelihood of children experiencing negative outcomes (Bouvette-Turcot et al., 2015).

To begin to tease apart some of the complexities inherent in an understanding of development in the context of adversity, this chapter will deal with current knowledge in two parts. First, it will outline the current literature relevant to the conceptualization of development over the life course, and second, it will discuss adversity as broken down into individual risk factors and outcomes. In the sections that follow, we examine risks in detail, offering insights regarding each by drawing on contemporary work in the fields of evolutionary biology and developmental psychology. These latter developments provide the developmental context in which such "risks" exert their influence.

THE CONTEXT OF HUMAN DEVELOPMENT

Advances in neuroscience, genetics, and developmental psychology have begun to illuminate the manner in which environmental influences interact, both with one another over time and with individual characteristics over the life course, to determine the course of development (Shonkoff et al., 2012). Early stressors alter children's physiology, although the child's genetic and physiological makeup determine the extent of this effect (McEwen, 2012). Furthermore, early dysfunction or delay in one domain of development can lead to a host of negative sequelae down the developmental chain.

Biological Embedding and Differential Susceptibility to Risk

Biological embedding refers to the process by which "the environment gets under the skin" (McEwen, 2012): that is, the manner in which early developmental contexts cause stable epigenetic modifications in the body which set lifelong patterns of physiological reactivity (McEwen, 2012). Epigenetic modifications refer to interactions between the genome and the environment in which the genome exists. Specifically, it refers to heritable alterations in genomic structure which are not due to DNA changes, but rather to changes in how DNA is expressed (Loscalzo & Handy, 2014). These processes regulate patterns of gene expression (Loscalzo & Handy, 2014). Epigenetic modifications interact with experiences over the life course, but the "embedded" patterns are enduring.

Biological embedding therefore constitutes the manner in which exposure to different social environments in childhood leads to different biological states, and how these biological differences affect development through the life course (Hertzman, 2012).

The environment to which children are exposed in their earliest years has a disproportionately large role in determining patterns of later development. When this early environment is characterized by adversity (abuse, neglect, or malnutrition, for instance) the later development of the individual must occur in a physiological context programmed, as it were, in adversity (McEwen, 2012).

For example, adverse early life events related to parental care in humans is predictive of subsequent negative mental and physical health outcomes in children. The amount, quality, and consistency of maternal care that an infant receives predicts subsequent emotional, social, and cognitive development (Levine et al., 1967; Meaney & Szyf, 2005), and these effects are related to the epigenetic effect of maternal care on infant physiology and brain development. That is, as mentioned earlier, maternal care may constitute an environmental influence by which a child's gene expression is altered (Champagne, 2008).

Much of what is known about the relationship between parental care and brain development and nervous system function comes from animal models: prenatal stress impairs hippocampal development in rats (Isgor et al., 2004), abusive maternal care in rodents results in impaired development of the amygdala (Moriceau & Sullivan, 2006), and maternal anxiety in rhesus monkeys leads to chronic anxiety in offspring (Coplan et al., 2001). However, data from human studies seem to point in the same direction: early adverse environments program the body to function in a certain way, heightening certain capacities and limiting others through their effect on neuronal and hormonal infrastructure (Champagne, 2008; Champagne & Curley, 2009).

Low SES, which increases the likelihood of stressors in the home, is related not only to deficiencies in language skills (Perkins, Finegood, & Swain, 2013), self-regulatory capacity (Evans & Kim, 2013), and memory abilities (Evans & Schamberg, 2009), but even more fundamentally, to smaller hippocampal volumes (Hanson et al., 2011) as well as prefrontal cortical gray matter (Gianaros et al., 2007) in humans. Importantly, exposure to a low-SES environment predicts greater subsequent amygdala reactivity (Gianaros et al., 2008).

Each of these brain and nervous system effects predicts later functioning. An infant exposed to chronic early stress, for instance, experiences greater amygdala reactivity in early childhood (Shonkoff et al., 2012; Tottenham et al., 2010). This, in turn, may lead to internalizing behaviors as the child struggles to manage anxiety resulting from an overactive hypothalamic–pituitary–adrenal axis (HPA) response (Granger, 1998; Hartman et al., 2013; Martinez-Torteya et al., 2016). Biological embedding goes a long way in explaining how differential exposure to harsh environments (which are socially stratified) results in differential health outcomes (which are also socially stratified) (Hertzman, 2012; Hertzman et al., 2001; Hertzman & Power, 2003). This social stratification refers to the fact that harsh environments, which are characterized by violence, high rates of substance use and abuse, and social stressors such as insecure housing, are more commonly environments that are also poor. Thus, people in the lower economic strata of a given society are more likely to experience multiple environmental stressors, and thus experience worse health outcomes. Furthermore, such social causation often involves mundane exposures to impoverished rather than abusive or neglectful rearing environments, sufficient to lead to compromised development and negative outcomes in later life (Hart & Risley, 1995; Hertzman, 2012; Kishiyama et al., 2009).

However, there is no one-to-one relationship between early stress and subsequent suboptimal development. Individuals exposed to harsh early environments may go on to thrive, or, if not thrive, show remarkable resilience. Such nuances in embedding of early experience is illuminated by research on gene–environment interactions (G × E). Of particular use in understanding such variance is differential susceptibility theory (Belsky, 1997; Ellis et al., 2011). Belsky's (Belsky, 1997) theory of differential susceptibility is an evolutionary-inspired proposition which posits that some individuals are more affected by their rearing experiences than are others. Belsky uses the phrase "for-better-and-for-worse" to refer to this proposed phenomenon. This model, a move away from conventional diathesis-stress models of G × E interactions, posits that individuals vary in susceptibility to both adverse and beneficial effects of rearing influences, and that moderators of individuals' susceptibility include temperamental, physiological, and genetic factors, markers of greater and lesser developmental plasticity (for reviews, see Belsky, 1997, 2005; Belsky, Bakermans-Kranenburg, & Van IJzendoorn, 2007a,b).

Studies involving measured genes and measured environments also document both for-better-and-for-worse rearing effects in the case of susceptible infants, specifically those with a particular allelic variant of a gene called DRD4, which codes for the D4 dopamine receptor. Given such findings, it would be simplistic to expect all individuals to respond to early environmental factors in the same way. Evidence shows that this is indeed not the case. For instance, work by Morgan et al. (2017) showed that children differed in their sensitivity to a parenting intervention, depending on whether they carried one form of a gene or another. Some individuals are less sensitive to their early environment and may experience better development in adverse contexts than their "sensitive" peers (Boyce & Ellis, 2005; Caspi et al., 2003; Suomi, 2006).

As a general rule, however, exposure to harsh early environments is a reliable predictor of suboptimal development. As noted, early effects of suboptimal early environments may set in motion a developmental pathway in which one suboptimal functioning results in another. Early experiences that produce early developmental states are the first step in a chain of events that carries with it a set of sequelae over the life course (Hertzman, 2012; Hertzman et al., 2001; Hertzman & Power, 2003), unfortunately often engendering further deprivation. One way concept of such pathways is that of developmental cascades.

Developmental Cascades

Since the early 1970s, and accelerated by advances in developmental psychology including a growing archive of longitudinal data sets, research has been trying to understand the complex linkages between early competencies and psychological symptoms (Ford & Lerner, 1992; Gottlieb, 2007; Gottlieb, Wahlsten, & Lickliter, 1998; Hinshaw, 2002; Masten, Burt, & Coatsworth, 2006; Sameroff, 2000). A growing body of literature attests to transactional and sequential effects between variables such as cognitive and social competence and internalizing and externalizing symptoms. Theoretically, these effects may be direct and unidirectional, direct and bidirectional, or indirect through different pathways, but the consequences are enduring (Bornstein, Hahn, & Haynes, 2010; Burt et al., 2008; Cicchetti & Cannon, 1999; Dodge et al., 2009; Dodge & Pettit, 2003; Dodge, Pettit, & Bates, 1994; Hanson & Gottesman, 2007; Masten & Cicchetti, 2010; Rutter, Kim-Cohen, & Maughan, 2006). One model of such interactions, which has gained traction in developmental psychology, sees these effects as "developmental cascades."

Developmental cascade theory holds that early functioning in one domain of adaptive behavior or emotional functioning, such as externalizing behavior in early childhood, spills over to influence functioning in other domains: for instance, by resulting in low academic competence in later childhood. These effects then influence subsequent development in yet another area (eg, low academic competence results in internalizing behavior in adolescence) (Capaldi & Stoolmiller, 1999; Moffitt et al., 2002; Sameroff, 2000).

There is evidence that domains of competence and psychopathology are interlinked over time through a complex temporal network of risk and outcome (Masten & Cicchetti, 2010; Sameroff, 2000). These interlinkages are recursive, and an outcome at one point in the child's life (such as aggressive behavior as a result of parental abuse) could subsequently become a risk factor for later cognitive development. Not only do symptoms undermine adaptive functioning, failures in adaptive functioning contribute to symptoms (Masten & Cicchetti, 2010). There is an ever-present possibility of spreading effects that result from dynamic interactions among capabilities, risks, and symptoms over time (Masten & Cicchetti, 2010; Masten et al., 2005; Sameroff, 2000).

What developmental cascade models contribute to our thinking about development over the life course is fourfold. First, they draw our attention to the complex networks of risk and protective factors that affect any individual child's long-term adjustment. Second, they highlight the necessity of taking a longitudinal perspective on child development, and on cumulative risk, rather than attempting to isolate the impacts of individual risks. Third, they allow us to direct attention to the predictors of first-tier cascade variables. For instance, if externalizing problems in early childhood is the first step in a certain negative developmental cascade, we must direct our attention to stymying the antecedents of externalizing problems in early childhood. Finally, by highlighting certain predictors as most salient in determining subsequent outcomes, they guide intervention priorities. Because developmental cascades may be positive in their consequences with respect to adaptive behavior, interventionists might be able to spur optimal long-term development if salient early domains of child functioning are targeted (Bornstein et al., 2010).

CONTEXTUAL RISK FACTORS

Low Socioeconomic Status and Poverty

Low SES and poverty are overarching risks that give rise to other risks, and which compound other risks. In this section, we examine the latest developments on the impacts of low SES and poverty on child development.

SES is a well-established predictor of child outcomes, including health outcomes (Backlund, Sorlie, & Johnson, 1996; Lantz et al., 1998; Schroeder,

2004; Winkleby et al., 1992), psychological outcomes (Caughy, O'Campo, & Muntaner, 2003; Rutter, 2003), and educational attainment (White, 1982). There have been notable advances in how we think about and research low SES, poverty, and children growing up in environments characterized by both. There have been important shifts in how poverty is imagined and measured in development economics (McLeod & Shanahan, 1993; Wolfensohn & Bourguignon, 2004). This shift has been from poverty defined by levels of income or consumption to a view of poverty that assesses access to a range of essential resources. In these so-called multidimensional approaches to poverty, being poor is defined as lacking access to a range of financial and social supports, which hinders the individual's capacity to attain a good quality of life (Sen, 1992, 1993). Such approaches allow us to see how being poor can affect a child's development: it is not only a matter of lacking household resources, but also the sequelae of this lack, such as reduced parental investment resulting from competing demands of job-seeking.

Poverty studies in the 1960s and 1970s thought about poverty as a fixed, static phenomenon. Today, the emphasis has shifted, largely thanks to the work of Elder (1998) and Duncan and Brooks-Gunn (1999), to a conceptualization of poverty as a life course phenomenon. Such work takes into account that the timing and duration of being poor influence how it will affect development. This shift in focus, McLeod and Shanahan (1993) noted, is rooted in two advances in child development studies: first, in the concepts and tenets of life course theory, which acknowledges the time-variant nature of causal processes (Elder, 1998); and second, in work which foregrounded the primacy of early experience (Bloom, 1964; Brooks-Gunn et al., 1993; Duncan et al., 1998; Zigler, 1994). This draws our attention not only to the effects of poverty experienced early in life but also to the fact that longer exposure to poverty and its environmental correlates (in a word, adversity) results in worse outcomes: a cumulative deficit model (Walker et al., 2011).

Developments in our conceptualization of low SES have drawn attention to the impact of the context in which being poor is experienced (McLeod & Shanahan, 1993). Is everyone around one poor, as well, or is the household in which the child grows up the only poor household in the area? Wilson (Wilson, 2012) showed how the impacts of low SES are strongest when that low SES characterizes an individual's earliest environments: sometimes, low SES in early life is a better predictor of developmental outcomes than current SES (Luo & Waite, 2005). It is worse, as it were, to have been poor then rather than now. Furthermore, persistent poverty has more detrimental effects on child development, including in the realm of IQ, school achievement, and psychological well-being, than transitory poverty. It is also worse to be consistently poor rather than poor for only a little while. Taken together, the worst effects of poverty are seen when it characterizes the child's developmental environment from before birth, and when it endures. Poverty is least likely to affect developmental outcomes negatively when it is encountered for a short period and/or later in life. Low SES is also worse when it is widespread. Poor individuals living in high-poverty communities are further disadvantaged by reduced access to jobs, high-quality services, and informal social supports (Wilson, 2012). Poor individuals in higher-SES communities are more likely to be able to draw on a range of social supports, better infrastructure, and other supports that buffer the impacts of household poverty. In addition, it is worst when it characterizes children's developmental environment from before birth and endures throughout their life, and when they come from a low-SES environment.

The "how" of the relationship between SES and child development is difficult to pick apart. However, we know that living in a low-SES environment and being poor diminishes access not only to resources (Brooks-Gunn & Duncan, 1997; Duncan & Brooks-Gunn, 2000; Duncan et al., 1998) but also to social capital. Children from higher-SES families have access to better resources, greater social capital, and richer environments than do children from low-SES families. Together, these factors result in drastically suboptimal environments for child development (Brooks-Gunn & Duncan, 1997; Hoff et al., 2002).

The "how" extends through generations. In a study by Bouvette-Turcot et al. (2015), women who reported higher levels of childhood adversity, and who were more depressed, were significantly more likely to live in low-SES environments. The interaction between low SES and maternal depression constitutes an adverse childhood environment (Cogill et al., 1986; Davis et al., 2007; Deave et al., 2008; Goodman et al., 2011). Maternal depression predicts mental disorders in children (Goodman et al., 2011). Thus, children of these women would be more likely to grow into adults in the same situation as their mothers: in low-SES environments with negative mental health outcomes (Murray et al., 2010). Low SES and one of its pernicious sequelae (mental disorders) can be intergenerationally transmitted (Aizer & Currie, 2014). Therefore, SES can be seen to be influenced by a life course pathway that begins in childhood and includes adversity-related mental health outcomes (Bouvette-Turcot et al., 2015): biological embedding resulting in a developmental cascade that compromises child development over generations within a family.

Maternal Depression

Antenatal Depression

The prevalence of antenatal depression/depressed mood in low- and middle-income countries (LMIC) ranges from 19.9% in Jamaica (Gardner et al., 1999) to 24.94 in Ethiopia (Biratu & Haile, 2015) and 39% in South Africa (Hartley et al., 2011; Manikkam & Burns, 2012) and Tanzania (Kaaya et al., 2010). There are significantly fewer studies on antenatal depression in LMIC than studies on postnatal depression. This partly because antenatal depression often goes undiagnosed owing to the ubiquity of mood changes during pregnancy. Depressed maternal mood is often taken to be a normative correlate of hormonal changes, including increased cortisol, during pregnancy (Field et al., 2004).

Nonetheless, researchers have begun to attempt to consider these potentially confounding variables (hormonal changes) and have found strong evidence for negative effects of prenatal depression on maternal and child outcomes (Deave et al., 2008; Luoma et al., 2001). Antenatal depression is associated with low birth weight, preterm delivery, and fetal growth restriction in LMIC (Grote et al., 2010; Rahman et al., 2007; Stewart et al., 2008). Pregnant women with depression are also more likely to experience obstetric complications such as preeclampsia (Evans et al., 2007; Field et al., 2004; Wisner et al., 2009).

Indeed, one mechanism that has been suggested to explain the relationship between antenatal depression and negative child outcomes, in particular, is preterm delivery. Among women with prenatal depression, the risk for preterm delivery increases significantly. In turn, preterm delivery contributes to significant cognitive, behavioral, and emotional problems in children (Li, Liu, & Odouli, 2009). Another mechanism which has received much attention in biological psychiatry is neonatal cortisol exposure. Antenatal depression causes elevated neonatal cortisol levels (Field et al., 2004). In turn, these elevated levels of the "stress hormone" negatively influence infant temperament and have been linked to childhood psychopathology (Davis et al., 2007). As noted, prenatal depression significantly predicts postpartum depression, and so the effects of prenatal depression on child cognitive outcomes are likely inasmuch as the condition is often premorbid to postpartum depression (Edwards et al., 2008; Milgrom et al., 2008).

However, in cases in which researchers managed to disentangle the impact of prenatal depression on fetal, infant, and child development, effects were negative. Fetuses of depressed women spent a significantly greater percentage of time being active (Dieter et al., 2001), and we know that excessive fetal activity is related to delayed fetal growth (Field, 2011). Women with prenatal depression were more likely to delivery prematurely and the infants to have low birth weight (Diego et al., 2009; Field et al., 2004).

Newborns of antenatally depressed mothers may also be less responsive to stimulation (Diego et al., 2009), have a difficult temperament (Diego et al., 2009; McGrath, Records, & Rice, 2008), and have increased crying (Milgrom et al., 2008; van der Wal, van Eijsden, & Bonsel, 2007).

Antenatal depression negatively affects infant sleep quality (Gaylor et al., 2005; Liu et al., 2005). Disturbances in sleep among infants, in turn, is associated with behavioral and physiological problems in childhood, including depression (O'Connor et al., 2007) and attention-deficit hyperactivity disorder (ADHD) (Gruber, Sadeh, & Raviv, 2000).

There is additional evidence of effects of prenatal depression on infant and child cognitive development when one considers cortisol exposure as a potential mediating variable in the relationship between prenatal depression and child cognitive outcomes. Contexts of adversity are often characterized by violence and other stressors. As such, it is worth examining the literature concerning elevated neonatal cortisol and its relation to infant and child cognitive development.

Maternal stress during pregnancy increases cortisol and corticotrophin-releasing hormone levels in both the mother and fetus (Field et al., 2004; Weinstock, 2008). During the prenatal period, fetal systems are uniquely vulnerable to both organizing and disorganizing influences. The effects of such influences, known as programming, are such that a stimulus or insult during a vulnerable developmental period has a nearly permanent or permanent impact on development (Cameron et al., 2005; Simmons et al., 2010).

Exposure to elevated levels of maternal stress (including antenatal depression) is associated with behavioral and emotional disturbances, as well as cognition during infancy and childhood (Bergman et al., 2007; Davis et al., 2007; Gutteling, de Weerth, & Buitelaar, 2005; Huizink et al., 2003).

Antenatal cortisol exposure negatively predicts cognitive ability in the infant, even when prenatal, obstetric, and socioeconomic factors are controlled for. However, the association between antenatal depression and infant cognitive development was moderated by child–mother attachment: In children with an insecure attachment, the correlation was significant, but not in children who had a secure attachment (Bergman et al., 2007). Still, the effects of prenatal maternal stress on cognitive development are less clear than the effect on behavior (Davis et al., 2007). Maternal stress and anxiety are associated with delayed infant cognitive and neuromotor development, and some of these deficits may persist into adolescence, although several studies found no such association (Brouwers, van Baar, & Pop, 2001; DiPietro et al., 2008). In line with this, elevated maternal cortisol late in gestation is associated with accelerated development over the first year and higher cognitive scores at 12 months (Rahman, Harrington, & Bunn, 2002).

Postnatal Depression

Depression affects many facets of the individual's interpersonal communication, including rate of speech, voice quality, eye contact, and emotional expressiveness and responsiveness (Murray et al., 1996). Postnatal depression may affect maternal child-rearing behaviors (Rahman et al., 2002); depressed mothers are less involved and show more negative affect when interacting with their infants (Cooper et al., 2009). Given the effects of maternal depression on maternal attunement, it is unsurprising that a great deal of research into the effects of postnatal depression on child development has focused on behavioral and psychosocial outcomes.

Kurstjens and Wolke (2001) found that the chronicity of maternal depression interacted with the sex of the child and low SES. Boys of chronically depressed mothers from low-SES families had the lowest cognitive scores of all children.

Infants of mothers with postnatal depression perform worse on tests of cognitive ability (Murray & Cooper, 1997), and this is worse for boys. Insensitive maternal interaction and stimulation at home predicts poorer cognitive functioning in children (Murray & Cooper, 1997; Murray et al., 1996). A potential explanation may lie in how mothers with postnatal depression focused their speech less on boys than girls (Murray & Cooper, 1997).

Timing of postnatal depression is also important; data show that the effects of maternal depression on child development are worst when mothers are depressed in the first year of the child's life (Cogill et al., 1986).

Therefore, the effects of maternal depression on child outcomes are worst when it is encountered early and when it endures. In the contexts of adversity, the effects of maternal depression are likely cumulative, following from one phase of child development to the next. Given the biological sequelae of prenatal depression for the infant's neurological development, subsequent exposure to compromised maternal care might be more deleterious. Advances in the study of maternal depression have also drawn attention to the intergenerational nature of maternal depression and its antecedents and sequelae. We noted earlier that maternal childhood adversity predicts the risk for mood disorders in the offspring, such that the effects of adversity are seemingly transmitted to the next generation (Plant et al., 2013). Maternal childhood adversity is associated with child developmental outcomes such as heightened levels of negative emotionality (Bouvette-Turcot et al., 2015), an increased risk for maltreatment (Berlin, Appleyard, & Dodge, 2011), and enhanced vulnerability to psychopathology (Collishaw et al., 2007). Mothers with childhoods characterized by adversity are more likely to be depressed. Maternal depression is a risk factor for child psychopathology (Caspi et al., 2003; Goodman et al., 2011; Weissman et al., 2006, 2005).

In terms of embedding and cascades, the sequelae of maternal depression for child developmental trajectories are numerous. Here, we deal with one possible example to make the point. First, a fetal environment compromised by maternal dysregulation and depression may alter brain development (Qiu et al., 2013). This may then put the child at risk for suboptimal development in its own right (via embedding), which is likely to be compounded if the maternal depression persists into infancy and early childhood. One consequence of maternal depression may be diminished maternal availability, a predisposing factor in suboptimal cognitive development in children (Brilli, Del Boca, & Pronzato, 2016). Early educational difficulty, in turn, predicts later externalizing behavior in children (Masten et al., 2005). In the context of chronic maternal depression, difficult child behavior may be exacerbated, because women who experience depression may have limited emotional resources to devote to the types of invested parenting required to promote positive behavior in their children (Kiernan & Huerta, 2008; Lovejoy et al., 2000; Webster-Stratton & Hammond, 1988). Ultimately, then, via maternal depression both before and after birth, diminished cognitive function, and externalizing behavior, a child born to a perinatally depressed mother might well be set on a path to future difficulties.

Exposure to Violence

Poverty is a predictor of both maternal depression and negative child outcomes, and a risk factor commonly associated with poverty. Violence is an extreme instance of adversity. It comes in many forms (interpersonal, intrafamilial, community, and structural). Community violence is defined as exposure to intentional acts of interpersonal violence committed in public areas by individuals who are not intimately related to the victim (including bullying, gang fighting, shootings, and attacks) (NCTSN). Low-SES environments often have high levels of crime and violence. Children born into lo- SES environments are therefore subject to increased exposure to life-threatening, pernicious environmental stressors, including violence and crime (Duncan, 1984; Duncan & Brooks-Gunn, 1999, 2000; Jargowsky, 1994; Shinn & Gillespie, 1994).

There are few studies from LMIC on the effect on infants and preschool children of exposure to armed conflict or community violence. Children can be exposed to community violence both directly, through victimization, and vicariously, through ambient community danger (Barbarin, Richter, & DeWet, 2001). Children exposed to community violence have higher levels of posttraumatic stress disorder (Magwaza et al., 1993), aggression (Liddell et al., 1994), attention problems, and depression (Barbarin et al., 2001). Ambient community violence is significantly and directly correlated with attention problems, aggression, and anxious depression (Barbarin et al., 2001), whereas victimization (like bullying) is significantly and directly correlated with oppositional behavior (Ford, 2002).

The negative effect of exposure to violence is likely to be increased when family cohesion or the mental health of primary caregivers is disrupted (Barenbaum, Ruchkin, & Schwab-Stone, 2004; Lustig et al., 2004; Shaw, 2003). Maternal distress is significantly associated with higher levels of community danger and family violence (Barbarin et al., 2001). It becomes easy to see how, in contexts of low SES and high violence, child outcomes might be cumulatively affected: Low SES is associated with violence, violence with maternal depression, and violence and maternal depression both with negative child outcomes (Evans & English, 2002; Goodman et al., 2009; Valentine et al., 2011; Westbrook & Harden, 2010).

Animal models have shown how an extreme instance of violence (parental abuse) impairs amygdala development in offspring (Moriceau & Sullivan, 2006). An infant exposed to chronic early stress of this nature experiences greater amygdala reactivity in early childhood (embedding), leading to anxiety resulting from an overactive HPA response. Such anxiety, in turn, predicts internalizing behaviors (such as suicidality and depression) in later childhood (cascades) (Goodwin, Fergusson, & Horwood, 2004). Biological embedding provides a plausible explanation of how differential exposure to harsh environments (often socially stratified) may result in differential health outcomes (Hertzman, 2012).

Human Immunodeficiency Virus

HIV presents a threat to child development in LMIC, particularly in sub-Saharan Africa, which bears a disproportionate burden of the global epidemic (Mathers, 2008). HIV stymies children via three main pathways: through its impact on maternal mental and physical health, through orphanhood, and through its impact on child physical health and development.

Maternal Health

Globally, between 34 and 39.8 million people are living with HIV (WHO, 2016). Of these, about 17.8 million are women of childbearing age, most of whom live in LMIC (Fair & Brackett, 2008). HIV infection greatly threatens parental physical and mental health; mothers, in particular, are at risk for anxiety (Stewart et al., 2008, 2010), depression (Murphy et al., 2002), and posttraumatic stress disorder (Olley et al., 2004). Women with perinatal depression and HIV are less likely to adhere adequately to antiretroviral therapy regimens and are more likely to abuse substances during pregnancy (Kapetanovic et al., 2009), which endangers their child's physical health to a greater degree than if they had either HIV or mental health disorders in isolation. Mental illness in the context of HIV is associated with stigma (Sinyangwe, 2012; Yator et al., 2016), being a single parent (Malee et al., 2014), housing instability (Lichtenstein, Sturdevant, &

Mujumdar, 2010; Sinyangwe, 2012), and a lack of education and family support (Yator et al., 2016).

Orphanhood

Perhaps the worst consequence of familial HIV infection is orphanhood. It has been estimated that 16% of children in HIV-affected families will be orphaned by age 18 years (PEPFAR, 2014). This has its own host of implications for child socioemotional development: for instance, children orphaned by HIV/AIDS or living with a caregiver with HIV/AIDS are at elevated risk for experiencing symptoms of anxiety (Cluver, Gardner, & Operario, 2007), and children orphaned by HIV are at increased risk for depression and posttraumatic stress symptoms (Cluver et al., 2012).

Child Health

More than 95% of HIV-infected children acquire the infection from their mother (Dabis & Ekpini, 2002; UNAIDS/WHO, 2001). Mortality rates among these children are high, especially in sub-Saharan Africa (UNAIDS/WHO, 2001; Spira et al., 1999; Taha et al., 1999). The morbidity of HIV-infected and exposed children has greatly improved since the introduction of highly active antiretroviral therapy (Gortmaker et al., 2001) for the rest of their lives (Dabis & Ekpini, 2002).

Given this improved longevity, the focus in child and adolescent HIV research has shifted from improving physical health outcomes to mental health. Mental health difficulties among children and adolescents with HIV include ADHD, anxiety, and depression (Brouwers et al., 2001, 1995; Brown & Lourie, 2000; Gadow et al., 2010). Many factors may contribute to the emergence of distress and mental health problems, such as postnatal neurotoxicity associated with HIV infection (Mekmullica et al., 2009).

Cumulative Effects

One of the most pernicious sequelae of HIV is its exacerbation of existing disadvantage. HIV in contexts of poverty greatly compromises parental mental health in a cumulative and mutually reinforcing package of risks facing children. HIV in itself may set in motion its own developmental cascade, one which begins with suboptimal brain development during the neonatal period (biological embedding), proceeds through insecure attachment in childhood (via maternal depression), and concludes in a host of problematic behaviors which entrench the cycle of poverty and risk for HIV.

Alcohol Abuse

The effects of alcohol use on child development fall into two broad categories: perinatal exposure, which has consequences for fetal development, and familial or social exposure to adult drinking and its sequelae. Here, we deal primarily with the former. Although outcomes for the child depend on timing, duration, and quantity of alcohol consumption, maternal drinking can and does affect fetal brain development (Marjonen et al., 2015) and pregnancy outcomes (McCarthy et al., 2013), and places the child at risk for fetal alcohol spectrum disorders (FASDs) (May et al., 2013). Evidence linking maternal drinking to FASD is substantial (May et al., 2013). The effects of heavy prenatal alcohol exposure are wide-ranging and devastating. The effects occur on a continuum, and qualitatively similar neuropsychological and behavioral features are seen across the spectrum of effect.

Drinking before pregnancy recognition, and continued drinking during pregnancy, have been associated with younger maternal age, being a single mother, smoking, a greater number of sexual partners, and experiences of intimate partner violence (O'Connor et al., 2011). Other risk factors include drug abuse, cohabiting with an alcoholic male partner, having alcohol-abusing parents, initiating drinking at an early age, and low self-efficacy (Day et al., 1991; Schlesinger, Susman, & Koenigsberg, 1990; Stratton, Howe, & Battaglia, 1996; Wilsnack et al., 1991; Wilsnack & Wilsnack, 1991). Importantly, depressive symptoms tend to be higher among women who drink before and during pregnancy (May et al., 2013; O'Connor et al., 2011).

The outcomes of maternal alcohol consumption during pregnancy vary. One of the most common sequelae of prenatal alcohol exposure is diminished intellectual ability (Abel & Sokol, 1987). The average IQ estimate of individuals with heavy prenatal alcohol exposure is 70 for those with FASD (Streissguth, Barr, & Sampson, 1990) and 80 for those not presenting with physical signs of the disorder (Mattson et al., 1997). Less research has examined intellectual abilities among individuals with lower levels of alcohol exposure (Mattson, Crocker, & Nguyen, 2011), and findings from studies which have been done are mixed (Alati et al., 2008; Fried & Watkinson, 1988; Willford, Leech, & Day, 2006).

In terms of higher-order cognitive processes, executive function is compromised in FASD. Executive function is extremely vulnerable to alcohol exposure in utero (Fryer et al., 2007); alcohol-exposed children experience delays with problem solving (Aragón et al., 2008), planning (Green et al., 2009), concept formation (McGee et al., 2008), and response inhibition (Burden et al., 2009). Children exposed to alcohol in the prenatal period may also experience deficits in language (Russell et al., 1991), deficits in attention (Burden, Jacobson, & Jacobson, 2005; Streissguth et al., 1986), and hyperactivity (Hanson, Jones, & Smith, 1976; O'Malley & Nanson, 2002), as well as a variety of difficulties and delays in motor function (Kalberg et al., 2006; Simmons et al., 2010; Wass et al., 2002).

TRAJECTORIES OF HUMAN DEVELOPMENT

For children living in contexts marked by adversity such as those outlined previously, the risk for negative developmental outcomes is substantial. Internalizing and externalizing behaviors, mental health disorders, violence perpetration, delayed cognitive development, peer problems, and compromised physical development may all result, each leading to a subsequent set of suboptimal outcomes, entrenching cycles of poverty, and morbidity in at-risk communities. Here we deal briefly with two major developmental cascade models (externalizing and internalizing behavior) that have gained prominence (Masten et al., 2005; Moilanen, Shaw, & Maxwell, 2010).

Externalizing problems in childhood (such as violence and aggression) undermine academic competence in adolescence. Children who are disruptive in class, for instance, are more likely to struggle academically. On the other hand, diminished competence in the early years of school is associated with internalizing problems (such as depression and suicidality) in young adulthood. The existence of these two temporal associations suggests the presence of a cascade effect (Masten et al., 2005). Masten and Roisman (Masten et al., 2005) showed how high levels of externalizing problems in early childhood were associated with both low levels of academic competence and high levels of internalizing problems during the early school-age period, and with elevations in internalizing problems during the transition to adolescence (Masten et al., 2005).

The most prominent explanatory theory in this regard, the adjustment erosion hypothesis, posits that initial externalizing symptoms reduce later academic competence, and that this increases future vulnerability to symptoms in other domains (Moilanen et al., 2010). In the case of a child with initial externalizing problems (for instance, hyperactivity), capacity for engagement in learning in the classroom is limited, which impedes academic performance (Chen, Rubin, & Li, 1997; Masten & Cicchetti, 2010; Masten et al., 2005). This may then engender disinterest in school, further reducing academic achievement (Chen et al., 1997; Schwartz et al., 2006), which negatively affects self-esteem, ultimately leading to depression.

Recall, briefly, the risk factors for externalizing behavior in early childhood: fetal alcohol syndrome, maternal substance abuse, and violence in the home. Consider the embedding of risk for early childhood attention-deficit disorder, for instance, which may occur when a mother consumes alcohol in the prenatal period and the child's developing brain is affected (Burden et al., 2005; Jacobson et al., 1993; Streissguth et al., 1986). Such a child may easily fall into this developmental trajectory, resulting in a fraught school career and stormy adolescence, as each developmental period is marked by the negative sequelae of that which preceded it. Taking this perspective further back, consider the risk factors that might lead a mother to drink during her pregnancy, such as poverty, spousal abuse, and maternal depression. Focusing on maternal depression, the intergenerational transmission of negative outcomes via embedding and cascade effects becomes apparent. The same adolescent or young adult experiencing internalizing symptoms as the result of academic failure, preceded by externalizing symptoms in childhood, preceded by maternal alcohol use during childhood, may go on to become a mother who drinks during pregnancy, therefore transmitting disadvantage to the next generation (Fig. 6.1).

There are also models suggesting that initial internalizing problems might lead to later academic difficulties or externalizing problems. Children with anxiety in early childhood, for instance, may go on to experience difficulties at school, which may lead to truancy, rebelliousness, and externalizing behavior in adolescence. Internalizing symptoms may undermine academic competence by eroding cognitive functioning (Maughan et al., 2003).

However, internalizing symptoms may also interfere with attentional focus and participation during class (Roeser, Eccles, & Sameroff, 2000). In this scenario, an adolescent with aggression may be traced back in developmental sequence to a child with anxiety resulting from dysregulation of the HPA axis, resulting from a mother with depression and anxiety during pregnancy. Maternal depression and anxiety during pregnancy, which embed risk, are in turn caused by their own host of risk factors, such as poverty, or experiencing intimate partner violence. If the child displaying externalizing behavior (say, aggression) were a boy who went on to perpetrate violence against his pregnant wife later in life, their

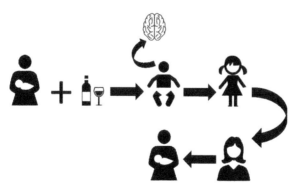

FIGURE 6.1   Maternal alcohol use during pregnancy, resulting in diminished attentional capacity in infancy. This results in externalizing behavior in early childhood, predisposing the individual to subsequent internalizing behavior in adolescence. If this child is female, she may then go on to consume alcohol during pregnancy, thus continuing the cycle of suboptimal development.

unborn child might experience the same developmental trajectory as his or her father (Fig. 6.2).

IMPLICATIONS FOR INTERVENTION

Progress in our understanding of developmental trajectories in contexts of adversity must necessarily constitute an impetus for change. Distilling implications for intervention from the foregoing discussion results in a clear set of guidelines for intervention programming.

If trajectories are to be altered, the starting point must be altered. The first 1000 days of a child's life is a critical window of opportunity during which nutrition, parenting, and health interventions will have the greatest impact on children's long-term trajectories (Department of Health, 2016; Martorell, 2013). Maternal and child health, and education interventions need to occur as early as possible (preferably before conception), to have the best effect.

However, the first 1000 days of life is not the only developmental period in which exposure to adversity can result in harm; and (if children are to be steered onto positive developmental courses) sustained "top-up" interventions and sustaining environments must be encountered over the life course. As noted, there are numerous mediating and moderating factors in the relationship between the adversities faced by a child and negative outcomes, and these are important points of intervention. The most salient mediators of the relationship between adversity and child outcomes vary across time, and sequential interventions should recognize

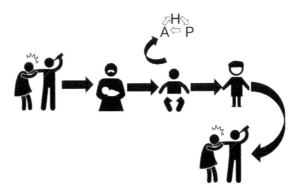

FIGURE 6.2   Maternal depression and anxiety during pregnancy, stemming from intimate partner violence perpetrated by her partner, may result in dysregulation of the infant's hypothalamic–pituitary–adrenal axis (HPA) function in infancy and early childhood. This, in turn, leads to internalizing behavior in early childhood, educational failure, and subsequent aggression in this example. This child may then go on to perpetrate violence against his intimate partner, thus continuing the cycle of suboptimal development.

this: In infancy, maternal attentiveness is important; in early childhood, parenting behavior; and in adolescence, positive peer groups. The developmental literature discussed earlier can inform interventions across the life course, as well. The concept of embedding points to the need to intervene early, and the idea of developmental cascades highlights the necessity of thinking about intervention with a life course perspective; programs should target phenomena that set in motion problematic cascades.

Despite the pervasiveness of many of the risks and stressors outlined in this chapter, however, not all exposed individuals require intervention support. There is a scarcity of resources with which to intervene in LMIC settings in which much adversity is encountered. To optimize these resources, a combination of lightweight, broad-based universal interventions and sustained, resource-intensive targeted interventions is necessary. Universal approaches might entail health promotion and awareness media campaigns, which chip away at the social factors that drive negative child outcomes (eg, intimate partner violence or a culture of alcohol use) (Harvey, Garcia-Moreno, & Butchart, 2007; Kyskan & Moore, 2005). More resource-intensive, targeted interventions could then be aimed at those most at risk. These include stepped-care approaches to health promotion, in which individuals who screen positive for mental health disorders, for instance, are enrolled into low-intensity and relatively brief evidence-based treatment (van Straten et al., 2015). However, if their distress or dysfunction proves to be severe and is not ameliorated by such treatment, they are "stepped up" into a higher tier of care (a treatment of higher intensity) (van Straten et al., 2015). This ensures that resources are invested on an "as-needed" basis, rather than applied in a blanket fashion where they may not be needed.

Finally, in addition to both of these types of interventions, efforts should be made to address the structural drivers of adversity and its sequelae. As discussed at the beginning of this chapter, poverty increases the likelihood of a host of other risks and thus negative child outcomes. Interventions targeting the structural drivers of poverty, violence, and mental disorders will complement other health promotion and disease prevention efforts. Such structural interventions include microfinance for mothers (DeLoach & Lamanna, 2011; Maldonado & González-Vega, 2008), conditional and unconditional cash transfers for families (Fernald, Gertler, & Neufeld, 2008, 2009; Gertler, 2004), and housing support for families (Leventhal & Newman, 2010; Meyers et al., 2005). Because structural risks place children at risk, but are largely beyond their caregivers' control, inequities in health will endure if these are not addressed. Conversely, if the structural drivers of health inequalities are dismantled, a foundation will have been laid upon which to build subsequent efforts at health promotion.

CONCLUSION

Adversity can weaken the developing architecture of the individual's brain and permanently set the body and mind on a negative developmental course. When an individual experiences toxic stress (adversity, poverty, abuse, and/or neglect) early in life, it can wreak cumulative havoc on that individual's physical and mental health. This relationship is proportionate, and the more (in number or severity) adverse the experiences are in childhood, the greater the likelihood is of negative developmental outcomes. Adults who experience more adversity in early childhood are more likely to have health problems, including substance abuse disorders, mental disorders, heart disease, and diabetes. The mechanisms posited to underlie many of these outcomes are biological embedding and developmental cascades.

The roots of health and illness, as well as inequality in outcomes between and within populations, lie in our earliest experiences and environments. What happens in early childhood will have repercussions for the individual that last a lifetime. To address inequalities successfully, it is essential to intervene with children when they are young. Providing stable, responsive, nurturing relationships and stimulating environments to children in their earliest years can prevent or even reverse the damaging effects of early adversity. First, we need to understand what types of adversity lead to what types of effects, and when and how. This chapter presents accumulated knowledge pertinent to thinking about child developmental trajectories in the context of adversity.

References

Abel, E. L., & Sokol, R. J. (1987). Incidence of fetal alcohol syndrome and economic impact of FAS-related anomalies. *Drug and Alcohol Dependence, 19*(1), 51−70.

Aizer, A., & Currie, J. (2014). The intergenerational transmission of inequality: Maternal disadvantage and health at birth. *Science, 344*(6186), 856−861.

Alati, R., et al. (2008). The developmental origin of adolescent alcohol use: Findings from the Mater University Study of Pregnancy and its outcomes. *Drug and Alcohol Dependence, 98*(1), 136−143.

Aragón, A. S., et al. (2008). Neuropsychological study of FASD in a sample of American Indian children: Processing simple versus complex information. *Alcoholism: Clinical and Experimental Research, 32*(12), 2136−2148.

Backlund, E., Sorlie, P. D., & Johnson, N. J. (1996). The shape of the relationship between income and mortality in the United States: Evidence from the National Longitudinal Mortality Study. *Annals of Epidemiology, 6*(1), 12−20.

Barbarin, O. A., Richter, L., & DeWet, T. (2001). Exposure to violence, coping resources, and psychological adjustment of South African children. *American Journal of Orthopsychiatry, 71*(1), 16.

Barenbaum, J., Ruchkin, V., & Schwab-Stone, M. (2004). The psychosocial aspects of children exposed to war: Practice and policy initiatives. *Journal of Child Psychology and Psychiatry, 45*(1), 41−62.

Belsky, J. (1997). Theory testing, effect-size evaluation, and differential susceptibility to rearing influence: The case of mothering and attachment. *Child Development, 68*(4), 598–600.

Belsky, J. (2005). Differential susceptibility to rearing influence: An evolutionary hypothesis and some evidence. In B. J. Ellis, & D. F. Bjorklund (Eds.), *Origins of the social mind: Evolutionary psychology and child development* (pp. 139–163). New York, NY, US: Guilford Press.

Belsky, J., Bakermans-Kranenburg, M. J., & Van IJzendoorn, M. H. (2007). For better and for worse: Differential susceptibility to environmental influences. *Current Directions in Psychological Science, 16*(6), 300–304.

Belsky, J., et al. (2007). Socioeconomic risk, parenting during the preschool years and child health age 6 years. *The European Journal of Public Health, 17*(5), 508–513.

Bergman, K., et al. (2007). Maternal stress during pregnancy predicts cognitive ability and fearfulness in infancy. *Journal of the American Academy of Child and Adolescent Psychiatry, 46*(11), 1454–1463.

Berlin, L. J., Appleyard, K., & Dodge, K. A. (2011). Intergenerational continuity in child maltreatment: Mediating mechanisms and implications for prevention. *Child Development, 82*(1), 162–176.

Biratu, A., & Haile, D. (2015). Prevalence of antenatal depression and associated factors among pregnant women in Addis Ababa, Ethiopia: A cross-sectional study. *Reproductive Health, 12*(1), 99.

Bloom, B. S. (1964). *Stability and change in human characteristics.* Wiley Online Library.

Bornstein, M. H., Hahn, C.-S., & Haynes, O. M. (2010). Social competence, externalizing, and internalizing behavioral adjustment from early childhood through early adolescence: Developmental cascades. *Development and Psychopathology, 22*(4), 717–735.

Bouvette-Turcot, A. A., et al. (2015). Maternal childhood adversity and child temperament: An association moderated by child 5-HTTLPR genotype. *Genes, Brain and Behavior, 14*(3), 229–237.

Boyce, W. T., & Ellis, B. J. (2005). Biological sensitivity to context: I. An evolutionary–developmental theory of the origins and functions of stress reactivity. *Development and Psychopathology, 17*(2), 271–301.

Brilli, Y., Del Boca, D., & Pronzato, C. D. (2016). Does child care availability play a role in maternal employment and children's development? Evidence from Italy. *Review of Economics of the Household, 14*(1), 27–51.

Brooks-Gunn, J., & Duncan, G. J. (1997). The effects of poverty on children. *The Future of Children,* 55–71.

Brooks-Gunn, J., et al. (1993). Do neighborhoods influence child and adolescent development? *American Journal of Sociology, 99*(2), 353–395.

Brouwers, P., et al. (1995). Correlation between computed tomographic brain scan abnormalities and neuropsychological function in children with symptomatic human immunodeficiency virus disease. *Archives of Neurology, 52*(1), 39–44.

Brouwers, E. P., van Baar, A. L., & Pop, V. J. (2001). Maternal anxiety during pregnancy and subsequent infant development. *Infant Behavior and Development, 24*(1), 95–106.

Brown, L. K., & Lourie, K. J. (2000). Children and adolescents living with HIV and AIDS: A review. *The Journal of Child Psychology and Psychiatry and Allied Disciplines, 41*(1), 81–96.

Burden, M. J., et al. (2009). The effects of fetal alcohol syndrome on response execution and inhibition: An event-related potential study. *Alcoholism: Clinical and Experimental Research, 33*(11), 1994–2004.

Burden, M. J., Jacobson, S. W., & Jacobson, J. L. (2005). Relation of prenatal alcohol exposure to cognitive processing speed and efficiency in childhood. *Alcoholism: Clinical and Experimental Research, 29*(8), 1473–1483.

Burt, K. B., et al. (2008). The interplay of social competence and psychopathology over 20 years: Testing transactional and cascade models. *Child Development, 79*(2), 359–374.

Cameron, N. M., et al. (2005). The programming of individual differences in defensive responses and reproductive strategies in the rat through variations in maternal care. *Neuroscience and Biobehavioral Reviews, 29*(4), 843–865.

Capaldi, D. M., & Stoolmiller, M. (1999). Co-occurrence of conduct problems and depressive symptoms in early adolescent boys: III. Prediction to young-adult adjustment. *Development and Psychopathology, 11*(1), 59–84.

Caspi, A., et al. (2003). Influence of life stress on depression: Moderation by a polymorphism in the 5-HTT gene. *Science, 301*(5631), 386–389.

Caughy, M. O. B., O'Campo, P. J., & Muntaner, C. (2003). When being alone might be better: Neighborhood poverty, social capital, and child mental health. *Social Science and Medicine, 57*(2), 227–237.

Champagne, F. A. (2008). Epigenetic mechanisms and the transgenerational effects of maternal care. *Frontiers in Neuroendocrinology, 29*(3), 386–397.

Champagne, F. A., & Curley, J. P. (2009). Epigenetic mechanisms mediating the long-term effects of maternal care on development. *Neuroscience and Biobehavioral Reviews, 33*(4), 593–600.

Chen, X., Rubin, K. H., & Li, D. (1997). Relation between academic achievement and social adjustment: Evidence from Chinese children. *Developmental Psychology, 33*(3), 518.

Cicchetti, D., & Cannon, T. D. (1999). Neurodevelopmental processes in the ontogenesis and epigenesis of psychopathology. *Development and Psychopathology, 11*(3), 375–393.

Cluver, L. D., et al. (2012). AIDS-orphanhood and caregiver HIV/AIDS sickness status: Effects on psychological symptoms in South African youth. *Journal of Pediatric Psychology, 37*(8), 857–867.

Cluver, L., Gardner, F., & Operario, D. (2007). Psychological distress amongst AIDS-orphaned children in urban South Africa. *Journal of Child Psychology and Psychiatry, 48*(8), 755–763.

Cogill, S., et al. (1986). Impact of maternal postnatal depression on cognitive development of young children. *British Medical Journal (Clinical Research Ed.), 292*(6529), 1165–1167.

Collishaw, S., et al. (2007). Maternal childhood abuse and offspring adjustment over time. *Development and Psychopathology, 19*(02), 367–383.

Cooper, P. J., et al. (2009). Improving quality of mother-infant relationship and infant attachment in socioeconomically deprived community in South Africa: Randomised controlled trial. *BMJ, 338*, b974.

Coplan, J. D., et al. (2001). Variable foraging demand rearing: Sustained elevations in cisternal cerebrospinal fluid corticotropin-releasing factor concentrations in adult primates. *Biological Psychiatry, 50*(3), 200–204.

Dabis, F., & Ekpini, E. R. (2002). HIV-1/AIDS and maternal and child health in Africa. *The Lancet, 359*(9323), 2097–2104.

Davis, E. P., et al. (2007). Prenatal exposure to maternal depression and cortisol influences infant temperament. *Journal of the American Academy of Child and Adolescent Psychiatry, 46*(6), 737–746.

Day, N. L., et al. (1991). The effects of prenatal alcohol use on the growth of children at three years of age. *Alcoholism: Clinical and Experimental Research, 15*(1), 67–71.

Deave, T., et al. (2008). The impact of maternal depression in pregnancy on early child development. *BJOG: An International Journal of Obstetrics and Gynaecology, 115*(8), 1043–1051.

DeLoach, S. B., & Lamanna, E. (2011). Measuring the impact of microfinance on child health outcomes in Indonesia. *World Development, 39*(10), 1808–1819.

Diego, M. A., et al. (2009). Prenatal depression restricts fetal growth. *Early Human Development, 85*(1), 65–70.

Dieter, N. I., Field, T., Hernandez-Reif, M., Jones, N. A., Lecanuet, J. P., Salman, F. A., et al. (2001). Maternal depression and increased fetal activity. *Journal of Obstetrics and Gynaecology, 21*(5), 468–473.

DiPietro, J. A., et al. (2008). Fetal responses to induced maternal relaxation during pregnancy. *Biological Psychology, 77*(1), 11–19.

Dodge, K. A., et al. (2009). A dynamic cascade model of the development of substance-use onset. *Monographs of the Society for Research in Child Development, 74*(3), vii–119.

Dodge, K. A., & Pettit, G. S. (2003). A biopsychosocial model of the development of chronic conduct problems in adolescence. *Developmental Psychology, 39*(2), 349.

Dodge, K. A., Pettit, G. S., & Bates, J. E. (1994). Socialization mediators of the relation between socioeconomic status and child conduct problems. *Child Development,* 649–665.

DoH, Department of Health. (2016). In D. O. Health (Ed.), *Western Cape Government introduces first 1000 days campaign.* Western Cape.

Duncan, G. J. (1984). Years of poverty years of plenty. *The Wilson Quarterly,* 44.

Duncan, G. J., & Brooks-Gunn, J. (1999). *Consequences of growing up poor.* Russell Sage Foundation.

Duncan, G. J., & Brooks-Gunn, J. (2000). Family poverty, welfare reform, and child development. *Child Development, 71*(1), 188–196.

Duncan, G. J., et al. (1998). How much does childhood poverty affect the life chances of children? *American Sociological Review,* 406–423.

Edwards, B., et al. (2008). Does antenatal screening for psychosocial risk factors predict postnatal depression? A follow-up study of 154 women in Adelaide, South Australia. *Australian and New Zealand Journal of Psychiatry, 42*(1), 51–55.

Elder, G. H. (1998). The life course as developmental theory. *Child Development, 69*(1), 1–12.

Ellis, B. J., et al. (2011). Differential susceptibility to the environment: An evolutionary–neurodevelopmental theory. *Development and Psychopathology, 23*(01), 7–28.

Evans, G. W., & English, K. (2002). The environment of poverty: Multiple stressor exposure, psychophysiological stress, and socioemotional adjustment. *Child Development, 73*(4), 1238–1248.

Evans, J., et al. (2007). Depressive symptoms during pregnancy and low birth weight at term. *The British Journal of Psychiatry, 191*(1), 84–85.

Evans, G. W., & Kim, P. (2013). Childhood poverty, chronic stress, self-regulation, and coping. *Child Development Perspectives, 7*(1), 43–48.

Evans, G. W., & Schamberg, M. A. (2009). Childhood poverty, chronic stress, and adult working memory. *Proceedings of the National Academy of Sciences, 106*(16), 6545–6549.

Fair, C., & Brackett, B. (2008). "I don't want to sit by you": A preliminary study of experiences and consequences of stigma and discrimination from HIV-positive mothers and their children. *Journal of HIV/AIDs Prevention in Children and Youth, 9*(2), 219–242.

Felitti, V. J., et al. (1998). Relationship of childhood abuse and household dysfunction to many of the leading causes of death in adults: The Adverse Childhood Experiences (ACE) Study. *American Journal of Preventive Medicine, 14*(4), 245–258.

Fernald, L. C., Gertler, P. J., & Neufeld, L. M. (2008). Role of cash in conditional cash transfer programmes for child health, growth, and development: An analysis of Mexico's Oportunidades. *The Lancet, 371*(9615), 828–837.

Fernald, L. C., Gertler, P. J., & Neufeld, L. M. (2009). 10-year effect of Oportunidades, Mexico's conditional cash transfer programme, on child growth, cognition, language, and behaviour: A longitudinal follow-up study. *The Lancet, 374*(9706), 1997–2005.

Field, T. (2011). Prenatal depression effects on early development: A review. *Infant Behavior and Development, 34*(1), 1–14.

Field, T., et al. (2004). Prenatal depression effects on the fetus and the newborn. *Infant Behavior and Development, 27*(2), 216–229.

Ford, J. D. (2002). Traumatic victimization in childhood and persistent problems with oppositional-defiance. *Journal of Aggression, Maltreatment and Trauma, 6*(1), 25–58.

Ford, D. H., & Lerner, R. M. (1992). *Developmental systems theory: An integrative approach.* Sage Publications, Inc.

Fried, P., & Watkinson, B. (1988). 12-and 24-month neurobehavioural follow-up of children prenatally exposed to marihuana, cigarettes and alcohol. *Neurotoxicology and Teratology, 10*(4), 305–313.

Fryer, S. L., et al. (2007). Prenatal alcohol exposure affects frontal–striatal BOLD response during inhibitory control. *Alcoholism: Clinical and Experimental Research, 31*(8), 1415–1424.

Gadow, K. D., et al. (2010). Co-occurring psychiatric symptoms in children perinatally infected with HIV and peer comparison sample. *Journal of Developmental and Behavioral Pediatrics, 31*(2), 116.

Gardner, J. M. M., et al. (1999). Behaviour and development of stunted and nonstunted Jamaican children. *Journal of Child Psychology and Psychiatry, 40*(5), 819–827.

Gaylor, E. E., et al. (2005). A longitudinal follow-up study of young children's sleep patterns using a developmental classification system. *Behavioral Sleep Medicine, 3*(1), 44–61.

Gertler, P. (2004). Do conditional cash transfers improve child health? Evidence from PRO-GRESA's control randomized experiment. *The American Economic Review, 94*(2), 336–341.

Gianaros, P. J., et al. (2007). Perigenual anterior cingulate morphology covaries with perceived social standing. *Social Cognitive and Affective Neuroscience, 2*(3), 161–173.

Gianaros, P. J., et al. (2008). Potential neural embedding of parental social standing. *Social Cognitive and Affective Neuroscience, 3*(2), 91–96.

Goodman, L. A., et al. (2009). When crises collide: How intimate partner violence and poverty intersect to shape women's mental health and coping? *Trauma, Violence, and Abuse, 10*(4), 306–329.

Goodman, S. H., et al. (2011). Maternal depression and child psychopathology: A meta-analytic review. *Clinical Child and Family Psychology Review, 14*(1), 1–27.

Goodwin, R. D., Fergusson, D. M., & Horwood, L. J. (2004). Early anxious/withdrawn behaviours predict later internalising disorders. *Journal of Child Psychology and Psychiatry, 45*(4), 874–883.

Gortmaker, S. L., et al. (2001). Effect of combination therapy including protease inhibitors on mortality among children and adolescents infected with HIV-1. *New England Journal of Medicine, 345*(21), 1522–1528.

Gottlieb, G. (2007). Probabilistic epigenesis. *Developmental Science, 10*(1), 1–11.

Gottlieb, G., Wahlsten, D., & Lickliter, R. (1998). The significance of biology for human development: A developmental psychobiological systems view. In *Handbook of child psychology.*

Granger, D. A. (1998). Children's salivary cortisol, internalising behaviour problems, and family environment: Results from the Concordia Longitudinal Risk Project. *International Journal of Behavioral Development, 22*(4), 707–728.

Green, C., et al. (2009). Executive function deficits in children with fetal alcohol spectrum disorders (FASD) measured using the Cambridge Neuropsychological Tests Automated Battery (CANTAB). *Journal of Child Psychology and Psychiatry, 50*(6), 688–697.

Grote, N. K., et al. (2010). A meta-analysis of depression during pregnancy and the risk of preterm birth, low birth weight, and intrauterine growth restriction. *Archives of General Psychiatry, 67*(10), 1012–1024.

Gruber, R., Sadeh, A., & Raviv, A. (2000). Instability of sleep patterns in children with attention-deficit/hyperactivity disorder. *Journal of the American Academy of Child and Adolescent Psychiatry, 39*(4), 495–501.

Gutteling, B. M., de Weerth, C., & Buitelaar, J. K. (2005). Prenatal stress and children's cortisol reaction to the first day of school. *Psychoneuroendocrinology, 30*(6), 541–549.

Hanson, J. L., et al. (2011). Association between income and the hippocampus. *PLoS One, 6*(5), e18712.

Hanson, D. R., & Gottesman, I. I. (2007). Choreographing genetic, epigenetic, and stochastic steps in the dances of developmental psychopathology. In *Multilevel dynamics in developmental psychopathology: Pathways to the future. Minnesota symposia on child psychology.*

Hanson, J. W., Jones, K. L., & Smith, D. W. (1976). Fetal alcohol syndrome: Experience with 41 patients. *JAMA, 235*(14), 1458–1460.

Hartley, M., et al. (2011). Depressed mood in pregnancy: Prevalence and correlates in two Cape Town peri-urban settlements. *Reproductive Health, 8*(1), 9.

Hartman, C. A., et al. (2013). Self-or parent report of (co-occurring) internalizing and externalizing problems, and basal or reactivity measures of HPA-axis functioning: A systematic evaluation of the internalizing-hyperresponsivity versus externalizing-hyporesponsivity HPA-axis hypothesis. *Biological Psychology, 94*(1), 175–184.

Hart, B., & Risley, T. R. (1995). *Meaningful differences in the everyday experience of young American children*. Paul H Brookes Publishing.

Harvey, A., Garcia-Moreno, C., & Butchart, A. (2007). In *Primary prevention of intimate-partner violence and sexual violence: Background paper for WHO expert meeting May 2–3, 2007*. Geneva: World Health Organization, Department of Violence and Injury Prevention and Disability.

Hertzman, C. (2012). Putting the concept of biological embedding in historical perspective. *Proceedings of the National Academy of Sciences, 109*(Suppl. 2), 17160–17167.

Hertzman, C., et al. (2001). Using an interactive framework of society and lifecourse to explain self-rated health in early adulthood. *Social Science and Medicine, 53*(12), 1575–1585.

Hertzman, C., & Power, C. (2003). Health and human development: Understandings from life-course research. *Developmental Neuropsychology, 24*(2–3), 719–744.

Hinshaw, S. P. (2002). Process, mechanism, and explanation related to externalizing behavior in developmental psychopathology. *Journal of Abnormal Child Psychology, 30*(5), 431–446.

Hoff, E., et al. (2002). Socioeconomic status and parenting. In *Handbook of parenting Volume 2: Biology and ecology of parenting* (Vol. 8(2), pp. 231–252).

Huizink, A. C., et al. (2003). Stress during pregnancy is associated with developmental outcome in infancy. *Journal of Child Psychology and Psychiatry, 44*(6), 810–818.

Isgor, C., et al. (2004). Delayed effects of chronic variable stress during peripubertal-juvenile period on hippocampal morphology and on cognitive and stress axis functions in rats. *Hippocampus, 14*(5), 636–648.

Jacobson, S. W., et al. (1993). Prenatal alcohol exposure and infant information processing ability. *Child Development, 64*(6), 1706–1721.

Jargowsky, P. A. (1994). Ghetto poverty among blacks in the 1980s. *Journal of Policy Analysis and Management, 13*(2), 288–310.

Kaaya, S., et al. (2010). Socio-economic and partner relationship factors associated with antenatal depressive morbidity among pregnant women in Dar es Salaam, Tanzania. *Tanzania Journal of Health Research, 12*(1), 23–35.

Kalberg, W. O., et al. (2006). Comparison of motor delays in young children with fetal alcohol syndrome to those with prenatal alcohol exposure and with no prenatal alcohol exposure. *Alcoholism: Clinical and Experimental Research, 30*(12), 2037–2045.

Kapetanovic, S., et al. (2009). Correlates of perinatal depression in HIV-infected women. *AIDS Patient Care and STDs, 23*(2), 101–108.

Kiernan, K. E., & Huerta, M. C. (2008). Economic deprivation, maternal depression, parenting and children's cognitive and emotional development in early childhood. *The British Journal of Sociology, 59*(4), 783–806.

Kishiyama, M. M., et al. (2009). Socioeconomic disparities affect prefrontal function in children. *Journal of Cognitive Neuroscience, 21*(6), 1106–1115.

Kurstjens, S., & Wolke, D. (2001). Effects of maternal depression on cognitive development of children over the first 7 years of life. *Journal of Child Psychology and Psychiatry, 42*(5), 623–636.

Kyskan, C. E., & Moore, T. E. (2005). Global perspectives on fetal alcohol syndrome: Assessing practices, policies, and campaigns in four English-speaking countries. *Canadian Psychology/Psychologie Canadienne, 46*(3), 153.

Lantz, P. M., et al. (1998). Socioeconomic factors, health behaviors, and mortality: Results from a nationally representative prospective study of us adults. *JAMA, 279*(21), 1703–1708.

Leventhal, T., & Newman, S. (2010). Housing and child development. *Children and Youth Services Review, 32*(9), 1165–1174.

Levine, S., et al. (1967). Physiological and behavioral effects of infantile stimulation. *Physiology and Behavior, 2*(1), 55–59.

Lichtenstein, B., Sturdevant, M. S., & Mujumdar, A. A. (2010). Psychosocial stressors of families affected by HIV/AIDS: Implications for social work practice. *Journal of HIV/AIDs and Social Services, 9*(2), 130–152.

Liddell, C., et al. (1994). Community violence and young South African children's involvement in aggression. *International Journal of Behavioral Development, 17*(4), 613–628.

Li, D., Liu, L., & Odouli, R. (2009). Presence of depressive symptoms during early pregnancy and the risk of preterm delivery: A prospective cohort study. *Human Reproduction, 24*(1), 146–153.

Liu, X., et al. (2005). Sleep patterns and sleep problems among schoolchildren in the United States and China. *Pediatrics, 115*(Suppl. 1), 241–249.

Loscalzo, J., & Handy, D. E. (2014). Epigenetic modifications: Basic mechanisms and role in cardiovascular disease (2013 Grover conference series). *Pulmonary Circulation, 4*(2), 169–174.

Lovejoy, M. C., et al. (2000). Maternal depression and parenting behavior: A meta-analytic review. *Clinical Psychology Review, 20*(5), 561–592.

Luoma, I., et al. (2001). Longitudinal study of maternal depressive symptoms and child well-being. *Journal of the American Academy of Child and Adolescent Psychiatry, 40*(12), 1367–1374.

Luo, Y., & Waite, L. J. (2005). The impact of childhood and adult SES on physical, mental, and cognitive well-being in later life. *The Journals of Gerontology Series B: Psychological Sciences and Social Sciences, 60*(2), S93–S101.

Lustig, S. L., et al. (2004). Review of child and adolescent refugee mental health. *Journal of the American Academy of Child and Adolescent Psychiatry, 43*(1), 24–36.

Magwaza, A., et al. (1993). The effects of chronic violence on preschool children living in South African townships. *Child Abuse and Neglect, 17*(6), 795–803.

Maldonado, J. H., & González-Vega, C. (2008). Impact of microfinance on schooling: Evidence from poor rural households in Bolivia. *World Development, 36*(11), 2440–2455.

Malee, K., et al. (2014). Prevalence, incidence and persistence of psychiatric and substance use disorders among mothers living with HIV. *Journal of Acquired Immune Deficiency Syndromes (1999), 65*(5), 526.

Manikkam, L., & Burns, J. K. (2012). Antenatal depression and its risk factors: An urban prevalence study in KwaZulu-Natal. *South African Medical Journal, 102*(12), 940–944.

Marjonen, H., et al. (2015). Early maternal alcohol consumption alters hippocampal DNA methylation, gene expression and volume in a mouse model. *PLoS One, 10*(5), e0124931.

Martinez-Torteya, C., et al. (2016). The influence of prenatal intimate partner violence exposure on hypothalamic–pituitary–adrenal axis reactivity and childhood internalizing and externalizing symptoms. *Development and Psychopathology, 28*(1), 55–72.

Martorell, R. (2013). The first 1000 days and human development: Implications for India. *Bulletin of the Nutrition Foundation of India, 34*(3).

Masten, A. S., Burt, K. B., & Coatsworth, J. D. (2006). *Competence and psychopathology in development*.

Masten, A. S., & Cicchetti, D. (2010). Developmental cascades. *Development and Psychopathology, 22*(3), 491–495.

Masten, A. S., et al. (2005). Developmental cascades: Linking academic achievement and externalizing and internalizing symptoms over 20 years. *Developmental Psychology, 41*(5), 733.

Mathers, C. (2008). *The global burden of disease: 2004 update.* World Health Organization.

Mattson, S. N., Crocker, N., & Nguyen, T. T. (2011). Fetal alcohol spectrum disorders: Neuropsychological and behavioral features. *Neuropsychology Review, 21*(2), 81–101.

Mattson, S. N., et al. (1997). Heavy prenatal alcohol exposure with or without physical features of fetal alcohol syndrome leads to IQ deficits. *The Journal of Pediatrics, 131*(5), 718–721.

Maughan, B., et al. (2003). Reading problems and depressed mood. *Journal of Abnormal Child Psychology, 31*(2), 219–229.

May, P. A., et al. (2013). Maternal alcohol consumption producing fetal alcohol spectrum disorders (FASD): Quantity, frequency, and timing of drinking. *Drug and Alcohol Dependence, 133*(2), 502–512.

McCarthy, F. P., et al. (2013). Association between maternal alcohol consumption in early pregnancy and pregnancy outcomes. *Obstetrics and Gynecology, 122*(4), 830–837.

McEwen, B. S. (2012). Brain on stress: How the social environment gets under the skin. *Proceedings of the National Academy of Sciences, 109*(Suppl. 2), 17180–17185.

McGee, C. L., et al. (2008). Children with heavy prenatal alcohol exposure demonstrate deficits on multiple measures of concept formation. *Alcoholism: Clinical and Experimental Research, 32*(8), 1388–1397.

McGrath, J. M., Records, K., & Rice, M. (2008). Maternal depression and infant temperament characteristics. *Infant Behavior and Development, 31*(1), 71–80.

McLeod, J. D., & Shanahan, M. J. (1993). Poverty, parenting, and children's mental health. *American Sociological Review,* 351–366.

Meaney, M. J., & Szyf, M. (2005). Environmental programming of stress responses through DNA methylation: Life at the interface between a dynamic environment and a fixed genome. *Dialogues in Clinical Neuroscience, 7*(2), 103.

Mekmullica, J., et al. (2009). Early immunological predictors of neurodevelopmental outcomes in HIV-infected children. *Clinical Infectious Diseases, 48*(3), 338–346.

Meyers, A., et al. (2005). Subsidized housing and children's nutritional status: Data from a multisite surveillance study. *Archives of Pediatrics and Adolescent Medicine, 159*(6), 551–556.

Milgrom, J., et al. (2008). Antenatal risk factors for postnatal depression: A large prospective study. *Journal of Affective Disorders, 108*(1), 147–157.

Moffitt, T. E., et al. (2002). Males on the life-course-persistent and adolescence-limited antisocial pathways: Follow-up at age 26 years. *Development and Psychopathology, 14*(1), 179–207.

Moilanen, K. L., Shaw, D. S., & Maxwell, K. L. (2010). Developmental cascades: Externalizing, internalizing, and academic competence from middle childhood to early adolescence. *Development and Psychopathology, 22*(3), 635–653.

Morgan, B., et al. (2017). Serotonin transporter gene (SLC6A4) polymorphism and susceptibility to a home-visiting maternal-infant attachment intervention delivered by community health workers in South Africa: Reanalysis of a randomized controlled trial. *PLoS Medicine, 14*(2), e1002237.

Moriceau, S., & Sullivan, R. M. (2006). Maternal presence serves as a switch between learning fear and attraction in infancy. *Nature Neuroscience, 9*(8), 1004.

Murphy, D. A., et al. (2002). Mothers living with HIV/AIDS: Mental, physical, and family functioning. *AIDS Care, 14*(5), 633–644.

Murray, L., & Cooper, P. J. (1997). Editorial: Postpartum depression and child development. *Psychological Medicine, 27*(02), 253–260.

Murray, L., et al. (1996). The impact of postnatal depression and associated adversity on early mother-infant interactions and later infant outcome. *Child Development,* 2512–2526.

Murray, L., et al. (2010). The effects of maternal postnatal depression and child sex on academic performance at age 16 years: A developmental approach. *Journal of Child Psychology and Psychiatry, 51*(10), 1150–1159.

NCTSN. Community violence. Available from http://www.nctsn.org/trauma-types/community-violence.

O'Connor, T. G., et al. (2007). Prenatal mood disturbance predicts sleep problems in infancy and toddlerhood. *Early Human Development, 83*(7), 451−458.

O'Malley, K. D., & Nanson, J. (2002). Clinical implications of a link between fetal alcohol spectrum disorder and attention-deficit hyperactivity disorder. *The Canadian Journal of Psychiatry, 47*(4), 349−354.

Olley, B. O., et al. (2004). Psychopathology and coping in recently diagnosed HIV/AIDS patients-the role of gender. *South African Journal of Psychiatry, 10*(1), 21−24.

O'Connor, M. J., et al. (2011). Predictors of alcohol use prior to pregnancy recognition among township women in Cape Town, South Africa. *Social Science and Medicine, 72*(1), 83−90.

PEPFAR. (2014). *Report highlights: Modeling the impact of HIV on affected children.* Available from: http://ovcsupport.org/wp-content/uploads/2014/10/highlights-modeling-report-final.pdf.

Perkins, S. C., Finegood, E. D., & Swain, J. E. (2013). Poverty and language development: Roles of parenting and stress. *Innovations in Clinical Neuroscience, 10*(4), 10.

Plant, D., et al. (2013). Intergenerational transmission of maltreatment and psychopathology: The role of antenatal depression. *Psychological Medicine, 43*(03), 519−528.

Qiu, A., et al. (2013). Maternal anxiety and infants' hippocampal development: Timing matters. *Translational Psychiatry, 3*(9), e306.

Rahman, A., et al. (2007). Association between antenatal depression and low birthweight in a developing country. *Acta Psychiatrica Scandinavica, 115*(6), 481−486.

Rahman, A., Harrington, R., & Bunn, J. (2002). Can maternal depression increase infant risk of illness and growth impairment in developing countries? *Child: Care, Health and Development, 28*(1), 51−56.

Roeser, R. W., Eccles, J. S., & Sameroff, A. J. (2000). School as a context of early adolescents' academic and social-emotional development: A summary of research findings. *The Elementary School Journal, 100*(5), 443−471.

Russell, M., et al. (1991). Measures of maternal alcohol use as predictors of development in early childhood. *Alcoholism: Clinical and Experimental Research, 15*(6), 991−1000.

Rutter, M. (2003). Poverty and child mental health: Natural experiments and social causation. *JAMA, 290*(15), 2063−2064.

Rutter, M., Kim-Cohen, J., & Maughan, B. (2006). Continuities and discontinuities in psychopathology between childhood and adult life. *Journal of Child Psychology and Psychiatry, 47*(3−4), 276−295.

Sameroff, A. J. (2000). Developmental systems and psychopathology. *Development and Psychopathology, 12*(3), 297−312.

Schlesinger, S., Susman, M., & Koenigsberg, J. (1990). Self-esteem and purpose in life: A comparative study of women alcoholics. *Journal of Alcohol and Drug Education, 36.*

Schroeder, S. A. (2004). Class-the ignored determinant of the nation's health. *The New England Journal of Medicine, 351*(11), 1137.

Schwartz, D., et al. (2006). Popularity, social acceptance, and aggression in adolescent peer groups: Links with academic performance and school attendance. *Developmental Psychology, 42*(6), 1116.

Sen, A. (1992). *Inequality reexamined.* Clarendon Press.

Sen, A. (1993). Capability and well-being 73. In *The quality of life* (p. 30).

Shaw, J. A. (2003). Children exposed to war/terrorism. *Clinical Child and Family Psychology Review, 6*(4), 237−246.

Shinn, M., & Gillespie, C. (1994). The roles of housing and poverty in the origins of homelessness. *American Behavioral Scientist, 37*(4), 505−521.

Shonkoff, J. P., et al. (2012). The lifelong effects of early childhood adversity and toxic stress. *Pediatrics, 129*(1), e232−e246.

Simmons, R. W., et al. (2010). Motor response programming and movement time in children with heavy prenatal alcohol exposure. *Alcohol, 44*(4), 371–378.

Sinyangwe, G. (2012). *Descriptive study of HIV/AIDS-related stigma experienced by people living with HIV/AIDS (PLWHA) in healthcare settings offering family planning and/or HIV services in Kapiri-Mposhi, Zambia*. Stellenbosch: Stellenbosch University.

Spira, R., et al. (1999). Natural history of human immunodeficiency virus type 1 infection in children: A five-year prospective study in Rwanda. *Pediatrics, 104*(5), e56.

Stewart, R. C., et al. (2008). Maternal common mental disorder and infant growth—a cross-sectional study from Malawi. *Maternal and Child Nutrition, 4*(3), 209–219.

Stewart, R. C., et al. (2010). Common mental disorder and associated factors amongst women with young infants in rural Malawi. *Social Psychiatry and Psychiatric Epidemiology, 45*(5), 551–559.

Stratton, K., Howe, C., & Battaglia, F. C. (1996). *Fetal alcohol syndrome: Diagnosis, epidemiology, prevention, and treatment*. National Academies Press.

Streissguth, A. P., Barr, H. M., & Sampson, P. D. (1990). Moderate prenatal alcohol exposure: Effects on child IQ and learning problems at age 7 1/2 years. *Alcoholism: Clinical and Experimental Research, 14*(5), 662–669.

Streissguth, A. P., et al. (1986). Attention, distraction and reaction time at age 7 years and prenatal alcohol exposure. *Neurobehavioral Toxicology and Teratology, 8*.

Suomi, S. J. (2006). Risk, resilience, and gene× environment interactions in rhesus monkeys. *Annals of the New York Academy of Sciences, 1094*(1), 52–62.

Taha, T. E., et al. (1999). Mortality after the first year of life among human immunodeficiency virus type 1-infected and uninfected children. *The Pediatric Infectious Disease Journal, 18*(8), 689–694.

Tottenham, N., et al. (2010). Prolonged institutional rearing is associated with atypically large amygdala volume and difficulties in emotion regulation. *Developmental Science, 13*(1), 46–61.

UNAIDS/WHO. (2001). *AIDS epidemic update December 2001*.

Valentine, J. M., et al. (2011). Recent intimate partner violence as a prenatal predictor of maternal depression in the first year postpartum among Latinas. *Archives of Women's Mental Health, 14*(2), 135–143.

van der Wal, M. F., van Eijsden, M., & Bonsel, G. J. (2007). Stress and emotional problems during pregnancy and excessive infant crying. *Journal of Developmental and Behavioral Pediatrics, 28*(6), 431–437.

van Straten, A., et al. (2015). Stepped care treatment delivery for depression: A systematic review and meta-analysis. *Psychological Medicine, 45*(2), 231–246.

Walker, S. P., et al. (2007). Child development: Risk factors for adverse outcomes in developing countries. *The Lancet, 369*(9556), 145–157.

Walker, S. P., et al. (2011). Inequality in early childhood: Risk and protective factors for early child development. *The Lancet, 378*(9799), 1325–1338.

Wass, T. S., et al. (2002). Timing accuracy and variability in children with prenatal exposure to alcohol. *Alcoholism: Clinical and Experimental Research, 26*(12), 1887–1896.

Webster-Stratton, C., & Hammond, M. (1988). Maternal depression and its relationship to life stress, perceptions of child behavior problems, parenting behaviors, and child conduct problems. *Journal of Abnormal Child Psychology, 16*(3), 299–315.

Weinstock, M. (2008). The long-term behavioural consequences of prenatal stress. *Neuroscience and Biobehavioral Reviews, 32*(6), 1073–1086.

Weissman, M. M., et al. (2005). Families at high and low risk for depression: A 3-generation study. *Archives of General Psychiatry, 62*(1), 29–36.

Weissman, M. M., et al. (2006). Offspring of depressed parents: 20 years later. *American Journal of Psychiatry, 163*(6), 1001–1008.

Westbrook, T. P. R., & Harden, B. J. (2010). Pathways among exposure to violence, maternal depression, family structure, and child outcomes through parenting: A multigroup analysis. *American Journal of Orthopsychiatry, 80*(3), 386–400.

White, K. R. (1982). The relation between socioeconomic status and academic achievement. *Psychological Bulletin, 91*(3), 461.

WHO. (2016). *HIV/AIDS factsheet 2016.*

Willford, J. A., Leech, S. L., & Day, N. L. (2006). Moderate prenatal alcohol exposure and cognitive status of children at age 10. *Alcoholism: Clinical and Experimental Research, 30*(6), 1051–1059.

Wilsnack, S. C., et al. (1991). Predicting onset and chronicity of women's problem drinking: A five-year longitudinal analysis. *American Journal of Public Health, 81*(3), 305–318.

Wilsnack, S. C., & Wilsnack, R. W. (1991). Epidemiology of women's drinking. *Journal of Substance Abuse, 3*(2), 133–157.

Wilson, W. J. (2012). *The truly disadvantaged: The inner city, the underclass, and public policy.* University of Chicago Press.

Winkleby, M. A., et al. (1992). Socioeconomic status and health: How education, income, and occupation contribute to risk factors for cardiovascular disease. *American Journal of Public Health, 82*(6), 816–820.

Wisner, K. L., et al. (2009). Major depression and antidepressant treatment: Impact on pregnancy and neonatal outcomes. *Focus, 7*(3), 374–384.

Wolfensohn, J. D., & Bourguignon, F. (2004). *Development and poverty reduction: Looking back, looking ahead.* Washington (DC).

Yator, O., et al. (2016). Risk factors for postpartum depression in women living with HIV attending prevention of mother-to-child transmission clinic at Kenyatta National Hospital, Nairobi. *AIDS Care, 28*(7), 884–889.

Zigler, E. (1994). Reshaping early childhood intervention to be a more effective weapon against poverty. *American Journal of Community Psychology, 22*(1), 37–47.

Infant Mental Health in Africa: Embracing Cultural Diversity

Astrid Berg[1,2], Anusha Lachman[2], Juané Voges[2]

[1] University of Cape Town, Cape Town, South Africa; [2] Stellenbosch University, Cape Town, South Africa

INTRODUCTION TO INFANT MENTAL HEALTH

Over half of the world's children aged less than 5 years live in Africa (The State of the World's Children 2014 in Numbers, n.d.). These infants and young children are raised in families with cultural worldviews that may be vastly different from those in the Western world, where most of the research and knowledge is generated. This chapter aims to fill some of the gaps.

A description of infant mental health (IMH) is given with a focus on why the first 1000 days are considered important for future development and mental health. This will be followed by research that has been conducted in Africa. Reflections on indigenous cultural practices will underline the adaptive and positive contributions these make to mental health. The need to be respectful of local customs and to integrate these with new information will be underlined throughout.

What Is Infant Mental Health?

The term "infant" refers to a child aged less than 3 years, whereas "mental health" encompasses the emotional, social, and cognitive domains of growing children within the context of their families.

IMH is therefore defined as the young infant's capacity to experience, regulate, and express emotions, form close and secure relationships, and explore and learn from his or her environment (DC:0—3R Diagnostic Classification of Mental Health and Developmental Disorders of Infancy and Early Childhood. Revised Edition, 2005).

FIGURE 7.1   Infant development.

The field of IMH is multidisciplinary concerning the well-being of infants and encompasses fundamental aspects (Zeanah, 2009), including early experiences that influence how babies view the world, respond to stressors, and negotiate challenges across the life span. The quality of caregiving relationships is important to a child's psychological health, and normal developmental trajectories that are sensitive need ongoing support. Infants and toddlers may also experience psychiatric symptoms, and the effects of this early psychopathology may be enduring.

IMH is closely connected to infant development, a product of continuous and dynamic transactions in which the timing may be genetic but the strength of connections depends on the early experiences (Fig. 7.1). The earliest experiences shape a baby's brain development and have a lifelong impact on that baby's mental and emotional health. IMH emphasizes the supports and positive attributes in a family system, as opposed to traditional mental health practices that focus on impairment and symptomatology (Simpson et al., 2016; Zeanah, 2009).

The First 1000 Days of Life

The first 3 years of an infant's life span are a critical time for brain development and growth (Schore, 2009). Starting in the third trimester of pregnancy and continuing through 18 months after birth, the human brain undergoes rapid growth, development, and specialization that help babies develop advanced emotional and cognitive capacities. Simple sensory connections (visual and auditory, for example) form first, followed by more complex neural circuits (such as early language

FIGURE 7.2 Core components essential in the first 1000 days of life.

and higher cognitive functions). Early experiences can change the structure of the developing brain, regulate genes and hormones, and affect the ability to develop into mentally resilient individuals later in life (Keller, Yovsi, et al., 2004; Simpson et al., 2016; Zeanah, 2009). Research indicates that the right care and nutrition during the first 1000 days help babies to develop their brains, fuel physical growth, strengthen the immune system, and improve school readiness and academic achievement, and reduce the risk for developing chronic diseases later in life (Kieling et al., 2011; Lewis, Galbally, Gannon, & Symeonides, 2014).

The three most important aspects of the first 1000 days are illustrated in Fig. 7.2. The components should first include a focus on health and nutrition, which implies taking care of the basic health and physical needs of both the mother and the developing infant from conception onward. A second essential component is love and attention, which includes responsive caregiving and support for both the baby and the mother. The final essential aspect is play and stimulation in an age-appropriate and safe environment to promote learning and emotional as well as social development (First 1000 Days Campaign | Western Cape Government, n.d.).

The Concept of Nurturing Care

Nurturing care should be considered the basic right of every child. On the basis of scientific advancements underscoring the importance of the early years, a child's brain is patterned by the nurturing care of trusted adults. Nurturing care is composed of attentive responses to children's efforts to connect to and learn about their world; it involves efforts to present children with learning experiences in a safe and mutually enjoyable way. IMH involves understanding that a child's overall behavior and functioning occur within specific cultural and environmental contexts, and that individual family experiences, beliefs, and cultural perspectives may influence child-rearing practices (Simpson et al., 2016). Nurturing care takes place in the context of families and through service providers across many sectors such as health, nutrition, education, and social services. This is part of essential care for children so that they will not only survive but also thrive and fulfil their social and developmental potential.

INFANT MENTAL HEALTH IN THE WORLD TODAY

The Evidence

Clinical and research findings on infant and child development over the past 50 years have profoundly changed how we conceptualize infants and altered our understanding of the formative importance of the relationship between infants and their caregivers.

Evidence has increasingly showed that investing in childhood and early intervention in these crucial years is cost-effective; moreover, it leads to improved adult health (Campbell et al., 2014). Although the scientific data have been growing internationally, the lack of policies regarding infancy and IMH has been striking. For example, in September, 2015, the Sustainable Development Goals (Sustainable Development Goals — United Nations, n.d.), spearheaded by the United Nations and involving 193 member state signatories, were unveiled without the inclusion of infant-specific indicators. Although this emphasizes the relative global neglect of infancy, for decades, numerous nongovernmental agencies and infant-affiliated organizations have been advocating for, engaging in quality research about, and delivering innovative infant and early childhood services (Tomlinson et al., 2015) (Box 7.1).

BOX 7.1

WORLD ASSOCIATION FOR INFANT MENTAL HEALTH

This association's mission is to promote the education, research, and study of the effects of mental, emotional, and social development during infancy on later normal and psychopathological development through international and interdisciplinary cooperation. See www.waimh.org to find out more information or to join the association.

The Rights of Infants

In their Position Paper on the Rights of Infants, the World Association for Infant Mental Health in 2014 affirmed the following:

> The United Nations Convention on the Rights of the Child (UNCRC, adopted 1990) in addressing the rights of children, does not sufficiently differentiate the needs of infants and toddlers from those of older children, in that infants and toddlers are totally dependent upon the availability of consistent and responsive care from specific adults for the adequate development of their basic human capacities. … There are unique considerations regarding the needs of infants during the first three years of life which are highlighted by contemporary knowledge, underscoring the impact of early experience on the development of human infant brain and mind. Further, specifying the unique needs and rights of the child in the first years of life is needed in order to motivate infant oriented actions and policies at both community and societal levels. In spite of the existence of the [Convention on the Rights of the Child], many societies around the globe still pay insufficient attention to infants, especially in times of stress and trauma. Additionally, consideration of infant needs and rights could guide policies of supports for mothers, fathers and caregivers, and in giving value to babies in contexts of risk and violence.
>
> WAIMH Position Paper on the Rights of Infants (2016).

Policy and Politics

Infants are not a constituency that can speak for themselves or mobilize resources. The early childhood agenda is truly global. Although there is a high need in low-income countries, infants living in disadvantaged homes in middle-income countries and high-income countries (HIC) are also at risk.

The allocation of scarce resources in low- and middle-income countries (LMIC) is often prioritized according to disease burden and more immediate health outcomes such as neonatal survival, rather than being focused on infant services where the greatest impact is likely to be seen only decades in the future. The 2016 "Every Woman Every Child Everywhere Work Stream" (Global Strategy — Every Woman Every Child, n.d.) highlighted that in targeting investments, priority should be given to populations in greatest need, while aiming to build more resilient systems in vulnerable environments to mitigate adversity in the face of conflict, violence, and natural disasters (Kieling et al., 2011).

Progress that has been made in the Millennium Development Goals on improving child survival has not been matched by an equivalent focus on ensuring that those who survive also thrive. Similarly, progress that has been made by the field of IMH in understanding brain development and the development of infants and children across time has not been matched by advocacy for greater funding and political priority. The economic case is clear for countries to invest in the early years.

An estimated 250 million children aged less than 5 years in LMIC are at risk for falling short of their full developmental potential because of exposure to early life adversities. Investing in early childhood development, and thereby improving their potential for developing physical, cognitive, and social capacities, will have profound implications for the future of society. Few countries have institutionalized mechanisms to implement policies; services remain fragmented and of variable quality; and programs at scale are rare and poorly evaluated. By continuing in this manner, we run the risk of exacerbating inequalities and social divisions globally (Chan & Anteby, 2016; Janse van Rensburg, 2009).

In keeping with the theme of investing in early childhood, in 2016, the World Bank announced the global launch of a *Lancet* series on Advancing Early Childhood Development: From Science to Scale (Richter et al., 2017) with the guiding message: "Nurturing care in the early years ensures individuals and societies thrive." Key messages from the *Lancet* series on Advancing Early Childhood Development are summarized in Fig. 7.3.

The burden and cost of inaction is high BLACK 2016	•A poor start in life limits infant's ability to benefit from education, leading to lower productivity and and social tension •Individuals: predicts loss of a quarter average adult income per year •Countries: may forfeit up to two times their current GDP expenditure on health, may risk the losing the dividend gained by improving child survival
Early means early BRITTO 2016	•Child development starts at conception, the young developing brain is dependent on good nutrition and types of experiences •Influence of stress and adversity may occur preconception and impact in utero •Families need support to provide nurturing care, via knowledge, time, skilled assistance and material resources •Affordable child care, provision of quality population based services assist in supporting families
A start can be made through health RICHTER 2016	•Expand maternal & child health care services to include interventions to promote nurturing care •Multisectoral collaborations are essential to support families and enhance existing childhood services. •Strengthen maternal, infant and child nutrition, child protection, social and financial support, access to quality education and early learning opportunities

FIGURE 7.3 Key messages from the *Lancet* Advancing Early Childhood Development series.

INFANT MENTAL HEALTH AWARENESS AND RESEARCH IN AFRICA

Infant Mental Health Research in Africa

The African continent is home to 1.2 billion people living in 54 recognized sovereign states and countries and nine territories (Africa Population, 2017). In most of these countries multiple cultures exist, each with their own behavioral patterns and organizations of caregiving relationships that underlie the development of attachment. Culture has a significant role in the variations observed in the manifestation, expression, and meaning of attachment behaviors. The specific behaviors and characteristics of parenting practices differ greatly depending on the individuals involved as well as the context in which they occur. Parenting practices are heavily influenced by the traditions, cultural beliefs, community practices, and availability of caregivers.

Mary Ainsworth, an American-Canadian developmental psychologist, conducted a study of mother—infant interaction in Uganda in the 1950s to investigate the application of attachment theory in a cross-cultural setting. From these detailed observations, she was able to identify the secure base concept (Ainsworth, 1985). When she replicated her observations in Baltimore, Maryland, she demonstrated how maternal sensitivity is important to fostering infant attachment and described how the infant uses the mother as a secure base (Posada, 2013). Since then, much of our knowledge about infant attachment has been shaped by research, assessment, and terminology that is situated in Western cultures. This imbalance in knowledge about infants was highlighted in a review of leading IMH journals from 1996 to 2001 by Tomlinson and Swartz (2003). They found that 94% of articles published in these journals were authored by individuals from Europe (16%) or North America (78%). Indeed, they underlined that infants from LMIC make up about 90% of the total infant population, but that most of the knowledge is generated in HIC, with different realities in terms of resources and living conditions. Most individuals from LMIC live in conditions that include extreme poverty and instability, which has a significant impact on parental experiences and stressors (Tomlinson, Cooper, & Murray, 2005). Given that the circumstances and parental experiences from HIC and LMIC differ so greatly, the question arises regarding whether findings from HIC can be applicable to LMIC families or parent—infant dyads.

In addition to the differences in the socioeconomic conditions of individuals from Western and African cultures, there are differences in the predominant cultural philosophies. In general terms, Western cultures tend to emphasize more individualist pursuits and African cultures tend to emphasize collectivist values; Table 7.1 lists central differences.

TABLE 7.1   Philosophical Differences Between Individualist and Collectivist Cultures

Individualist Cultures	Collectivist Cultures
Tend to value independence	Tend to value cooperation and interdependence
Pursuit of individual or immediate family's self-interest	Pursuit of group goals (eg, family, peers) and preference for group decisions
Individual needs take precedence over collective needs	Often individual needs take back seat to what is best for the majority
Promotion of personal autonomy, self-realization, and individual initiative	Embodies a sense of community among individuals
Personal identity regarded as sum of individual's attributes	Personal identity understood as knowing place in the group, less personal privacy
	Loyalty to group is highly regarded
Examples include Australia, Great Britain, Canada, and United States	Examples include many African cultures, China, and Japan

Modified from Darwish, A.E., & Huber, G.L.(2003). Individualism vs Collectivism in Different Cultures: A cross-cultural study. Intercultural Education, 14(1), 47-55.

Infant Attachment in Africa

A literature review of African attachment studies by Voges, Berg, and Niehaus (2017) identified only nine studies from five African countries that published quantitative data on attachment classifications over the past 50 years. The Strange Situation Paradigm was used to evaluate infant attachment in six studies, two used the Attachment Q-sort, and one developed an attachment scoring system derived from the Circle of Security, the Attachment assessment score sheet. Most studies were from dyads living in periurban, township, or slum areas; only two were conducted in a rural setting. Despite significant adversity in living conditions, relatively high rates of secure attachment were found in the majority of studies; secure attachment rates reported to range between 53.7% and 90.2% when considering the two-way attachment classification. Thus, most mothers had the ability to create a safe environment for their infants amidst adversity, unpredictability, or turmoil, and were able to facilitate the healthy socioemotional development of their children. It is important to consider whether there are overlapping factors that may assist parents in creating an environment conducive to secure attachment and that help parents to overcome these challenges. One possible protective factor is the notion of *Ubuntu*, a concept that is common to all African traditional cultures. Berg (2003) described this concept in terms of a Xhosa proverb (*Umtu ngumtu ngabantu*), meaning "A person is a person because of another person," which embodies the centrality of compassion for others and a sense of community among individuals. The self is seen in relation to the broader community, and personal development is marked by rituals that involve the community within which they live. Another philosophy common to the African societies is depicted by the proverb "It takes a village to raise a child" (Mooya, Sichimba, & Bakermans-Kranenburg, 2016). Within this perspective, the infant is thought of as also belonging to the community, and the well-being of children within that community is considered a collective responsibility (Tomlinson, et al., 2005).

The literature review identified that disorganized attachment was assessed in only four African studies; three studies reported relatively high rates of infant disorganization (Cooper et al., 2009; Mooya et al., 2016; Tomlinson et al., 2005; True, Pisani, & Oumar, 2001). The examination of disorganized attachment behavior is important because it is an early indicator for later psychopathology that can be identified in infancy (Lyons-Ruth & Jacobvitz, 2008). The presence of prominent psychosocial stressors caused by social adversity or the presence of HIV may be of concern to the mother and affect how available and sensitive she is able to be in her parenting responses toward her infant.

An interesting finding from the Dogon tribe in Mali was the apparent lack of avoidant infant attachment (True, et al., 2001) Some parenting practices of Mali mothers may explain this phenomenon: Infants are fed on demand, are carried or worn in a sling for most of the day, and are in constant proximity to a caregiver, and infants and mothers often sleep together. It was proposed that these caregiving practices do not lend themselves to the patterns of caregiving usually associated with the development of avoidant attachment, such as rejection of attachment bids and a lack of availability or close physical contact. The practice of offering the breast when an infant is in distress was common. Breastfeeding is considered the dominant strategy to comfort infants who are in distress and the primary manner in which infants seek comfort (True, et al., 2001). Ainsworth also discussed this pattern among Ugandan infants whom she studied, for whom the source of nourishment and comfort and the attachment figure was the same person, a practice that may further make it difficult to develop avoidant attachment styles of interaction (Ainsworth, Blehar, Waters, & Wall, 1978).

Although the attachment networks of most cultures in the world include nonparental attachment figures, only two studies assessed infant attachment to nonmaternal individuals. In Zambia, infant attachment to older siblings was assessed; 42% were rated as securely attached (Mooya et al., 2016). Among the Gusii in Kenya, a rate of secure infant attachment to child caretakers of 53.8% was reported (Kermoian & Leiderman, 1986).

Knowledge about infant attachment in the African setting is still sparse despite the recognition that there is a need for greater diversity of research on infant attachment from developing countries.

Alternative Cultural Parenting Practices

Most attachment research methodologies support the view that mothers are central in the social development of infants. The majority of studies reporting on mother—infant relationships and the assessment measures used often focus on mother—infant interaction. However, there is growing recognition of the importance that individuals other than the mother figure, such as fathers, siblings, and peers, have in the social development (experiences) of infants, especially in societies with less technological complexity (Tronick, Morelli, & Ivey, 1992). Nonmaternal or allomaternal care provides a wide range of benefits to the infant, including improved cognitive development and increased survival (Meehan, 2009).

Parenting behaviors and strategies are mechanisms by which cultural values and practices are transmitted from generation to generation, with significant cultural and contextual variation (Keller, Lohaus, et al., 2004). Different cultures adapt to factors within their environment and social structures through specific caregiving practices, and despite variations in the organization of the environment and caregiving responsibilities, all cultures have adapted to ensure the infant's survival during a particularly vulnerable period of life (Marvin, VanDevender, Iwanaga, LeVine, & Levine, 1977). Two notable examples include child caregivers of Kenya and the polymatric Hausa society.

Child Caregivers: Gusii Tribe in Kenya

The Gusii tribe from the Kisii district in the southwestern area of Kenya is unique in its caregiving practices in that mothers are significantly involved in activities related to the gathering and preparation of food whereas older children of both genders are expected to share child care responsibilities. The division of roles is clearly defined: Mothers typically take care of the infant's physical needs, such as breastfeeding and bathing, and child caregivers spend time playing and socializing with the infants. A study by Kermoian and Leiderman (1986) noted that the Gusii tended to involve younger child caregivers and for more substantial activities than those observed in other communities. Caretaking was usually delegated to a sibling between age 7 and 12, but because more of them attend school, the role is typically fulfilled by a preschool-aged sibling; about half of their sample was aged 6 years or younger and eight of the caretakers were aged 4 years or younger. Over half of the infants observed had secure attachments to either their mother or child figure. It was noted that around the time of weaning, Gusii infants appeared to be more vulnerable to anxious attachment to the mother, because breastfeeding (one of the primary sources of interaction with the mother) was being withdrawn. Despite the differentiation in roles between mother and child caretaker, activities that make up the interaction with the infants are sufficient to establish a secure attachment relationship. The role that each caregiver fulfils in relation to the infant seems to be associated with a particular aspect of functioning. Security of attachment to their mothers was associated with physical growth, and security of attachment to the child caretaker was associated with cognitive development of the infant.

Kermoian and Leiderman observed several differences among the Gusii compared with their American counterparts. Gusii infants are typically greeted with a handshake and appeared to anticipate this greeting, much like "American infants anticipate a hug" (p. 460, 1986). Infants classified as secure would reach toward an adult with one arm, whereas insecure infants would turn away or reach and pull away after contact was made with the caregiver. The infants' exploration of their environment was primarily visual (scanning their environment) rather than manipulative (handling of objects), and infants who were securely attached displayed visual exploration that differed with or without the presence of the attachment figure. From an early age, Gusii infants are trained to remain on a mat, largely because of the presence of dangers within the compound, such as open fires, livestock, and tools; during the experimental procedure, not a single infant left the mat when in the company of another person. During periods when the infant was alone, some left the mat to search for the attachment figure after a long hesitation. The infants' motor development was described as being more advanced than that of their American counterparts; many of the 8-month-old infants were already crawling or walking.

Polymatric Society of Hausa, Nigeria

Marvin et al. (1977) conducted a descriptive observational study of the caregiving practices of the Hausa, a polymatric tribe from Nigeria. For an explanation of the differences between monomatric and polymatric societies, please see Box 7.2. The participants were mostly Muslim and, in keeping with Islamic law, men were allowed as many as four wives at a time. Each compound was a round, walled grouping of huts. There were separate huts for the compound-head and each wife, with a common cooking and working area. The men pursued agricultural activities outside the compound, and married women did not assist the men in the fields but maintained individual gardens in the living compounds. Inside the common area, there were usually cooking fires and it was common for

BOX 7.2

POLYMATRIC VS. MONOMATRIC CAREGIVING

This polymatric organization refers to the coincidental sharing of caregiving activities, even in the mother's presence.

In a monomatric society, a single caregiver (usually the mother) has complete or at least primary responsibility for the infant.

Marvin, R. S., Van Devender, T. L., Iwanaga, M. I., LeVine, S., & Levine, R. A. (1977). Infant-caregiver attachment among the Hausa of Nigeria. In H. McGurk (Ed.), Ecological factors in human development (pp. 247–260). Amsterdam, North Holland.

chickens and other small animals to roam freely. The infants grew up in a context of high social density. There were usually two to three wives in each compound, a number of children, grandparents, and siblings of the compound-head, and co-wives. The co-wives interacted on a continuing basis within an informal hierarchy, with the first wife being dominant. There was minimal conflict between the wives and a substantial amount of cooperation and sharing of responsibilities, which allowed time for relaxing, talking, and leisurely keeping eye on children.

Sharing of responsibilities included the care of infants and children, which significantly influenced the attachment and exploratory behavior of infants. Similarly, to the Dogon, Hausa mothers were also largely responsible for the physical caregiving of their infants, which included feeding, bathing, and other physical activities. Other caregiving activities were shared among familiar adults and older children. These included comforting, keeping infants away from danger, vocalizing, and playing with and encouraging infants' vocal and motor skills. The number of familiar adult caregivers with whom infants regularly interacted ranged between 1 and 10, with an average of 3.8. Hausa infants were almost always in physical contact with someone, even when they were able to crawl and walk; when they were not held, they would play on a mat beside the caregiver. When seated, the infants were in a caregiver's lap, facing outward and interacting with others across a distance. Compared with an American sample, Hausa caregivers appeared indulgent and restrictive: indulgent in terms of constant physical contact and rapid responsiveness to almost all signals, but restrictive in terms of limiting exploration beyond the caregiver's immediate proximity. This practice appeared to result largely from an adaptation to the physical and social setting. The high mortality rate from injury and illness influenced caregivers to be watchful and responsive. The presence of four to five continuously available caregivers meant that essentially all signals could be responded to. It was observed that Hausa infants did not use caregivers as secure bases for locomotor exploration, but did for manipulatory exploration, which would cease when the caregiver moved away.

The question was posed whether infants in a polymatric environment become attached to one or multiple caregivers. Marvin et al. found that all 15 infants observed were attached to more than one caregiver, with an average of three to four. Most displayed a clear preference to one person despite multiple attachments. Interactions were further investigated to determine whether infants became attached to the person who most often fed them or interacted with them. All but one displayed greater attachment to the person who held and interacted with the infant the most.

Different cultures adapt to contextual factors in different ways through specific caregiving practices. The Hausa adapted to the high infant mortality rate and dangerous physical environment by responding to almost all of the infant's signals and restricting the infant through social means.

Socioemotional Risks to the Mental Health of Infants in Africa

There is convincing evidence that psychosocial factors, including low socioeconomic status, pose a significant risk to infant development. A metaanalysis of factors affecting attachment security in high-risk samples found that the cumulative effect of socioeconomic risk factors poses as significant a risk to attachment insecurity and disorganization as does parental maltreatment (Cyr, Euser, Bakermans-Kranenburg, & Van Ijzendoorn, 2010). The risk to attachment security and disorganization appears to be compounded when multiple risk factors are present.

The African review of attachment by Voges, Berg, and Niehaus (in press) identified multiple socioeconomic factors that affected the living conditions of the African populations examined. Among others, unemployment, financial difficulties or a low income, low levels of education, poor quality or unstable housing, being a single parent, lacking the support of a partner, being an adolescent mother, the presence of substance abuse, and depression are factors that have been associated with more significant risk to the caregiver—infant attachment relationship. Most communities reported in the review experienced at least one of these risk factors, and in many cases, several of them. The particular contribution of each of these factors to the climate of caregiving is unclear, but it may be inferred that the parents, caregivers, and infants who live under these conditions are exposed to significant psychological stress. This will presumably have an impact on the quality of the infant's attachment relationships and subsequent development. In addition, the

---

BOX 7.3

THE INTERNATIONAL CHILD DEVELOPMENT PROGRAM

The International Child Development Program has projects world-wide (including in 14 African countries) that focus on communities experiencing significant adversity. The program recognizes that assistance to caregivers in providing empathic and sensitive parenting may be the most effective way of early intervention to infants and children. Their objective is to sensitize parents' caregivers to "enhance their ability to provide good quality care and to release empathic feelings towards their children." See www.icdp.info for more information.

---

mother or caregiver who contends with this level of adversity and associated uncertainty is more challenged when she is required to respond in a sensitive, caring, and attuned manner to an infant who requires her attention.

Maternal depression, in particular, remains a condition that has a significantly detrimental effect on maternal and IMH. Depression among African women is widespread in the postpartum period; it is reported by an average of 18% of women (Sawyer, Ayers, & Smith, 2010). Under conditions of social adversity, the impact of maternal depression appears particularly potent, because infants exposed to both conditions display a range of disturbances in interactional behavior (Murray, Fiori-Cowley, Hooper, & Cooper, 1996). The International Child Development Programme is an example of an early intervention for families experiencing significant adversity. For more information, please see Box 7.3.

INFANT MENTAL HEALTH IN AFRICA: REFLECTION ON INDIGENOUS CULTURAL PRACTICES AND WHAT WE CAN LEARN FROM IT

The previous section addressed published research from Africa. Here we focus on qualitative findings from practicing IMH in Africa with an emphasis on the cultural richness that is present in the practices of a culturally diverse continent.

To obtain a sense of what perception mental health professionals have of Africa, an informal survey of mental health professionals, mostly psychiatrists, was conducted. All nine respondents, who resided in Central and East Africa as well as South Africa, were certain that there is an interplay between IMH knowledge and local cultural practices, and that at times a conflict existed between what is locally known and what is understood by the Western worldview regarding infants' development and needs. In the words of one respondent from Central Africa:

> For a long time, high burden of infectious diseases causing high infant mortality rate directed the focus of where resources and energy should be put at individual, community, and national level. This, I believe, led to the understanding of the development of a child not beginning "until a certain age." Now that the infant mortality rate is reducing and infectious diseases are fairly under control, the chances of an infant surviving beyond 5 years has increased and because of this, I believe there should be fewer barriers to local adaptations of Western understanding of infant developmental needs.

Another respondent, from South Africa, stated that

> To me it seems that with more knowledge about IMH the Western world is moving toward some more traditional African practices, for example co-sleeping, carrying babies close to the body for extended periods, breastfeeding on demand and often exclusively for longer periods, breastfeeding in public spaces, etc. On the other hand, other aspects challenge the more African approaches, for example, reading, talking, and playing with infants basically from birth.

These two quotations introduce the importance of the different contexts in which infants grow up and how these affect the view of young children's developmental and emotional needs, as well as the universally evolving nature of infant care practices. It is important to pay attention and give credence to age-old customs, because they grew out of environmental necessities as well as parental belief systems. If they are not respected and considered for what they represent, there is the risk of advocating a one size fits all approach, which could result in a two-dimensional, flat approach to child rearing.

The Developmental Niche

Culture is the shared framework by which the group understands and gives meaning to the reality in which the family and community live (Kagawa Singer et al., 2016) Culture is a socially interactive process composed of shared activity (cultural practices) and shared meaning (cultural interpretation) (Greenfield, Keller, Fuligni, & Maynard, 2003).

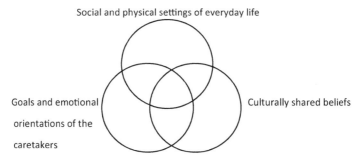

Social and physical settings of everyday life

Goals and emotional
orientations of the
caretakers

Culturally shared beliefs

FIGURE 7.4   The developmental niche. *From Harkness, S., & Super, C. M. M. (1994). The developmental niche: A theoretical framework for analyzing the household production of health.* Social Science & Medicine, 38(2), 217–226. https://doi.org/10.1016/0277-9536(94)90391-3.

The developmental niche is a theoretical framework for studying cultural regulation of the microenvironment of the child (Harkness & Super, 1994). Three components operate as a homeostatic system to promote stability among the setting (the physical environment), the customs (practices), and the psychology of the caregivers. As can be seen in Fig. 7.4, the three circles of settings, beliefs, and caretaker orientations overlap and interconnect.

From the beginning, the infant is shaped by parents' interactions with him. These are influenced by their own as well as their society's ideas of whom they wish the child to become. Ultimately, the developmental task for children is to adapt to the environment into which they are born.

Two prototypical environments were examined by Keller (2007): rural, subsistence-based ecologies with families who closely cooperate for their joint economy and in which formal education was not the norm; and urban, middle-class, Western families. These two environments inform the underlying dimensions of relatedness (rural, subsistence-based ecology) and autonomy (urban, middle-class), leading to two models of parenting styles. The interdependent model values relationships, cooperation with others in the group, and respect for the elders; the independent model focuses on the development of autonomy, individual rights, and personal achievement.

These models are not cognitive, conscious constructs, but are deeply embedded in the unconscious mind of the group. Mothers' spontaneous, daily interactions with their very young infants arise in large part from psychological layers that are outside consciousness. A comparison between mother–infant interactions in two distinct groups (one in an urban setting in Germany and the other in a rural setting in Cameroon) illustrates how cultural expectations are mediated in early infancy. The German mothers established interactions that facilitated proto-conversations, turn-taking, and bestowing a sense of agency in the infant. The Cameroon mothers were more structuring of their infant's behavior; there was more joint rhythmic co-participation through the establishment of bodily proximity and rhythmic patterning of the mothers' speech and movements (Demuth, Keller, & Yovsi, 2012).

Indigenous African Child-Rearing Practices

Indigenous child-rearing practices are informed by the environmental conditions of the family and social group, as well as the belief systems of the caretakers. What follows are some examples from a rich tapestry of child care customs and traditions.

Back-Carrying

Physical closeness continues throughout infancy and most of toddler-hood, as is more visibly noticed through practices such as back-carrying. In most parts of central and sub-Saharan Africa, the baby is carried on the back of the mother or caregiver; this is a method of transport for infants from 6 weeks to 2 years of age (Graham, Manara, Chokotho, & Harrison, 2015) and reflects an adaptation to the physical environment.

From an attachment perspective, back-carrying provides multiple opportunities for bonding: physical closeness, being swaddled and feeling "held," being in tune with the mother's physical rhythm, and generally feeling safe in the high position on the mother's body. Medically speaking, there are also advantages, such as protection against conditions such as hip dysplasia (Graham et al., 2015), which is rarely encountered in infants in sub-Saharan Africa. Thus, the Wolof proverb rings true that "The mother's back is the baby's medicine" (Timyan, 1988, p. 15). Even when the child is bigger and still unable to walk, the mother sees it as her duty to carry the child on her back; as the isiXhosa saying goes, "Does the elephant complain about its trunk?" However, back-carrying has been proposed to have the potential for negative consequences for sensory integration owing to the possible lack of crawling opportunities (Pretorius & Naudé, 2002), which may result in visual perceptual and spatial deficiencies.

Breastfeeding

Other customs, such as breastfeeding, mirror not only the reality of a readily available milk supply but also attitudes and beliefs (Timyan, 1988).

Maiello (2003) describes an infant observation in a community in South Africa showing the physical oneness between the mother and her young baby. This is the phase of *Mdlezana* and could be understood in terms of Winnicott's "primary maternal preoccupation":

> The transition from "breast" to "no-breast" remained fluid. She (the mother) was surprised when I asked how often she fed her baby and replied "Always." This included day and night. She was equally surprised when I told her that European babies usually sleep in a cot separated from their mothers. (2003, p. 83)

A practice that ensures the infant's unlimited access to the breast during the first 2 years of life is the *madzawde* practice among the Gusii peoples in Mozambique. During the *madzawde* period the mother is free to devote her entire attention to her child in a symbiotic manner. Two years after the birth, the parents have to perform an important ritual called *madzawde*. This marks the end of the infant–mother symbiotic relationship, and unless it is performed, it is believed that the child could become ill and even die (Igreja, 2003).

The Meaning of Babies

For all human groups, babies carry the hope for the future economically (that is, one day, they will provide for the parents when they are old) and spiritually (they will remember their parents and ensure that the clan continues to exist and thrive).

Most cultures in Africa have a powerful clan structure along patriarchal lines and a belief system that reveres the ancestors. However, in some, such as those of the Beng people of the Ivory Coast, the belief is articulated differently: Each baby is said to be a reincarnation of someone who died, and infants have been living their lives in the previous, invisible existence. When a baby is unhappy for no obvious reason, it is believed that it is trying to communicate a spiritual need; for this, a diviner may be consulted (Gottlieb, 1998). Much of the behavior of the infant as well as the older child is explained from the basis of the child's being the reincarnation of an ancestor. This an example of a particular way of viewing the child and it may well have changed over time. However, the depth of the spiritual role that is attributed to infants and young children needs to be acknowledged and respected in this community as in that of all other people.

A golden thread that runs through African culture is reverence for ancestors. It is a worldview that is introduced to the child from early on, such as the practice of "praising the child in his clan"; this is a rhythmical incantation that names the child and the child's forebears one by one, going increasingly further back into ancestral history. This could be regarded as an abstraction of the back-carrying and general bodily proximity that the infant experiences; the child is not alone, but is embedded in the weft and warp of the clan structure. It could also be regarded as part of the concept of *Ubuntu*, which signifies our humanity and our dependence on others to make us human (Berg, 2012a, 2012b).

The Evolution of Cultures: The Role of Formal Education

Cultures are not static, and change as the microenvironment and macroenvironment change. This change may be abrupt, such as moving from a rural to an urban environment; or it may be more gradual, as with compulsory education for children, especially girls who will become mothers.

Keller (2007) argues that formal education "initiates a trend toward the cultural model of independence" (p. 264), which runs counter to the model of interdependence seen in many African families. The South African Schools Act of 1996 requires all children between ages 7 and 15 years to attend school. This means that even children in rural and more traditional settings are exposed to a form of learning that differs from what their parents or grandparents may have had. Learning no longer take place through observation and imitation of practical skills (the "apprenticeship model"); children learn abstract forms of communication such as reading and writing, and are encouraged to think independently. The child's individuality and autonomy are fostered through this form of education. Because most parents wish their children to be educated, it is challenging to prepare their children for this form of learning, while honoring age-old customs such as respect for the elders.

The challenge for health care and educational providers is to respect cultural practices and incorporate these into programs of early childhood development, building on local strengths and using familiar languages (Serpell & Nsamenang, 2014). At the same time, it cannot be ignored that children from traditional settings whose parents did not receive significant formal education are not exposed to intellectually stimulating activities. At the same time, they may find themselves in an urban, industrialized setting (such as a semiformal community setting outside a big city), and they may have to incorporate ways of being with their child that might be unfamiliar. The shared reading of books is an example. Clinical experience in a primary health care setting (Berg, 2012a, 2012b) found that older infants and toddlers were delighted when offered books and that their caregiver was often surprised by the excitement the children displayed when looking at pictures. The delight of the children could be regarded as an endorsement that this activity should be encouraged.

This clinical experience is being investigated through a randomized controlled trial which evaluates the cognitive and socioemotional development of toddlers exposed to a book-sharing intervention (Dowdall et al., 2017). A previous trial showed that training in book sharing benefited infant cognitive development (Murray et al., 2016). As expected in research, the intervention consisted of training caregivers to conduct book sharing in a systematic and structured way.

These research findings verify the clinical experience and suggest that providing caregivers of infants and toddlers with books, accompanied by suggestions of co-reading, would be a respectful way to bring into the parent–infant relationship an aspect that is novel but not alien, and one that would facilitate learning from an early age.

THE WAY FORWARD

Prevention Through Sharing New Information and Knowledge

Given that most of the research has been conducted in North American and European countries (Tomlinson, Bornstein, Marlow, & Swartz, 2014), there is an assumption that the Western model of child rearing is the ideal. There needs to be an awareness of this Eurocentric approach lest we unconsciously continue to disregard African beliefs and practices.

When there is the opportunity for experience on the ground with other cultures, there is a realization that much thought and wisdom lies behind traditional practices and beliefs (Berg, 2012a, 2012b):

> We must recognize that what is considered a "good" practice in one socio-cultural context may not be considered so in another. Careful attention must be paid to the cultural rationale for childrearing practices and their adaptive function for a given society in order to be able to identify those that are "positive," and therefore to be encouraged, as well as those that are "negative" and to be discouraged. Western notions of "good" and "bad" childrearing practices cannot be uncritically accepted. They must be juxtaposed to the reality of local cultures and to the reality of today's African families, doing their best to adapt to new information, new requirements for survival, and new expectations. (Timyan, 1988, p. 24).

The question then arises: How do we inform parents about what we believe are universal human needs? All parents have the right to know what modern research reveals about the development of the infant brain. What are those universal needs? The Infant Rights Position Paper is an attempt to name these universal needs (WAIMH, 2016).

The focus here would be on the following:

1. Besides physical care, protection, and nutrition, the infant relies on the relationship with adults in his or her world to develop emotionally and cognitively.

2. Infants make attachments to their primary caregivers, and disrupting these attachments during the first 3 years of life constitutes a trauma.

3. Caregivers require emotional support. Their mental health is pivotal in enabling them to provide an alive and stimulation environment for the child.

4. Relational trauma, such as is evident in domestic violence, constitutes toxic stress and damages the developing infant brain.

One way to inform parents of these needs is through audiovisual means. The use of video material is well-established in general education, and there is evidence that parents favor video-based presentation of information (Morrongiello, Zdzieborski, Sandomierski, & Lasenby-Lessard, 2009) A DVD was created in 2010 (executive producer: Astrid Berg, UCT Ethics Approval for this 150/2006). The funding for this project was obtained from the Schoenberg Trust of the Red Cross War Memorial Children's Hospital. The DVD lasts 20 min and focuses on the developmental needs of infants and toddlers. The writing of the script was informed by current research findings as well as clinical experience in working psychotherapeutically with mothers and babies from various communities.

Several features made this DVD unique: It was locally produced and describes three infants in different developmental stages coming from three different communities within the surrounds of Cape Town; the DVD can be played in any one of the three official languages of the Western Cape. A particular and exceptional feature is that the main narrators are the infants themselves: Using children's voices, the baby and toddler "speak" about their feelings and needs. All of this was been done with the aim of facilitating parents' identification with their young children.

The links to it are:

English—https://vimeo.com/11356560/25d40f9a49
IsiXhosa—https://vimeo.com/11528378/d690068e28
Afrikaans—https://vimeo.com/11524725/aef8dc7928

Early Identification Through Universally Accepted/"Culture-Free" Screening Tools

In South Africa, the *National Road to Health Booklet* (About us — Road to Health, n.d.) is issued at birth to all infants. It is a patient-held record of essential basic health information about the baby, including birth, immunization and vitamin A, growth parameters, development, oral health, and hospital admissions. It also contains age group—related feeding recommendations and play and stimulation messages. A complementary tool has been developed, called the postnatal checklist tool, to assist with implementation of a Western Cape Postnatal Care Policy, which provides guidance for care of mothers and infants during the first 6 weeks after the baby's birth. A copy of this tool is added to the *Road to Health Book* after birth. The postnatal checklist has two components, one for the mother and one for infant, and both are completed at various set time points during this 6-week period (https://perspectives.waimh.org).

Five questions have been added that are the result of a collaboration with colleagues in Finland, where IMH has been integrated into primary care through the Basic Infant Mental Health Screen:

1. Are you (the caregiver) worried about your infant/child?
2. How have you (the caregiver) been feeling?
3. Please give the weight and height of the child.
4. Please describe the infant's eye contact with the caregiver and the health care worker.
5. Please observe shared pleasure between the infant and the caregivers.

These five questions have been found to be useful tools for detecting psychological distress in infants and young children (Puura, Malek, & Berg, 2018).

Acceptable and Feasible Interventions

Interventions should aim to promote nurturing care: that is, the establishment of a stable environment that is sensitive to children's needs, protects them from threats, and provides opportunities for early learning as well as responsive interactions (Britto et al., 2017).

Providing information about infants' abilities and their basic needs helps many parents to provide their children with nurturing care.

A useful model is the *Ububele Baby Mat Service*, a community-based parent—IMH intervention offered at primary health care clinics in a community in Johannesburg (Frost, 2012). The aim of the intervention is to promote healthy caregiver—infant attachments. A therapeutic couple is present on a mat in a primary health care context and invites caregivers to engage with their infants on the mat. A respectful and curious stance about the infant's behavior is adopted and is integrated with cultural understandings (Dawson, Richards, & Frost, 2017).

A more individually based model was used in a community clinic near Cape Town, where faltering weight was the presenting problem in most cases. Supportive infant–parent psychotherapy was offered within a confidential space in the clinic. Bestowing personhood onto the infant and talking to the infant was an important modeling action for mothers whose sense of competence had been impaired. Improved infant functioning and mother–infant relationships attested to the appropriateness of this intervention for the more in-need mothers (Berg, 2012a, 2012b).

For caregivers who are more vulnerable and need extra emotional support, a more intensive parenting intervention may be required. Nancy Suchman at the Yale School of Medicine developed the Parenting from the Inside Out model; this was pilot-tested in five sites in the Western Cape, South Africa. It is an attachment-based reflective parenting intervention, with the goal of improving a parent's capacity to recognize and respond sensitively to the child's emotional cues (Suchman et al., 2010). This intervention is indicated for parents who are particularly vulnerable, either because of their own mental health issues or because of having children whose problems are especially challenging, such as children who have sustained burn injuries or those with severe developmental delays.

CONCLUSION

The great majority of infants, toddlers, and young children live in Africa in families whose worldviews are different from those of Europe and the United States, from where most of the research comes. These families provide mental health practitioners with the opportunity to learn about parenting practices that have been shaped by the cultural environment in which communities live. Gaining knowledge and understanding of indigenous practices is important when entering into the space of infants and their families. The value of a cultural perspective on IMH raises the importance of not making assumptions about child rearing. Our key messages in Box 7.4 convey the central message of the need for nurturing care for all infants, together with a respect for indigenous cultural practices through which this care is provided.

As some of the examples given in this chapter illustrate, there is often a deep wisdom that informs the way in which parents relate to and raise their children, one from which the Western world could learn. An "African" style of parenting with physical closeness and attuned mothering, particularly during the first year of life, is one that is gaining ground globally. Learning from each other (that is, Africa from the Western world, and vice versa) will contribute to a global culture in which human infants receive the nurturant care to which they are entitled.

BOX 7.4

KEY MESSAGES

- Infant mental health should be a key priority in promoting maternal and infant well-being.
- The first 1000 days of life begins from conception, and recognition of the potential for positive intervention and for adversity in this critical period is essential.
- Nurturing care should be considered a fundamental human right of all babies regardless of psychosocial or economic standing.
- Maternal and paternal mental health influence caregiving capacity as well as the impact on providing sensitive and nurturing caregiving, so mental health screening of primary caregivers should be routine when screening infants.
- There is wide variation in parenting practices that is influenced by traditions, cultural beliefs, and community practices; there is no one size fits all approach.
- Different cultures adapt to factors within their environment and social structures through caregiving practices to ensure an infant's survival during a vulnerable period of life.
- Indigenous cultural practices should be known and respected.
- Children should be equipped and have the opportunity to be formally educated.
- Early identification and intervention are the most cost-effective ways of ensuring mental health.

References

About us — Road to Health. (n.d.). Retrieved October 25, 2017, from https://roadtohealth.co.za/about-us/.

Africa Population 2017 (2017, October, 23). Retrieved October 25, 2017, from http://worldpopulationreview.com/continents/africa-population/.

Ainsworth, M. D. S. (1985). Patterns of infant-mother attachments: Antecedents and effects on development. *Bulletin of the New York Academy of Medicine, 61*(9), 771–791. https://doi.org/10.2307/23082925.

Ainsworth, M. D. S., Blehar, M. C., Waters, E., & Wall, S. (1978). *Patterns of attachment: A psychological study of the strange situation.* Oxford UK: Erlbaum.

Berg, A. (2003). Beyond the dyad: Parent-infant psychotherapy in a multicultural society - Reflections from a South African perspective. *Infant Mental Health Journal, 24*(3), 265–277. https://doi.org/10.1002/imhj.10055.

Berg, A. (2012a). *Connecting with South Africa - cultural comunication and understanding* (College Station).

Berg, A. (2012b). Infant-parent psychotherapy at primary care level: Establishment of a service. *South African Medical Journal, 102*(6), 582–584.

Britto, P. R., Lye, S. J., Proulx, K., Yousafzai, A. K., Matthews, S. G., Vaivada, T., et al. (2017). Nurturing care: Promoting early childhood development. *The Lancet, 389*(10064), 91–102. https://doi.org/10.1016/S0140-6736(16)31390-3.

Campbell, F., Conti, G., Heckman, J. J., Moon, S. H., Pinto, R., Pungello, E., et al. (2014). Early childhood investments substantially boost adult health. *Science, 343*(6178), 1478–1485. https://doi.org/10.1126/science.1248429.

Chan, C. K., & Anteby, M. (2016). Task segregation as a mechanism for within-job inequality. *Administrative Science Quarterly, 61*(2), 184–216. https://doi.org/10.1177/0001839215611447.

Cooper, P. J., Tomlinson, M., Swartz, L., Landman, M., Molteno, C., Stein, A., et al. (2009). Improving quality of mother-infant relationship and infant attachment in socioeconomically deprived community in South Africa: Randomised controlled trial. *British Medical Journal, 338*, b974. https://doi.org/10.1136/bmj.b974.

Cyr, C., Euser, E. M., Bakermans-Kranenburg, M. J., & Van Ijzendoorn, M. H. (2010). Attachment security and disorganization in maltreating and high-risk families: A series of meta-analyses. *Development and Psychopathology, 22*(1), 87–108. https://doi.org/10.1017/S0954579409990289.

Dawson, N., Richards, J., & Frost, K. (2017). The Ububele Baby Mat Service - a primary preventative mental health intervention in a culturally diverse setting. *Journal of Child and Adolescent Mental Health, 29*(1), 85–97. https://doi.org/10.2989/17280583.2017.1297308.

Revised Edition. DC:0–3R *Diagnostic classification of mental health and developmental disorders of infancy and early childhood* (2005). Washington, D.C: ZeroToThree Press.

Demuth, C., Keller, H., & Yovsi, R. D. (2012). Cultural models in communication with infants: Lessons from Kikaikelaki, Cameroon and Muenster, Germany. *Journal of Early Childhood Research, 10*(1), 70–87. https://doi.org/10.1177/1476718X11403993.

Dowdall, N., Cooper, P. J., Tomlinson, M., Skeen, S., Gardner, F., & Murray, L. (2017). The benefits of early book sharing (BEBS) for child cognitive and socio-emotional development in South Africa: Study protocol for a randomised controlled trial. *Trials, 18*(1), 118. https://doi.org/10.1186/s13063-017-1790-1.

First 1000 Days Campaign | Western Cape Government. (n.d.). Retrieved October 25, 2017, from https://www.westerncape.gov.za/general-publication/first-1-000-days-campaign.

Frost, K. (2012). The ububele baby mat project: a community-based parent-infant intervention at primary health care clinics in Alexandra Township, Johannesburg. *South African Journal of Psychology, 42*(4), 608–616.

Global Strategy — Every Woman Every Child. (n.d.). Retrieved October 25, 2017, from http://www.everywomaneverychild.org/global-strategy/.

Gottlieb, A. (1998). Do infants have religion? The spiritual lives of Beng babies. *American Anthropologist, 100*(1), 122–135. https://doi.org/10.1525/aa.1998.100.1.122.

Graham, S. M., Manara, J., Chokotho, L., & Harrison, W. J. (2015). Back-carrying infants to prevent developmental hip dysplasia and its sequelae. *Journal of Pediatric Orthopedics, 35*(1), 57–61. https://doi.org/10.1097/BPO.0000000000000234.

Greenfield, P. M., Keller, H., Fuligni, A., & Maynard, A. (2003). Cultural pathways through universal development. *Annual Review of Psychology, 54*(1), 461–490. https://doi.org/10.1146/annurev.psych.54.101601.145221.

Harkness, S., & Super, C. M. (1994). The developmental niche: A theoretical framework for analyzing the household production of health. *Social Science & Medicine, 38*(2), 217–226. https://doi.org/10.1016/0277-9536(94)90391-3.

Igreja, V. (2003). The effects of traumatic experiences on the infant-mother relationship in the former war zones of central Mozambique: The case of madzawde in Gorongosa. *Infant Mental Health Journal, 24*(5), 469–494. https://doi.org/10.1002/imhj.10068.

Janse van Rensburg, A. B. R. (2009). A changed climate for mental health care delivery in South Africa. *African Journal of Psychiatry, 12*(2), 157–165.

Kagawa Singer, M., Dressler, W., George, S., Baquet, C. R., Bell, R. A., Burhansstipanov, L., et al. (2016). Culture: The missing link in health research. *Social Science & Medicine, 170*, 237–246. https://doi.org/10.1016/j.socscimed.2016.07.015.

Keller, H. (2007). *Cultures of infancy.* New York and London: Psychology Press.

Keller, H., Lohaus, A., Kuensemueller, P., Abels, M., Yovsi, R., Voelker, S., et al. (2004). The bio-culture of parenting: Evidence from five cultural communities. *Parenting.* https://doi.org/10.1207/s15327922par0401_2.

Keller, H., Yovsi, R., Borke, J., Kärtner, J., Jensen, H., & Papaligoura, Z. (2004 Dec 1). Developmental consequences of early parenting experiences: self-recognition and self-regulation in three cultural communities. *Child development, 75*(6), 1745–1760.

Kermoian, R., & Leiderman, P. H. (1986). Infant attachment to mother and child caretaker in an East African community. *International Journal of Behavioural Development, 9*, 455–469.

Kieling, C., Baker-Henningham, H., Belfer, M., Conti, G., Ertem, I., Omigbodun, O., et al. (2011). Child and adolescent mental health worldwide: Evidence for action. *The Lancet, 378*(9801), 1515–1525. https://doi.org/10.1016/S0140-6736(11)60827-1.

Lewis, A. J., Galbally, M., Gannon, T., & Symeonides, C. (2014). Early life programming as a target for prevention of child and adolescent mental disorders. *BMC Medicine, 12*(1), 33. https://doi.org/10.1186/1741-7015-12-33.

Lyons-Ruth, K., & Jacobvitz, D. (2008). Attachment Disorganization: Genetic factors, parenting contexts and developmental transformation from infancy to adulthood. In J. Cassidy, & P. R. Shaver (Eds.), *Handbook of attachment* (pp. 666–697). New York: Guilford.

Maiello, S. (2003). The rhythmical dimension of the mother-infant relationship - transcultural considerations. *Journal of Child and Adolescent Mental Health, 15*(2), 81–86. https://doi.org/10.2989/17280580309486552.

Marvin, R. S., VanDevender, T. L., Iwanaga, M. I., LeVine, S., & Levine, R. A. (1977). Infant-caregiver attachment among the Hausa of Nigeria. In H. McGurk (Ed.), *Ecological factors in human development* (pp. 247–260). Amsterdam, North Holland.

Meehan, C. L. (2009). Maternal time allocation in two cooperative childrearing societies. *Human Nature, 20*(4), 375–393. https://doi.org/10.1007/s12110-009-9076-2.

Mooya, H., Sichimba, F., & Bakermans-Kranenburg, M. (2016). Infant–mother and infant–sibling attachment in Zambia. *Attachment & Human Development, 18*(6), 618–635. https://doi.org/10.1080/14616734.2016.1235216.

Morrongiello, B. A., Zdzieborski, D., Sandomierski, M., & Lasenby-Lessard, J. (2009). Video messaging: What works to persuade mothers to supervise young children more closely in order to reduce injury risk? *Social Science & Medicine, 68*(6), 1030–1037. https://doi.org/10.1016/j.socscimed.2008.12.019.

Murray, L., De Pascalis, L., Tomlinson, M., Vally, Z., Dadomo, H., MacLachlan, B., et al. (2016). Randomized controlled trial of a book-sharing intervention in a deprived South African community: Effects on carer–infant interactions, and their relation to infant cognitive and socioemotional outcome. *The Journal of Child Psychology and Psychiatry and Allied Disciplines, 57*(12), 1370–1379. https://doi.org/10.1111/jcpp.12605.

Murray, L., Fiori-Cowley, A., Hooper, R., & Cooper, P. (1996). The impact of postnatal depression and associated adversity on early mother-infant interactions and later infant outcome. *Child Development, 67*(5), 2512–2526. https://doi.org/10.2307/1131637.

Posada, G. (2013). Piecing together the sensitivity construct: Ethology and cross-cultural research. *Attachment & Human Development, 15*(5–6), 637–656. https://doi.org/10.1080/14616734.2013.842753.

Pretorius, E., & Naudé, H. (2002). Results from an empirical study: The impact of carrying a child on the back on the development of visual integration pathways. *Early Child Development and Care, 172*(6), 585–594. https://doi.org/10.1080/03004430215106.

Puura, Malek, & Berg, 2018. http://perspectives.waimh.org.

Richter, L. M., Daelmans, B., Lombardi, J., Heymann, J., Boo, F. L., Behrman, J. R., et al. (2017). Investing in the foundation of sustainable development: Pathways to scale up for early childhood development. *The Lancet, 389*(10064), 103–118. https://doi.org/10.1016/S0140-6736(16)31698-1.

Sawyer, A., Ayers, S., & Smith, H. (2010). Pre- and postnatal psychological wellbeing in Africa: A systematic review. *Journal of Affective Disorders, 123*(1–3), 17–29. https://doi.org/10.1016/j.jad.2009.06.027.

Schore, A. N. (2009). Relational trauma and the developing right brain: An interface of psychoanalytic self psychology and neuroscience. *Annals of the New York Academy of Sciences, 1159*, 189–203. https://doi.org/10.1111/j.1749-6632.2009.04474.x.

Serpell, R., & Nsamenang, A. B. (2014). Locally relevant and quality ECCE programmes: Implications of research on indigenous African child development and socialization. *Early Childhood Care and Education Working Papers Series, 3.*

Simpson, T. E., Condon, E., Price, R. M., Finch, B. K., Sadler, L. S., & Ordway, M. R. (2016). Demystifying infant mental Health: What the primary care provider needs to know. *Journal of Pediatric Health Care, 30*(1), 38–48. https://doi.org/10.1016/j.pedhc.2015.09.011.

The State of the World's Children 2014 in Numbers. (n.d.). Retrieved October 25, 2017, from https://www.unicef.org/sowc2014/numbers/.

Suchman, N. E., DeCoste, C., Castiglioni, N., McMahon, T. J., Rounsaville, B., & Mayes, L. (2010). The mothers and toddlers program, an attachment-based parenting intervention for substance using women: Post-treatment results from a randomized clinical pilot. *Attachment & Human Development, 12*(5), 483–504. https://doi.org/10.1080/14616734.2010.501983.

Timyan, J. (1988). *Cultural aspects of psychosocial development: An examination of West African childrearing practices.* Washington, D.C.

Tomlinson, M., Bornstein, M. H., Marlow, M., & Swartz, L. (2014). Imbalances in the knowledge about infant mental health in rich and poor countries: Too little progress in bridging the gap. *Infant Mental Health Journal, 35*(6), 624–629. https://doi.org/10.1002/imhj.21462.

Tomlinson, M., Cooper, P., & Murray, L. (2005). The mother-infant relationship and infant attachment in a South African settlement. *Child Development, 76*(5), 1044–1054.

Tomlinson, M., Rotheram-Borus, M. J., Harwood, J., le Roux, I. M., O'Connor, M., & Worthman, C. (2015). Community health workers can improve child growth of antenatally-depressed, South African mothers: A cluster randomized controlled trial. *BMC Psychiatry, 15*(1), 225. https://doi.org/10.1186/s12888-015-0606-7.

Tomlinson, M., & Swartz, L. (2003). Imbalances in the knowledge about infancy: The divide between rich and poor countries. *Infant Mental Health Journal, 24*(6), 547–556. https://doi.org/10.1002/imhj.10078.

Tronick, E. Z., Morelli, G. A., & Ivey, P. K. (1992). The Efe forager infant and toddler's pattern of social relationships: Multiple and simultaneous. *Developmental Psychology, 28*(4), 568–577. https://doi.org/10.1037/0012-1649.28.4.568.

True, M. M., Pisani, L., & Oumar, F. (2001). Infant-mother attachment among the Dogon of Mali. *Child Development, 72*(5), 1451–1466. https://doi.org/10.1111/1467-8624.00359.

United Nations — Sustainable Development Goals. (n.d.). Retrieved October 30, 2017, from http://www.un.org/sustainabledevelopment/sustainable-development-goals/.

Voges, J., Berg, A. M., & Niehaus, D. J. H. (2017). *Revisiting the origins of attachment research - 50 years on from Ainsworth, A descriptive review.* Manuscript submitted for publication.

WAIMH Position Paper on the Rights of Infants, Edinburgh, 14-18 June, 2014 (amended March 2016). https://www.waihm,org.

Zeanah, C. H. (2009). *Handbook of infant mental health* (3rd ed.). New York: Guilford Press.

Mental Health Service Provision for Child and Adolescent Refugees: European Perspectives

Joerg M. Fegert, Thorsten Sukale, Rebecca C. Brown

University of Ulm, Ulm, Germany

THE SITUATION IN EUROPE

According to the United Nations High Commissioner for Refugees (UNHCR) (UNHCR, 2017b), in 2017, 65.6 million people were forcibly displaced, 22.5 million of whom were refugees. In other words, 28,300 people had to leave their homes every day because of persecution or conflict (UNHCR, 2017b). Over 50% of those refugees originated from Syria, Afghanistan, and South Sudan. Whereas most refugees were hosted in Africa (30%) or the Middle East and North Africa (26%), Europe hosted 17% of all refugees. There were few first-time asylum seekers in the European Union (EU) between 2006 and 2012 (less than 200,000/year), but numbers increased rapidly from 431,000 in 2013 to 1.3 million in both 2015 and 2016 (Eurostat, 2017b). These were the highest numbers since a peak in 1992, with 672,000 asylum seekers arriving in the EU, mainly from former Yugoslavia (Eurostat, 2017b). Numbers increased particularly in Germany, from 442,000 in 2015 to 722,000 in 2016, thus hosting 60% of all asylum seekers in the EU. Germany was followed by Italy and Greece, both of which reported an increase of around 30,000 first-time asylum seekers from 2015 to 2016. On the contrary, countries such as Austria, Belgium, and all Scandinavian countries reported a decline in numbers, with less than 50% of the number of asylum seekers in 2016 compared with 2015. These changes mainly result from the agreement between the EU and Turkey in March, 2016, stating that Turkey would host most refugees wanting to migrate from the Middle East to Europe, and that it

*Understanding Uniqueness and Diversity in Child and
Adolescent Mental Health*
https://doi.org/10.1016/B978-0-12-815310-9.00008-3

195

would receive financial compensation in return. In the following months, numbers of refugees from the Middle East decreased significantly in all European countries in late 2016 and 2017 (e.g., a decrease of −47% in the first quarter of 2017 compared with 2016), whereas Italy and other Mediterranean countries continued to receive large numbers of refugees from Africa (Eurostat, 2017a).

In general, refugees in Europe represent a young, predominately male group of people. A large majority of refugees (83%) are aged less than 35 years; 32% are aged less than 18 years (Eurostat, 2017b). An unaccompanied refugee minor (URM) is defined as a person under age 18 years who arrives in the host country without an adult responsible for his or her care, or who is left unaccompanied after arriving in the host country. In total, around 16% of all refugee minors were URM in 2016 throughout the EU; numbers were much higher in Italy and Slovenia (Eurostat, 2017b). In total numbers, Germany had accommodated over 60,000 URM by the end of January, 2016, with most URM coming from Afghanistan, Syria, Iraq, Eritrea, and Somalia (Bundesamt für Migration und Flüchtlinge, 2016).

PSYCHOSOCIAL NEEDS, PSYCHIATRIC ILLNESSES, AND CONSEQUENCES OF TRAUMATIZATION IN MINOR REFUGEES

Refugee children come from areas with ongoing war, armed conflict, prosecution, or immense poverty. Many of them have experienced death or the loss of close relatives or significant others, have not had access to education or fostering environments, or have been subject to domestic violence and physical abuse. To escape hardship in their home countries, they risk forced labor, sexual abuse, beatings, detention, and death during migration. Of the 4579 refugees who died on the Central Mediterranean Route (from Africa across the Mediterranean Sea to Europe) in 2016, around 700 were children (UNICEF, 2017). Many refugee children have to watch the death of other refugees or become separated from their family members or friends during migration. According to Eurostat data (Eurostat, 2017b), around one in four refugee children worldwide travels without a parent or adult guardian and around 9 in 10 refugee children tries to cross the Mediterranean Sea without a caregiver (UNICEF, 2017).

When arriving in Europe, new stressors arise in the form of insecure asylum status, unemployment, inadequate housing, and the challenge of having to integrate into a foreign culture and society. In a Belgian study by Vervliet et al. (2014) reported a significant effect of everyday stressors on URM. Next to medical treatment, living and financial situations were reported, especially problems with gaining or maintaining positive social contacts. Furthermore, refugees might be faced with negative or even hostile attitudes displayed by the population of hosting countries. Especially in Germany, which is the country that hosts most refugees in the EU, attitudes changed in 2016 from a generally pronounced "welcome culture" to a more hesitant (and sometimes hostile) atmosphere in 2016. A shift in attitudes is probably caused by many factors, one of which is media coverage of current events. Whereas in May and October, 2015, 31% and 32%, respectively, of the general population said that it was possible for Germany to host more refugees (Koecher, 2015), in the beginning of 2016 this was answered positively with regard to URM by only 23% (Plener, Groschwitz, Brahler, Sukale, & Fegert, 2017). This shift in attitudes was temporally associated with events on New Year's Eve 2015—2016, when apparently planned sexual harassment of a large number of women in the market square of Cologne by mainly non-German young men was linked in the media to increasing numbers of refugees in Germany (Michel, Schoenian, Thurm, & Steffen, 2016). When asking whether URM should be deported to their country of origin immediately after arriving in Germany, 38.6% of a representative sample of the German population agreed with this statement (Plener et al., 2017). Interestingly, this question generated lower rates than did the mean level of agreement when the sample was asked about URM differentiated by their country of origin. In this case, 35.3% of participants agreed to deport URM from the Middle East, thus regarding them as the most "eligible" group for asylum, whereas agreement rates for deporting URM from Africa (51%) and the Balkan region (62%) were much higher. Generally, those attitudes were stronger in participants with right-extremist (and right-wing) or Islamophobic tendencies, males, and older participants (Plener et al., 2017). However, high rates of approval (almost three-quarters of participants agreed) were found with regard to questions about offering URM equal education to German children and granting them the right to stay in Germany after successfully completing school or an apprenticeship or being integrated into the labor force.

Apart from these studies, media debates linking increasing numbers of refugees to an increased risk for terrorist attacks and crime seem to have fostered negative and hostile public attitudes and stereotypes in Germany and Europe. Especially in 2016, a debate on crimes committed by refugees was widespread in international media. This debate mainly resulted from numbers released by the German Federal Criminal Police Office. For example, the *Daily Mail* stated that German chancellor Angela Merkel was under pressure owing to 142,500 crimes committed by refugees in Germany in the first 6 months of 2016 (Robinson, 2016). However, what was not reported and discussed in most mainstream media was that most refugees in Germany were young men, a group that has an eightfold risk of being involved in criminal activity in the general population. Furthermore, war refugees such as those from Syria were the least likely to commit crimes (deutschlandfunk, 2017). Because of this debate about crime, violence, and sexual violence, public attention has focused mainly on young male refugees. This has led to the neglect of public awareness regarding female URM and children who migrated with their families. This focus of attention probably also exists because most URM are male, because often the oldest or most intelligent son is chosen to take on the journey to Europe and is equipped with financial and other support to do so, thus often leaving girls in devastating conditions back in their home countries and denying them the chance of a better life. Furthermore, girls are of greater risk to be victims of sexual violence or sexual exploitation during migration (UNHCR, 2017c). However, these topics are neglected by the media compared with crime and violence committed by young male refugees.

As a result of all of these stressors, refugee children comprise an especially vulnerable group for the development of mental disorders (Huemer, Karnik, & Steiner, 2009; Stotz, Elbert, Muller, & Schauer, 2015). However, different people react differently to potentially traumatic experiences and not every potentially traumatic experience leads to the development of a psychiatric disorder with the same chance. Fully developed posttraumatic stress disorders (PTSDs) are seen more often in adults than in children, because children more often develop age-appropriate developmental delays or other posttraumatic stress symptoms (PTSSs). Having said this, interpersonal traumatic events (e.g., rape, torture, or other interpersonal violence) usually cause more severe impairment than do traumatic events without direct interpersonal contact such as accidents or natural disasters. Most important, the "dose" of traumatic events seems to be associated with the likelihood of developing PTSD; i.e., an increasing number of traumatic events is associated with an increased risk for developing PTSD, a finding that holds true for adults and children (Catani, Jacob, Schauer, Kohila, & Neuner, 2008; Neuner et al., 2004). To date, no explicit numbers can be determined for prevalence rates of mental disorders in refugee children. However, one study on a representative sample of Syrian refugee children living with their families in a German refugee camp provides first evidence (Soykoek, Mall, Nehring, Henningsen, & Aberl, 2017). Prevalence rates of PTSD of 26% in 0- to 6-year-olds and 33% in 7- to 14-year-olds were found. These prevalence rates were therefore much higher than those in the German general population of 3% (Maercker, Forstmeier, Wagner, Glaesmer, & Brahler, 2008).

Among child and adolescent refugees, URM are a particularly vulnerable group for developing mental disorders (Huemer et al., 2009), owing to the lack of protective factors such as a supportive family environment and increased feelings of loneliness and fear for relatives back in their home countries (Derluyn & Broekaert, 2007; Derluyn,

Broekaert, & Schuyten, 2008). Furthermore, URM living together with other URM show an increased fear of being sent back to their home countries, because they are at increased risk for witnessing this happening to their befriended URM (Malmsten, 2014).

In a systematic review on mental health issues of URM, Witt, Rassenhofer, Fegert, and Plener (2015) found studies reporting traumatic experiences to be present in almost all URM, and that URM were more likely to have experienced traumatic events than were children who were accompanied by families or guardians. Most consistent results on the prevalence rates of psychiatric disorders were drawn from two studies using clinical interviews; 42%—56% of URM met criteria for psychiatric disorders. For example, a study from Norway interviewing 160 male URM aged 15—18 years found that 42% of all refugees met criteria for at least one psychiatric disorder, but 96% had experienced at least one stressful life event (Jakobsen, Demott, & Heir, 2014). The other study using clinical interviews was conducted in Austria. It included 41 URM, 85% of whom were male, and it reported slightly higher prevalence rates of at least one psychiatric disorder (56%). Studies using other methodologies, such as questionnaires, screenings, or reports from caregivers, reported rates of internalizing or externalizing disorders between 20% and 81.5%. Those studies originated from Sweden, Austria, the United Kingdom, Norway, Belgium, Italy, and the Netherlands. There were probably several reasons for differences in those prevalence rates: different questionnaires were used, refugees came from different countries, different amounts of time were in Europe before refugees were assessed, and samples contained different ratios of male to female participants and ages. Across all studies, PTSD or PTSSs showed the highest prevalence rates compared with other psychiatric impairments (Witt et al., 2015). Prevalence rates for PTSD or PTSS ranged from 17% to 71% in studies using questionnaires and 19.5% to 30% when assessing PTSD via diagnostic interviews. The lowest rate of 17% was assessed in a study from Austria (Volkl-Kernstock et al., 2014), using the University of California at Los Angeles (UCLA) PTSD reaction index. However, whereas only 17% met all criteria for PTSD in that sample, around 30% met partial criteria for PTSD according to UCLA. In a study from the United Kingdom differentiating between female and male URM, female URM showed slightly higher rates of the risk for developing PTSD (73%) compared with males (61.5%) (Hodes, Jagdev, Chandra, & Cunniff, 2008). Other common psychiatric symptoms included depressive symptoms, with prevalence rates for major depression of 9% in clinical interviews (Jakobsen et al., 2014) and 44% depressive symptomatology via self-report in a Belgian study (Vervliet et al., 2014). Again, female URM (23%) showed higher prevalence rates than did males (11.5%) (Hodes et al., 2008). The prevalence for anxiety symptoms ranged from 4% in clinical interviews (generalized anxiety disorder and agoraphobia) (Huemer et al., 2011) to 38% in self-report questionnaires (Vervliet et al., 2014). In studies using self-report questionnaires, rates of externalizing symptoms were lower than those in the general population (Witt et al., 2015). Longitudinal studies identified in this systematic review showed a high stability of psychiatric symptoms over time. Furthermore, an increase, rather than a decrease, in negative life events was reported by URM after having arrived in the host country, which may have hindered remittance of mental health issues. These numbers show that refugees, especially URM, are of elevated risk for developing mental health issues. Interestingly, although Germany was the country that received most refugees compared with all other countries in Europe, Witt et al. were not able to detect any studies on the situation of URM in Germany. Walg, Fink, Grossmeier, Temprano, and Hapfelmeier (2016) were the first to provide these data. However, analyses are based on retrospective data of a selective group of refugees in a clearing center in Duesseldorf, Germany. Of the 75 male URM living in this clearing center between May, 2013 and December, 2015, 56 (75%) were referred to a clinic for child and adolescent psychiatry owing to emotional and behavioral problems as observed by staff at the clearing center. PTSD was diagnosed in 36% of those 75 URM, followed by 27% who were diagnosed with major depression. Most URM (80%–84%) reported disordered sleeping, 55% headaches, and 29% stomachaches.

On the other hand, considering all of these risk factors, a substantial number of refugees (estimated at around 50%) (Witt et al., 2015), did not develop significant psychiatric symptoms. Factors fostering resilience seemed to be social support (Afifi & Macmillan, 2011) and being in contact with family members in the country of origin. Furthermore, learning the language of the host country and attending school were the two most common needs expressed by URM (Fegert, Plener, & Koelch, 2015; Witt et al., 2015). Access to the education system provides URM with a much-needed daily structure and an opportunity for integration (Fegert, Plener, et al., 2015). However, because studies on the resilience of URM are rare and this group seems to be particularly heterogeneous, further studies are needed on specific risk and protective factors (Witt et al., 2015).

URM receive support in most European countries (e.g., living in foster homes, having access to psychotherapeutic treatment), which offers protection and possibilities for integration, but young refugees arriving with their families often receive less support in this regard. In German refugee camps, for example, access to adequate schooling is sometimes difficult, because often school attendance is not compulsory (Bundesfachverband unbegleitete minderjährige Flüchtlinge, 2015), which is a practice contrary to Article 28 of the United Nations Resolution on the Rights of the Child, which emphasizes the right to education for every child (Fegert, Plener, et al., 2015). Gambaro, Liebau, Peter, and Weinhardt (2017) published encouraging data (sampling June to December, 2016) from a representative sample of more than 4500 adult refugees concerning a subgroup of 4405 children to age 12 years who were living in 1643 households in Germany. More than two-thirds of those families came from Syria, Afghanistan, and Iraq. Most of the school-aged children attended school (95%) and half of that group acquired special language training; 25% of the school-aged children attended special preparation and adaptation classes for refugee children. In the kinder-garten group, around 80% were in institutional care, compared with 95% in the overall population in Germany. In the youngest age group, 0- to 3-year-olds, only 15% of children attended care facilities. Families often have to stay in refugee camps, which do not offer adequate privacy for the family (e.g., only one room for the whole family, with no private bath-rooms). Children and adolescents are at pronounced risk for physical and sexual abuse in those camps, especially when families are housed together with single men. The German Independent Commissioner for Issues Related to Child Sexual Abuse released guidelines for protection in institutions working with or housing refugee children, to protect them from sexual violence or intervene efficiently in case there was suspicion of it (UBSKM, 2017) (see Box 8.1 for further information).

Furthermore, family constellations may have changed before or during the flight, e.g., by having lost or left behind family members. Often, parents themselves are traumatized or mentally changed from experiences before or during migration and lack social support from other relatives or friends. This can make it difficult to provide adequate parenting and a stable, nurturing, and safe environment (Fegert, Diehl, Leyendecker, & Hahlweg, 2017). In families in which parents are traumatized from war, inadequate parenting and physical violence against women and children is significantly more common than in non-traumatized parents (Catani et al., 2008; Saile, Ertl, Neuner, & Catani, 2014). Although the underlying processes for these associations have not yet been explored, symptoms of increased arousal in particular (increased irritability, fits of rage, and hypervigilance) might explain increased violence in families with a family member experiencing PTSD. This association was found in a number of studies. For example, whereas 70% of veterans of the Vietnam War with PTSD and their partners reported clinically relevant relationship issues and physical aggression, this was reported by only 30% of veterans without PTSD and their partners (Riggs, Byrne, Weathers, & Litz, 1998). Furthermore, increased use of alcohol in traumatized men seems to be related to more domestic violence (Catani et al., 2008; Saile et al., 2014). Unfortunately, especially children with mental disorders are at higher risk for experiencing verbal or physical violence (Sriskandarajah, Neuner, & Catani, 2015b). Especially in the case

---

BOX 8.1

CHECKLIST FOR A MINIMUM STANDARD TO PROTECT CHILDREN FROM SEXUAL VIOLENCE IN REFUGEE ACCOMMODATIONS (UBSKM, 2017)

1. Professional standards
   a. Were professionals and volunteers well-sensitized and informed about sexual violence?
   b. Were helpers made aware of the necessity for an unprejudiced and culturally sensitive attitude toward refugees?
   c. Are there equal numbers of male and female helpers?
   d. Do helpers working with refugees have to submit an extended certificate of good conduct or, alternatively, sign a commitment statement?
2. Building Standards
   a. Can toilets be locked?
   b. Are showers separated by gender available?
   c. Can children and adolescents spend time in supervised playground and spare-time areas?
   d. Can single mothers and their children be accommodated in separate areas?
3. Information and help offers
   a. Is culturally sensitive and easily understood information available in all relevant languages?
   b. Has a contact person been appointed who can be turned to in case of suspected sexual violence?
   c. Is support available from interpreters?
   d. Is there separate information for refugee children, especially concerning their rights?
   e. Is there an emergency plan regarding how to act in case of suspected sexual violence?
   f. Does the facility cooperate with counseling services?

---

of posttraumatic symptomatology, children often display externalizing behaviors such as irritability, anger, or tantrums, which might provoke physical disciplinary actions in parents. Furthermore, children with PTSS are often less able to concentrate or fulfill scholarly or domestic chores. Parents might perceive these deficits to be signs of laziness or unwillingness, and therefore might also be more likely to display inadequate parenting behaviors. In these cases, parental violence can be a sign of helplessness or the lack of more positive parenting strategies to deal with externalizing or internalizing symptoms displayed by their children. This is particularly important for planning possible interventions, because a study conducted in families after the civil war in Sri Lanka showed that a high level of parental support was associated with less severe post-traumatic psychiatric impairment in children (Sriskandarajah, Neuner, & Catani, 2015a).

DIAGNOSTIC ISSUES AND SCREENING AFTER ARRIVAL IN A HOST COUNTRY

When they newly arrive in a host country, adolescents and children are not usually able to understand or speak the language. Although adolescents, and especially children, often quickly make good progress in learning new languages, more complex topics such as mental health issues can be difficult to assess within the first months after arrival. Furthermore, some adolescents are illiterate and therefore cannot be recruited to complete (screening) questionnaires. Although the possibility exists of involving translators and can be helpful, many obstacles might occur. First, translators are not always available or affordable. Furthermore, not many translators have training in child and adolescent mental health and therefore the might not always be appropriate partners to ask delicate questions, or they might even be negatively psychologically affected when they hear stories of traumatizing events. Another issue is that some adolescents might not feel comfortable talking about intimate details when too many persons are in the room. On the other hand, a study by Keselman, Cederborg, Lamb, and Dahlstroem (2010) showed that in a sample of 26 URM from Russia, all participants were willing and able to reveal information about themselves, even when confronted with stressful or difficult topics in the presence of a translator. Most translations were accurate, but some problems in validity arose, especially when translators were trying to improve adolescents' choices of words or grammar in their translation. Furthermore, the authors noticed that some questions or replies were translated in a suggestive or judgmental way. Therefore, clinicians, translators, and refugees should be aware of these issues and the possibility of decreased validity of replies to questions. Although the use of translators can be helpful, because of these issues mentioned, it seems feasible to have validated diagnostic tools available in the language of the host country as well as that of the country of origin.

In addition to language barriers, cultural norms, stigma, and acceptance of child and adolescent psychiatric services can present major obstacles. Often, young refugees have no concept or a different concept of mental health compared with the conceptualization of and professionals such as psychotherapists or psychiatrists. In many cultures, people with mental illnesses are discriminated against (Amuyunzu-Nyamongo, Owuor, & Blanchard, 2013). Often, patients present with somatic symptoms (e.g., headache or stomachache) rather than mental health issues (Hofmeister, 2014). In a first contact, it is therefore important to explain the concept and appraisal of psychiatric disorders in Western cultures (Reher & Metzner, 2016). Furthermore, some patients might be hesitant to report their experiences before or during their migration, because they may have had negative experiences when being asked to tell their story when they were evaluated for asylum status (Reher & Metzner, 2016).

Another cultural difference is the expression of certain psychiatric symptoms in ways different from those frequently used in Europe. For example, whereas most adolescents in Western cultures engage in non-suicidal self-injury (NSSI) by cutting their skin (Yates, 2004), adolescents from the Middle East seem to engage in NSSI most often by hitting their hands or heads against a wall or hitting themselves (Gholamrezaei, Heath, & Panaghi, 2016). These injuries can be overlooked or not attributed to being NSSI by Western-trained clinicians or other medical or youth-welfare staff. Furthermore, although rare, some adolescents from African countries or certain minority Muslim groups might engage in self-injury as part of a religious ritual (Baasher, 2001).

Another issue when first screening for or diagnosing mental health issues in adolescent refugees is assessing suicidality in a culturally sensitive way. Because suicide is strictly forbidden in Islam (Pridmore & Pasha, 2004), Muslim refugees might feel ashamed of discussing this topic and might negate suicidal tendencies that are actually present. However, religiosity has shown to be a protective factor for suicidality (Caribe et al., 2012), and Islam in particular can be protective owing to its strict rules on suicide and the regularity of prayers. Whereas Ruf et al. (2010) found prevalence rates of 13% lifetime suicidality in 98 refugee minors who arrived in Germany with their families, prevalence rates were much higher in children and adolescents (aged 7–16 years) who were diagnosed with PTSD. Of those refugee minors, 32% indicated lifetime suicidality, whereas 16% had had suicidal thoughts within the past month. However, those suicidal thoughts may often express being overwhelmed by excessive demands, without the concrete intention or plan for actions (Reher & Metzner, 2016). On the other hand, although suicide is strictly forbidden in Islam, dying as a martyr can be viewed as rewarding. Thus, Islamic radicalization, and therefore turning a wish to die from suicide into a "meaningful" death, might be a danger with which especially young URM are faced. Radical Islamic influence can stem directly from mosques visited by URM, often to compensate for the lack of stability and safety within a family. Furthermore, the Internet, which is crucial for gaining information and for staying in touch with their family and friends in their home countries, can be used by radical Islamists to lure young refugees into their community.

On a last note, assessment of traumatic experiences can be difficult owing to PTSD symptoms (e.g., avoidance, lack of ability to concentrate or strong emotional arousal). This is particularly true for URMs when no other person is available to give an account of what happened to the young person or to validate or support the story. Especially in the case of URM, some information, especially on the early development of the adolescent, might be unattainable (Zindler & Metzner, 2016). Therefore it is necessary to make diagnostic evaluations using as little information as possible.

Rassenhofer, Fegert, Plener, and Witt (2016) thus defined the following requirements for diagnostic tools used to assess emotional and behavioral problems in URM: The instrument should be available in a large number of different languages, and it should be culturally adapted and also be available for use with illiterate adolescents (i.e., by being able to apply the instrument in the form of an interview or by providing adequate visual or audio resources). Because studies have shown that URM are mainly affected by symptoms associated with PTSD, depression, and anxiety (Witt et al., 2015), instruments should have a certain focus on those symptomatic clusters. Furthermore, all instruments completed by others than the adolescents themselves should include the option of being completed by a number of different persons (e.g., teachers, social workers, legal guardians) and it should be possible to complete those questionnaires with little previous knowledge about the developmental history of the adolescent. Because timely resources are often scarce for professionals working with URM, instruments (besides good reliability and validity) should also be efficient in their use, and freely available.

In their systematic review, Rassenhofer et al. (2016) identified four screening and diagnostic tools for which validated versions for URM are available in different languages. All of those questionnaires were validated by one research group from the Netherlands, led by Tammy Bean and Philip Spinhoven. The group evaluated a questionnaire to assess PTSS (Reactions of Adolescents to Traumatic Stress Questionnaire) (Bean, Derluyn, Eurrelings-Bontekoe, Broekaert, & Spinhoven, 2006) and the Hopkins Symptoms Checklist (Bean, Derluyn, Eurelings-Bontekoe, Broekaert, & Spinhoven, 2007) to assess internalizing and externalizing behaviors in reaction to traumatic events via self-report. Both instruments were evaluated in 19 languages (Albanian, Amharic, Arabian, Badini, Dari, German, English, Farsi, French, Mongolian, Dutch, Portuguese, Russian, Serbo-Croatian, Sorani, Somali, Spanish, and Turkish) in four independent samples of 3535 adolescent URM, immigrants, and native Dutch and Belgian students. Both questionnaires were shown to be reliable and valid for assessing emotional and behavioral issues in URM and culturally diverse groups via self-report (Bean, Derluyn, et al., 2007, 2006). Apart from self-report measures, it is also important to be able to assess emotional and behavioral problems via the report of others. Bean, Mooijaart, and Spinhoven (2007) evaluated the Dutch version of the Teacher's Report Form (TRF), which assessed internalizing and externalizing behaviors in a sample of 486 teachers of adolescent URM. Although generally showing good reliability, the scale "thought problems" could not be validated. Furthermore, overall scores showed just acceptable construct and concurrent validity compared with the original Dutch TRF. Similar results were found when evaluating the Child Behavioral Checklist (CBCL) in a sample of 920 URM and their legal guardians (caseworkers) (Bean, Mooijaart, Eurelings-Bontekoe, & Spinhoven, 2006). Main problems concerning the validity of those questionnaires was the limited time caregivers or teachers had spent with the adolescents (especially compared with parents for whom the CBCL was originally designed) and the experience of teachers and caregivers with URM in general. The authors therefore recommended collecting information from different sources (e.g., legal guardians, teachers, caregivers, and adolescents themselves) to arrive at a more valid conclusion about the actual emotional and behavioral problems of the adolescent (Bean, Mooijaart, et al., 2007). Although the evaluated questionnaires are suitable for a first screening of psychiatric impairment in URM, neither the CBCL nor the TRF is freely available. This might cause financial problems, especially for nongovernmental organizations (NGOs) taking care of URM in many countries. Rassenhofer et al. (2016) therefore suggested the possibility of using other questionnaires, such as the Strength and Difficulties Questionnaire (SDQ) (www.sdq.info). This questionnaire is available in 80 languages, has been validated as a self-report and others-report instrument, and is widely used internationally. Although the SDQ is not specific to common symptoms in URM because it assesses emotional problems, hyperactivity, problems with others, and behavioral problems, it can be used acceptably as a screening tool. Furthermore, the Refugee Mental Health Project, by Canada's Mental Health and Addiction Network, offers a wide variety of screening tools available in different languages (https://www.porticonetwork.ca/web/rmhp/toolkit/screening-assessment), some of which are freely available online. However, some of these instruments are not available with open access online but have to be ordered. Furthermore, some instruments are available only in languages which are not relevant to most refugees living in European countries (i.e., the Harvard Trauma Questionnaire is available in English, Vietnamese, Cambodian, Laotian, Japanese, Croatian, and Bosnian).

Because most URM in European countries live in youth-welfare institutions, those institutions often carry the burden of having to decide whether a URM needs psychotherapeutic help. This is also true for refugee camps where many families live, or for social workers or volunteers who support refugee families in the integration process. To facilitate a screening of stressors and impairment of young refugees in welfare institutions or refugee camps, or when they are first assessed at a mental health institution, Sukale et al. (2016) developed an online screening tool based on the National Child Traumatic Stress Network core stressor overview. Using the Providing Online Resource and Trauma Assessment for Refugees (PORTA), professionals as well as volunteer helpers can assess the stressors and possible further needs of young refugees. One reason for developing this tool arose from the realization that the level of expertise of people helping refugees ranged from psychiatrists or child and adolescent therapists to youth welfare workers, teachers, and volunteer helpers with no explicit training. This online tool can be used only if the child or adolescent has been in contact with a person within the care system for a sufficient amount of time for that person to give appropriate information about the adolescent or child of concern. Furthermore, children or adolescents have the opportunity to provide self-report, either without further assistance or guided by an adult. The tool is available in German, English, French, Arabic Dari, Pashto, and Tigrinya. In a first step, general impairment in different areas of life is assessed. An algorithm then gives automated standardized suggestions for improvement and possible further steps in the health care system. Results are easily understood because they are presented in a graph with each area of life colored according to the assessed impairment in the form of a traffic light system (green for no impairment, yellow for medium impairment, and red for severe impairment). For example, areas of life can be mental health or social functioning. In a further step, more specific impairment is assessed using the Refugee Health Screener, the SDQ, the Child and Adolescent Trauma Screening, and parts of the Self-injurious Thoughts and Behaviors Interview. The PORTA tool has been validated in a pilot study including 33 boys (mean age, 16.2 years; standard deviation = 1.03 years) and their helpers during a time span of 4 weeks. Helpers came from different professional backgrounds (e.g., trainee in child and adolescent behavioral therapy, social workers, psychologists, psychiatrists), with a broad age range of 19–50 years. All adolescents lived in preclearing institutions or clearing institutions and originated from Syria (58%); Afghanistan (27%); Iran (6%); and Somalia, Sudan, and Iraq (3% each). Whereas adolescents in Germany stay in preclearing institutions for a limited amount of time until their legal status has been cleared, adolescents in clearing institutions can stay there until their 18th birthday, and a stay includes schooling as well as other integration programs. Concerning general impairment, adolescents in the preclearing-institution were significantly more impaired than were adolescents in the more permanent clearing institution. Adolescents who had spent more than 7 months in one institution were significantly less distressed than were those who had arrived at an institution less than a month ago. Overall, PORTA is an easy-to-use screening tool which assesses different aspects of possible stressors or impairment in young refugees' lives, but it also assesses possible resources to build upon. Furthermore, it provides refugees and their helpers with guidance as to where to seek further help or in which areas in life further support is needed. However, of course, screening tools such as PORTA do not replace psychiatric evaluation when a psychiatric diagnosis is likely.

IMMEDIATE INTERVENTIONS, CRISES MANAGEMENT AFTER SUICIDALITY AND AGGRESSIVE CONFLICTS, AND THE ROLE OF INPATIENT SERVICES

Because of the high vulnerability of refugee minors, which is caused by acute and chronic stressors as well as psychiatric symptoms related to PTSD, strategies are needed for immediate interventions and crisis management. This can be particularly challenging owing to language barriers and the often distressed emotional state of refugees in those situations. Furthermore, because often refugees are not familiar with psychotherapeutic or psychiatric treatment, they might be skeptical or scared, because they might be reminded of how they were treated by institutions in their home country or even of being detained (especially when police are recruited to take adolescents to the psychiatric ward) (Walg et al., 2016). A study by Walg et al. (2016) showed that emergency situations, which are highly distressing to all parties involved, can be reduced by offering special consultation sessions for refugees at a department for child and adolescent psychiatry and psychotherapy. These consultation sessions can be used by young refugees living, e.g., in youth-welfare institutions or clearing centers, who present with psychiatric impairment. Adolescents would already be familiar with the staff and procedures at the department before possible emergency situations. Therefore, those situations could be handled much more calmly, because adolescents would know what to expect and would show higher compliance related to reduced mistrust and anxiety (Walg et al., 2016).

As another example, 562 URM were accommodated in the State of Saarland, Germany, and later dispersed to different parts of the country in 2015 and 2016. In those first few days or weeks of arrival, many URM were obviously deeply distressed and in need of stabilization (Dixius & Moehler, 2017). Although a maximum level of transparency was offered about all processes, and a "safe place" for living, adolescents were also in high need for emotional security and help to develop strategies to reduce stress and regulate emotion (Dixius & Moehler, 2017). Physiological symptoms such as erosive gastritis and head and muscle pains were highly prevalent, but URMs also reported disordered sleeping or regular nightmares and emotional distress owing to worries about the safety of family members, homesickness, or missing loved ones. In addition to these issues, all refugees were constantly worried about their future, because none had yet been granted asylum or knew to which part of Germany they would be taken. Progressive muscle relaxation (PMR) and skills groups, which were assisted by translators, showed subjectively good effects, but they were not sufficient to cater to all needs of the URM. This was mainly because of language barriers and because translators were not always available, particularly not in most sudden acute stressful situations. Therefore, a structured short intervention (such as Students and Refugees Together [START]) was developed using nonverbal material and providing verbal instructions in the most common languages spoken by URM (Dixius & Moehler, 2017). The basis of this intervention is the idea of evoking feelings of self-efficacy and control over one's own behavior by successfully learning and implementing skills in stressful situations. These skills are supposed to be behaviors which help in the short term, giving immediate stress reduction and emotional regulation. Therefore, the intervention is not designed specifically to reduce PTSD symptomatology. Being able to administer coping skills might also strengthen resiliency, facilitate an easier integration into the new surroundings (by having less adverse experiences with other adolescents or care providers, or even delinquent behaviors) and prevent youth from self-medicating with alcohol or other substances (Dixius & Moehler, 2017). Skills used in START are taken from other therapeutic concepts such as dialectic behavioral therapy for adolescents and cognitive behavioral therapy (CBT), and incorporate relaxation techniques such as PMR. The training incorporates different modules, each teaching skills serving emotion regulation and awareness (to enhance perception of feelings and thoughts and be able to react as soon as possible) as well as relaxation skills to enhance the ability to calm down, the perception of emotions, and the enhancement of self-efficacy. The START intervention is delivered in groups, ideally by two therapists. Therefore, one therapist can lead through the exercises while the other can offer support individually to patients experiencing acute distress. Most of the modules can be delivered without translators, because materials are visually explanatory (pictures explaining behaviors or emotions) or language-based input is available in several languages. The program is conceptualized for adolescents aged 13–18 years. First experiences with the program showed good feasibility and acceptance among adolescents and caregivers (Dixius & Moehler, 2017). Because the program can be delivered in youth-welfare institutions or refugee camps, it is less stigmatizing and reduces strain caused by regular visits to psychiatric departments. An important issue is voluntary participation. Because being mentally ill is highly stigmatized in many countries, especially male URM have shown high aversion to being treated in a psychotherapeutic setting. By offering a group intervention focused on teaching skills, high acceptance was seen by the authors (Dixius & Moehler, 2017).

One issue often described by URM, but also accompanied refugee minors, is sleeping difficulties. Therefore, one module of START focuses on implementing skills and relaxation models for sleeping. Furthermore, techniques for describing and modifying nightmares are used. However, this module often requires the use of translators and individual sessions (Dixius & Moehler, 2017). Apart from this specific intervention, discussing sleeping hygiene strategies (e.g., not sleeping during the day, not eating or drinking just before going to bed) can be helpful to improve sleep quality. Furthermore, psychopharmacological treatment is often used successfully in this case, because refugee minors are often severely impaired in everyday functioning owing to disturbed sleep. However, further studies are needed on appropriate medication so that empirically based recommendations may be made to treat refugee minors, who also often experience PTSD and nightmares, (Reher & Metzner, 2016).

Another short intervention for traumatized URM, which can be delivered by youth-welfare staff, is the CBT group intervention My Way (Pfeiffer & Goldbeck, 2018). The intervention consists of six sessions including psychoeducation, relaxation, creation of a trauma narrative, and cognitive restructuring. A pilot evaluation study including 29 male URM, aged 14–18 years (Pfeiffer & Goldbeck, 2018), showed first positive effects on the reduction of PTSS symptoms. This was especially true for symptoms such as reexperiencing negative alterations in cognitions and mood, and avoidance. Thus, My Way could be a feasible and effective option to provide a large number of URM with a low-threshold intervention targeting PTSS symptoms.

In the case of acute aggression or suicidality, refugee minors might have to be treated in inpatient units of psychiatric hospitals. Here, problems arise concerning language and cultural barriers. Therefore, medical and nonmedical staff in those units need to receive specific training to be capable of dealing with such highly stressful situations. Helping young refugees become accustomed to psychiatric hospitals before emergency situations happen, i.e., by offering special consultation sessions, can have a positive effect by reducing anxiety and mistrust and thus enhancing compliance during emergencies. Short trainings such as START or My Way could also be used in those units to offer first relief and skills to adolescents. Furthermore, critical situations are often caused by acute stressors such as the rejection of asylum status, or a sudden loss of contact with family members in the home country. Those situations need to be dealt with, and networking with members of the youth-welfare as well as the legal system is of utmost importance.

TRAUMA-SPECIFIC PSYCHOTHERAPEUTIC INTERVENTIONS

As described previously, language difficulties are not only a concern regarding the diagnostic process or crisis interventions, they provide a similar problem with regard to psychotherapy. Because there will not be enough psychotherapists in Europe who speak all of the languages of refugee minors, even when considering a long-term perspective, the use of translators or therapy involving minimal language is and will continue to be a constant necessity. Despite the lack of randomized controlled trials, first studies report promising results from translator-assisted therapy and report positive practical experiences (Brune, Eiroa-Orosa, Fischer-Ortman, Delijaj, & Haasen, 2011; d'Ardenne, Ruaro, Cestari, Fakhoury, & Priebe, 2007). However, therapy including a third person usually requires some sessions for all parties involved to become used to each other. Therapists need to learn to speak in short, simple sentences which can be translated easily, and to speak directly to the patient and not the translator. On their side, patients have to learn to accept another person in the room and to wait for translations to go back and forth, which can be difficult, particularly in emotionally stressful situations. The translator has to stay neutral and translate accurately, and not to bring personal interpretations into the translation process. Furthermore, many translators themselves are refugees or have experienced similarly distressing situations. Therefore, translators should be assessed for their ability to deal with distressing topics and to be able to concentrate in stressful situations, as well as to have good social and communicative skills. Translators should also be able to separate themselves from patients' feelings and wishes and to be able to obtain help from supervisors if needed (Mehus & Becher, 2015). In the case of Germany and other European countries, however, there are no official rules for minimum qualifications of translators being paid for by health insurance or other help networks, which makes it difficult to ensure a quality standard (Metzner, Reher, Kindler, & Pawils, 2016). Online resources such as the Refugee Mental Health Project of Canada's Mental Health and Addiction Network offer practical information and online courses for translators. However, those resources are specific to the Canadian culture and infrastructure and might have to be adapted to the European situation to be of service there.

Because most refugees may bring with them conceptualizations of mental illness different from those of European psychotherapists, it is important to spend enough time with the patient on the construction of an explanatory model for the mental illness (Reher & Metzner, 2016). According to Schepker and Toker (2009), it is helpful to discuss differential concepts of psychiatric illnesses (e.g., to be possessed by a "Jinn" or to be punished by God, as opposed to Western rational-scientific concepts). Often, it can be easier for adolescents to accept Western rationales as well if their own concepts are not being considered incorrect but are integrated into the model. Many refugees are relieved when considering Western rational-scientific explanatory models, because they can take away blame or feelings of failure.

In a metaanalyses on psychosocial interventions for children and adolescents after man-made and natural disasters, Brown et al. (2017) found high overall effect sizes for pre-post comparisons (Hedges' $g = 1.34$) and medium effect sizes for intervention groups that were compared with control groups (Hedges' $g = 0.43$). Interestingly, there were no significant differences among the three most commonly evaluated interventions: eye movement desensitization and reprocessing (EMDR), narrative exposure therapy for children (kid narrative exposure therapy [KIDNET]), and CBT. During EMDR, patients are encouraged to remember the worst moment of the traumatic event as vividly as possible and are stimulated bilaterally (e.g., by rapid eye movement or tapping on hands or legs), during this exposure *in sensu*. This process is repeated until the patient can think about the traumatic event without significant arousal. In the process of EMDR, individual resources are activated and integrated. In both KIDNET and CBT, patients are encouraged to write a script of their traumatic experiences. While in KIDNET, a narrative lifeline is developed to integrate traumatic events into the biography and reconsolidate them; CBT focuses on dysfunctional cognitions and emotions expressed throughout the script and on restructuring them in a further step. When looking at similarities of those different treatment methods, all methods use confrontation techniques (mainly *in sensu*), which seems to be a significant factor in treating PTSD. Furthermore, all techniques start with psychoeducation, which has shown to be greatly important when working with refugees. Especially the emotion of fear and its physiological symptoms should be addressed in great detail. This can be done using general examples of frightening situations as well as simple pictures depicting behaviors such as fight, flight, and freezing, and showing typical physiological reactions. Practical experience has shown that despite cultural differences and insufficient knowledge about the physiology of the human body, most refugees can understand that fear and its physiological reactions are normal reactions which currently occur unnecessarily in safe situations (Reher & Metzner, 2016). Furthermore, motivational aspects have to be considered for all types of therapy, because confrontation with painful memories is incompatible with avoidance and is therefore highly aversive. This is especially true when refugees have a different concept of psychotherapy or mental health, or none at all. It is therefore important to establish compliance and motivation, e.g., by using simple metaphors linking to physiological issues, such as having to clean a wound before it can heal.

In general, no recommendation based on clear empirical evidence from large studies can be given for the specific treatment of young refugees. However, available information points to the need for a stepped-care approach. First, needs such as safety, sufficient sleep, and skills for acute stress and emotion regulation should be addressed. Once the young refugee's situation is stable, psychoeducation, development of an explanatory model, and enhancing motivation are important before being able to start therapeutic processes focused on traumatic events. Therapeutic methods involving confrontation in vivo and *in sensu* seem to be promising. EMDR has the advantage of not having to use much language, and might therefore be delivered without translators, whereas methods such as CBT or KIDNET can be advantageous to children and adolescents who feel the need to tell their story in detail to someone else. Therefore, treatment should be delivered individually according to local conditions, catering to the needs of each child and adolescent.

With regard to young refugees who arrive and live with their families, parental training and involvement should always be fostered according to these aspects. In addition to detailed psychoeducation, parents should be equipped with skills to deal with their offsprings' symptomatology and should be referred to psychotherapy for themselves if needed.

FORMAL POSITIONS OF EUROPEAN CHILD AND ADOLESCENT PSYCHIATRISTS AND ALLIED PROFESSIONS ON FLIGHT-RELATED POLITICS CONCERNING CHILDREN AND ADOLESCENTS AND THEIR FAMILIES

Starting in 2014, the German Association for Child and Adolescent Psychiatry, Psychosomatics and Psychotherapy, together with the Professional Association for Child and Adolescent Psychiatry, Psychosomatics, and Psychotherapy in Germany and the Federal Consortium of the Leading Hospital Doctors for Child and Adolescent Psychiatry,

Psychosomatics, and Psychotherapy, published position statements on political decisions and suggestions concerning the situation of young refugees in Germany. The first paper called for fixed legal rules to support and protect adolescent URM who were turning age 18 years and were therefore facing the loss of support from youth-welfare institutions and child and adolescent psychiatric treatment (Banaschewski, 2016; Fegert, Ludolph, & Wiebels, 2014). Other position statements objected to genital or radiological age diagnosis of URM, for ethical reasons and the lack of scientific evidence regarding its validity (Fegert, Jung, & Berg, 2015). The statements calls for the need to provide extended certificates of good conduct for all persons working with young refugees, psychiatric evaluation to prevent deportation to be conducted by trained child and adolescent psychiatrists, and not to refuse family members of URM from joining them in Germany (Banaschewski, Berg, & Jung, 2016). The scientific council for family affairs in Germany is an interdisciplinary committee advising the government in issues regarding families and children in Germany. For example, it has advised not underestimating the psychosocial risks of families coming from crisis regions, and initiating culture-sensitive and family-oriented interventions for refugee families, expanding the availability of trained interpreters, and establishing (online) training programs for professional and volunteer helpers (Fegert et al., 2017). As an NGO, the World Childhood Foundation is calling for the need of protection and "safe places" for refugee children in Germany (World Childhood Foundation, 2017).

The Swiss Association for Child and Adolescent Psychiatry and Psychotherapy raised similar issues (Di Gallo, Bessler, Beutler, Schlueter-Mueller, & Vertone, 2016). Most important, the society called for guaranteed humanitarian basics such as protection from discrimination and the right for education. In addition, the provision of developmentally adequate environments (e.g., no separation from family members, and the provision of family privacy) were mentioned. Special focus was on the training of staff at the borders and in refugee camps, to facilitate adequate psychiatric assessment and treatment.

The European Society for Child and Adolescent Psychiatry (ESCAP) reviewed important information for clinicians in Europe concerning the refugee situation, and initiated an online forum (Hebebrand et al., 2016). ESCAP also called for action in a position paper published in 2016 (Anagnostopoulos et al., 2016). Major points of this call to action are presented in Box 8.2. This joint call to action of ESCAP is especially important because political debates on the refugee crisis have led to political segregation and separation in the EU, which making it crucial for European health care professionals to stand together and publish shared calls and statements.

BOX 8.2

CALL FOR ACTION OF THE EUROPEAN SOCIETY FOR CHILD AND ADOLESCENT PSYCHIATRY (ANAGNOSTOPOULOS ET AL., 2016, P. 675).

- For all governments and political groups with influence in regions of conflict and war to draft solutions to resolve these conflicts.
- For all basic health care to be provided to migrants, with joint focus on children's physical and mental health.
- For all activities of professionals and organizations to apply the principles of best interests identified in the United Nations Convention on the Rights of the Child (Article 3) to all children independent of their immigration status.
- For hosting countries to make steps leading to a legalization of the residential status and granting asylum as transparent as possible.
- For children not to be separated from their families as long as this is consistent with their best interest.
- For optimal use of limited funding concerning provision of a safe environment, appropriate schooling, and youth welfare system.
- For adolescent refugees turning age 18 years to be able to finish the education/apprenticeship they have started.
- For young refugees with developing or preexisting serious mental disorders to receive appropriate mental health care.
- For adopting a public health approach using screening, stepped care, task sharing, and task shifting in current structures, health care financing, and ways of working and for enhancing cultural competence of professionals.
- For all stakeholders to gather and distribute state-of-the-art-knowledge, taking into consideration the different needs and available resources of the various EU countries.

CONCLUSION

During the refugee crisis in Europe in 2015 and 2016, many countries struggled to cope with the large numbers of refugees arriving in a short time and were unable to provide appropriate care and integration. Since the agreement of the EU and Turkey, which stated that newly arrived refugees in Turkey would be settled there rather than move to EU countries for financial compensation in return, only small numbers of refugees from the Middle East have traveled to the EU. However, Italy is still struggling with the large number of refugees traveling across the Mediterranean Sea, and several countries are trying to stop trafficking via this dangerous route, which regularly causes many deaths. Facing those new realities, most European countries could now change from "crisis interventions" and spontaneous, sometimes chaotic support to more organized, long-term plans for help, including appropriate health care, education, and integration. To achieve this plan, the education of professionals is a key effort. Because of the large number of professionals and voluntary helpers who need training, online courses seem to be appropriate to educate the large number of participants simultaneously across Europe. In Germany, the Ministry for Education and Research funded the development, implementation, and evaluation of three online courses from September, 2016 to August, 2019. The first course provides basic information on the consequences of traumatic events and mental health issues in the context of migration and asylum seeking. The course is available in two versions: one for professionals working in therapeutic contexts and the other for nontherapeutic professionals and volunteers. The second course contains specific information about self- and other-related aggression in child and adolescent refugees. The third course communicates specific protection plans for organizations caring for child and adolescent refugees. The online courses contain 20 sessions lasting 45 min each and include literature, case examples, questionnaires, and other screening tools. In short videos, interactions between professionals and refugees on specific topics are demonstrated. Following the example of the Refugee Mental Health Project by Canada's Mental Health and Addiction Network, which provides a large pool of teaching resources and tools, similar projects could be useful to health care professionals and other professions to provide appropriate help for refugee minors.

One problem with offering specific interventions to refugees is that not many interventions have been sufficiently evaluated for the specific group of refugee minors. Research funding is usually granted after time-consuming peer review, which delays the start of intervention studies by 2 or 3 years after most refugee minors have arrived in Europe.

Furthermore, systematic research and long-term follow-up are needed on the situation of integrating refugees into society. Because speaking the language of the host country is associated with less psychopathology in refugee minors (Fazel, Wheeler, & Danesh, 2005), providing access to language courses should be a major focus of host countries. Furthermore, integration can be fostered by including children and adolescents into public schools and publicly organized spare-time activities such as sports clubs with children and adolescents from the host country as soon as possible after arrival. This holds true for accompanied minors and URMs. However, whereas URM automatically come into contact with professionals from their host country and are surrounded by Western norms because they live in foster homes or foster families, special attention needs to be drawn to young refugees who arrive with their families. These children and adolescents are confronted with cultural differences on a daily basis (i.e., changing from a Western school environment to the norms and language of their families after school) and might therefore find it harder to adapt to the different situation in the host country. However, family reunion should also have an important role in the case of URM, because this could significantly improve their mental health and well-being. Because family reunions are often impossible, for many different reasons, contact with their families should be facilitated whenever possible via the Internet or phone. A study by the UNHCR (UNHCR, 2017a) found that refugees often spend up to a third of their monthly allowance or income on staying connected with their families or other contacts. Not being in contact with their families means increased psychological distress, and a lack of access to the Internet can prevent refugees from making informed decisions about how to improve their lives, health, or education (UNHCR, 2017a). However, especially in young refugees, the Internet also has the danger of radicalization and influences that are negatively associated with their integration into a new society.

Overall, because the large numbers of new arrivals of young refugees seem to have ceased in most European countries, Europe faces the task of integrating refugee minors and helping them to grow up to become healthy individuals who can contribute positively to Europe's cultural, economic, and political development, or to return to their home countries once safe living conditions can be achieved.

References

Afifi, T. O., & Macmillan, H. L. (2011). Resilience following child maltreatment: A review of protective factors. *Canadian Journal of Psychiatry, 56*(5), 266–272. https://doi.org/10.1177/070674371105600505.

Amuyunzu-Nyamongo, M., Owuor, J. O., & Blanchard, C. (2013). The Consortium for NCD Prevention and Control in sub-Saharan Africa (CNCD-Africa): From concept to practice. *Global Health Promotion, 20*(4 Suppl.), 97–103. https://doi.org/10.1177/1757975913500682.

Anagnostopoulos, D. C., Hebebrand, J., Eliez, S., Doyle, M. B., Klasen, H., Crommen, S., et al. (2016). European Society of Child and Adolescent Psychiatry: Position statement on mental health of child and adolescent refugees. *European Child & Adolescent Psychiatry, 25*, 673–676.

Baasher, T. A. (2001). Islam and mental health. *Eastern Mediterranean Health Journal, 7*(3), 372–376.

Banaschewski, T. (2016). *Stellungnahme der Deutschen Gesellschaft für Kinder- und Jugendpsychiatrie, Psychosomatik und Psychotherapie (DGKJP)*. Retrieved from http://www.dgkjp.de/images/files/stellungnahmen/2016/Stellungahme%20Gesundheitsversorgung%20Flchtlinge.pdf.

Banaschewski, T., Berg, G., & Jung, M. (2016). *Gemeinsame Stellungnahme der kinder- und jugend-psychiatrischen Fachgesellschaft und der Fachverbände DGKJP, BAG KJPP, BKJPP in Abstimmung mit der DAKJ zum Gesetzentwurf zur Einführung beschleunigter Asylverfahren (Asylpaket II)*. Retrieved from http://www.dgkjp.de/stellungnahmen-positionspapiere/stellungnahmen-2016/355-asylpaket-2.

Bean, T., Derluyn, I., Eurelings-Bontekoe, E., Broekaert, E., & Spinhoven, P. (2007). Validation of the multiple language versions of the Hopkins symptom checklist-37 for refugee adolescents. *Adolescence, 42*(165), 51—71.

Bean, T., Derluyn, I., Eurrelings-Bontekoe, E., Broekaert, E., & Spinhoven, P. (2006). Validation of the multiple language versions of the reactions of adolescents to traumatic stress questionnaire. *Journal of Traumatic Stress, 19*, 241—255.

Bean, T., Mooijaart, A., Eurelings-Bontekoe, E., & Spinhoven, P. (2006). Validation of the child behavior checklist for guardians of unaccompanied refugee minors. *Children and Youth Services Review, 28*, 867—887.

Bean, T., Mooijaart, A., & Spinhoven, P. (2007). Validation of the teacher's report form for teachers of unaccompanied refugee minors. *Journal of Psychoeducational Assessment, 25*, 53—68.

Brown, R. C., Witt, A., Fegert, J. M., Keller, F., Rassenhofer, M., & Plener, P. L. (2017). Psychosocial interventions for children and adolescents after man-made and natural disasters: A meta-analysis and systematic review. *Psychological Medicine, 47*(11), 1893—1905. https://doi.org/10.1017/S0033291717000496.

Brune, M., Eiroa-Orosa, F. J., Fischer-Ortman, J., Delijaj, B., & Haasen, C. (2011). Intermediated communication by interpreters in psychotherapy with traumatized refugees. *International Journal of Culture and Mental Health, 4*, 144—151.

Bundesamt für Migration und Flüchtlinge. (2016). *Das Bundesamt in Zahlen 2015*. Nuernberg: Asyl, BAMF.

Bundesfachverband unbegleitete minderjährige Flüchtlinge. (2015). *Ausbildungsverbote und weitere Bildungseinschränkungen ab 24. Oktober 2015*. Retrieved from http://www.b-umf.de/images/Neuregelung_Bildung-2015.pdf.

Caribe, A. C., Nunez, R., Montal, D., Ribeiro, L., Sarmento, S., Quarantini, L. C., et al. (2012). Religiosity as a protective factor in suicidal behavior: A case-control study. *The Journal of Nervous and Mental Disease, 200*(10), 863—867. https://doi.org/10.1097/NMD.0b013e31826b6d05.

Catani, C., Jacob, N., Schauer, E., Kohila, M., & Neuner, F. (2008). Family violence, war, and natural disasters: A study of the effect of extreme stress on children's mental health in Sri Lanka. *BMC Psychiatry, 8*, 33. https://doi.org/10.1186/1471-244X-8-33.

d'Ardenne, P., Ruaro, I., Cestari, I., Fakhoury, W., & Priebe, S. (2007). Does interpreter-mediated CBT with traumatized refugee people work? *Behavioral and Cognitive Psychotherapy, 35*, 293—301.

Derluyn, I., & Broekaert, E. (2007). Different perspectives on emotional and behavioural problems in unaccompanied refugee children and adolescents. *Ethnicity and Health, 12*(2), 141—162. pii:772413672.

Derluyn, I., Broekaert, E., & Schuyten, G. (2008). Emotional and behavioural problems in migrant adolescents in Belgium. *European Child & Adolescent Psychiatry, 17*(1), 54—62. https://doi.org/10.1007/s00787-007-0636-x.

deutschlandfunk. (2017). *Kriminalstatistik 2016-Flüchtlinge sind nicht diejenigen, die Probleme bereiten*. From http://www.deutschlandfunk.de/kriminalstatistik-2016-fluechtlinge-sind-nicht-diejenigen.694.de.html?dram:article_id=384547.

Di Gallo, A., Bessler, C., Beutler, H., Schlueter-Mueller, S., & Vertone, L. (2016). *Stellungnahme der SGKJPP zur Situation und Versorgung minderjähriger Flüchtlinge in der Schweiz*. Retrieved from http://www.sgkjpp.ch/oeffentlichkeit/projekte-themen/oeffentliche-stellungnahmen/index.php?eID=tx_securedownloads&u=0&g=0&t=

1508952539&hash=6a381ec43be66d51ff52379b33d5f6d7bf172b8d&file=/fileadmin/ SGKJPP/user_upload/documents/Oeffentlichkeit/Themen___PosPapiere/d_ Stellungnahme_SGKJPP_minderjaehrige_Fluechtlinge_SSM_def.pdf.

Dixius, A., & Moehler, E. (2017). START — development of an intervention for a first stabilization and arousal-modulation for highly stressed minor refugees. *Praxis der Kinderpsychologie und Kinderpsychiatrie, 66*(4), 277—286. https://doi.org/10.13109/ prkk.2017.66.4.277.

Eurostat. (2017a). *Asylum quarterly report*. Retrieved from http://ec.europa.eu/eurostat/ statistics-explained/index.php/Asylum_quarterly_report.

Eurostat. (2017b). *Asylum statistics*. Retrieved from http://ec.europa.eu/eurostat/statistics-explained/index.php/Asylum_statistics.

Fazel, M., Wheeler, J., & Danesh, J. (2005). Prevalence of serious mental disorder in 7000 refugees resettled in western countries: A systematic review. *Lancet, 365*(9467), 1309—1314. pii:S0140-6736(05)61027-6.

Fegert, J. M., Diehl, C., Leyendecker, B., & Hahlweg, K. (2017). *Kinder mit traumatisierten Angehörigen in aus Kriegsgebieten geflüchteten Familien: Enwicklungsrisiken, Behandlungsangebote, Versorgungsdefizite*. Kurzgutachten des Wissenschaftlichen Beirats für Familienfragen beim BMFSFJ.

Fegert, J. M., Jung, M., & Berg, G. (2015). *Gemeinsame Stellungnahme der kinder- und jugendpsychiatrischen Fachgesellschaft und der Fachverbände DGKJP, BKJPP, BAGKJPP zu Methoden der Altersfeststellung bei unbegleitetend minderjährigen Flüchtlingen*. Retrieved from http:// www.dgkjp.de/stellungnahmen-positionspapiere/stellungnahme-2015/339-altersfeststellung.

Fegert, J., Ludolph, A. G., & Wiebels, K. (2014). *Gemeinsame Stellungnahme der kinder- und jugendpsychiatrischen Fachgesellschaft und der Fachverbände DGKJP, BAG KJPP, BKJPP zur Perspektive unbegleiteter minderjähriger Flüchtlinge (UMF) bei Erlangnung der Volljährigkeit*. Retrieved from http://www.dgkjp.de/images/files/stellungnahmen/ 2014/unbegleitete%20minderjhrige%20Flchtlinge_final.pdf.

Fegert, J. M., Plener, P. L., & Koelch, M. (2015). Traumatisierung von Flüchtlingskindern - Häufigkeiten, Folgen und Interventionen. *Recht der Jugend und des Bildungswesens, 4*, 380—389.

Gambaro, L., Liebau, E., Peter, F., & Weinhardt, F. (2017). Viele Kinder von Geflüchteten besuchen eine Kita oder Grundschule — Nachholbedarf bei den unter Dreijährigen und der Sprachförderung von Schulkindern. *DIW Wochenbericht, 19*, 379—386.

Gholamrezaei, M., Heath, N., & Panaghi, L. (2016). Non-suicidal self-injury in a sample of university students in Tehran, Iran: Prevalence, characteristics and risk factors. *International Journal of Culture and Mental Health*, 1—14.

Hebebrand, J., Anagnostopoulos, D. C., Eliez, S., Linse, H., Pejovic-Milovancevic, M., & Klasen, H. (2016). A first assessment of the needs of young refugees arriving in Europe: What mental health professional need to know. *European Child & Adolescent Psychiatry, 25*, 1—6.

Hodes, M., Jagdev, D., Chandra, N., & Cunniff, A. (2008). Risk and resilience for psychological distress amongst unaccompanied asylum seeking adolescents. *Journal of Child Psychology and Psychiatry, 49*(7), 723—732. https://doi.org/10.1111/j.1469-7610.2008.01912.x.

Hofmeister, C. (2014). *Hat Migration Auswirkung auf den psychischen Gesundheitszustand?* Hamburg: Diplomica Verlag.

Huemer, J., Karnik, N., & Steiner, H. (2009). Unaccompanied refugee children. *Lancet, 373*(9664), 612—614. https://doi.org/10.1016/S0140-6736(09)60380-9.

Huemer, J., Karnik, N., Voelkl-Kernstock, S., Granditsch, E., Plattner, B., Friedrich, M., et al. (2011). Psychopathology in African unaccompanied refugee minors in Austria. *Child Psychiatry and Human Development, 42*(3), 307—319. https://doi.org/10.1007/s10578-011-0219-4.

II. UNIQUENESS AND RISK IN MARGINALIZED GROUPS

Jakobsen, M., Demott, M. A., & Heir, T. (2014). Prevalence of psychiatric disorders among unaccompanied asylum-seeking adolescents in Norway. *Clinical Practice and Epidemiology in Mental Health, 10*, 53—58. https://doi.org/10.2174/1745017901410010053.

Keselman, O., Cederborg, A., Lamb, M. E., & Dahlstroem, Ö. (2010). Asylum-seeking minors in interpreter-mediated interviews: What do they say and what happens to their responses? *Child & Family Social Work, 15*, 325—334.

Koecher, R. (2015, Oct 29, 2016). *Kontrollverlust - die Besorgnis der Bürger wächst.* Dokumentation des Beitrags. Retrieved from http://www.ifd-allensbach.de/uploads/tx_reportsndocs/FAZ_Oktober_Flu__chtlinge.pdf.

Maercker, A., Forstmeier, S., Wagner, B., Glaesmer, H., & Brahler, E. (2008). Post-traumatic stress disorder in Germany. Results of a nationwide epidemiological study. *Der Nervenarzt, 79*(5), 577—586. https://doi.org/10.1007/s00115-008-2467-5.

Malmsten, J. (2014). Unaccompanied children living in transitional houses — voices from Sweden. *International Journal of Migration, Health and Social Care, 10*, 18—35.

Mehus, C. J., & Becher, E. H. (2015). Secondary traumatic stress, burnout, and compassion fatigue in a sample of spoken-language interpreters. *Traumatology.* https://doi.org/10.1037/trm0000023.

Metzner, F., Reher, C., Kindler, H., & Pawils, S. (2016). Psychotherapeutische Versorgung von begleiteten und unbegleiteten minderjährigen Flüchtlingen und Asylbewerbern mit Traumafolgestörung in Deutschland. *Bundesgesundheitsblatt.* https://doi.org/10.1007/s00103-016-2340-9.

Michel, A. M., Schoenian, V., Thurm, F., & Steffen, T. (October 29, 2016). Was geschah in Koeln? *Zeit Online.* Retrieved from http://www.zeit.de/gesellschaft/zeitgeschehen/2016-01/koeln-silvester-sexuelle-uebergrifferaub-faq.

Neuner, F., Schauer, M., Karunakara, U., Klaschik, C., Robert, C., & Elbert, T. (2004). Psychological trauma and evidence for enhanced vulnerability for posttraumatic stress disorder through previous trauma among West Nile refugees. *BMC Psychiatry, 4*, 34. pii:1471-244X-4-34.

Pfeiffer, E., & Goldbeck, L. (October 30, 2017). Evaluation of a trauma-focused group intervention for unaccompanied young refugees: A pilot study. *Journal of Traumatic Stress*, (5), 531—536. https://doi.org/10.1002/jts.22218. Epub 2017 Oct 9.

Plener, P. L., Groschwitz, R. C., Brahler, E., Sukale, T., & Fegert, J. M. (2017). Unaccompanied refugee minors in Germany: Attitudes of the general population towards a vulnerable group. *European Child & Adolescent Psychiatry.* https://doi.org/10.1007/s00787-017-0943-9.

Pridmore, S., & Pasha, M. I. (2004). Psychiatry and Islam. *Australasian Psychiatry, 12*(4), 380—385. pii:APY2131.

Rassenhofer, M., Fegert, J. M., Plener, P. L., & Witt, A. (2016). Validated instruments for the psychological assessment of unaccompanied refugee minors — a systematic review. *Praxis der Kinderpsychologie und Kinderpsychiatrie, 65*(2), 97—112. https://doi.org/10.13109/prkk.2016.65.2.97.

Reher, C., & Metzner, F. (2016). Entscheidungshilfe zur Therapieplanung bei jugendlichen Flüchtlingen und Asylbewerbern mit Traumafolgestörungen in der ambulanten Praxis. *Praxis der Kinderpsychologie und Kinderpsychiatrie, 65*, 707—728.

Riggs, D. S., Byrne, C. A., Weathers, F. W., & Litz, B. T. (1998). The quality of the intimate relationships of male Vietnam veterans: Problems associated with posttraumatic stress disorder. *Journal of Traumatic Stress, 11*(1), 87—101. https://doi.org/10.1023/A:1024409200155.

Robinson, J. (2016). Angela merkel under more pressure over refugee policy as it is revealed migrants committed 142,500 crimes in Germany during the first six months of 2016. *Daily Mail.* Retrieved from http://www.dailymail.co.uk/news/article-3893436/Angela-Merkel-pressure-refugee-policy-revealed-migrants-committed-142-500-crimes-Germany-six-months-2016.html.

Ruf, M., Schauer, M., Neuner, F., Catani, C., Schauer, E., & Elbert, T. (2010). Narrative exposure therapy for 7- to 16-year-olds: A randomized controlled trial with traumatized refugee children. *Journal of Traumatic Stress, 23*(4), 437—445. https://doi.org/10.1002/jts.20548.

Saile, R., Ertl, V., Neuner, F., & Catani, C. (2014). Does war contribute to family violence against children? Findings from a two-generational multi-informant study in Northern Uganda. *Child Abuse & Neglect, 38*(1), 135—146. https://doi.org/10.1016/j.chiabu.2013.10.007.

Schepker, R., & Toker, M. (2009). *Transkulturelle Kinder- und Jugendpsychiatrie*. Berlin: Medizinisch Wissenschaftliche Verlagsgesellschaft.

Soykoek, S., Mall, V., Nehring, I., Henningsen, P., & Aberl, S. (2017). Post-traumatic stress disorder in Syrian children of a German refugee camp. *Lancet, 389*(10072), 903—904. pii: S0140-6736(17)30595-0.

Sriskandarajah, V., Neuner, F., & Catani, C. (2015a). Parental care protects traumatized Sri Lankan children from internalizing behavior problems. *BMC Psychiatry, 15*, 203. https://doi.org/10.1186/s12888-015-0583-x.

Sriskandarajah, V., Neuner, F., & Catani, C. (2015b). Predictors of violence against children in Tamil families in northern Sri Lanka. *Social Science & Medicine, 146*, 257—265. https://doi.org/10.1016/j.socscimed.2015.10.010.

Stotz, S. J., Elbert, T., Muller, V., & Schauer, M. (2015). The relationship between trauma, shame, and guilt: Findings from a community-based study of refugee minors in Germany. *European Journal of Psychotraumatology, 6*, 25863. https://doi.org/10.3402/ejpt.v6.25863.

Sukale, T., Hertel, C., Möhler, E., Joas, J., Müller, M., Banaschewski, T., et al. (2016). Diagnostik und Ersteinschätzung bei minderjährigen Flüchtlingen. *Der Nervenarzt*. https://doi.org/10.1007/s00115-016-0244-4.

UBSKM. (2017). *Checkliste Mindeststandards zum Schutz von Kindern in Flüchtlingsunterkünften*. Retrieved from https://beauftragter-missbrauch.de/presse-service/meldungen/detail/news/checkliste-mindeststandards-zum-schutz-von-kindern-in-fluechtlingsunterkuenften/.

UNHCR. (2017a). *Connectivity for refugees*. Retrieved from http://www.unhcr.org/connectivity-for-refugees.html.

UNHCR. (2017b). *Figures at a glance*. http://www.unhcr.org/figures-at-a-glance.html.

UNHCR. (2017c). *Refugee children: Guidelines on protection and care*. Retrieved from http://www.unhcr.org/protection/children/3b84c6c67/refugee-children-guidelines-protection-care.html.

UNICEF. (2017). *A deadly journey for children — The Central Mediterranean Migration Route*. UNICEF child alert.

Vervliet, M., Meyer Demott, M. A., Jakobsen, M., Broekaert, E., Heir, T., & Derluyn, I. (2014). The mental health of unaccompanied refugee minors on arrival in the host country. *Scandinavian Journal of Psychology, 55*(1), 33—37. https://doi.org/10.1111/sjop.12094.

Volkl-Kernstock, S., Karnik, N., Mitterer-Asadi, M., Granditsch, E., Steiner, H., Friedrich, M. H., et al. (2014). Responses to conflict, family loss and flight: Posttraumatic stress disorder among unaccompanied refugee minors from Africa. *Neuropsychiatry, 28*(1), 6—11. https://doi.org/10.1007/s40211-013-0094-2.

Walg, M., Fink, E., Grossmeier, M., Temprano, M., & Hapfelmeier, G. (2016). Häufigkeit psychischer Störungen bei unbegleiteten minderjährigen Flüchtlingen in Deutschland. *Zeitschrift für Kinder- und Jugendpsychiatrie und Psychotherapie, 45*, 58—68.

Witt, A., Rassenhofer, M., Fegert, J., & Plener, P. L. (2015). Hilfebedarf und Hilfsangebote in der Versorgung von unbegleiteten minderjährigen Flüchtlingen. *Kindheit und Entwicklung, 24*, 209—224.

World Childhood Foundation. (2017). *Activity report 2015*. Retrieved from http://www.childhood.org/wp-content/uploads/2016/05/childhoodactivityreport2015.pdf.

Yates, T. M. (2004). The developmental psychopathology of self-injurious behavior: Compensatory regulation in posttraumatic adaptation. *Clinical Psychology Review, 24*(1), 35–74. https://doi.org/10.1016/j.cpr.2003.10.001.

Zindler, A., & Metzner, F. (2016). Die Geister der Flucht vertreiben. *Projekt Psychotherapie, 3,* 27–29.

Sexuality and Gender Identity in Child and Adolescent Mental Health: Some Reflections on Social, Psychiatric, and Mental Health Service Changes

Gordon Harper[1], Mari Dominguez[2],
Angels Mayordomo-Aranda[3], Matthew Hodes[4,5]

[1] Harvard Medical School, Boston, United States; [2] Imperial College London, London, United Kingdom; [3] Enfield and Haringey Mental Health NHS Trust, London, United Kingdom; [4] Imperial College London, London, United Kingdom; [5] Central and North West London NHS Foundation Trust, London, United Kingdom

INTRODUCTION

Increasing attention has been given in child psychiatry and child mental health to topics related to gender. Increased coverage in both the lay press and scientific journals (Oldehinkel, 2017; Zeanah & Myint, 2017) reflects increased interest in topics that were for many years inconspicuous in or often totally absent from many professional discussions.

Topics include gender as an explanatory variable in development and occupational outcomes, gender-based victimization of various kinds, variations in sexual orientation (with homosexuality no longer considered a disorder), gender dysphoria, and transgender identity. New discussion has drawn on and supported advocacy for previously unrecognized groups. Although this change may be partly due to the increased real or administrative prevalence of some disorders, there is also a new readiness among professionals to acknowledge a topic in human development brought forward by previously unheard voices of lived experience.

This chapter addresses the growth of interest in sexuality, especially nonbinary sexuality, and gender identity, gender dysphoria, and transgender that has been seen in many high-income countries since 2000. Some of the salient social and associated psychiatric changes are outlined. The final section considers the increases in help seeking and service provision that have followed.

This chapter arose from the gender work group of the International Association for Child and Adolescent Psychiatry and Allied Professions (IACAPAP), in which the topic of gender dysphoria was one work stream. The inspiration for the work group came from the late esteemed child and adolescent psychiatrist and psychoanalyst Colette Chiland. She had been an early spokesperson for sympathetic understanding and scientific study of gender (further information about her contribution is given in Appendix 1).

CHILDREN'S RIGHTS AND THE GROWTH OF TOLERANCE

After centuries of being seen simply as "miniature adults," children were gradually recognized in the 19th and 20th centuries as occupying a distinct phase of life (Aries, 1962), a change influenced by the Enlightenment of the 18th century (Pinker, 2011). In the West, children had been tainted with original sin, but Rousseau replaced this belief with the idea of original innocence. He argued that children had not yet developed their ideas and so should be allowed to learn from their experiences. John Locke argued that children were like a blank slate and should be treated leniently. He suggested teachers should try and understand their pupils and help them enjoy studying. Throughout the 19th century, leniency and valuation of children gradually increased.

Corporal punishment subsided across North America and Europe, and by 1979 had become illegal in Sweden. The attention given to bullying among the general public and psychiatric field (Arseneault, 2017) reflects increased awareness of children's suffering (an excellent account of these historical changes is given by Pinker (2011)). Children's rights, according to both moral and legal perspectives, are increasingly recognized, both nationally and internationally (Archard, 1993).

A further example of increased tolerance and respect for human rights and well-being relevant to this chapter is the change in views toward one form of sexual difference, homosexuality. Montesquieu and Voltaire argued that homosexuality should be decriminalized. Homosexuality was decriminalized in France after the French Revolution (Pinker, 2011). In the 19th century, only a small number of countries decriminalized homosexuality, but the numbers increased significantly in the mid-20th century. Civil rights, equal opportunities, and growing tolerance were extended to homosexuality and gender nonconformity across North America and Europe, although in many countries homosexuality is still illegal and highly stigmatized.

Support for greater tolerance and understanding has come from cross-cultural studies. People in the West have learned of cultures in which gender variation is not only allowed but been seen as offering individuals a special relationship with deities. Such knowledge relativized our understanding of children and the variety of sexual behaviors, practices, and rituals associated with puberty (Montgomery, 2009). High levels of migration and the need for tolerance in multicultural societies has been associated with increased tolerance toward those with sexual differences in North America and Europe.

In the same spirit, the United Nations (UN) has linked protection of those with gender differences to human rights, as in a UN System-wide Action Plan towards gender quality and the empowerment of women (UN-SWAP at http://www.who.int/gender-equity-rights/understanding/gender-definition/en/). Recognition of the individual's right to self-determination, especially when in opposition to societal expectations, has required persistent (and sometimes lonely) advocacy.

UNDERSTANDING SEXUALITY IN CHILD AND ADOLESCENT MENTAL HEALTH

Changes in Societal Acceptance of Childhood Sexuality and Difference

During the 19th century and for much of the 20th century, childhood was regarded as an age of sexual innocence. Sexuality did not fit with the romanticized view of children and adolescents as presexually "innocent." Public attention to adolescent sexuality, often shaming and punitive, focused on preventing pregnancy rather than appreciating the relationship aspects of sexuality and implications for emotional states (Montgomery, 2009). These attitudes have been changing with increased psychological understanding of children, attention to their rights, and popular interest in adolescent peer romantic relationships.

With regard to gender nonconformity, change has come increasingly fast. In popular culture, movies and television shows have featured new terms and categories (in movies such as *Albert Nobbs* and *The Danish Girl*, and in the widely reported transition of public figures such as Caitlyn Jenner). In the law, new advocacy (often engendering opposition) has supported the rights of trans people to serve in the military, to have access to health care (especially for medical and surgical care in transitioning), and to have access to bathrooms of their choice. Although these changes have encountered some opposition, the public debate is new and probably irreversible.

Conversations challenging conventional definitions of gender have been heard in surprising quarters. For instance, a rabbi has asked whether the God of the Hebrew Bible was transgender, noting, "To the Israelites, identify was fluid, for humans and for deities" (NYTimes 13 August 2016). Some religious organizations have seen divisions regarding whether to allow or discourage gender-nonconforming behavior in young children. For instance, a directive called "Valuing All God's Children," arguing against bullying or harassing of nonconforming children, was contested by "conservative" members of the Church of England (cf Cowell, 2017).

Changes in Child and Adolescent Psychiatric Understanding

These decades of inattention to, and even silence regarding, sexuality and gender are paradoxical given the prominence in early child psychiatry, child mental health, and psychoanalysis of the hypothesized role of infantile sexuality (that is, in early childhood) in shaping personality and mental health. For many, Freud's legacy went silent and became an "elephant in the room." From overemphasis, we went to exclusion. Many believe that increasingly biological study of child development blocked clinical observations of gender-dysphoric children, who both challenged cultural norms and expressed psychological distress with their observable biological state.

The growth of biopsychosocial approaches in child and adolescent psychiatry (CAP) in the second half of the 20th century was associated with new interest in gender, adolescent sexuality and romantic relationships, and gender nonconformity. For instance, one of the world's leading textbooks includes a chapter on atypical psychosexual development (Green, 1985). This chapter addresses hormonal influences on development as well as cross-gender behavior and follow-up of those presenting with atypical development. Some pediatricians took an inclusive view, recommending questions about sexuality as a part of routine care. One format used, Home & environment Education & employment Activities Drugs Sexuality Suicide/depression (HEADSS), "A Psychosocial Interview for Adolescents," is available at http://www.bcchildrens.ca/Youth-Health-Clinic-site/Documents/headss20assessment20guide1.pdf.

Inclusion of the topic of gender identity and gender dysphoria has been inconsistent. For instance, Stearns' reviews of gender in childhood discusses social expectations of role differences and children's needs for adult supervision, but nothing about discordant gender identity or differences in sexual interest or orientation (Stearns, 2015a,b).

It has become standard for CAP texts to discuss childhood sexuality. For instance, content related to sexuality and gender is included in the IACAPAP online *Textbook of Child and Adolescent Mental Health* (available at http://iacapap.org/iacapap-textbook-of-child-and-adolescent-mental-health). Introductory chapters on child development and assessment mention gender identity. Another chapter discusses "Children with Atypical Gender Development." A Practice Parameter published by the American Academy of Child and Adolescent Psychiatry in 2012 addressed "Gay, Lesbian, or Bisexual Sexual Orientation, Gender Nonconformity, and Gender Discordance in Children and Adolescents."

More rapid change has occurred. Previously ignored (and often victimized) groups such as gay youth and gender-dysphoric youth are widely acknowledged, initiating new and more open discussion and advocacy. Recognition that gay and lesbian youth and gender-dysphoric youth were at increased risk of self-harm and suicide has contributed to the emergence of this field of study (Aitken, VanderLaan, Wasserman, Stojanovski, & Zucker, 2016). Among gender-dysphoric youth, suicide risk seems to be lower in those who transition and persist in the new gender.

GENDER IDENTITY, GENDER DYSPHORIA, AND TRANSGENDER

Recognition of the many forms of gender uncertainty or gender non-concordance calls for a new way of thinking in child and adolescent mental health. Are things changing, or are our ideas about them changing?

For most of the 20th century, sexual differentiation (including gender identity) was seen in binary terms. This view was supported when the genetic and endocrinological bases of previously unrecognized conditions were discovered and labeled *abnormal* sexual development (Federman, 1967; italics added). The contribution of each level of sexual differentiation was shown: chromosomal (XX, XY, etc.), gonadal (testes and ovaries), anatomic/genital (internal and external), physiological (hormones and puberty), and psychological (binary identity, and sexual orientation). Differentiation could proceed "abnormally" at any of these levels, although less space was given to psychological variation and to the individual, family, and cultural factors that contribute to such variation.

The defining paradigm was binary: male or female. What fell within these two classes was "normal"; what lay outside was "abnormal." "Abnormal" conditions included, on a genetic level, extra sex chromosomes; on a physiological and anatomic level, congenital adrenal hyperplasia, testicular feminization, etc.; and on the psychological level, nonheterosexual sexual orientation and gender nonconformity.

Later in the 20th century this paradigm was extended. This happened in response to clinical experience with those whose anatomical and physiological development was characterized as "intersex" and to advocacy on behalf of those previously considered abnormal.

This new way of seeing indeterminate or mixed gender was supported by recognition that "gender" was in part a social construction and by a cultural critique of power relationships and the privilege that comes with membership in a dominant group. Clinical recognition of gender-dysphoric and transgender individuals gave rise to a new clinical specialty and affected psychiatric classification systems (Turban & Ehrensaft, 2017).

CHANGES IN THE CLASSIFICATION OF GENDER IDENTITY AND GENDER DYSPHORIA

Classification systems have changed in the way they define gender identity and gender dysphoria, evident in a shift in diagnostic categories, names, and criteria. The four main diagnostic systems (*Diagnostic and Statistical Manual of Mental Disorders*, Fourth Edition [DSM-IV] (2000), International Classification of Diseases, 10th Revision [ICD-10] [1992] DSM-5 [2013], and ICD-11 [2015]) have varied in the criteria required for diagnosing gender identity and gender dysphoria. These criteria address: (1) the individual's wish for treatment to make body congruent with experienced gender, (2) symptom duration, and (3) requirement of clinical distress or impairment.

Wish to Transition: From Binary to a Continuum

In ICD-11 and DSM-5, the "wish to transition" was dropped as the requirement for a diagnosis of gender identity disorder or gender dysphoria. The experiences of service users had an important role in this change. This change reflected a shift from the earlier view of gender identity in binary terms (either male or female) in favor of understanding gender identity within a continuum: historical classification systems had seen gender identity, gender role, and gender problems dichotomously rather than dimensionally (Cohen-Kettenis & Pfäfflin, 2010).

New assessment tools were developed and used. A psychometric tool, the Utrecht Gender Dysphoria Scale, was used to measure gender identity and gender dysphoria dimensionally (Schneider et al., 2016); the Gender Identity/Gender Dysphoria Questionnaire for Adolescents and Adults, developed by the North American Task Force on Intersexuality Research (Deogracias et al., 2007), measured both experienced gender and the relational, social, and legal impact on the individual's life. This shift has also been translated to clinical practice, because users may request a variation in treatment goals other than complete sex reassignment.

Symptom Duration: A Criterion Affecting Public Health

Time frames for many diagnoses have been decided without adequate empirical basis (Maj, 2011). Cutoff points on symptom duration affect clinical management as well as public health. New diagnostic systems reduce symptom length requirements for gender dysphoria. This may reflect increased awareness of the need for nosological systems to be useful clinically (Maj, 2011), because the ability to give a diagnosis affects clinicians' ability to care for individuals with a wish for gender reassignment, which is problematic in some developing countries (Saxena, Thornicroft, Knapp, & Whiteford, 2007; Wang et al., 2007). At the same time, these revisions have epidemiological consequences, because a decision to lower the required symptom duration may result in higher prevalence rates (International Advisory Group for the Revision of ICD Mental and Behavioural Disorders, 2011).

Required symptom duration has been reduced: from 2 years to 6 months for DSM-5, and for gender incongruence in ICD-11. The reduction in time makes criteria for gender incongruence in children more like those required for diagnosis in adolescents and adults. This prevents the anomalous situation in which a child could meet criteria for childhood gender identity disorder but lose the diagnosis upon reaching adolescence, because the required duration was formerly 2 years for the adolescent group.

Clinical Distress: A Controversial Criterion

The American and international diagnostic systems show disparity with regard to the requirement of "clinically significant distress or impairment" for gender dysphoria diagnosis, a criterion that has been controversial. Some argue that the distress or impairment should stay as a diagnostic criterion because a strong desire for gender reassignment indicates "inherent" distress (Lawrence, 2010). By defining gender incongruence as distressing in itself, as the condition is ego dystonic, clinicians would no longer have to make a separate estimation of distress in deciding whether someone meets threshold for diagnosis and thus can access treatment (Cohen-Kettenis & Pfäfflin, 2010). This is especially relevant where, as in the United Kingdom, access to services for gender identity is available for adolescents and their families via the National Health Service, without financial burden, if a diagnosis of gender identity disorder is fulfilled.

Arguing against this requirement, some point out that some applicants without high reported levels of distress would thus be excluded from services (Meyer-Bahlburg, 2010). The ICD advisory group (Drescher, Cohen-Kettenis, & Winter, 2012) advocates the exclusion of functional impairment as a diagnostic criterion in favor of a separate rating of severity (mild, moderate, or severe) (International Advisory Group for the Revision of ICD-10 Mental and Behavioural Disorders, 2011). The rationale reflects the push to abandon the psychopathological model of transgender people.

In adolescents, absence of impairment or distress is most clearly illustrated by those who want sex reassignment (Cohen-Kettenis & Pfäfflin, 2010). Adolescents whose parents support their experienced gender, who already knew in childhood that they could access puberty-delaying treatment early on, and who had accepting peers and teachers, report less impairment or distress (de Vries, Doreleijers, Steensma, & Cohen-Kettenis, 2011). This observation has been hypothesized as the reason why adolescent applicants for sex reassignment function psychologically better than do their adult counterparts.

This controversy regarding the distress criterion reflects the larger debate about whether to consider gender dysphoria a psychiatric diagnosis. This controversy dates back to DSM-II and the question in the American Psychiatric Association about whether homosexuality was a mental disorder (Spitzer, 1981). The decision then that homosexuality was not a mental disorder if it was not accompanied by subjective distress or generalized impairment, as with gay people living functional lives who did not see the need to change their sexual orientation, was a novel definition of a mental condition. Before that time, anything psychiatrists defined as psychopathological was viewed as such.

This definition was later used as a framework for the DSM-III. Homosexuality was gradually removed, a new diagnosis of sexual orientation disturbance (SOD) was introduced in DSM-II (homosexuality regarded as an illness only if the same-sex attractions were experienced as distressing), and then SOD was replaced by ego dystonic homosexuality (Drescher, 2010), which again highlights the importance of perceived distress as crucial to determine whether variance from the norm qualifies as a disorder.

A similar evolution of attitudes and criteria is likely to occur with gender identity disorder, in which only those who are distressed and wishing to pursue sex reassignment will qualify for a diagnosis, and eventually the "diagnosis" may be removed from the psychiatric classification system and regarded as a variant of normal development.

INCREASING DEMAND FOR HELP AND GROWTH OF SERVICES FOR GENDER DYSPHORIA

The experience of children regarding sexuality and gender, particularly when their experience differs from society's expectations, now receives sympathetic and clinical support. The need to care for the health of children and trans people is reflected in calls for equity in health care, for instance by *The Lancet*, in a special section in June, 2016, on "Transgender Health: An Opportunity for Global Health Equity" (Lo, Horton, 2016).

We can see the individual child or youth presenting with gender dysphoria in several ways:

- as one going through a phase (for whom the term "nonpersistence" or "de-sistence" is used). The age at which dysphoria presents affects the later course. Data from Sweden and elsewhere indicate that only a minority (about 20%) of prepubertal children with gender dysphoria will persist in a wish to transition; a larger percentage of those presenting later will persist;
- as one for whom gender dysphoria, an increasingly culturally available explanatory model or identity, gives meaning to a nonspecific sense of "not being right" (this group also includes those who, for individual reasons, do not conform to "standard" gender-specific stereotypes);
- as a variation of human development, long suppressed in many cultures, now increasingly acknowledged and permitted.

The range of clinical presentations, and the corresponding need for clinicians to respond judiciously to those who present with dysphoria, with a possible request to support transition, is illustrated by scenarios such as these:

- a child surviving caretaking and medical trauma for whom a new gender represents, at least, a strong turning away from a bad past;
- a young child frightened by gender-typical traits (sports and aggression in boys, and doll play in girls) feeling safer in another gender;
- a child of parents with their own reasons to overperceive the child's tendency to identify one way or the other;
- a mid-teen with longstanding trans identification, whose family, with strong religious backing, suppresses any discussion of dysphoria, let alone transitioning;
- an early teen whose parents, and the first consultants seen, endorse transition with a certainty that goes beyond that of the teen. The youth takes this as unhelpful endorsement and encouragement, missing the teen's own uncertainty;
- a male teen for whom assertion of nonbinary gender is a way to respond to years of bullying brought on by gender nonconformity, but who may not (at least not yet) seek transition to the "other" binary gender;
- a late teen emerging from serious trauma who criticizes her professionals' failure to appreciate her posttraumatic state and what she now sees as quick endorsement of medical transition.

To assist such youth, specialized clinical services have been developed that combine assessment of youth and family, psychological support to both, support for decision making such as delaying ("puberty-blocking") or initiating medical transition, and transition support (which entails psychosocial, medical, and surgical care) (Turban & Ehrensaft, 2017). These groups have produced guidelines for care, outlining the many psychological, social, and medical aspects of care, including the possibility of puberty delay or of medical and surgical transition (for example, see American Academy of Child and Adolescent Psychiatry, 2012; Newman, 2012; Zucker & Seto, 2015).

These guidelines emphasize the heterogeneity of those seen, which range from questioners (brief or long-term) to those seeking transition (on a continuum from social to medical to surgical). Of those who transition, most will continue in the new gender ("persisters"); some will not ("de-sisters"). The specialized programs recognize this continuum and the roles played by age, developmental level, duration of dysphoria, and family and community response. The degree to which gender dysphoria co-occurs with a mental disorder, or indeed is a mental disorder itself, continues to be debated, as reviewed earlier (Zucker & Seto, 2015).

Nevertheless, the field has a weak evidence base. No randomized controlled trials have been published regarding interventions with youngsters with gender dysphoria, and most evidence comes from single case or multiple single-case studies. The vignettes described previously illustrate the range of considerations regarding clinical management.

As a result, management and care require the integration of patient preference (child and parents), child development, and ethical perspectives (Zucker & Seto, 2015).

Clinical services for gender-dysphoric youth exist in many countries, such as the VU Medical Center Amsterdam, the Center of Expertise on Gender Dysphoria (https://www.vumc.com/branch/gender-dysphoria/), and the Gender Management Service at Boston Children's Hospital (http://www.childrenshospital.org/centers-and-services/disorders-of-sexual-development-dsd-and-gender-management-service-program/disorders-of-sexual-development-program). Similar programs have been established in (among others) Australia, France, Germany, Sweden, and the United Kingdom.

The social changes discussed previously and acceptance of gender dysphoria as a problem requiring attention have resulted in rapid growth of such services. In the United Kingdom, the Gender Identity Development Service, founded in 1989, saw relatively small numbers (less than 100/year) during its first 2 decades, whereas in the past decade the number referred has risen nearly 30-fold (Doward, 2017). In Toronto, referral rates showed a fivefold increase between 2008 and 2011 (Wood et al., 2013).

For many professionals, surprise is a frequent response: "I never knew that ..." This reaction from members of dominant groups, upon hearing about the experience of the disempowered, is seen in other contexts as well (Harper, Norris, & Woo, 1995). It is hoped that growing awareness of the difficulties associated with gender dysphoria and access to specialist help will make health services more welcoming to such individuals.

CONCLUSION

Gender dysphoria is a "model" condition for CAP and mental health, in the sense that what it teaches us about the occurrence of and the mechanisms behind a condition, and the principles of caring for those affected, are applicable to other conditions in our work. In a few decades gender dysphoria has gone from unacknowledged (but shamed and punished) to acknowledged as a disorder (pathologized), and to acknowledged as a difference in human development, sometimes amounting to a clinical condition requiring care.

The condition varies according to chronological and developmental age. Care must be integrated across medical, cultural, social, and psychological realms (Turban & Ehrensaft, 2017). The evolving autonomy of the child/youth must be balanced with the child's need for parental support and guidance. The complexity of etiology must guide care, as well: care must proceed, acknowledging much that is uncertain.

While offering dilemmas in choosing how to respond to those presenting with gender dysphoria, the history of its "discovery" and the ensuing debates also reminds us that our professional views, like our personal views, are culturally bound. The corresponding challenge is always: How can we in psychiatry/mental health see the cultural blind spots of our day, and affirm more consistently our shared humanity?

References

Aitken, M., VanderLaan, D. P., Wasserman, L., Stojanovski, S., & Zucker, K. J. (2016). Self-harm and suicidality in children referred for gender dysphoria. *Journal of the American Academy of Child & Adolescent Psychiatry, 55*(6), 513–520. https://doi.org/10.1016/j.jaac.2016.04.001.

American Academy of Child, Adolescent Psychiatry. (2012). Practice parameter on gay, lesbian, or bisexual sexual orientation, gender nonconformity, and gender discordance in children and adolescents. *Journal of the American Academy of Child & Adolescent Psychiatry, 51*(9), 957–974.

American Psychiatric Association. (2013). Gender dysphoria. In (5th ed.,*Diagnostic and statistical manual of mental disordersHighlights of changes from DSM-IV-TR to DSM-5* (pp. 814–815). Arlington VA: American Psychiatric Publishing.

Archard, D. (1993). *Children. Rights and childhood*. London and New York: Routledge.

Aries, P. (1962). *Centuries of childhood: A social history of family life*. London: Jonathan Cape.

Arseneault, L. (2017). Annual research review: The persistent and pervasive impact of being bullied in childhood and adolescence: Implications for policy and practice. *Journal of Child Psychology and Psychiatry.* https://doi.org/10.1111/jcpp.12841.

Cohen-Kettenis, P. T., & Pfäfflin, F. (2010). The DSM diagnostic criteria for gender identity disorder in adolescents and adults. *Archives of Sexual Behavior, 39*(2), 499–513. https://doi.org/10.1007/s10508-009-9562-y.

Cowell, A. (November 13 , 2017). Tutus and tool belts: Church of England urges children to explore gender identity. *New York Times.*

Deogracias, J. J., Johnson, L. L., Meyer-Bahlburg, H. F., Kessler, S. J., Schober, J. M., & Zucker, K. J. (2007). The gender identity/gender dysphoria questionnaire for adolescents and adults. *The Journal of Sex Research, 44*(4), 370–379.

Doward, J. (November 2017). Take these children seriously': NHS clinic in the eye of trans rights storm. *The Guardian, 18.*

Drescher, J. (2010). Queer diagnoses: Parallels and contrasts in the history of homosexuality, gender variance, and the diagnostic and statistical manual. *Archives of Sexual Behavior, 39*(2), 427–460.

Drescher, J., Cohen-Kettenis, P., & Winter, S. (2012). Minding the body: Situating gender identity diagnoses in the ICD-11. *International Review of Psychiatry, 24*(6), 568–577.

Federman, D. D. (1967). *Abnormal sexual development: A genetic and endocrine approach to differential diagnosis.* Philadelphia: W B Saunders.

Green, R. (1985). Atypical psychosexual development. Chapter 40. In M. Rutter, & L. Hersov (Eds.), *Child and adolescent psychiatry. Modern approaches* (2nd ed., pp. 638–649). Oxford: Blackwell Scientific Publications.

Harper, G., Norris, D., & Woo, B. (1995). Physician education in a diverse society: Listening to and learning from new voices. *The Pharos, 58*(2), 39–42.

International Advisory Group for the Revision of ICD-10 Mental and Behavioural Disorders. (2011). A conceptual framework for the revision of the ICD-10 classification of mental and behavioural disorders. *World Psychiatry, 10*, 86–92.

Lawrence, A. (2010). Proposed revisions to gender identity disorder diagnoses in the DSM-5. *Archives of Sexual Behavior, 39*(6), 1253–1260. https://doi.org/10.1007/s10508-010-9660-x.

Lo, S., & Horton, R. (2016). Transgender health: An opportunity for global health equity. *Lancet, 388,* 316–318.

Maj, M. (2011). Psychiatric diagnosis: Pros and cons of prototypes vs. operational criteria. *World Psychiatry, 10*(2), 81–82.

Meyer-Bahlburg, H. F. (2010). From mental disorder to iatrogenic hypogonadism: Dilemmas in conceptualizing gender identity variants as psychiatric conditions. *Archives of Sexual Behavior, 39*(2), 461–476.

Montgomery, H. (2009). *An introduction to childhood.* Chichester: Wiley-Blackwell.

Newman, L. (2012). Children with atypical gender development. Chapter H.3. In J. M. Rey (Ed.), *IACAPAP e-textbook of child and adolescent mental health.* Geneva: International Association for Child and Adolescent Psychiatry and Allied Professions.

Oldehinkel, A. J. (2017). Editorial: Let's talk about sex - the gender binary revisited. *Journal of Child Psychology and Psychiatry, 58*(8), 863–864. https://doi.org/10.1111/jcpp.12777.

Pinker, S. (2011). *The better angels of our nature. A history of violence and humanity.* London: Penguin.

Saxena, S., Thornicroft, G., Knapp, M., & Whiteford, H. (2007). Resources for mental health: Scarcity, inequity, and inefficiency. *Lancet, 370*(9590), 878–889.

Schneider, C., Cerwenka, S., Nieder, T. O., Briken, P., Cohen-Kettenis, P. T., De Cuypere, G., et al. (2016). Measuring gender dysphoria: A multicenter examination and comparison of the utrecht gender dysphoria scale and the gender identity/gender dysphoria questionnaire for adolescents and adults. *Archives of Sexual Behavior, 45*(3), 551–558.

Spitzer, R. L. (1981). The diagnostic status of homosexuality in DSM-III: A reformulation of the issues. *The American Journal of Psychiatry, 138*(2), 210−215.

Stearns, P. (2015a). *Gender in world history* (3rd ed.). New York: Routledge.

Stearns, P. N. (2015b). History of childhood. In J. M. Rey (Ed.), *IACAPAP e-textbook of child and adolescent mental health*. Geneva: International Association for Child and Adolescent Psychiatry and Allied Professions.

Turban, J. L., & Ehrensaft, D. (October 26, 2017). Research Review: Gender identity in youth: treatment paradigms and controversies. *Journal of Child Psychology and Psychiatry.* https://doi.org/10.1111/jcpp.12833 [Epub ahead of print].

de Vries, A. L., Doreleijers, T. A., Steensma, T. D., & Cohen-Kettenis, P. T. (2011). Psychiatric comorbidity in gender dysphoric adolescents. *Journal of Child Psychology and Psychiatry, 52*(11), 1195−1202.

Wang, P., Aguilar-Gaxiola, S., Alonso, J., Angermeyer, M., Borges, G., Bromet, E., & Wells, J (2007). Use of mental health services for anxiety, mood, and substance disorders in 17 countries in the WHO world mental health surveys. *Lancet, 370*(9590), 841−850. https://doi.org/10.1016/s0140-6736(07)61414-7.

Wood, H., Sasaki, S., Bradley, S. J., Singh, D., Fantus, S., Owen-Anderson, A., et al. (2013). Patterns of referral to a gender identity service for children and adolescents (1976-2011): Age, sex ratio, and sexual orientation. *Journal of Sex & Marital Therapy, 39*(1), 1−6. https://doi.org/10.1080/0092623x.2012.675022.

Zeanah, C. H., & Myint, M. T. (2017). Editorial: Minding the gap - research on sexual minority and gender nonconforming children and adolescents. *Journal of Child Psychology and Psychiatry, 58*(11), 1177−1179. https://doi.org/10.1111/jcpp.12836.

Zucker, K. J., & Seto, M. C. (2015). Gender dysphoria and paraphilic sexual disorders. Chapter 69. In A. Thapar, et al. (Eds.), *Rutter's child and adolescent psychiatry* (6th ed.). London: John Wiley & Sons.

APPENDIX 1

Colette Chiland, MD, PhD (1928−2016)

Colette Chiland was a leader in helping child psychiatry embrace gender and its vicissitudes. The IACAPAP Working Group on Gender now bears her name. This chapter is dedicated to her memory.

Her life was notable in many ways. From a working-class background and a family that was not supportive of medical education for women, she needed determination and persistence to obtain training in medicine, as well as in philosophy and psychology. She was both a student and practitioner of psychoanalysis. She was mentored by senior individuals in her fields of study, including Piaget, Pierre Ferrari, Serge Lebovici, René Diatkine, and Julian de Ajuriaguerra.

Her writing and personal qualities led to early distinction, both academically and professionally. She turned to international CAP as a visiting professor abroad and through IACAPAP to link French practice and theory to the larger community. In IACAPAP, she served as President, and later as Honorary President, and chaired two international Congresses in Paris. Her work was characterized not only by scientific interest (she was a lifelong student as well as a teacher with a towering intellect) but also by sympathetic understanding of all parties, child and parent alike. Personally, she is recalled by all for her friendly enthusiasm, her caring for colleagues as well as patients, and her great sense of humor. Her stories could induce laughter to the point of tears.

Colette Chiland's personal style is captured in the slightly different ways in which the word "elephant" is used in expressions in English and French. Like *l'éléphant dans le magasin de porcelain* (in English, "the bull in the china shop"), she disrupted discussions in fields that had become overly staid and complacent. She was often the one who drew attention to important topics visible in plain sight but ignored, the proverbial "elephant in the room."

In the IACAPAP Working Group on Gender, she championed diversity in our professions (worried about the preponderance of women and the dwindling number of men among young CAP/Centre for Addiction and Mental Health professionals), advocated for girls and women who had been victims of gender-based discrimination or violence, and spoke up for professional training schedules that were more supportive of women (and men) trying to strike a work–life balance.

Regarding sexuality and gender, she saw gender dysphoria as an underrecognized clinical phenomenon. She followed and studied, over more than 15 years, 40 families with dysphoric youth, work reflected in *Changer de Sexe: Illusion et Réalité* and *Exploring Transexualism*. She was active in the debates regarding whether sexual "difference" was a mental disorder or a variation of the human condition.

More details about her life and work, as well as a list of her publications, are included in a Memorial Minute (in French): Bourrat M-M and Raynaud J-P, "Colette Chiland, a pioneer in child and adolescent psychiatry and psychoanalysis," which appears in *Neuropsychiatrie d'Enfance et de l'Adolescence*, 2017: Vol 65, pp 1–4, and in the *Bulletin of IACAPAP, the International Association for Child and Adolescent Psychiatry and Allied Professions*, for November, 2016.

PART III

SUPPORTING UNIQUENESS AND DIVERSITY THROUGH INTERVENTIONS AND SERVICES

Pharmacogenomics in the Treatment of Child and Adolescent Psychiatric Disorders

Salma Malik[1], Sophia A. Walker[2], Sasha Malik[3], Lisa Namerow[4]

[1] Qatar Foundation, Doha, Qatar; [2] University of Connecticut School of Medicine, Farmington, CT, United States; [3] Miss Porter's School, Farmington, CT, United States; [4] Institute of Living/Hartford Hospital, Hartford, CT, United States

INTRODUCTION

The era of personalized medicine has arrived, and its impact on child and adolescent psychiatry is no exception. Research in genetics historically was limited to the study of individual genes and their patterns of inheritance; however, the completion of the Human Genome Project has brought with it the area of genomics, the study of the entire genome, its functions, and associated analytical techniques. In addition, research has focused on identifying genetic differences in the genes involved with both medication metabolism and medication targets, particularly those in the brain. This is called pharmacogenomics. The evolving role of this discipline in patient care has led to an exciting time in child and adolescent psychiatry, especially with regard to exploring the nuances of drug metabolism and activity at the enzyme and receptor level. Furthermore, because psychotropic medications prescribed to children (aged 6–17 years) account for about 9% of all office visits to US physicians (Comer, Olfson, & Mojtabai, 2010), it is unsurprising that research in pharmacogenomics has a focus associated with psychopharmacology. Moreover, that most drugs are on average only 40%–50% efficacious raises the question of why there is such variability in drug responses (Leucht, Hierl, Kissling, Dold, & Davis, 2012).

Understanding Uniqueness and Diversity in Child and Adolescent Mental Health
https://doi.org/10.1016/B978-0-12-815310-9.00010-1

239

As a result of these efforts, it is clear that a significant component of the variability in drug responses can be explained by genetics, even when empirical approaches to drug and dose selection are implemented. The focus of much of the work being done is the individuality in drug response. The use of genotyping tests to inform clinical decision making is becoming more prevalent, mainly owing to the increasing availability of genomic technology and clinicians becoming more comfortable with using this type of clinical data. Historically, prescribers have used trial-and-error processes, family history, and close patient monitoring to guide medication selection and monitor response (Malik, Program, & Hospital, 2016). During this process, the patient may either continue to experience distressing symptoms or be at risk for significant medication side effects (Mrazek, 2010). However, with the advent of pharmacogenomics, there is great potential to alter, and even improve, the status quo for patients and their clinicians.

Child and adolescent psychiatrists have the tasks of examining the possible role of integrating genetic information into clinical decision making, beginning to understand the impact of genetics on the treatment of their patients, and ultimately incorporating all of a patient's complex genetic information into daily decision making. Because such testing is increasingly available and the meaningful application of results is rapidly evolving, it is especially important for the clinician to become familiar with the evidence regarding genes often found to be associated with commercially available pharmacogenomics products. This chapter will discuss this specific aspect of personalized medicine (pharmacogenomics), including the basic science behind it, established evidence and guidelines, new discoveries in this area, applications to the clinical setting, and its implications for the future practice of child and adolescent psychiatry (Malik et al., 2016).

BASICS OF PHARMACOGENOMICS (FABBRI & SERRETTI, 2015; MRAZEK, 2010)

Pharmacogenomics combines the principles of genetics and pharmacotherapy, ultimately to derive an understanding of the connections between genetic variation and individual drug responses (Lerer & Macciardi, 2002). Its goal is to maximize drug efficacy and minimize side effects, thus reducing the risk of adverse effects and increasing the likelihood of treatment success (Weinshilboum, 2003). In this section, the general principles governing pharmacogenomics are described.

Genomics is the study and application of analytical techniques to the entire genome, which is the totality of the hereditary material, DNA, that encodes all of the molecular information about the components of the body. The **genome** is composed of about 3 billion individual nucleotide bases (adenine, guanine, cytosine, and thymine), whose sequence determines the genetic information necessary for the formation and maintenance of all of the components of an organism. About 99% of these bases are similar among all people; the other 1% accounts for all of the genetic variability of the human genome. The bases are connected to each other in long strands via the sugar and phosphate backbones from the nucleotides. Two corresponding strands assemble into the double-helix conformation via the pairing of adenine and thymine bases and guanine and cytosine bases, respectively. Each strand of DNA in the double helix can serve as a pattern for duplicating the sequence of the nucleotide bases, which occurs during DNA replication and cell division. The total amount of DNA constituting the human genome, when fully uncoiled, would be about 2 m in length. So, to fit into cells, DNA strands coil compactly, forming **chromosomes**, of which there are 46 in humans.

When DNA is copied to form a protein through the process of **transcription**, the strand opens and unravels sufficiently to allow a copy of a single strand of the DNA to be made. This copy is called messenger ribonucleic acid (mRNA). Through a process called **translation**, ribosomes then use the mRNA strand to encode the correct amino acid strand that would ultimately constitute a protein. Proteins are the essential building blocks of the cells throughout the human body, constituting enzymes, receptors, channels, and so on, all of which are important in every aspect of life function. Thus, variability within the human genome accounts for varying degrees of protein functionality throughout the body.

The single unit of nucleotide bases that fully encode a functional protein is referred to as a **gene**. The position of each gene on a chromosome is called the gene's **locus**. Genes are passed on from parents to offspring through recombination of loci and assortments of chromosomes during germ cell division, resulting in 23 chromosomes being provided from each parent. Thus, every gene generally has two discrete and possibly alternative forms, or **alleles**, available in the cells of each organism: one inherited from the mother and one inherited from the father. The **genotype** of an individual refers to this combined genetic information available about a given gene, whereas the ultimate observable characteristic of the organism corresponding to the genetic information is called the **phenotype**. The process of a given genotype being manifested into a corresponding phenotype is called **gene expression**. Thus, **genetics** is the study of the inherited contributions to various phenotypic manifestations.

The recombination and assortment of chromosomes into the parent's germ cells contribute enormously to genetic variability passed on to each generation of offspring because genes from each parent may or may not have different forms. **Mutations** are referred to as any differences in the sequence of nucleotide bases from the "**wild-type**," or that which most of the population exhibits. They are generally permanent and heritable alterations (i.e., insertions, deletions, or replacements) in the gene in question. Most of the time, these changes in DNA have minimal effects or cause little to no harm, but sometimes they can significantly affect the functioning of an encoded protein. With improvements in functioning there may be an increased chance of passing on the beneficial change to offspring; contrarily, a mutation may be detrimental, and while still passed on, it may harm the offspring. Much of this depends on the modes of inheritance and gene expression unique to each gene. When an offspring inherits identical alleles from each parent, they are called **homozygous** at that gene locus, whereas if the offspring were to inherit different alleles from the parents, they would be called **heterozygous** at the gene locus. When there is a replacement of a single nucleotide in a gene with another that is present within at least 1% of the general population, the mutation is referred to as a **single nucleotide polymorphism** (SNP). SNPs occur throughout the genome, occurring at a frequency of about one in every 300 nucleotide base pairs, corresponding to about 10 million SNPs within the human genome. Because of the myriad technological advances in genetics, especially with regard to computerized database systems, it is possible to run assays that look at the entire genome, sequencing thousands of SNPs at various loci. This technique, referred to as **genome-wide association studies**, allows for the identification of associations among various SNPs and specific phenotypic manifestations (Bush, Moore, Li, McDonnell, & Rabe, 2012). This is especially relevant to more common and complex phenotypic characteristics or disease states, which is especially helpful in understanding their genetic components.

Through genomics, it has been understood that nearly every mechanism in drug metabolism and activity is susceptible to the multifarious array of alterations in gene expression (Mrazek, 2010). In fact, of the 200 top-selling prescription drugs, 59% of the 27 most frequently cited in adverse drug reaction studies are metabolized by at least one enzyme known to have genetic variation coding for reduced or absent functionality (Phillips, Veenstra, Oren, Lee, & Sadee, 2001). Because it is recognized that genetic polymorphisms within genes that code for proteins involved in the metabolism and the targets of drug therapy can have an even more significant influence on the efficacy and toxicity of medications than clinical variables, the intersection of genetics and pharmacology is all the more relevant.

The two main branches of pharmacology that inform the various aspects of drug metabolism, effects, and actions in the body are pharmacokinetics (PKs) and pharmacodynamics (PDs). **PKs** refers to the processes by which a drug is absorbed, distributed, biologically available, and ultimately excreted from the body. **PDs** refers to the interaction of the active ingredient of the drug with the intended target (usually a receptor) at specific locations in the body. Pharmacogenomics explores gene variations associated with both fields. PKs essentially answers the question, "What does the body do to the drug?" PDs answers the question, "What does the drug do to the body?" As such, there is an enormous complexity to the factors associated with drug response beyond genetics:

- other PK factors (absorption, distribution, metabolism, and elimination),
- individual health variables (liver and renal function, medical comorbidities, age, weight, etc.),
- drug-to-drug interactions with metabolism or target sites, and
- psychosocial factors (family dynamics, life stressors, diet, treatment compliance, substance use, tobacco use, psychodynamic factors, etc.).

For this reason, it must be known that regardless of how a clinician may use pharmacogenomic information, it cannot entirely predict or ensure a positive treatment outcome. As such, data from pharmacogenomic testing should be used in conjunction with assessing these additional factors throughout the treatment course, so that clinicians can make more informed and individualized decisions to improve treatment outcomes.

CONSENSUS GUIDELINES IN PHARMACOGENOMICS

Given the vast array of accumulating data on pharmacogenomics, which would be impossible for the clinician to review and assess, some working groups have developed websites to serve as databases for the level of evidence known about any particular gene related to pharmacogenomics.

PharmGKB Levels of Evidence (Whirl-Carrillo et al., 2012)

PharmGKB is a knowledge database that aggregates primary pharmacogenomics literature and knowledge and extrapolates relevant information with the aim of providing clinical interpretations and support the development of clinical guidelines. Initially, it was started as a simple database with specific pharmacogenomic data; it expanded to include clinically useful and relevant information. Currently, the site includes information about pharmacogenomics-based drug dosing guidelines, drug labels, drug metabolic pathways, clinically relevant gene–drug and gene–phenotype associations, and summaries of important genes. This information is disseminated so as to illustrate the various levels of evidence of the pharmacogenomics literature using criteria such as replication, statistical significance, and study size.

Level 1A (high evidence): Annotation for a variant—drug combination in a Clinical Pharmacogenetics Implementation Consortium (CPIC) or medical society—endorsed pharmacogenomics guideline, or implemented at a pharmacogenomics research network site or another major health system.

Level 1B (high evidence): Annotation of a variant drug combination in which the preponderance of evidence shows an association. The association must be replicated in more than one cohort with significant P values and strong effect size.

Level 2A (moderate evidence): Annotation of a variant-drug combination that qualifies for level 2b, in which the variant is within an important pharmacogene as defined by PharmGKB.

Level 2B (moderate evidence): Annotation of a variant-drug combination with moderate evidence of an association. The association must be replicated but there might be some studies that do not show statistical significance and or the effect size may be small.

Level 3 (low evidence): Annotation of a variant-drug combination based on a single significant study which is not yet replicated, or multiple studies but lacking clear evidence.

Level 4 (preliminary evidence): Annotation based on case report, nonsignificant study, or in vitro, molecular, or functional assay evidence only.

Clinical Pharmacogenetics Implementation Consortium Level of Evidence for Genes/Drugs (Prioritization of Genes/Drugs — CPIC, 2017)

Consortium groups such as CPIC are actively seeking ongoing review of expanding gene research in an attempt to reach consensus guidelines regarding how best to apply the science to clinical practice. In one such example, CPIC published Guidelines on selective serotonin reuptake inhibitor (SSRI) dosing (escitalopram, citalopram, and sertraline) using the PK status of 2D6, 2C19, which may be relevant to child and adolescent clinical practice (Hicks et al., 2015). Consensus guidelines by CPIC are being developed around drug—gene pairs, which are intended to help clinicians understand how available genetic results should be used to optimize drug therapy. The relevance of this information to younger patient populations has not been directly assessed, because pharmacogenomics evaluations of antidepressant medications are largely derived from adult study samples owing to data availability. The smaller study samples in younger patients make direct comparisons of kinetic and clinical pharmacogenomics relationships challenging. However, because these genes remain consistent throughout life, the same principles generally ought to apply. In the CPIC database, the following designations are used:

Level A: Preponderance of evidence is high or moderate in favor of changing prescribing, so prescribing action is recommended.

Level B: Preponderance of evidence is weak with little conflicting data, so genetic information could be used to change prescribing of the affected drug because alternative therapies are extremely likely to be as effective as no genetically based dosing. At least one optional action is recommended.

Level C: Evidence levels vary. Published studies are of varying evidence; no prescribing actions are recommended.

Level D: Evidence levels vary. There are few published studies, mostly weak evidence. No prescribing actions are recommended.

PHARMACOKINETIC GENES AND RELEVANT POLYMORPHISMS

A key role associated with drug PKs is the metabolism and detoxification of drugs that occur in the liver through different groups of reactions called phase I and II reactions. In **phase I reactions,** drugs are chemically oxidized or reduced via the cytochrome P450 (CYP450) enzyme complex. Developmental changes also occur in this system throughout childhood and adolescence that may affect metabolism when these drugs are prescribed in pediatric patients (Anderson & Lynn, 2009). **Phase II reactions** involve other secondary reactions including conjugation, glucuronidation, and acetylation. The genetics associated with enzymes that engage in these reactions have the potential to affect a drug's PKs in individual patients.

Currently, the best and most expedient opportunity for clinicians to begin understanding the relevance of genetics to psychiatric treatment is by examining **CYP450 enzymes** and their genetic variation among patients. Almost all psychotropic medications are subject to extensive metabolism by a number of enzymes, most specifically CYP450 enzymes. In fact, several drugs have CYP450 genotyping information included in their US Federal Drug Administration (FDA) or European Medicines Agency—approved product labeling. Particularly relevant to psychiatry are CYP450 1A2, 2B6, 2C9, 2C19, 2D6, and 3A4 enzymes; genotyping of these CYP450 enzymes is currently available (Malik et al., 2016). The nomenclature of the enzymes is purely on the basis of genetics and has no bearings on or implications for enzyme function. Each enzyme is assigned a family number, a subfamily letter, and then a specific enzyme number (Wilkinson, 2005).

Polymorphisms in these genes can alter the rate at which affected enzymes can metabolize medications (Malik et al., 2016; Mrazek, 2010). These enzymes have a critical role in drug metabolism and account for high percentages of the drugs metabolized by the CYP450 system; thus, genotyping CYP450 enzymes can assist in the selection of an appropriate drug and dosing scheme. According to the affinity of each enzyme for different drugs, interactions between them may vary. A drug may act as a **substrate** for an enzyme, meaning that the enzyme acts on the drug to modify it directly. Furthermore, a few different enzymes in the complex may act on a drug; certain enzymes have a greater role than others and are referred to as primary or secondary metabolizers. Fig. 10.1 shows an illustration of the CYP450 metabolism of the PK pathway of fluoxetine, which is metabolized by CYP450 enzymes 2C9 and 2D6.

In addition, drugs can act on enzymes in the CYP450 complex by making them more or less active in their metabolic activity. When a drug acts to increase the activity of an enzyme in the CYP450 complex, it is called an **inducer**; when a drug decreases activity, it is called **an inhibitor** of the enzyme (Malik et al., 2016). This is a direct result of the interaction between the drug and enzyme and has little to do with the patient's own genetic profile. However, because certain medications will alter the metabolic rates of individual CYP450 enzymes, it is essential to take this into account when prescribing, especially in patients who are prescribed multiple medications.

Polymorphisms in alleles in the CYP450 enzymes can result in varying degrees of functional significance. This has resulted in the description of four distinct metabolizer statuses (Black, O'Kane, & Mrazek, 2007). For each enzyme, a patient is categorized according to the following descriptions: extensive (normal) metabolizer (EM), intermediate metabolizer (IM), poor metabolizer (PM), and ultrarapid metabolizer (UM). Extremes in metabolic rates (i.e., PM or UM) resulting from gene polymorphisms may contribute to either poor tolerability (in the PMs) or poor efficacy (in the UMs), even when using psychotropic medications that are dosed empirically. Guidelines for characterizing a patient's genetically determined metabolizer status (i.e., the phenotypic manifestation of their metabolic rate) are described accordingly (Black et al., 2007; Malik et al., 2016):

Extensive Metabolizers

EMs have normal metabolic capacity. Genotypes that are consistent with the EM phenotype have two active functional forms of the gene, producing an enzyme with complete drug metabolizing capacity. They are also referred to as the "wild type" by molecular biologists. This is the

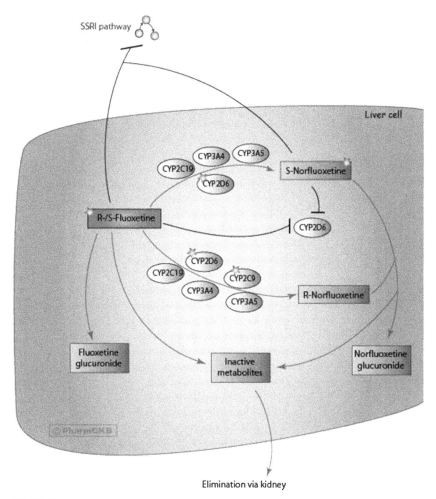

FIGURE 10.1   **Fluoxetine Pharmacokinetic Pathway.** Above is depicted SSRI (specifically fluoxetine) metabolism through cytochrome P450 pathways in the liver. *CYP,* cytochrome P450; *SSRI,* selective serotonin reuptake inhibitor.

most common genotype in Caucasians. EMs exhibit normal activity and can be treated in accordance with standard dosing practices.

Intermediate Metabolizers

IMs have a decreased level of metabolic capacity. Genotypes consistent with this phenotype are those with only one active or functional form of the gene producing the drug metabolizing enzyme and therefore have reduced metabolic capacity. They have one nonfunctional allele, which results in overall lower activity levels, although the group tends to demonstrate a wide range of enzyme activity. Patients who have this genotype may require medication doses that are lower than average.

Poor Metabolizers

PMs have absent metabolic capacity. Genotypes consistent with the PM phenotype are those with genes that encode inactive enzymes, so these patients have two nonfunctional alleles. Therefore, these individuals are unable to metabolize substrates through the affected enzymatic pathway. Using standard dosing practices, these patients are at increased risk for accumulating a medication, experiencing drug-induced side effects, or having a lack of therapeutic effect, all owing to a failure to generate downstream metabolites of the drug.

Ultrarapid Metabolizers

UMs have a metabolic capacity that is greater than normal. Genotypes that are consistent with a UM phenotype include three or more active genes, each coding for the production of a drug metabolizing enzyme. The rate of metabolism is often correlated directly to the number of copies present (Wilkinson, 2005). These patients are more likely to require an increased dosage owing to higher than normal rates of drug metabolism. The drug can be cleared so rapidly that UM patients are usually nonresponders as a result of the drug not reaching therapeutic levels.

It is well-established that for a medication to generate the intended therapeutic response for a patient, it must be given at a sufficient dose over a sufficient duration of time. This allows the patient the best opportunity to respond appropriately, by providing the appropriate dose to reach the desired concentration at receptor targets in the brain. However, when clinically relevant gene polymorphisms are present for specific CYP450 enzymes pertinent to a given drug's metabolism, the corresponding alteration in metabolic rates and thus target site concentrations can lead to poor treatment outcomes. For example, a patient who is a PM would be more likely to experience drug toxicity or other adverse reactions that are out of proportion with the recommended dose, whereas a UM may experience no improvement in target symptoms at recommended doses. Thus, awareness of a patient's CYP450 genotyping can have a significant therapeutic impact. Although this is the case, beyond PKs, there is also the impact of receptor target function and interaction with the active molecule; alteration in this genetics may also greatly influence drug response (Table 10.1).

TABLE 10.1 Cytochrome P450 Enzyme Drug Metabolism, by Drug Class (Drugs@FDA; Flockhart Table, 2016; Micromedex (c) Healthcare Series, n.d.)

Drug Class	Drug Name	Cytochrome P (CYP) 450 Enzyme					
		CYP1A2	CYP2B6	CYP2C9	CYP2C19	CYP2D6	CYP3A4/5
Selective serotonin reuptake inhibitors	Citalopram				•	•	•
	Escitalopram				•	•	•
	Fluoxetine			•	•	•	•
	Fluvoxamine	•				•	
	Paroxetine					•	
	Sertraline			•	•	•	•
Serotonin–norepinephrine reuptake inhibitors	Desvenlafaxine					•	•
	Duloxetine	•				•	
	Levomilnacipran						•
	Venlafaxine			•	•	•	•
Tricyclic antidepressants	Amitriptyline	•		•	•	•	•
	Clomipramine	•			•	•	•
	Desipramine					•	
	Imipramine	•		•	•	•	•
	Nortriptyline				•	•	
Other antidepressants	Bupropion		•				
	Mirtazapine	•				•	•
Sleep	Trazodone	•				•	•

Continued

TABLE 10.1 Cytochrome P450 Enzyme Drug Metabolism, by Drug Class (Drugs@FDA; Flockhart Table, 2016; Micromedex (c) Healthcare Series, n.d.)—cont'd

Drug Class	Drug Name	Cytochrome P (CYP) 450 Enzyme					
		CYP1A2	CYP2B6	CYP2C9	CYP2C19	CYP2D6	CYP3A4/5
Stimulants	Amphetamine Salts					•	
	Dexmethylphenidate						
	Dextroamphetamine					•	
	Lisdexamfetamine					•	
	Methylphenidate						
Nonstimulants	Atomoxetine	•			•	•	•
	Clonidine					•	•
	Guanfacine						•
Typical antipsychotics	Chlorpromazine	•				•	•
	Fluphenazine	•		•	•	•	•
	Haloperidol	•				•	•
Atypical antipsychotics	Aripiprazole					•	•
	Asenapine	•					•
	Clozapine	•		•	•	•	•
	Lurasidone						•
	Olanzapine	•				•	•
	Paliperidone					•	•
	Quetiapine					•	•
	Risperidone					•	•
	Ziprasidone	•					•

RELEVANT PHARMACODYNAMIC GENES AND POLYMORPHISMS

Pharmacogenomics has become integrated into clinical practice and is used as a potential additional tool to improve the efficacy and tolerability of psychotropic medications. This technology has evolved to include genes influencing the PD response of medications, primarily downstream mechanisms such as receptors and second messenger mechanisms (Table 10.2).

Human Leukocyte Antigen-B27 to B*1502 and A*3101

Human leukocyte antigen (HLA) genetic variation is implicated in the development of specific cutaneous adverse reactions to aromatic anticonvulsants. HLA-B is a gene that encodes a cell surface protein involved in presenting antigens to the immune system. HLA-B*1502 is associated with increased risk of Stevens-Johnson syndrome (SJS) and toxic epidermal necrolysis (TEN) in patients who are being treated with carbamazepine. The allele is seen with high frequency in many Asian populations (Ferrell & McLeod, 2008).

Genetic Test Interpretation

Genotyping identifies HLA-B and HLA-A alleles. The results are either positive if one or two copies of the variant alleles are present or negative if no copy of the variant allele is present. The absence of the variant alleles suggests a lower risk for dermatological adverse events, which include TEN and SJS when patients are taking certain mood stabilizers (Leckband et al., 2013).

Serotonin Transporter Gene

Serotonin transporter gene (SLC6A4) is a presynaptic transmembrane protein that is responsible for terminating the action of 5-hydroxytryptamine

TABLE 10.2   Important Pharmacodynamic Genes

1. Human leukocyte antigen (HLA)-B*1502 and HLA-A*3101 (only need to be considered with certain mood stabilizers
2. SLC6A4: serotonin transporter gene: CPIC B/C evidence and PharmGKB 2A evidence, so moderate evidence
3. MTHFR: Methylenetetrahydrofolate reductase
4. COMT: Catechol-O-methyltransferase: CPIC level C/D and PharmGKB 2A
5. ADRA2A: α-2A-adrenergic receptor
6. DRD2: dopamine receptor: CPIC level C and PharmGKB 2A

CPIC, Clinical Pharmacogenetics Implementation Consortium.

(5-HT) in the synaptic cleft. Released serotonin is transported back into the presynaptic terminals via this integral membrane protein. The molecular target for SSRI is SLC6A4, which results in an inhibition of 5-HT reuptake in the presynapse from the synaptic cleft. SSRIs have a high affinity for 5-HT uptake transporters (Katrin, Klein, & Altman, 2009).

The observation that current antidepressant therapies need sustained treatment of 2—4 weeks to be effective suggests that adaptive changes in both serotonergic and noradrenergic neurotransmission and downstream neural adaptation (e.g., the brain-derived neurotrophic factor receptor signaling pathway) rather than only the elevation in synaptic monoamine levels itself are responsible for the therapeutic effects (Hashimoto, 2009; Vidal, Valdizán, Mostany, Pazos, & Castro, 2009) (Fig. 10.2).

There are two variations of SLC644 within the transporter-linked promoter polymorphic region (5-HTTLPR). There is a 43—base pair deletion of DNA in SLC6A4. Individuals with this deletion are termed "short" or S patients. Individuals who do not have this deletion are termed "long" or L patients. The short variant is associated with a reduction in both the expression and function of serotonin transporter (Porcelli, Fabbri, & Serretti, 2012; Shiroma, Drews, Geske, & Mrazek, 2014; Staeker, Leucht, Laika, & Steimer, 2014). Data suggest that individuals with the short transporter allele are less likely to respond to SSRIs and to achieve remission (Altar et al., 2013). Studies also show that L-allele carriers have a faster and better response to SSRI in the Caucasian population. The data were not robust in other populations (Karlovic & Serretti, 2013). In addition, there is also an SNP within the long, or L, 43 base pair which also disrupts the function of the transporter. This variation is represented as L (A) or L (G). Patients who have the L (G) allele have poor expression and function of the serotonin transporter (Staeker et al., 2014). Some data suggest that patients with an SLC6A4 variant may be more likely to respond to medications that are nonselective for the serotonin transporter (Smits, Smits, Schouten, Peeters, & Prins, 2007; Yoshida et al., 2004).

Methylenetetrahydrofolate Reductase

Methylenetetrahydrofolate reductase (MTHFR) is an enzyme responsible for the conversion of folic acid and folate to methyl folate. Methyl folate is the active form of folic acid and a precursor for the synthesis of the monoamine transmitters norepinephrine, dopamine, and serotonin. Two variations have been reported within this gene. An SNP in the MTHFR gene known as the C677T variant replaces cytosine with thymine, which results in a decrease in activity by 30%—35%. The second variant in the MTHFR gene is known as A1298C, resulting from adenine to cytosine replacement, but the change in enzymatic activity related to this is smaller

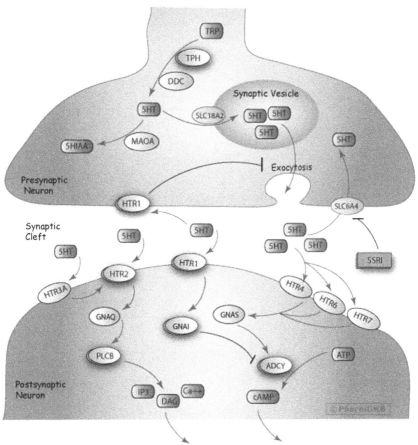

Neurotransmitter Release from Central Serotonergic,
Noradrenergic, and Dopaminergic Neurons

FIGURE 10.2   **Selective Serotonin Reuptake Inhibitor Pathway.** Depiction of genes involved in serotonin synthesis, release, and reuptake and effects of selective serotonin reuptake inhibitor (SSRI) antidepressants in the brain. *5-HT*, 5-hydroxytryptamine i.e. serotonin; *5HIAA*, 5-hydroxyindoleacetic acid; *ADCY*, adenylate cyclase; *ATP*, adenosine triphosphate; *CA++*, Calcium ion; *cAMP*, cyclic adenosine monophosphate; *DAG*, diacylglycerol; *DDC*, aromatic decarboxylase; *GNAI*, G protein alpha subunit, group I; *GNAQ*, Guanine nucleotide-binding protein (G protein) alpha subunit, group Q; *GNAS*, G protein alpha subunit, group S; *HTR*, hydroxytryptamine receptor i.e. serotonin receptor; *IP3*, inositol triphosphate; *MAOA*, monoamine oxidase A; *PLCB*, phospholipase C type B; *SLC18A2*, solute carrier family 18 member 2 i.e. serotonin presynaptic vesicular transporter; *SLC6A4*, solute carrier family 6 member 4 i.e. serotonin reuptake transporter; *TPH*, tryptophan hydroxylase; *TRP*, tryptophan.

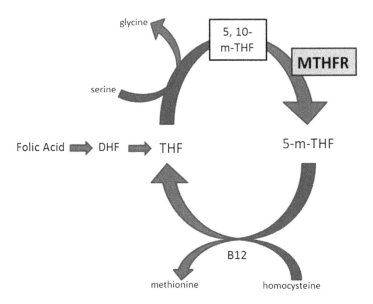

FIGURE 10.3 **MTHFR enzymatic activity.** Above is depicted the rate limiting step of active metabolite formation by conversion of 5, 10 methylene folate to 5-methylene folate via MTHFR activity. *DHF*, dihydrofolate; *m-THF*, methylene-tetrahydrofolate; *MTHFR*, methylenetetrahydrofolate reductase; *THF*, tetrahydrofolate.

compared with the C677T variant (Gilbody, Lewis, & Lightfoot, 2007) (Fig. 10.3).

Studies show that patients with the C677T variant have a greater risk of developing depression (Wu et al., 2013). There are data to support that methyl folate can be effective as an augmentation to antidepressants in patients with this polymorphism (Papakostas et al., 2012).

Catechol-O-Methyltransferase

Catechol-O-methyltransferase is a central enzyme responsible for the breakdown of dopamine, which is a neurotransmitter important for memory, attention, and other executive functions. A valine (Val) to methionine (Met) variation, called val158met, results in individual variation that is caused by a varied capacity of the enzyme to degrade dopamine. Met allele results in lower enzymatic activity and thus leads to higher dopamine levels, whereas the Val allele results in higher enzymatic activity leading to lower dopamine levels (Shield, Thomae, Eckloff, Wieben, & Weinshilboum, 2004).

If clinically indicated, a patient with a Val/Val genotype may benefit from agents that result in an increase in dopamine in the synapse (Hamidovic, Dlugos, Palmer, & de Wit, 2010).

α-2A-Adrenergic Receptor

The α-2A-adrenergic receptor (ADRA2A) is a subtype of α2-adrenergic receptors primarily located in the prefrontal cortex of the brain and stimulated by norepinephrine, which is critical for memory, attention, impulse control, and executive functioning (Cinnamon Bidwell, Dew, & Kollins, 2010).

An SNP at 1291 within the ADRA2A gene is caused by the replacement of cytosine (C) by guanine (G). This results in vulnerability to attention-deficit hyperactivity disorder symptoms (Polanczyk et al., 2007). The G allele has also been implicated in improved response to methylphenidate (Da Silva et al., 2008).

Dopamine Receptor

Dopamine 2 receptor is a D2 subtype of dopamine receptor involved in regulating dopamine neurotransmission (Beaulieu & Gainetdinov, 2011). The mechanism of action of most antipsychotics is via blockade of the D2 receptors. Affinity for the receptor has shown to correlate with side effects (Strange, 2001).

The genetic variation of −141 C insertion/deletion can lead to altered treatment response because a deletion in the promoter region of the gene leads to reduced gene expression and poor response and increased risk for side effects (Zhang, Lencz, & Malhotra, 2010). Caution is needed regarding antipsychotics, and agents with a lower binding affinity to the D2 receptor are preferred.

SELECTED LITERATURE REVIEW AND CLINICAL APPLICATIONS

Studies in the field of pharmacogenomics linking gene polymorphisms with treatment outcomes generally have had four designs: pairing single genes (either PK or PD) with single medications to assess the impact on a treatment outcome, pairing single genes with treatment outcomes in a certain disorder (i.e., major depression), looking for relevant genes associated with a particular illness or treatment outcome (i.e., Sequenced Treatment Alternatives to Relieve Depression study or Genome-Based Therapeutic Drugs for Depression project [GENDEP]), or applying a panel of pharmacogenomic genes to assess the impact of pharmacogenomic guidance on treatment outcome. There have been mixed but interesting findings.

Among the PK genes, CPIC, which has been maintaining an increasing database of these gene−medication associations of the current level of evidence which supports those associations, believed that there was enough evidence to publish guidelines for SSRI doses in patients being treated with SSRIs who were found to have vulnerabilities with PK genes 2D6 and 2C19 (Hicks et al., 2015).

Among the PD genes, the most robust findings have involved the SLC6A4 and the polymorphism 5-HTTLPR. In a meta-analysis of numerous studies, the long allele has been associated with both a better response and remission in patients treated with SSRIs for depression (Porcelli et al., 2012). In GENDEP, the effect of 5-HTTLPR on the efficacy of escitalopram compared with nortriptyline was explored. The results indicated a preferential impact of 5-HTTLPR on escitalopram over nortriptyline, with more robust findings in males than females. In that study, an additional polymorphism, rs2020933, influenced the outcome (Huezo et al., 2009). However, in another genome-wide study looking for relevant genes associated with treatment outcome in patients with depression, no associative genes were found, which suggests the difficulty of detecting relevant genes within an entire genome (Uher et al., 2013). Despite these contrasting findings, it was concluded that there is sufficient evidence among Caucasians for this polymorphism to be applied to clinical practice (Karlovic & Serretti, 2013). A newer finding is that polymorphisms within the norepinephrine transporter gene may influence response to treatment of depression with venlafaxine (Marshe et al., 2017).

Although mostly industry supported, there is evidence to support that the use of pharmacogenomic panels that combine PD and PK genes to guide in medication selection results in better outcomes than unguided treatment (Altar et al., 2015; Pérez et al., 2017). That most of those studies have been supported by industry resulted in speculation regarding the validity of the findings (Carlat, 2016). In addition, in an article by Rosenblat, Lee, and McIntyre (2017) in a systematic review of cost-effectiveness studies, the authors concluded that although the clinical use of the application of pharmacogenomic testing has shown promise, its cost-effectiveness is not yet well-supported.

CONCLUSIONS AND FUTURE DIRECTIONS

The field of pharmacogenomics is rapidly expanding as more polymorphisms are being identified that either confer vulnerability regarding the metabolism of psychiatric medications (i.e., PK genes) or confer vulnerability regarding the response to psychiatric medications. However, as an industry, this testing is available often in terms of a panel of genes which are integrated based on an internal algorithm or weighted importance to yield results in which medications are categorized within color domains indicating which medications to use, use with caution, or avoid. Although the individual gene results are also shared, many practitioners are not yet sufficiently well-versed to be able to combine the gene results themselves and will often defer to the industry-based results. Therefore, there continues to be pressure on providers themselves to be sure they have an adequate knowledge base before ordering such testing and applying the results within their clinical practice.

Despite these caveats, because the method of trial-and-error prescribing is not satisfactory to either the patient or practitioner, there clearly seems to be a role for pharmacogenomics. However, as the field continues to explore the efficacy and clinical situations for its application and more studies are published, practitioners must remain vigilant to the age-old medical school teaching that you should order a test only if you know how to apply the results in terms of both its potential benefit and its potential risk. In addition, it may be that ordering individual relevant genes, depending on the illness being treated and the medication being selected, rather than using preselected gene panels, may be more efficacious, relevant, and cost-effective. Within the research community, both genome-wide association studies such as GENDEP as well as gene-specific studies should serve as models to guide all pharmacological studies to perform relevant pharmacogenomic analyses in evaluating all study subjects to better understand the genetic basis for the categories of clinical outcomes: response, failures, and adverse events.

Regardless of whether this is within the research community or the clinical community, it is clear that the near future will continue to enhance our understanding of the role of pharmacogenomics in the field of child and adolescent psychiatry.

HELPFUL RESOURCES FOR CLINICIANS

- **PharmGKB** (pharmgkb.org) provides information that encompasses information related to the literature review, an illustration of drug pathways, phenotype relationships with drug metabolism, relevant gene–drug associations, and clinical guidelines for drug dosing.
- **CPIC** (https://cpicpgx.org) is an international group that develops peer-reviewed, evidence-based, and regularly updated clinical practice guidelines.
- **Flockhart Table** (http://medicine.iupui.edu/clinpharm/ddis/main-table), developed by the Indiana University Clinical Pharmacology Department, identifies drugs (psychotropic and otherwise) that are substrates, inducers, and inhibitors of specific CYP450 enzymes, especially those which are clinically the most relevant.

- **Human CYP450 allele nomenclature committee** (http://www.cypalleles.ki.se) provides genetic information and nomenclature guides for CYP450 enzymes and corresponding alleles.
- **Dutch Pharmacogenetics** Working Group (www.pharmgkb.org/page/dpwg) is the sister group of the US-based PharmGKB, established by the Royal Dutch Pharmacist's Association. It provides additional, differing levels of evidence and clinical relevance for drug guidelines.
- **FDA Pharmacogenomics** (https://www.fda.gov/Drugs/ScienceResearch/ResearchAreas/Pharmacogenetics) provides information about drug development and labeling, including genomics guidances, relevant publications, lists of biomarkers and related evidence, and more.

References

Altar, C. A., Carhart, J. M., Allen, J. D., Hall-Flavin, D. K., Dechairo, B. M., & Winner, J. G. (2015). Clinical validity: Combinatorial pharmacogenomics predicts antidepressant responses and healthcare utilizations better than single gene phenotypes. *The Pharmacogenomics Journal, 15*(5), 443–451. https://doi.org/10.1038/tpj.2014.85.

Altar, C. A., Hornberger, J., Shewade, A., Cruz, V., Garrison, J., & Mrazek, D. (2013). Clinical validity of cytochrome P450 metabolism and serotonin gene variants in psychiatric pharmacotherapy. *International Review of Psychiatry, 25*(5), 509–533. https://doi.org/10.3109/09540261.2013.825579.

Anderson, G. D., & Lynn, A. M. (2009). Optimizing pediatric dosing: A developmental pharmacologic approach. *Pharmacotherapy: The Journal of Human Pharmacology and Drug Therapy, 29*(6), 680–690. https://doi.org/10.1592/phco.29.6.680.

Beaulieu, J.-M., & Gainetdinov, R. R. (2011). The physiology, signaling, and pharmacology of dopamine receptors. *Pharmacological Reviews, 63*(1), 182–217. https://doi.org/10.1124/pr.110.002642.182.

Black, J. L., O'Kane, D. J., & Mrazek, D. A. (2007). The impact of CYP allelic variation on antidepressant metabolism: A review. *Expert Opinion on Drug Metabolism & Toxicology, 3*(1), 21–31. https://doi.org/10.1517/17425255.3.1.21.

Bush, W. S., Moore, J. H., Li, J., McDonnell, S., & Rabe, K. (2012). Chapter 11: Genome-wide association studiesF. Lewitter, & M. Kann (Eds.). *PLoS Computational Biology, 8*(12), e1002822. https://doi.org/10.1371/journal.pcbi.1002822.

Carlat, D. (2016). The GeneSight genetic test: A review of the evidence. *The Carlat Report Psychiatry, 13*(5). https://thecarlatreport.com/print/10531.

Cinnamon Bidwell, L., Dew, R. E., & Kollins, S. H. (2010). Alpha-2 adrenergic receptors and attention-deficit/hyperactivity disorder. *Current Psychiatry Reports, 12*(5), 366–373. https://doi.org/10.1007/s11920-010-0136-4.

Comer, J. S., Olfson, M., & Mojtabai, R. (2010). National trends in child and adolescent psychotropic polypharmacy in office-based practice, 1996–2007. *Journal of the American Academy of Child & Adolescent Psychiatry*. https://doi.org/10.1016/j.jaac.2010.07.007.

Da Silva, T. L., Pianca, T. G., Roman, T., et al. (2008). Adrenergic Alpha 2A receptor gene and response to methylphenidate in attention-deficit/hyperactivity disorder-predominantly inattentive type. *Journal of Neural Transmission, 115*(2), 341–345. https://doi.org/10.1007/s00702-007-0835-0.

Drugs@FDA: FDA Approved Drug Products. U.S. Food & Drug Administration https://www.accessdata.fda.gov/scripts/cder/daf/.

Fabbri, C., & Serretti, A. (2015). Pharmacogenetics of major depressive Disorder: Top genes and pathways toward clinical applications. *Current Psychiatry Reports, 17*(7). https://doi.org/10.1007/s11920-015-0594-9.

Ferrell, P. B., & McLeod, H. L. (2008). Carbamazepine, HLA-B*1502 and risk of Stevens-Johnson syndrome and toxic epidermal necrolysis: US FDA recommendations. *Pharmacogenomics, 9*(10), 1543—1546. https://doi.org/10.2217/14622416.9.10.1543.

Flockhart Table. (2016). Trustees of Indiana University. http://medicine.iupui.edu/clinpharm/ddis/main-table/.

Gilbody, S., Lewis, S., & Lightfoot, T. (2007). Methylenetetrahydrofolate reductase (MTHFR) genetic polymorphisms and psychiatric disorders: A HuGE review. *American Journal of Epidemiology, 165*(1), 1—13. https://doi.org/10.1093/aje/kwj347.

Hamidovic, A., Dlugos, A., Palmer, A. A., & de Wit, H. (2010). Catechol-O-methyltransferase val158met genotype modulates sustained attention in both the drug-free state and in response to amphetamine. *Psychiatric Genetics, 20*(3), 85—92. https://doi.org/10.1097/YPG.0b013e32833a1f3c.

Hashimoto, K. (2009). Emerging role of glutamate in the pathophysiology of major depressive disorder. *Brain Research Reviews, 61*(2), 105—123. https://doi.org/10.1016/j.brainresrev.2009.05.005.

Hicks, J. K., Bishop, J. R., Sangkuhl, K., et al. (2015). Clinical Pharmacogenetics Implementation Consortium (CPIC) guideline for CYP2D6 and CYP2C19 genotypes and dosing of selective serotonin reuptake inhibitors. *Clinical Pharmacology & Therapeutics, 98*(2), 127—134. https://doi.org/10.1002/cpt.147.

Huezo, D. P., Uher, R., Smith, R., et al. (2009). Moderation of antidepressant response by the serotonin transporter gene. *British Journal of Psychiatry, 195*, 30—38.

Karlovic, D., & Serretti, A. (2013). Serotonin transporter gene (5-Httlpr) polymorphism and efficacy of selective serotonin reuptake inhibitors - do we have sufficient evidence for clinical practice. *Acta Clinica Croatica, 52*(3), 353—362.

Katrin, S., Klein, T. E., & Altman, R. B. (2009). Selective serotonin reuptake inhibitors pathway. *Pharmacogenet Genomics*.

Leckband, S., Kelsoe, J., Dunnenberger, H., et al. (2013). Clinical pharmacogenetics implementation Consortium guidelines for HLA-B genotype and Carbamazepine dosing. *Clinical Pharmacology & Therapeutics, 94*(6), 324—328. https://doi.org/10.1038/clpt.2013.172.

Lerer, B., & Macciardi, F. (2002). Pharmacogenetics of antidepressant and mood-stabilizing drugs: A review of candidate-gene studies and future research directions. *International Journal of Neuropsychopharmacology, 5*(3), 255—275. https://doi.org/10.1017/S1461145702002936.

Leucht, S., Hierl, S., Kissling, W., Dold, M., & Davis, J. M. (2012). Putting the efficacy of psychiatric and general medicine medication into perspective: Review of meta-analyses. *British Journal of Psychiatry*. https://doi.org/10.1192/bjp.bp.111.096594.

Malik, S., Program, F., & Hospital, H. (2016). Psychopharmacogenomics in pediatric psychiatry with a focus on cytochrome P450 testing. *Psychiatric Annals, 46*(1), 52—57.

Marshe, V. S., Maciukiewicz, M., Rej, S., et al. (2017). Norepinephrine transporter gene variants and remission from depression with venlafaxine treatment in older adults. *American Journal of Psychiatry*. https://doi.org/10.1176/appi.ajp.2016.16050617.

Micromedex (c) Healthcare Series (n.d.). Greenwood Village, CO: Thomson Micromedex. http://thomsonhc.com.

Mrazek, D. A. (2010). Psychiatric pharmacogenomic testing in clinical practice. *Dialogues in Clinical Neuroscience, 12*(1), 69—76. https://doi.org/10.1517/17410541.2.2.93.

Mrazek, M. D. D. (2010). *Psychiatric pharmacogenomics*. Oxford University Press. https://doi.org/10.1093/med/9780195367294.001.0001.

Papakostas, G. I., Shelton, R. C., Zajecka, J. M., et al. (2012). L-methylfolate as adjunctive therapy for SSRI-resistant major depression: Results of two randomized, double-blind, parallel-sequential trials. *The American Journal of Psychiatry, 169*(12), 1267−1274. https://doi.org/10.1176/appi.ajp.2012.11071114.

Pérez, V., Salavert, A., Espadaler, J., et al. (2017). Efficacy of prospective pharmacogenetic testing in the treatment of major depressive disorder: Results of a randomized, double-blind clinical trial. *BMC Psychiatry.* https://doi.org/10.1186/s12888-017-1412-1.

Phillips, K. A., Veenstra, D. L., Oren, E., Lee, J. K., & Sadee, W. (2001). Potential role of pharmacogenomics in reducing adverse drug reactions: A systematic review. *JAMA, 286*(18), 2270−2279. https://doi.org/10.1001/jama.286.18.2270.

Polanczyk, G., Zeni, C., Genro, J. P., et al. (2007). Association of the adrenergic alpha2A receptor gene with methylphenidate improvement of inattentive symptoms in children and adolescents with attention-deficit/hyperactivity disorder. *Arch Gen Psychiatry, 64*(2), 218−224. https://doi.org/10.1001/archpsyc.64.2.218.

Porcelli, S., Fabbri, C., & Serretti, A. (2012). Meta-analysis of serotonin transporter gene promoter polymorphism (5-HTTLPR) association with antidepressant efficacy. *European Neuropsychopharmacology, 22*(4), 239−258. https://doi.org/10.1016/j.euroneuro.2011.10.003.

Prioritization of genes/drugs − CPIC. August 17.(2017). https://cpicpgx.org/prioritization/#cpicLevels.

Rosenblat, J. D., Lee, Y., & McIntyre, R. S. (2017). Does pharmacogenomic testing improve clinical outcomes for major depressive disorder? *Journal of Clinical Psychiatry, 78*(6), 720−729. https://doi.org/10.4088/JCP.15r10583.

Shield, A. J., Thomae, B. A., Eckloff, B. W., Wieben, E. D., & Weinshilboum, R. M. (2004). Human catechol O-methyltransferase genetic variation: Gene resequencing and functional characterization of variant allozymes. *Molecular Psychiatry, 9*(2), 151−160. https://doi.org/10.1038/sj.mp.4001386.

Shiroma, P. R., Drews, M. S., Geske, J. R., & Mrazek, D. A. (2014). SLC6A4 polymorphisms and age of onset in late-life depression on treatment outcomes with citalopram: A sequenced treatment alternatives to relieve depression (STAR???D) report. *The American Journal of Geriatric Psychiatry, 22*(11), 1140−1148. https://doi.org/10.1016/j.jagp.2013.02.012.

Smits, K. M., Smits, L. J. M., Schouten, J. S. A. G., Peeters, F. P. M. L., & Prins, M. H. (2007). Does pretreatment testing for serotonin transporter polymorphisms lead to earlier effects of drug treatment in patients with major depression? A decision-analytic model. *Clinical Therapeutics, 29*(4), 691−702. https://doi.org/10.1016/j.clinthera.2007.04.018.

Staeker, J., Leucht, S., Laika, B., & Steimer, W. (2014). Polymorphisms in serotonergic pathways influence the outcome of antidepressant therapy in psychiatric inpatients. *Genetic Testing and Molecular Biomarkers, 18*(1), 20−31. https://doi.org/10.1089/gtmb.2013.0217.

Strange, P. G. (2001). Antipsychotic drugs: Importance of dopamine receptors for mechanisms of therapeutic actions and side effects. *Pharmacological Reviews, 53*(1), 119−133.

Uher, R., Tansey, K. E., Rietschel, M., et al. (2013). Common genetic variation and antidepressant efficacy in major depressive disorder: A meta-analysis of three genome-wide pharmacogenetic studies. *The American Journal of Psychiatry, 170*(2), 207−217. https://doi.org/10.1176/appi.ajp.2012.12020237.

Vidal, R., Valdizán, E. M., Mostany, R., Pazos, A., & Castro, E. (2009). Long-term treatment with fluoxetine induces desensitization of 5-HT4 receptor-dependent signalling and functionality in rat brain. *Journal of Neurochemistry, 110*(3), 1120−1127. https://doi.org/10.1111/j.1471-4159.2009.06210.x.

Weinshilboum, R. (2003). Inheritance and drug response. *New England Journal of Medicine, 348*(6), 529−537. https://doi.org/10.1056/NEJMra020021.

Whirl-Carrillo, M., McDonagh, E. M., Hebert, J. M., Gong, L., Sangkuhl, K., Thorn, C. F., et al. (2012). Pharmacogenomics knowledge for personalized medicine. *Clinical Pharmacology & Therapeutics, 92*(4), 414–417.

Wilkinson, G. R. (2005). Drug metabolism and variability among patients in drug response. *New England Journal of Medicine, 352*(21), 2211–2221. https://doi.org/10.1056/NEJMra032424.

Wu, Y.. Le, Ding, X. X., Sun, Y. H., et al. (2013). Association between MTHFR C677T polymorphism and depression: An updated meta-analysis of 26 studies. *Progress in Neuro-Psychopharmacology & Biological Psychiatry, 46*, 78–85. https://doi.org/10.1016/j.pnpbp.2013.06.015.

Yoshida, K., Takahashi, H., Higuchi, H., et al. (2004). Prediction of antidepressant response to milnacipran by norepinephrine transporter gene polymorphisms. *The American Journal of Psychiatry, 161*(9), 1575–1580. https://doi.org/10.1176/appi.ajp.161.9.1575.

Zhang, J.-P., Lencz, T., & Malhotra, A. K. (2010). D2 receptor genetic variation and clinical response to antipsychotic drug treatment: A meta-analysis. *The American Journal of Psychiatry, 167*(7), 763–772. https://doi.org/10.1176/appi.ajp.2009.09040598.

11

Telepsychiatry and Digital Mental Health Care in Child and Adolescent Psychiatry: Implications for Service Delivery in Low- and Middle-Income Countries

Savita Malhotra, Ruchita Shah

Postgraduate Institute of Medical Education and Research, Chandigarh, India

Nick Bostrom[1] wrote:

> ...a technological revolution (is) a dramatic change brought about relatively quickly by the introduction of some new technology. *Bostrom (2006)*

INTRODUCTION

Ours is an era of accelerated technological progress characterized not only by new innovations but also by their application and diffusion. Information and communication technologies (ICTs) have entered every walk of our lives with unprecedented speed and depth. We have moved from desktop computers to laptops, handheld tablets, and smartphones, with ever-increasing apps that facilitate our enterprises from banking to

---

[1] Bostrom is the director of the Future of Humanity Institute and the Strategic Artificial Intelligence Research Centre, University of Oxford, and the author of *Superintelligence*.

buying, holidaying, and health care. Technology has transformed how people communicate, learn, work, and even appraise and take care of their health. With this backdrop, it is unsurprising that technological advancements are being increasingly applied to health care needs. Although the use of ICT for health care delivery (mainly in the form of videoconferencing [VC]) has a long history, newer methods based on medical informatics and artificial intelligence are rapidly being incorporated into the health care delivery system. These range from mobile apps (Hollis et al., 2017), some with wearable gadgets that monitor patient parameters including activity and even mood, CD-ROM or app-based interventions (Boydell et al., 2014) and patient portals (Kendrick & Benson, 2017), to decision support systems that assist remote providers (Koposov et al., 2017). Such rapid technological advancements make it imperative to be aware about how (methods and models) and what (content and evidence) ICT has to offer to child and adolescent mental health (CAMH) care delivery systems.

THE PROMISE OF TECHNOLOGY

Epidemiological studies show that the prevalence of child and adolescent behavioral and mental disorders ranges from 18% to 22.5% in high-income countries (HIC) (Costello, Mustillo, Keller, & Angold, 2004; Merikangas, Nakamura, & Kessler, 2009). Studies from low- and middle-income countries (LMIC) such as India put these figures a little lower, at 6%–15% (Malhotra & Patra, 2014). Although the prevalence is relatively low, the sheer numbers of children and adolescents in LMIC with expansive (broader-base) population pyramids are staggering. The early years of life are the most important from a developmental perspective, given that CAMH disorders, many of which are developmental in nature, are often associated with lifelong morbidity and disability, and place an enormous burden on the family, society, and economy (Merikangas et al., 2009). Compounding the matter further, CAMH care services are grossly deficient or even nonexistent in most LMIC, and often inaccessible even in HIC. This huge discrepancy between the need for services on the one hand and its availability and accessibility on the other, often referred to as the mental health gap, is caused by two major factors: inadequate resources and inequity. In LMIC such as India, where there are 0.2 psychiatrists per 100,000 people (Sinha & Kaur, 2011), the number of psychiatrists who are trained, qualified, or even working in child and adolescent psychiatry as an area of interest is dismal, approximately at 1 per 4–5 million children and adolescents (Malhotra & Padhy, 2015). Furthermore, professionals working in this field are either affiliated with major institutions or based in large cities. The cost of receiving specialized care is high because of direct costs involved, such as fees or transportation, or as a result of indirect costs related to child care. The task of increasing specialized staff to the extent that it serves most of those who need it in an affordable and accessible manner is daunting and almost unachievable in India and many other LMIC. From the perspective of service use, there are also other important barriers such as stigma and a lack of awareness in the community. Interestingly, the acceptability and popularity of ICT have increased exponentially among the general public and professionals, and more so among young people. The use of smartphones and video-chats or video-calls serves as a classical example. Telepsychiatry and other related health care innovations using various platforms and technologies have the potential to bridge this mental health gap. These can increase the reach of the services and overcome hurdles such as stigma and cultural barriers.

DEFINING TELEPSYCHIATRY AND DIGITAL HEALTH CARE

Telepsychiatry or telehealth can be broadly defined as the use of tele-communication technology (ICT) to provide or support psychiatric services and treatment across distances. Such services can be delivered using various virtual care technologies include interactive (real-time) video, telephones, smartphones and tablets, secure messaging and mailing portals, and shared electronic health (eHealth) records. The therapeutic bandwidth, i.e., the ability of the provider and the patient to hear and see each other (Mohr, Cuijpers, & Lehman, 2011), varies across these technologies. The better the therapeutic bandwidth, the more the verbal and nonverbal communication and cues exchanged between doctor and patient, and better the treatment. Broadly, the technology may be synchronous or real-time (live), or asynchronous or store-forward.

eHealth has been defined as Internet-based health care delivery, or anything health-related that uses ICT, incorporating computers or the Internet in its delivery. Mobile-delivered health (mHealth) is a branch of eHealth focusing on delivering health care-related information, interventions, and monitoring through portable electronic/mobile devices and technologies such as smartphones, tablets, and wearable devices: for example, mobile apps or short message service (SMS)-based interventions (Hollis et al., 2017). Broadly, digital health interventions (DHI) are those that provide information, support, and therapy (emotional, decisional, behavioral, and neurocognitive) for physical and/or mental health problems via a technological or digital platform (e.g., website, computer, mobile phone app, SMS, email, VC, wearable device) (Hollis et al., 2017).

Medical informatics (also called health informatics or health care informatics) is the interdisciplinary study of the design, development, adoption, and application of information technology (IT)-based innovations in health care services delivery, management, and planning (as quoted by the Healthcare Information and Management Systems Society) (Medical Informatics, n.d., para 1). Such technologies include computerized prescriber order entry (CPOE), which allows prescribers to enter orders directly into an electronic system and clinical decision support (CDS) tools that provide information and recommend treatments to prescribers at the point of care; and electronic medical records, which can integrate information from CPOE, CDS, and other systems (Walker, 2008).

The US Food and Drug Administration defines digital health as including categories such as mHealth, health IT, wearable devices, telehealth and telemedicine, and personalized medicine (Digital Health, n.d., para 8).

Traditionally, telepsychiatry models involve a provider at the hub site who provides direct care to the patient at the remote site or provides consultation to the doctor at the remote site, who in turn delivers care locally. On the other hand, Internet-based services or app-based interventions may not include a provider or facilitator. Such eHealth/mHealth undoubtedly increases the accessibility of such services but it is less efficient and increases the risk for unsupervised interventions. Also, human support may be beneficial for better adherence and effectiveness (Hollis et al., 2017). This may be more relevant for children and adolescents compared with adults. A depressed and suicidal adolescent seeking remedy on the Web may encounter one of many hundreds such apps. Except for a few, these apps have not been researched adequately for their efficacy or effectiveness, benefits, and risks. On the other hand, an online CDS system that guides local providers in service delivery may be particularly useful and acceptable to all stakeholders (Malhotra, Chakrabarti, Shah, Mehta, et al., 2015; Malhotra, Chakrabarti, Shah, Sharma, et al., 2015; Peters, 2016).

MODELS OF TECHNOLOGY-BASED HEALTH CARE DELIVERY

As explained in the previous section, technology-based health care delivery can be in the form of telepsychiatry or other types of eHealth/mHealth that may or may not use medical informatics. DHIs for CAMH disorders that directly empower clients or patients to make health care decisions have been reviewed extensively by Hollis et al. (2017), Schueller, Stiles-Shields, and Yarosh (2017), and Siemer et al. (2011). We shall briefly delve into the pros, cons, and future of such interventions, and toward the end of this section we will consider whether they can find a place within provider-based services. We shall describe in detail the various conventional models of telepsychiatry and its emerging interface with medical informatics and other modes of digital health. In addition, we shall present examples of each model for better understanding and an overview of evidence if available.

Hilty, Yellowlees, Cobb, et al. (2006) and later Fortney et al. (2015) described various telepsychiatry models based mainly on their resource-intensiveness. Theoretically, the more resources that are devoted to treating an individual patient, the greater the effectiveness of the treatment (for that patient) (Fortney et al., 2015). However, when more clinical resources are devoted to an individual patient, fewer numbers of patients can be reached (i.e., treated). From a population health perspective, the ultimate goal is to maximize "population-level effectiveness" given the fixed capacity of mental health providers. Population-level effectiveness is the product of how many patients are reached and the clinical effectiveness of the treatment provided to those who are reached (Fortney, Enderle, et al., 2013; Fortney, Pyne, et al., 2013; Zatzick et al., 2009). Hilty, Yellowlees, Cobb, et al. (2006) originally described a three-tier model of direct care, consultation-liaison, and collaborative care. Fortney et al. (2015) expanded the model to a five-tiered pyramid from a least resource-intensive model at the base to the most resource-intensive model at the top. The theoretical assumption that the more resource-intensive an approach is the more effective it would be for the individual patient has clearly not been borne out in research. For example, the telepsychiatry referral model is most resource-intensive because it is characterized by direct care by the telepsychiatrist or mental health specialist at the hub site. However, that this might be the most effective model for the individual patient may not be true, because cultural barriers and incompetency may hinder quality care. On the other hand, collaborative care that involves collaboration between local providers and mental health specialists with care delivery by the local team has been shown to be superior (Hilty, Yellowlees, Cobb, et al., 2006). Thus, resource-intensiveness may not be an ideal proxy marker for effectiveness of the telepsychiatry models. Also, with the growing number of ICT applications in mental health, distinctions between such traditional telepsychiatry models and eHealth, mHealth, and health informatics are blurring. Elements of several of these technologies may provide a less resource-intensive and yet a more effective model of technologically based mental health care delivery.

Conventional Models of Telepsychiatry

Telepsychiatry Referral Model

This is the traditional model in which the primary care provider refers the patient for telepsychiatry. In this model, the telepsychiatrist/mental health specialist assumes all of the responsibilities of patient care including diagnostic assessments, treatment, and follow-up. There may be varying degrees of communication with the primary care referral provider (PCP). The PCP may or may not attend the session, but the primary responsibility rests with the telepsychiatrist. Direct care can be provided for diagnostic assessment, pharmacological treatment, and psychotherapeutic interventions. Myers, Valentine, Morganthaler, and Melzer (2006) reported on telepsychiatry services provided through a Children's Health Access Regional Telemedicine program. Services were provided by child and adolescent telepsychiatrists at the University of Washington School of Medicine to children and adolescents in four nonmetropolitan sites. They met via high-bandwidth interactive video with parents and youths together, and then separately as clinically indicated and tolerated. After completion of each session, the telepsychiatrist sent a note by faxing summarized findings, followed by a full report 2–3 weeks later to the referring physician. Although referring physicians were invited to attend the sessions, none of them did so (Myers et al., 2006). Also, although referring providers endorsed high satisfaction with telepsychiatric care, pediatricians were consistently more satisfied than were family physicians. In India, a telepsychiatry project (Thara, John, & Rao, 2008) offered service to 156 villages by means of a bus that was custom-built to contain a consultation room and pharmacy. After a tele-consultation, a prescription was advised by the psychiatrist located at the nodal center to the telepsychiatry clinic facilitator in the bus and dispensed by the onboard pharmacy. Real-time VC for psychiatric care and capacity-building in remote areas has also been attempted in Pakistan (Impact Evaluation, n.d., para 1) and reported from a few other LMIC (Nepal Sets Up Telepsychiatry Program, 1998).

Although this model increases reach and helps to establish geographic equity, it merely redistributes resources (Fortney et al., 2015). The mental health specialist cannot see a patient face-to-face (FTF) at the same time as providing video-consultation to a patient who is located remotely. In other words, the telepsychiatrist does not see a higher number of patients, but merely different patients (i.e., from rural and geographically inaccessible areas). From the public health perspective, therefore, it does not increase the reach of psychiatric services. Good-quality, evidence-based service is provided to the same number of people, albeit in different locations. Fortney et al. (2015) suggested that because this is the most resource-intensive model, it must ideally be reserved only for difficult cases or where there has been poor response after several trials to treatment. This is similar to stepped-up care. In addition, engaging and retaining patients remains an issue with telepsychiatry referral clinics, which have high no-show and dropout rates similar to those of FTF mental health clinics (Frueh et al., 2007). Telepsychiatrists may not be culturally competent to provide direct consultations because they may not be familiar with several important aspects of the child's culture, such as child-rearing practices, norms of child behavior, and views of illness causation (Savin, Glueck, Chardavoyne, Yager, & Novins, 2011). This may have direct negative implications for therapeutic alliance, diagnostic assessment, treatment recommendations, the family's adherence to those recommendations, and follow-up. Also, major concern of duty of care remains an issue because the telepsychiatrist is solely responsible for care of a patient who is remotely located (Malhotra, Chakrabarti, & Shah, 2013). This is especially important in case of emergencies such as suicidal patients or medical emergencies after drug treatment. Thus, this model may be suitable only for follow-up of patients after initial FTF consultation. Also, this model provides no opportunities for PCP to improve knowledge or skills, and thus does not increase the capacity of services in any manner.

Collaborative Care Model/Behavioral Health Consultation

Thus far, collaborative care or integrated care has been considered the best model (Fortney et al., 2015; Hilty, Yellowlees, Cobb, et al., 2006). This model is more resource-intensive than those at the base of the pyramid, but the services are more effective. Several providers and researchers have used the terms "collaborative care" and "behavior health consultation models" interchangeably. However, Fortney et al. (2015) distinguished between the two. They defined the two models in accordance to practice-based models of care (i.e., not using telepsychiatry) with the aim of integrating mental health into primary health care. Fortney et al. described collaborative care as the model originally developed by Katon et al. (1995, 1996) at the University of Washington and demonstrated it to be clinically effective in randomized control trials. The collaborative care model attempts to improve access to evidence-based mental health treatments for primary care patients. Fortney et al. (2015) defined the behavioral health consultant model as the model of care developed simultaneously and independently at Cherokee Health Systems, Tennessee, United States, and the White River Junction VA Medical Center, Vermont, United States. This model lacks rigorous scientific evidence regarding its impact on clinical outcomes. Although it was found to be effective (Fortney et al., 2015), the greatest challenge in implementing such a model in practice is the paucity of child and adolescent psychiatrists. This is where telepsychiatry can have an important role.

In a collaborative care model, the central person acts as the care manager. The care manager may be located on-site (at the primary care level) or off-site (at the provider level). A care manager co-located with the mental health specialist may be in a better position to cover several primary care sites and to conduct case reviews with the mental health specialist. The care manager contacts patients in between their primary care visits to assess the follow-up and progress. During case reviews, the mental health specialist can ask a certain case to be reviewed using telepsychiatry. Here a consultation can be raised by the telepsychiatrist, as opposed to a referral raised by the PCP in the direct model. The telepsychiatrist has the treatment history and access to case records. This can be electronic or scanned copies of case notes. In this model, the telepsychiatrist therefore has better access to previous records, compared with the consultation-liaison model, and the consultation can be more focused and comprehensive. Ideally, the primary care provider and care manager are present during the telepsychiatry consultation. The telepsychiatrist can clarify the diagnosis, make the treatment plan, and provide recommendations. Recommendations are taken up by the primary care provider. The case can be reviewed from time to time by the mental health specialist, but day-to-day care is provided by the primary care provider. Structured assessments have also been incorporated in some such projects to monitor progress and flag consultation with the telepsychiatrist. Telephone or email contact may also be maintained between the care manager and the psychiatrist. The care manager also acts as a go-between with the primary care provider.

According to Hilty et al. (2013), collaborative care via telepsychiatry is a co-provision of medication for primary care patients by the telepsychiatrist and PCP in rural communities, based on earlier models of in-person care. This model is often integrated with stepped-up models of care, which use "less-intensive or less expensive interventions" first. If a patients fail to improve, care is then "stepped up" to more intensive services. Collaborative care as applied to telepsychiatry has been found to be feasible and effective as well as cost-effective compared with in-person collaborative care for the treatment of depression (Fortney, Enderle, et al., 2013; Fortney, Pyne, et al., 2013; Hilt, 2017; Pyne et al., 2010). This model is ideal, especially for children and adolescents, because most childhood disorders such as developmental disabilities require a multidisciplinary approach (Szeftel et al., 2011).

The Michigan Child Collaborative Care Program run by the University of Michigan uses principles of collaborative care as well as the consultation model (see subsequent discussion) to provide care through PCPs using telepsychiatry (Michigan Child Collaborative Care Program, n.d.). The Children's Attention-Deficit Hyperactivity Disorder (ADHD) Telemental Health Treatment Study (CATTS) was a randomized, controlled trial that demonstrated the superiority of a telehealth service delivery model using some principles of collaborative care to treat ADHD with combined pharmacotherapy and behavior training, compared with management in primary care augmented with a telepsychiatry consultation (Myers, Vander Stoep, & Lobdell, 2013; Rockhill, Tse, Fesinmeyer,

Garcia, & Myers, 2016; Vander Stoep et al., 2017). The telepsychiatrists used the Texas Children's Medication Algorithm Project for ADHD to guide pharmacotherapy. The algorithms were part of a Web-based decision-making and tracking tool termed WebCATTS (Vander Stoep & Myers, 2013), which improved telepsychiatrists' fidelity with guidelines. Although this model is considered to be better among conventional models, there is still a substantial need for child and adolescent psychiatrists' services as telepsychiatrists. The telepsychiatry behavioral consultant model is not well-researched and data in this field regarding effectiveness, superiority vis-à-vis other models, and importantly, cost-effectiveness are still emerging (Fortney et al., 2015).

Consultation-Liaison/Consultation Care Model

Consultation—liaison refers to two related clinical processes: first, that of a psychiatrist providing expert advice on the consultee's patient, and second, that of a "liaison" or linking person to help with signposting or directing to appropriate services or next steps. Conventionally, the latter suggested that the psychiatrist was based in close proximity to the medical team, and/or worked as a member of it. Over time, the term has been expanded to indicate the educational function of the consulting psychiatrist, who provides the consultee with knowledge and skills (Katon & Gonzales, 1994; Leigh, 2015). In the consultation model, the request is raised by the primary care provider. Here the mental health specialist gives a telepsychiatry consultation, provides an opinion about the diagnosis, and makes treatment recommendations. However, it is up to the PCP to follow proposed recommendations. In the telepsychiatry consultation—liaison model, the telepsychiatrist may conduct a traditional diagnostic assessment via interactive video or phone. It is also feasible to conduct telepsychiatry consultation asynchronously using store and forward technologies (Yellowlees et al., 2010). The treatment plan could include a recommendation to deliver brief psychotherapy (e.g., problem-solving therapy) and/or prescribe psychotropic medication. The telepsychiatrist does not take over the treatment of the patient, which frees up time to treat or consult with other patients. Such a model of telepsychiatry has been followed in Asian countries such as India and Pakistan. Balasinorwala, Shah, Chatterjee, Kale, and Matcheswalla (2014) reported the feasibility of asynchronous telepsychiatry for providing consultation to PCP. A study from Rawalpindi in Pakistan demonstrated the feasibility of using "store and forward," through the use of the Internet and a dedicated email address to train and supervise staff in diagnosing and managing children and adolescents aged 16 years or less at no extra cost (Rahman, 2006). Furthermore, most of these programs are run as part of telemedicine programs rather than stand-alone services. Although less resource-intensive than other conventional models, it has not been shown to improve patient outcomes (Fortney et al., 2015; Hilty, Marks, Wegelin, Callahan, & Nesbitt, 2007; Myers, Vander Stoep, Zhou, McCarty, & Katon, 2015). Thus, although the telepsychiatry consultation–liaison model improves access and reach, it does not appear to increase population-level effectiveness (Fortney et al., 2015).

Evidence for Effectiveness and Feasibility of Conventional Telepsychiatry

The literature related to these conventional models of telepsychiatry mainly using VC has been reviewed extensively (Diamond & Bloch, 2010; Myers, Palmer, & Geyer, 2011; Pesamaa et al., 2004) and a number of randomized clinical trials have been conducted in this field (Elford et al., 2001; Fortney, Enderle, et al., 2013; Fortney, Pyne, et al., 2013; Myers et al., 2013; Nelson, Barnard, & Cain, 2003; Rockhill et al., 2016; Vander Stoep et al., 2017). Studies mainly pertained to the reliability of psychiatric and neuropsychological assessments and satisfaction with and acceptability of telepsychiatry; there was limited literature on clinical outcome (i.e., improvement in symptoms and functioning), quality of life, or treatment adherence. Furthermore, there were few robust data on the cost-effectiveness of telepsychiatry, especially accounting for the psychiatrists' time, using any model. Overall child and adolescent (and general) telepsychiatry literature is mainly restricted to VC, with few reports on the use of asynchronous telepsychiatry for clinical, training, and educational purposes.

A number of studies reported on child/adolescent and caregiver satisfaction, as well as provider satisfaction, with the overall positive conclusion that there is high satisfaction and acceptability with VC (Elford et al., 2001; Hilty, Yellowlees, Nesbitt, et al., 2006; Kopel, Nunn, & Dossetor, 2001; Myers, Valentine, & Melzer, 2007; Myers et al., 2006). Other descriptive studies suggested the feasibility and acceptability of telepsychiatry for providing CAMH care (Cloutier, Cappelli, Glennie, & Keresztes, 2008; Myers et al., 2010). However, problems with audiovisual quality because of the lack of technical support were perceived as major hurdles to satisfaction. Also, it was reported that parents would have preferred to see the psychiatrist in person (Savin et al., 2011). Although this was attributed to parents' discomfort with or feeling intimidated by technology, preference for in-person consultation with the doctor for personal satisfaction cannot be ruled out (Savin et al., 2011). Only one study (Wagnild et al., 2006) reported a low rate of satisfaction with VC among psychiatrists (26%). There is the possibility of publication bias for positive reports of satisfaction with VC, as pointed out previously by Pesamaa et al. (2004). In addition, Chakrabarti and Shah (2016) commented on the low uptake of telepsychiatry by the wider psychiatry fraternity despite the huge promise and potential.

Comparison of videoconference-based assessments and in-person assessments in children found the former to be reliable, feasible, and satisfactory to patients and their parents (Elford et al., 2001; Keilman et al., 2005; Myers et al., 2007, 2008). A randomized trial for the treatment of ADHD with combined pharmacotherapy and behavior training using telepsychiatry (CATTS) found that children assigned to the telehealth service model showed significantly more improvement on several measures compared with care by PCPs augmented with a teleconsultation. The CATTS telepsychiatrists showed high fidelity to evidence-based algorithms (Myers et al., 2013; Rockhill et al., 2016; Vander Stoep et al., 2017). A retrospective analysis (Yellowlees, Hilty, Marks, Neufeld, & Bourgeois, 2008) on the diagnostic and clinical outcomes for children who were evaluated via VC found significant improvement in symptoms over follow-up. Individual case reports described the delivery of telepsychiatric care (VC) for children with anorexia nervosa (Goldfield & Boachie, 2003), depression (Alessi, 2002), posttraumatic stress disorders (Alessi, 2003), and ADHD (Hilty, Sison, Nesbitt, & Hales, 2000). Hilt et al. (2015) reported on a statewide child telepsychiatry consult system which included televideo consults, medication reviews, and provider-telephone consults. They found that there was a significant decrease in the number of children aged less than 5 years using psychotropic medications, in children using psychotropic doses greater than 150% of the maximum approved, and in children referred by caseworkers for psychiatric residential treatment facility admission. Nelson et al. (2003) evaluated an 8-week cognitive behavior therapy intervention for childhood depression in 28 youths who received the intervention either FTF or via VC. Participants were evaluated on depression inventories before and after treatment. Cognitive behavioral therapy treatment was shown to be effective and comparable across the two conditions.

Cost-effectiveness is the least studied dimension of telepsychiatry. Most studies report on cost savings through decreased travel and expenditure, days lost of work, and days lost owing to prolonged illness vis-à-vis the infrastructure and telecommunication costs. Overall positive findings have been reported (Elford et al., 2001; Hilt et al., 2015; Myers et al., 2015; Spaulding, Belz, DeLurgio, & Williams, 2010). However, there is a huge risk of publication bias, and cost accounting might have not considered variables such as the child and adolescent psychiatrists' time to give a teleconsultation in the context of any model of care.

Issues Specific to Children and Adolescents in the Context of Conventional Models of Telepsychiatry

Acceptability of newer and advanced telecommunication modalities has been found to be higher in young people. A case series also suggested that a subset of children and adolescents preferred to use VC over

FTF given the novelty of the VC consultation and the extra distance (both psychological and physical) provided by VC, which made it easier for adolescents to talk about drug problems (Pakyurek, Yellowlees, & Hilty, 2010). Also, adolescents perceived that they had freedom to end the session if they wished. Pakyurek et al. (2010) therefore suggested that telepsychiatry may be a better mode of offering services to certain clients.

We acknowledge that there might be certain difficulties in assessing and treating younger children. Observations of activity and behavior may be difficult. Hyperactive toddlers may often go out of the frame. Also, engagement might be difficult with toddlers and younger children because it is common during in-person practice for the child psychiatrist to move along with the child, trying to engage the child. This is especially so while evaluating children with developmental disabilities such as intellectual disability and autism spectrum disorder. The problems with bandwidth may further compound the problems.

Curbside Consultation Model

Apart from the traditional models of telepsychiatry described, Fortney et al. (2015) described another model, referred to as the "curbside consultation" model. This model does not involve direct patient care, is similar to grand rounds, albeit virtual, and is considered to be the least resource-intensive.

Informal consultations are sometimes referred to as "curbside," "hallway," "elevator," or "sidewalk" consults (Curbside Consultations, 2010). In a curbside consultation, the treating physician seeks informal information or advice about patient care or the answer to an academic question from a colleague. Often the colleague has a particular expertise or talent that can be brought to bear. Curbside consults are typically based on the treater's presentation of the case or by posing direct questions. The colleague consultant does not see the patient or review the chart and is not paid for the consultation. Thus, management of that particular case may or may not benefit, depending on the information elicited and provided by the PCP. The Extension of Community Health Outcomes project from the University of New Mexico (Arora et al., 2011) is an example of curbside consultation. The model works on a hub-and-spoke knowledge-sharing arrangement using multipoint VC to create a virtual network of experts at the hub site and PCP at the spokes. Usually, a case is presented, followed by group discussion of the case, and related clinical issues are moderated by the experts at the hub. This model may be considered as virtual grand rounds offering some direct benefit to the patient whose case is discussed and indirect benefits to others. Although it seems promising, such effectiveness has not yet been established. Traditional randomized, controlled trials are needed to demonstrate the clinical effectiveness of the telepsychiatry curbside consultation model in children and adolescents (Fortney et al., 2015).

INNOVATIVE MODELS OF TECHNOLOGY-BASED HEALTH CARE DELIVERY

Here we describe newer innovative model of health care that aim to empower PCPs to diagnose and manage psychiatric disorders and provide for supervision at varying levels. Although these models use VC mainly for training or education, these are primarily capacity-building models. In this way, they differ from conventional models of telepsychiatry in which service provision invariably needs a child and adolescent psychiatrist with varying degrees of intensity. In already resource-constrained settings, it would be practically impossible to develop and sustain a collaborative care model beyond funded research programs.

Tele-Enabling Model

An innovative model combining medical informatics for clinical decision making and VC for training of PCP in the use of a clinical decision support system (CDSS) and video-consult, if needed, has been developed and implemented in India (Malhotra, Chakrabarti, & Shah, 2016). As highlighted earlier, traditional telepsychiatry models have the disadvantage of being relatively resource-intensive, with the need for a telepsychiatrist at different levels of care at different intensities. A technology-based model of care that does not overburden the already very scarce specialist resources and simultaneously builds the capacity of services by training PCPs would be ideal in LMIC or even in resource-deficient rural areas of HIC. Such a model could have the advantages of a collaborative care model without stretching resources. A medical informatics application, namely CDSS, which is designed to help general practitioners and PCP make sound clinical decisions in real time is promising in training and enables professionals to deliver mental health care (Koposov et al., 2017). CDSS is defined as "providing clinicians or patients with computer-generated clinical knowledge and patient-related information, intelligently filtered or presented at appropriate times, to enhance patient care" (Sittig et al., 2008). In its simplest form, CDSS can be a collection of electronic rules and alerts. However, to provide the biggest impact, it should have more advanced operations such as documentation templates (history and physical clinic visit progress notes), relevant data presentation (flowsheets), protocol support (clinical pathways), reference information (info buttons), unsolicited alerts (proactive warnings), advanced dosing guidance (incorporating patient information), and advanced checking of drug–disease interactions and contraindications (Walker, 2008). Furthermore, CDSS that provide recommendations are considered superior.

We present here our model of the CDSS, a comprehensive tele-enabling model (Malhotra et al., 2016), that has most of the attributes described by Walker (2008). This CDSS was developed as a part of a project to develop and implement a model telepsychiatry application, using a medical knowledge-based CDSS, to deliver mental health care in remote areas through nonspecialists. It is a comprehensive system for diagnosing and managing psychiatric disorders in adults, and separately in children and adolescents, in which the nodal center at the Department of Psychiatry at the Postgraduate Institute of Medical Education and Research, Chandigarh, India, was connected with three peripheral sites located in adjoining hill states in northern India covering a population of 24 million people with 70 general psychiatrists and no child psychiatrist. Telepsychiatric centers were established in district-level hospitals at each peripheral site. The teams at each site consisted of a general physician or a general psychiatrist if available, psychologists or social workers, and computer operators. The application applied a logical decision support system (for diagnosis and management) with facilities for real-time as well as store-forward (Web-based) video recording, teleconferencing, and creation of electronic medical records. The nonspecialist team at the peripheral sites undertook the diagnosis and treatment of patients with psychiatric disorders attending their hospitals after online training in the use of the newly developed CDSS.

The CDSS is Internet-based and bilingual (English and Hindi), and covers 18 psychiatric disorders of children, adolescents, and adults. The diagnostic and management decision support systems are logically linked through a diagnosis–management interface. The diagnostic system consists of a screening module for all disorders followed by detailed questioning for specific disorders as indicated by responses to screening and a "core" diagnostic tool based on the standardized classification systems with a criterion-based approach. The system guides the interviewer in rating responses. Based on built-in thresholds and hierarchies, it autogenerates a multiaxial psychiatric diagnosis. Thereafter, the diagnostic system is linked to the management decision support system based on psychiatric diagnosis, severity, associated medical disorders (if any), age, and gender. Management includes modules for investigations, pharmacological and psychosocial treatment, follow-up care, and referrals for complicated presentations. Pharmacological treatment algorithms are designed on considerations of the diagnosis and severity of symptoms for initial dosing, and on the level of improvement and side effects for follow-up care. Psychosocial treatments include general and disorder-specific guidelines and printable modules for psychoeducation, counseling, and stress management. Also, a brief self-guided relaxation exercise based on principles of self-relaxation is provided in an audiovisual format and a printable form (instruction pamphlet). Furthermore, the application includes a system for longitudinal follow-up with provision for elicitation and recording of symptoms and signs, level of improvement, drug side effects, compliance and level of functioning; and recording and ordering of investigations on every visit. Core diagnostic interviewing can be carried out by a nonspecialist doctor or other mental health para-professional. After going through the system-generated management options, the physician prescribes the drug as guided by the recommended choices or his or her own choice. Psychological interventions can be carried out by either the doctor or other professionals (Malhotra, Chakrabarti, Gupta, et al., 2013; Malhotra et al., 2014; Malhotra, Kumar, et al., 2013; Malhotra, Chakrabarti, Shah, Mehta, et al., 2015; Malhotra, Chakrabarti, Shah, Sharma, et al., 2015). Fig. 11.1 show the workflow; Fig. 11.2 shows the functioning of the CDSS.

The different components of the CDSS were tested for their validity, reliability, and feasibility of use and underwent several revisions (Malhotra, Chakrabarti, Gupta, et al., 2013; Malhotra et al., 2014; Malhotra, Kumar, et al., 2013; Malhotra, Chakrabarti, Shah, Mehta, et al., 2015; Malhotra, Chakrabarti, Shah, Sharma, et al., 2015). The diagnostic module of the application for children and adolescents was examined separately in randomly selected child and adolescent patients (aged <18 years) by comparing it with a diagnosis made by independent interviewers in separate interviews using the Mini-International Neuropsychiatric Interview for Children and Adolescents and with clinician-led diagnoses. Results from these studies conducted at the nodal center suggested that the application has acceptable levels of accuracy, reliability, and feasibility. Most patients and interviewers were satisfied with the diagnostic process (Malhotra, Chakrabarti, Shah, Mehta, et al., 2015). Physicians, psychologists, or social workers were trained in using the application via VC. The CDSS was also used by nonspecialists at the remote sites (Malhotra et al., 2017), and indicated acceptable validity and reliability. Importantly, across all studies, the average time taken was 5 min for screening and 20 min for a detailed diagnostic assessment. A majority of patients, their relatives, and interviewers were satisfied with the assessment. Pharmacological management done by nonspecialists at remote sites according to the recommendations of the CDSS was found to concur with specialists' opinions (Malhotra, Kumar, et al., 2013). Psychoeducation and counseling modules were helpful and easy to use by paraprofessionals, and patients and their relatives found these to be

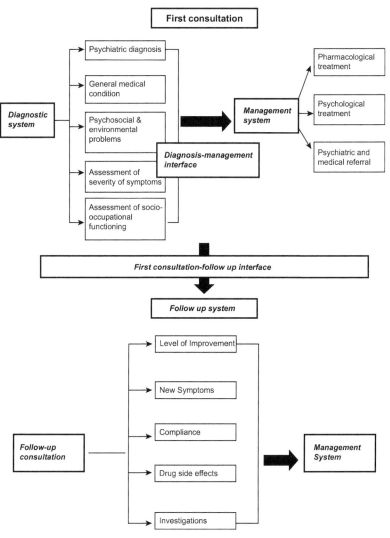

FIGURE 11.1 Workflow of telepsychiatry application. The figure shows the three logically interlinked modules: i.e., diagnostic module, management module, and follow up module. Diagnostic interview can be done by a nonmedical professional or a general practitioner. Data gathered from the patient and/or the accompanying family, or the key person, in various domains such as socio-demography, presenting problems, diagnostic interview, family and past history, examination findings, and rating of symptom severity and dysfunction, as guided by the application generate a summary of positive findings and a clinical descriptive diagnosis as per the International Statistical Classification of Diseases and Related Health Problems, 10th Revision. Management and follow-up modules guide the general practitioner into prescribing medication and psychosocial intervention, as well as recording and monitoring progress.

Tele-Psychiatry Application – Inputs / Outputs

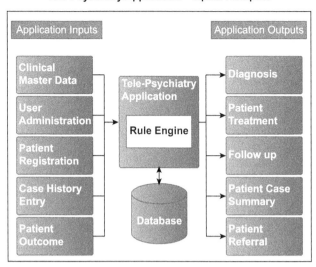

FIGURE 11.2   Graphic representation of the application's input/output datasets and internal processing by a rule engine. The rule engine is composed of diagnostic and management algorithms and rules and supported by domain knowledge such as drug prescribing information.

helpful. Training of physicians, psychologists, or social workers was carried out by didactic, observational, and hands-on experience, using real-time VC for about 2 weeks. The application is password protected and has provisions for storage and continuous upgrading. Longitudinal effectiveness studies were planned to evaluate the effect on health-related and service delivery-related outcome measures.

Apart from its feasibility, this modality of training was cost-effective. Overall, the application is expected to act as a self-educating tool, improving the skills and capability of nonspecialists with repeated use, as was evident in their performance and self-appraisal. VC with the supplementary use of email and telephone has been successfully applied for booster training sessions, support, supervision, and monitoring of staff at peripheral centers.

This model is unique because the diagnostic and management systems are logically linked, compared with most existing CDSS that are stand-alone programs (Koposov et al., 2017). Logically linked management protocols at baseline as well as follow-up make this CDSS amenable to integration into routine clinical practice. This is crucial because Koposov et al. (2017) noted that CDSS was not integrated in clinical practice, including the use of assessment, treatment, and follow-up monitoring of patients, which reduced the potential utility and application of these systems.

Krishna (2017) reviewed the impact of health IT on the doctor−patient relationship in child and adolescent psychiatry. The limited data suggest that health IT does not affect the patient−provider relationship negatively. Use of computers may lead to disengagement with the patient and his or her family. Therefore, thoughtful interaction strategies are crucial. The author suggested simple measures such as arranging the office space so that the computer can be operated while facing the patient or family and avoiding arrangements that place the computer physically between the provider and patient. This arrangement maximizes opportunities to monitor affect and nonverbal cues even while attending to the electronic health record, and in case of the tele-enabling model, the CDSS. The CDSS that is part of the tele-enabling model has meaningfully incorporated sections for open-ended questions, as well as module-based questions are semistructured and the doctor can record patient's problems and concerns ad verbatim. These measures are expected to help in rapport-building exercises; they stand in contrast to CDSS, which was built mainly for research purposes. Data on acceptability and satisfaction with this model of care for patients and their families, as well as providers, support this conjecture (Malhotra, Chakrabarti, Shah, Mehta, et al., 2015; Malhotra, Chakrabarti, Shah, Sharma, et al., 2015). Moreover, these systems fill the gap in CAMH services in LMIC settings, which otherwise is impossible to address, and should be viewed against the backdrop of some service versus no service.

The system is built on a dynamic and flexible platform, supports a multilingual format, and can be deployed in other settings after translation into their respective languages. Although it was tested in three sites, it is scalable to a state or a country in any number of sites and at the primary or secondary care setting, with a psychiatrist providing backup service and who could be located elsewhere. It is highly cost-effective because it requires a simple computer, a broadband connection, and a telephone line at the remote end. The staff required is a mental health paraprofessional and a general physician at each site. The diagnostic and management algorithms can be modified or updated as necessary.

Digital Health in the Hands of Patients

There are digital health models in which clients can seek certain forms of therapies that may be available online, such as a downloadable app that can be used offline or in a CD format, or through patient portals. The mental health problems addressed range from mood disorders to anxiety disorders and autism spectrum disorder. Hollis et al. (2017), Schueller et al. (2017) and Siemer et al. (2011) reviewed these DHIs extensively.

CD-ROMs and Mobile Apps Offering Therapies

DHIs are developed based on theoretically grounded concepts and offer good potential for improving health-related behaviors (Siemer et al., 2017). Some of these interventions direct users through the modules. This is achieved by using a hard-coded program or through the direct instruction of a mediating health care specialist. A metareview (Hollis et al., 2017) found some support for the clinical benefit of the DHIs, particularly computerized cognitive behavioral therapy, for depression and anxiety in adolescents and young adults. Mood-Gym, StressBusters, and The Journey (Lillevoll, Vangberg, Griffiths, Waterloo, & Eisemann, 2014; Smith et al., 2015; Stasiak, Hatcher, Frampton, & Merry Sally, 2014) are some of the well-researched programs. Randomized, controlled trials on DHIs for ADHD, autism spectrum disorder, anxiety, depression, psychosis, eating disorders, and posttraumatic stress disorder show insufficient evidence of benefits, and evidence is lacking regarding the cost-effectiveness of the DHIs. Based on their review, Siemer et al. (2017) suggested that children and adolescents may be more likely to respond to alternative delivery strategies such as Internet-based video or games.

Despite these highly promising, exponentially growing DHIs, certain cautions are necessary. Unsupervised use of such programs without parental involvement, engaging in programs with little research evidence, engagement by severely and seriously ill children and adolescents such as those who are suicidal or psychotic are some of the dangers. It has been pointed out that such DHIs place the responsibility of treatment on patients and lack of improvement may be conceived by patients as personal failure. Also, there are suggestions that before entering into such a program, the client must be aware of security, confidentiality, data storage, and sharing policies of the software provider.

Patient Portals

Patient portals are secure websites that give patients access to personal health information and the ability to communicate securely with their providers (Kendrick & Benson, 2017). Such portals are available for several medical specialties. These portals present a unique opportunity to interact with young patients who, by virtue of their developmental age, need autonomy and independence. However, few data exist about their use in child and adolescent psychiatry. Kendrick and Benson (2017) suggest that confidentiality can be a major issue in developing such portals, and what information can be made available on the portal and what cannot should be well-defined. Also, the portals can be accessed by patients alone, parents alone, or jointly, i.e., confidentiality model, parent orientation model, and family engagement model. The latter appears to be the best model for implementing patient portals in this age group.

THE FUTURE OF TELEPSYCHIATRY AND DIGITAL MENTAL HEALTH

The technological revolution has much to offer to the field of CAMH services. Telepsychiatry in various forms is much in vogue in many countries such as Australia and the United States and is rapidly expanding. CDSSs and expert systems are forms of artificial intelligence (AI), in which the logic, reasoning, and analytical skills of humans are programmed into computers by which functions are automated. These technologies can be further expanded to incorporate machine learning, artificial neural networks, and robotics to be useful in diagnosing and treating various psychiatric conditions. They have been used in a few conditions such as autism spectrum disorders, cognitive disabilities, or schizophrenia (Luxton, 2016). Medical knowledge is no longer the sole preserve of medical professionals. Use of AI is increasingly making the expert systems and machines function more efficiently, reliably, and without error. Moreover, unlike humans, these are not liable to fatigue, boredom, disinterest, or forgetfulness. Extreme shortage of child and adolescent psychiatrists in countries such as India and other LMIC and the impossibility of having the needed numbers in the foreseeable future requires innovative solutions. Use of digital technologies and AI seems to be one of the ways forward to deal with the problem. It would revolutionize the way we think about and practice mental health care service delivery.

> In a few years, the idea of receiving medical treatment exclusively at a doctor's office or hospital will seem quaint. Subramanian et al. (2015).

Conflict of interest

SM developed the tele-enabling model and RS worked in the capacity of research staff.

References

Alessi, N. E. (2002). Telepsychiatric care for a depressed adolescent. *Journal of the American Academy of Child and Adolescent Psychiatry, 41*(8), 894–895.
Alessi, N. E. (2003). Quantitative documentation of the therapeutic efficacy of adolescent telepsychiatry. *Telemedicine Journal and e-Health, 9*(3), 283–289.

Arora, S., Kalishman, S., Dion, D., Som, D., Thornton, K., Bankhurst, A., et al. (2011). Partnering urban academic medical centers and rural primary care clinicians to provide complex chronic disease care. *Health Affairs (Millwood), 30*, 1176–1184.

Balasinorwala, V. P., Shah, N., Chatterjee, S. D., Kale, V. P., & Matcheswalla, Y. A. (2014). Asynchronous telepsychiatry in Maharashtra, India: Study of feasibility and referral pattern. *Indian Journal of Psychological Medicine, 36*(3), 299–301.

Bostrom, N. (2006). Technological revolutions: Ethics and policy in the dark. In N. Cameron, & M. E. Mitchell (Eds.), *Nanoscale: Issues and perspectives for the nano century* (pp. 129–152). New Jersey: John Wiley.

Boydell, K. M., Hodgins, M., Pignatiello, A., Teshima, J., Edwards, H., & Willis, D. (2014). Using technology to deliver mental health services to children and youth: A scoping review. *Journal of Canadian Academy of Child and Adolescent Psychiatry, 23*(2), 87–99.

Chakrabarti, S., & Shah, R. (2016). Telepsychiatry in the developing world: Whither promised joy? *Indian Journal of Social Psychiatry, 32*, 273–280.

Cloutier, P., Cappelli, M., Glennie, J. E., & Keresztes, C. (2008). Mental health services for children and youth: A survey of physicians' knowledge, attitudes and use of telehealth services. *Journal of Telemedicine and Telecare, 14*(2), 98–101.

Costello, E. J., Mustillo, S., Keller, G., & Angold, A. (2004). Prevalence of psychiatric disorders in childhood and adolescence. In B. L. Levin, J. Petrila, & K. D. Hennessy (Eds.), *Mental health services: A public health perspective* (Ed 2, pp. 111–128). Oxford, UK: Oxford University Press.

Curbside Consultations. (2010). *Psychiatry (Edgmont), 7*(5), 51–53.

Diamond, J. M., & Bloch, R. M. (2010). Telepsychiatry assessments of child or adolescent behavior disorders: A review of evidence and issues. *Telemedicine Journal and e-Health, 16*(6), 712–716.

Digital Health. (n.d.). In, *US food and drug adminstration.* Retrieved November 27, 2017 from https://www.fda.gov/medicaldevices/digitalhealth/.

Elford, R., White, H., St John, K., Maddigan, B., Ghandi, M., & Bowering, R. (2001). A prospective satisfaction study and cost analysis of a pilot child telepsychiatry service in Newfoundland. *Journal of Telemedicine and Telecare, 7*(2), 73–81.

Fortney, J. C., Enderle, M. A., Clothier, J. L., Otero, J. M., Williams, J. S., & Pyne, J. M. (2013). Population level effectiveness of implementing collaborative care management for depression. *General Hospital Psychiatry, 35*, 455–460.

Fortney, J. C., Pyne, J. M., Mouden, S. B., Mittal, D., Hudson, T. J., Schroeder, G. W., et al. (2013). Practice based versus telemedicine based collaborative care for depression in rural federally qualified health centers: A pragmatic randomized comparative effectiveness trial. *American Journal of Psychiatry, 170*(4), 414–425.

Fortney, J. C., Pyne, J. F., Turner, E. E., Farris, K. M., Normoyle, T. M., Avery, M. D., et al. (2015). Telepsychiatry integration of mental health services into rural primary care settings. *International Review of Psychiatry, 27*(6), 525–539.

Frueh, B. C., Monnier, J., Yim, E., Grubaugh, A. L., Hamner, M. B., & Knapp, R. G. (2007). A randomized trial of telepsychiatry for post-traumatic stress disorder. *Journal of Telemedicine and Telecare, 13*, 142–147.

Goldfield, G. S., & Boachie, A. (2003). Delivery of family therapy in the treatment of anorexia nervosa using telehealth. *Telemedicine Journal and e-Health, 9*, 111–114.

Hilt, R. J. (2017). Telemedicine for child collaborative or integrated care. *Child and Adolescent Psychiatric Clinics of North America, 26*(4), 637–645.

Hilt, R. J., Barclay, R. P., Bush, J., Stout, B., Anderson, N., & Wignall, J. R. (2015). A statewide child telepsychiatry consult system yields desired health system changes and savings. *Telemedicine Journal and e-Health, 21*(7), 533–537.

Hilty, D. M., Ferrer, D. C., Parish, M. B., Johnston, B., Callahan, E. J., & Yellowlees, P. M. (2013). The effectiveness of telemental health: A 2013 review. *Telemedicine and e-Health, 19*(6), 444–454. https://doi.org/10.1089/tmj.2013.0075.

Hilty, D. M., Marks, S., Wegelin, J., Callahan, E. J., & Nesbitt, T. S. (2007). A randomized, controlled trial of disease management modules, including telepsychiatric care, for depression in rural primary care. *Psychiatry (Edgmont), 4,* 58–65.

Hilty, D. M., Sison, J. I., Nesbitt, T. S., & Hales, R. E. (2000). Telepsychiatric consultation for ADHD in the primary care setting. *Journal of the American Academy of Child and Adolescent Psychiatry, 39*(1), 15–16.

Hilty, D. M., Yellowlees, P. M., Cobb, H. C., Bourgeois, J. A., Neufeld, J. D., & Nesbitt, T. S. (2006). Models of telepsychiatric consultation – liaison service to rural primary care. *Psychosomatics, 47,* 152–157.

Hilty, D. M., Yellowlees, P. M., & Nesbitt, T. S. (2006). Evolution of telepsychiatry to rural sites: Changes over time in types of referral and in primary care providers' knowledge, skills and satisfaction. *General Hospital Psychiatry, 28*(5), 367–373.

Hollis, C., Falconer, C., Martin, J. L., Whittington, C., Stockton, S., Glazebrook, C., et al.Bethan Davies, E. (2017). Annual research review: Digital health interventions for children and young people with mental health problems – a systematic and meta-review. *The Journal of Child Psychology and Psychiatry, 58*(4), 474–503.

Impact Evaluation: Assessing the Effectiveness of Telepsychiatry Consultations in Pakistan. (n.d.). In, *Aga Khan development network eHealth resource centre.* Retrieved November 27, 2017 from http://www.akdn.org/what-we-do/health/ehealth-resources-centre/effectiveness-telepsychiatry-consultations.

Katon, W., & Gonzales, J. (1994). A review of randomized trials of psychiatric consultation—liaison studies in primary care. *Psychosomatics, 35,* 268–278.

Katon, W., Robinson, P., Von Korff, M., Lin, E., Bush, T., Ludman, E., et al. (1996). A multifaceted intervention to improve treatment of depression in primary care. *Archives of General Psychiatry, 53,* 924–932.

Katon, W., Von Korff, M., Lin, E., Walker, E., Simon, G. E., Bush, T., et al. (1995). Collaborative management to achieve treatment guidelines. Impact on depression in primary care. *JAMA, 273,* 1026–1031.

Keilman, P. (2005). Telepsychiatry with child welfare families referred to a family service agency. *Telemedicine Journal and e-Health, 11*(1), 98–101.

Kendrick, E. J., & Benson, C. (2017). Patient portals in child and adolescent psychiatry. *Child and Adolescent Psychiatric Clinics of North America, 26,* 43–54.

Kopel, H., Nunn, K., & Dossetor, D. (2001). Evaluating satisfaction with a child and adolescent psychological telemedicine outreach service. *Journal of Telemedicine and Telecare, 7*(2), 35–40.

Koposov, R., Fossum, S., Frodl, T., Nytrø, O., Leventhal, B., Sourander, A., et al. (2017). Clinical decision support systems in child and adolescent psychiatry: A systematic review. *European Child & Adolescent Psychiatry, 26*(11), 1309–1317.

Krishna, R. (2017). The impact of health information technology on the doctor-patient relationship in child and adolescent psychiatry. *Child and Adolescent Psychiatric Clinics of North America, 26*(1), 67–75.

Leigh, H. (2015). The function of consultation-liaison psychiatry. In H. Leigh, & J. Streltzer (Eds.), *Handbook of consultation-liaison psychiatry* (pp. 12–15). Boston, MA: Springer.

Lillevoll, K. R., Vangberg, H. C. B., Griffiths, K. M., Waterloo, K., & Eisemann, M. R. (2014). Uptake and adherence of a self-directed internet-based mental health intervention with tailored e-mail reminders in senior high schools in Norway. *BMC Psychiatry, 14,* 14. https://doi.org/10.1186/1471-244X-14-14.

Luxton, D. D. (2016). An introduction to artificial intelligence in behavioural and mental health care. In D. D. Luxton (Ed.), *Artificial intelligence in behavioural and mental health care* (pp. 1–26). San Diego: Academic Press.

Malhotra, S., Chakrabarti, S., Gupta, A., Mehta, A., Shah, R., Kumar, V., et al. (2013). A self-guided relaxation module for telepsychiatric services: Development, usefulness, and feasibility. *International Journal of Psychiatry in Medicine, 46*, 325–337.

Malhotra, S., Chakrabarti, S., & Shah, R. (2013). Telepsychiatry: Promise, potential, and challenges. *Indian Journal of Psychiatry, 55*(1), 3–11.

Malhotra, S., Chakrabarti, S., & Shah, R. (2016). Telepsychiatry in child and adolescent mental healthcare. In S. Malhotra, & P. Santosh (Eds.), *Child and adolescent psychiatry.* New Delhi: Springer.

Malhotra, S., Chakrabarti, S., Shah, R., Gupta, A., Mehta, A., Nithya, B., et al. (2014). Development of a novel diagnostic system for a telepsychiatric application: A pilot validation study. *BMC Research Notes, 7*, 508. https://doi.org/10.1186/1756-0500-7-508.

Malhotra, S., Chakrabarti, S., Shah, R., Kumar, V., Nithya, B., Gupta, A., et al. (2013). Computerised system of diagnosis and treatment in telepsychiatry: Development and feasibility of the pharmacological treatment module. *Indian Journal of Psychiatry, 55*, S129–S130.

Malhotra, S., Chakrabarti, S., Shah, R., Mehta, A., Gupta, A., & Sharma, M. (2015). A novel screening and diagnostic tool for child and adolescent psychiatric disorders for telepsychiatry. *Indian Journal of Psychological Medicine, 37*, 288–298.

Malhotra, S., Chakrabarti, S., Shah, R., Sharma, M., Sharma, K. P., Malhotra, A., et al. (2017). Telepsychiatry clinical decision support system used by non-psychiatrists in remote areas: Validity and reliability of diagnostic module. *Indian Journal of Medical Research, 146*(2), 196–204.

Malhotra, S., Chakrabarti, S., Shah, R., Sharma, M., Sharma, K. P., & Singh, H. (2015). Diagnostic accuracy and feasibility of a net-based application for diagnosing common psychiatric disorders. *Psychiatry Research, 230*, 369–376.

Malhotra, S., & Padhy, S. K. (2015). Challenges in providing child and adolescent psychiatric services in low resource countries. *Child and Adolescent Psychiatric Clinics of North America, 24*, 777–797.

Malhotra, S., & Patra, B. (2014). Prevalence of child and adolescent psychiatric disorders in India: A systematic review and meta-analysis. *Child and Adolescent Psychiatry and Mental Health, 8*, 22. https://doi.org/10.1186/1753-2000-8-22.

Medical Informatics. (n.d.). In, *Healthcare information and management systems society.* Retrieved November 26, 2017 from http://www.himss.org/clinical-informatics/medical-informatics.

Merikangas, K. R., Nakamura, E. F., & Kessler, R. C. (2009). Epidemiology of mental disorders in children and adolescents. *Dialogues in Clinical Neuroscience, 11*(1), 7–20.

Michigan Child Collaborative Care Program. (n.d.). In, *Michigan child collaborative care program website.* Retrieved November 26, 2017 from https://mc3.depressioncenter.org/about/.

Mohr, D. C., Cuijpers, P., & Lehman, K. (2011). Supportive accountability: A model for providing human support to enhance adherence to eHealth interventions. *Journal of Medical Internet Research, 13*, e30.

Myers, K. M., Palmer, N. B., & Geyer, J. R. (2011). Research in child and adolescent telemental health. *Child and Adolescent Psychiatric Clinics of North America, 20*(1), 155–171.

Myers, K. M., Valentine, J. M., & Melzer, S. M. (2007). Feasibility, acceptability, and sustainability of telepsychiatry with children and adolescents. *Psychiatric Services, 58*, 1493–1496.

Myers, K. M., Valentine, J. M., & Melzer, S. M. (2008). Child and adolescent telepsychiatry: Utilization and satisfaction. *Telemedicine Journal and e-Health, 14*, 131–137.

Myers, K., Valentine, J., Morganthaler, R., & Melzer, S. (2006). Telepsychiatry with incarcerated youth. *Journal of Adolescent Health, 38*(6), 643−648.

Myers, K., Vander Stoep, A., & Lobdell, C. (2013). Feasibility of conducting a randomized controlled trial of telemental health with children diagnosed with attention-deficit/hyperactivity disorder in underserved communities. *Journal of Child and Adolescent Psychopharmacology, 23*(6), 372−378.

Myers, K. M., Vander Stoep, A., McCarty, C. A., Klein, J. B., Palmer, N. B., et al. (2010). Child and adolescent telepsychiatry: Variations in utilization, referral patterns and practice trends. *Journal of Telemedicine and Telecare, 16*(3), 128−133.

Myers, K., Vander Stoep, A., Zhou, C., McCarty, C. A., & Katon, W. (2015). Effectiveness of a telehealth service delivery model for treating attention-deficit/hyperactivity disorder: A community-based randomized controlled trial. *Journal of the American Academy of Child and Adolescent Psychiatry, 54*(4), 263−274.

Nelson, E. L., Barnard, M., & Cain, S. (2003). Treating childhood depression over videoteleconferencing. *Telemedicine Journal and e-Health, 9*, 49−55.

Nepal Sets Up Telepsychiatry Program. (1998). *Telemedicine and Virtual Reality, 3*(4), 46.

Pakyurek, M., Yellowlees, P., & Hilty, D. (2010). The child and adolescent telepsychiatry consultation: Can it be a more effective clinical process for certain patients than conventional practice? *Telemedicine Journal and e-Health, 16*(3), 289−292.

Pesamaa, L., Ebeling, H., Kuusimaki, M. L., Winblad, I., Isohanni, M., & Moilanen, I. (2004). Videoconferencing in child and adolescent telepsychiatry: A systematic review of the literature. *Journal of Telemedicine and Telecare, 10*(4), 187−192.

Peters, T. E. (2016). Transformational impact of health information technology on the clinical practice of child and adolescent psychiatry. *Child and Adolescent Psychiatric Clinics of North America, 26*(1), 55−66.

Pyne, J. M., Fortney, J. C., Tripathi, S. P., Maciejewski, M. L., Edlund, M. J., & Williams, D. K. (2010). Cost-effectiveness analysis of a rural telemedicine collaborative care intervention for depression. *Archives of General Psychiatry, 67*(8), 812−821.

Rahman, A. (2006). E-mental health in Pakistan: A pilot study of training and supervision in child psychiatry using the internet. *Psychiatric Bulletin, 30*, 149−152.

Rockhill, C. M., Tse, Y. J., Fesinmeyer, M. D., Garcia, J., & Myers, K. (2016). Telepsychiatrists' medication treatment strategies in the children's attention-deficit/hyperactivity disorder telemental health treatment study. *Journal of Child and Adolescent Psychopharmacology, 26*(8), 662−671.

Savin, D., Glueck, D. A., Chardavoyne, J., Yager, J., & Novins, D. K. (2011). Bridging cultures: Child psychiatry via videoconferencing. *Child and Adolescent Psychiatric Clinics of North America, 20*(1), 125−134.

Schueller, S. M., Stiles-Shields, C., & Yarosh, L. (2017). Online treatment and virtual therapists in child and adolescent psychiatry. *Child and Adolescent Psychiatric Clinics of North America, 26*, 1−12.

Siemer, C. P., Fogel, J., & Van Voorhees, B. (2011). Telemental health and web-based applications in children and adolescents. *Child and Adolescent Psychiatric Clinics of North America, 20*, 135−153.

Sinha, S. K., & Kaur, J. (2011). National mental health programme: Manpower development scheme of eleventh five-year plan. *Indian Journal of Psychiatry, 53*(3), 261−265.

Sittig, D. F., Wright, A., Osheroff, J. A., Middleton, B., Teich, J. M., Ash, J. S., et al. (2008). Grand challenges in clinical decision support v10. *Journal of Biomedical Informatics, 41*(2), 387−392.

Smith, P., Scott, R., Eshkevari, E., Jatta, F., Leigh, E., Harris, V., et al. (2015). Computerised CBT for depressed adolescents: Randomised controlled trial. *Behaviour Research and Therapy, 73*, 104−110.

Spaulding, R., Belz, N., DeLurgio, S., & Williams, A. R. (2010). Cost savings of telemedicine utilization for child psychiatry in a rural Kansas community. *Telemedicine Journal and e-Health, 16*(8), 867–871.

Stasiak, K., Hatcher, S., Frampton, C., & Merry Sally, N. (2014). A pilot double blind randomized placebo controlled trial of a prototype computer-based cognitive behavioural therapy program for adolescents with symptoms of depression. *Behavioural and Cognitive Psychotherapy, 42*, 385–401.

Subramaian, S., Dumont, C., Dankert, C., & Wong, A. (2015). *Personalized Technology will Upend the Doctor Patient Relationship, in Harvard Business Review.*

Szeftel, R., Mandelbaum, S., Sulman-Smith, H., Naqvi, S., Lawrence, L., Szeftel, Z., et al. (2011). Telepsychiatry for children with developmental disabilities: Applications for patient care and medical education. *Child and Adolescent Psychiatric Clinics of North America, 20*(1), 95–111.

Thara, R., John, S., & Rao, K. (2008). Telepsychiatry in Chennai, India: The SCARF experience. *Behavioral Sciences & the Law, 26*, 315–322. https://doi.org/10.1002/bsl.816.

Vander Stoep, A., McCarty, C. A., Zhou, C., Rockhill, C. M., Schoenfelder, E. N., & Myers, K. (2017). The children's attention-deficit hyperactivity disorder telemental health treatment study: Caregiver outcomes. *Journal of Abnormal Child Psychology, 45*(1), 27–43.

Vander Stoep, A., & Myers, K. (2013). Methodology for conducting the children's attention-deficit hyperactivity disorder telemental health treatment study in multiple underserved communities. *Clinical Trials, 10*(6), 949–958.

Wagnild, G., Leenknecht, C., & Zauher, J. (2006). Psychiatrists' satisfaction with telepsychiatry. *Telemedicine Journal and E Health, 12*(5), 546–551.

Walker, K. A. (2008). Transforming healthcare with information technology. *In Medscape Informatics and Clinical Decision Support.* Retrieved November 28, 2017 from http://www.medscape.org/viewarticle/571099.

Yellowlees, P. M., Hilty, D. M., Marks, S. L., Neufeld, J., & Bourgeois, J. A. (2008). A retrospective analysis of a child and adolescent e-mental health program. *Journal of the American Academy of Child and Adolescent Psychiatry, 47*, 103–107.

Yellowlees, P. M., Odor, A., Parish, M. B., Iosif, A. M., Haught, K., & Hilty, D. (2010). A feasibility study of the use of asynchronous telepsychiatry for psychiatric consultations. *Psychiatry Services, 61*(8), 838–840.

Zatzick, D. F., Koepsell, T., & Rivara, F. P. (2009). Using target population specification, effect size, and reach to estimate and compare the population impact of two PTSD preventive interventions. *Psychiatry, 72*, 346–359.

EUROPEAN PERSPECTIVES ON CHILD AND ADOLESCENT MENTAL HEALTH SERVICES AND TRAINING

Child and Adolescent Mental Health: Knowledge, Practice, and Services in Central Europe

Helmut Remschmidt[1], Michal Goetz[2], Patrick Haemmerle[3]

[1] Philipps-University, Marburg, Germany; [2] Charles University Second Faculty of Medicine, Prague, Czech Republic; [3] FMH, Freiburg/Fribourg, Switzerland

Child and Adolescent Psychiatry in the Czech Republic

Michal Goetz

INTRODUCTION

Definition

Child and adolescent psychiatry (CAP) in the Czech Republic is understood to be a clinical field providing diagnosis and treatment of mental disorders for people aged under 18 years. Compared with other medical disciplines, however, it has a totally unique overlap with nonmedical sciences such as pedagogy, psychology, psychometry, sociology, philosophy, and forensic science. The boundaries of the field are therefore less sharp and child psychiatric work requires the ability to assess behavioral and mental phenomena in broad contexts and from different perspectives.

Understanding Uniqueness and Diversity in Child and Adolescent Mental Health
https://doi.org/10.1016/B978-0-12-815310-9.00012-5

Historical Development

The early development of CAP in the Czech Republic reflects several stages as described by Moritz Tramer (1882–1963): The first stages were characterized by care for youths with mental disabilities and later also with antisocial behavior, followed by different types of disorders distinguished according to their clinical picture and etiology with a growing emphasis on social factors. In the following periods, specific goals of CAP were defined and counseling services as well as inpatient units were established within general hospitals.

Important milestones included:

- 1871: Karel Slavoj Amerling (1807–84) founded the first institute for children with intellectual disabilities called Ernestinum. Besides medical care, children staying at the asylum received education in basic skills.
- 1911: A law was passed concerning the rights of children and duties of parents.
- 1920: Dr. Karel Herfort (1871–1940), professor of pediatric psychopathology at Charles University in Prague, established the first child psychiatric outpatient service in the regions of Bohemia and Moravia and became the editor of the country's first journal on pediatric mental health.
- 1923: Part of an adult psychiatry facility in a former Jesuit's convent in Oparany was turned into the first hospital for children and adolescents with mental disorders. The hospital had its own school, swimming pool, and facilities for work-therapy. Czech counties experienced the expansion of a network of child psychiatric outpatient services.
- 1947: Dr. Josef Apetauer, physician and psychologist, founded the first child psychiatric inpatient unit at the Department of Adult Psychiatry, affiliated with Charles University Hospital.
- 1953: The Czechoslovak Ministry of Health issued a conceptual plan for child and adolescent mental health care.
- 1961: Professor Jan Fischer established a department of child psychiatry as a branch of the Institute of Postgraduate Training in Medical Professions.
- 1963: The first Czechoslovak textbook of pedopsychiatry, edited by Professor Fischer, was published.
- 1971: A department of CAP within Motol University Hospital in Prague was established consisting of inpatient as well as outpatient units.
- The team of professor Zdeněk Matějček (1922–2004) published important papers on the long-term consequences of the failure to meet children's social and emotional needs as a result of institutional care.

- Since the 1980s, and especially the 1990s, the psychotherapeutic approach to child psychiatric disorders expanded.
- 2015: The reform of the postgraduate education aimed to abolish child psychiatry as an independent training program (5 years) and replace it with a 2-year course to be followed after passing the board examination in adult psychiatry. This system of training was established in 2009–12. The numbers of trainees radically decreased during this period. With the help of an intensive campaign in the media as well as the government, it was possible to maintain CAP as an independent specialty.

Professional Organizations

Specialists in the field of child and adolescent mental health are organized into the two professional organizations:

- The Czech Psychiatric Association was founded in 1919 and belongs to the oldest physicians' professional organization. The Section of Child and Adolescent Psychiatry of the Czech Psychiatric Association is the co-organizer of the 2018 International Association for Child and Adolescent Psychiatry and Allied Professions (IACAPAP) Congress in Prague.
- The Association of Child and Adolescent Psychiatry of the Czech Republic (ADDP) is an independent, professional nonprofit organization. ADDP, which was founded in 1993, is the strongest professional organization of child and adolescent psychiatrists in the Czech Republic and has been a member of European Society for Child and Adolescent Psychiatry (ESCAP) since 2016. Members of the association are involved in the transformation of psychiatric care in the Czech Republic. ADDP is also the co-organizer of the 2018 IACAPAP Congress.

KNOWLEDGE

Specialist Knowledge

CAP is no longer regarded merely as a specialization of psychiatry, but also as a separate field requiring long-term specialized training.

A modern textbook on CAP was published, which provides a comprehensive overview of etiology, phenomenology, development, and therapy (Hort, Hrdlička, Kocourková, & Malá, 2000). Chapters on CAP are part of all three major psychiatric textbooks.

Czech child and adolescent psychiatrists participated in translating the American *Diagnostic and Statistical Manual*, Fifth Edition (DSM-5)

(American Psychiatric Association, 2013). International scales and questionnaires for the assessment of attention-deficit hyperactive disorder (ADHD), child autism, and quality of life have been validated and put into clinical practice.

In 1999, the Czech Psychiatric Society issued treatment guidelines (Raboch, 1999b), which are updated regularly after a previous discussion of experts and patient organizations in a special conference.

Research projects funded by both national and international grants are developing and child psychiatrists also serve as mentors in doctoral programs.

Three psychiatric journals are published in Czech Republic; child psychiatrists are members of editorial boards. A separate child psychiatric journal does not exist.

Every second year, a nationwide multidisciplinary congress is held dedicated to children's mental health. Child psychiatrists regularly organize symposia at national meetings of the Czech Psychiatric Association, Society of Biological Psychiatry, etc.

Public Knowledge

There has been a growing public interest in child and adolescent mental health. In the media, information on ADHD is relatively frequent; in particular, autism spectrum disorders have attracted the attention of various media.

Czech professionals authored or translated a number of educational materials for parents and patients. Programs on destigmatization, awareness campaigns, education of professionals, and the area of psychiatric care are included in the goals of ongoing major reform in psychiatry.

Epidemiology

According to data collected by the Institute of Health Information and Statistics of the Czech Republic (2013), 56,940 children and adolescents used psychiatric services (3.19%). Disorders requiring treatment at services were categorized according to the International Statistical Classification of Diseases and Related Health Problems, 10th Revision (ICD-10) (WHO, 1992). A total of 57% were treated for disorders of psychological development and behavioral and emotional disorders; onset usually occurred in childhood and adolescence (F80–F98), followed by neurotic, stress-related and somatoform disorders (F40–F48) (23%), mental retardation (F70–F79) (8%), mood disorders (F30–F39) (5%), mental and behavioral disorders caused by psychoactive substance use (F10–F19) (4%), and psychotic disorders (F20–F29) (2%).

TABLE 12.1 Personnel Load and Coverage by Services in the Czech Republic

Number of Services and Personal Load	Inpatient Beds/ Units	Inpatient Beds per 100,000 Persons Aged <18 Years	Outpatient Clinics	Outpatient Clinics per 100,000 Persons Aged <18 Years	C&A Psychiatrists per 100,000 Persons Aged <18 Years	C&A Psychologists per 100,000 Person Aged <18 Years
N	590/14	22.7	80	4	2.8 (at full service)	4.4

C&A, child and adolescent.

STAFFING LEVELS AND STRUCTURE OF SERVICES

Table 12.1 shows personnel load and coverage by services. The ratio of child and adolescent psychiatrists per 100,000 young people in the Czech Republic is unsatisfactorily low compared with other countries (Signorini et al., 2017) (see Table 12.7); one goals of the ongoing reformation of the care is to increase the number of child and adolescent psychiatrists and psychologists.

Structure of Services

Psychiatry in the Czech Republic has not experienced major systemic changes since the beginning of the 1990s and faces long-term under-funding as a health care profession.

In 2014, on the basis of a joint resolution of the Ministry of Foreign Affairs and the Czech Psychiatric Association, preparatory steps were taken for a major reform of psychiatry and CAP by introducing mental health centers, regional services, mobile teams, etc. The main goals of the reform are to provide sufficient treatment and support for patients in their own environment, and enhance cooperation and coordination between individual components of mental health care providers.

Inpatient Services

There is a satisfactory number of child and adolescent psychiatric beds; however, they are not distributed equally across different regions of the Czech Republic. Of 14 counties of the Czech Republic, only 10 have inpatient child and adolescent inpatient units. Furthermore, most of these beds are reserved for long-term care and rehabilitation; therefore, there is a lack of short-term beds. Finally, 78% of beds are concentrated in psychiatric hospitals (which results in the risk for stigmatization).

TABLE 12.2   Inpatient Services in the Czech Republic

Inpatient Services	University and Local Hospitals	C&A Psychiatric Hospitals	Children Departments in Adult Psychiatric Hospitals
Units/beds, N	5/139	3/210	6/241

C&A, child and adolescent.

Outpatient Services

A shortage of outpatient psychiatric and psychological services including day care services for children and adolescents is a significant deficit in the Czech system of mental health care. There are 80 outpatient psychiatric clinics in the country and these are not equally distributed across the republic. Only in 4 of the 14 counties, there is an average of only 1 child and adolescent psychiatrist per 100,000 inhabitants (21,000 children and adolescents). This leads to long waiting lists for examination by a child psychiatrist (2—6 months, varying according to county).

Day Care Services

The only child psychiatric day care service (age range, 14—21 years) in the Czech Republic is located in the Department of Psychiatry of the General University Hospital, Charles University, in Prague. There are also day care services organized by nonprofit organizations, in particular for children and adolescents with intellectual disabilities and combined disabilities.

Services for Addicted Children and Adolescents

There is only one specialized detoxification unit for children and adolescents in the Czech Republic, consisting of 14 beds and located in Prague. Only one facility in the country provides long-term treatment of addicted CAP patients.

Diagnosis-Specific Services

Specialized services exist only for children and adolescents with autistic spectrum disorders. An outpatient-based center in the capital focuses on diagnostic assessments, education, and therapy of children and adolescents with autism spectrum disorders. Furthermore, a comprehensive diagnostic program for autistic spectrum disorders exists at the Department of CAP in Motol University Hospital in Prague.

PRACTICE

Child and adolescent mental health care in the Czech Republic consists of social care (family support, child protection, and financial support), special education (classroom assistants, learning, and behavior support in regular or special classrooms and schools, and pedagogical-psychological counseling centers), and medical care (psychological and psychiatric services). Organization and budgeting are divided among the Ministry of Labor and Social Affairs, the Ministry of Education, Youth and Sports, and the Ministry of Health and nonprofit organizations. The systemic cooperation of individual yet relatively separate and regionally unevenly represented services dealing with child and adolescent mental health is one of the objectives of the reform of psychiatric care.

Funding of Care

Medical care in the Czech Republic is funded partly by the state budget and partly by the insurance companies. From the 7.6% of the gross domestic product going to health care in the Czech Republic, only 3% is reserved for psychiatry, including CAP. This is much lower than in other West European countries. Health care services are basically paid for by one of the public health insurance companies. All individuals in the Czech Republic are required to have insurance, which amounts to 13.5% of the calculated base income.

Access to Care

Access to child psychiatric care is possible without the recommendation of an expert. Only in exceptional cases defined by the law can a child psychiatric assessment be carried out without the caregiver's consent. For such cases, there are special regulations.

Classification System

In all Czech inpatient and outpatient establishments, the ICD-I0 classification system is used. The DSM-5 classification is used for research purposes.

Practice Guidelines

In 1999, the Czech Psychiatric Society issued treatment guidelines (Raboch, 1999a) which are updated every 4 years after a discussion of experts and patient organizations in a special conference. With each new release, the number of child psychiatric topics has expanded. Diagnoses include eating disorders, anxiety disorders, schizophrenia, depression, hyperkinetic disorders, childhood autism, and sleeping disorders (Raboch, Anders, Hellerová, Uhlíková, & Šusta, 2014).

Diagnostic Methods

Clinical interviews and observation measures performed by child psychiatrists (medical doctors) are the principal methods of psychiatric assessment. For several diagnoses, clinical questionnaires and rating scales are used (autism spectrum, mood, anxiety, ADHD, etc.). Structured interviews or assessments for autism spectrum disorders are performed (Autism Diagnostic Observation Schedule, Autism Diagnostic Interview, Revised, etc). The assessment at inpatient units includes a psychological examination and a couple of somatic investigations including a neurological examination and EEG and, if indicated, imaging techniques.

Therapeutic Methods

Most outpatient and inpatient child and adolescent psychiatric units use pharmacotherapy combined with psychotherapy.

COOPERATION WITH OTHER MEDICAL AND NONMEDICAL DISCIPLINES

Clinical Psychologists

Child psychologists are the closest partners of child psychiatrists in the Czech Republic. The staffing levels of psychologists are relatively good in CAP inpatient facilities. In outpatient care, clinical child psychologists are difficult to access.

Pediatricians/Somatic Medicine

Pediatricians do not provide systematic treatment of mental disorders in children and adolescents in the Czech Republic; however, they are allowed to prescribe most basic psychotropic medication (except stimulants and atomoxetine). There is an established system of preventive checkups, physical health care, and monitoring of the development of children and adolescents with the possibility of early detection of mental illnesses. A screening program for children with autism spectrum disorders has been introduced in primary care pediatric clinics.

Pedagogic-Psychological Counseling Services

These facilities provide counseling in the field of education and special education under the jurisdiction of the Ministry of Education and Youths. In case of doubt about behavior or academic performance, the teacher recommends children for counseling. The classification system of behavioral difficulties that these services use is not in line with the ICD-10 system. Sometimes this creates problems regarding diagnosis and treatment.

Child Protection Services

The Department of Care for Children and Families, which has an office in each city, is under the jurisdiction of the Ministry of Labor and Social Affairs. It addresses concerns about children at risk and in danger (e.g., special care, placement in foster homes).

Forensic Practice

Some child and adolescent psychiatrists work as forensic experts appointed by the Ministry of Justice or the court on the basis of specialized training. Experts prepare reports mainly on the basis of a court or police order, or exceptionally at the request of another state administration or private person. These reports relate to crimes involving children or adolescents as victims or offenders. Furthermore, a large part of forensic expert opinion deals with divorce disputes between parents and child care arrangements.

PROFESSIONAL TRAINING STRUCTURE

Undergraduate Training

Psychiatry is included in the curriculum of all medical faculties in the Czech Republic. However, teaching in CAP is carried out only in faculties that are affiliated with child and adolescent psychiatric departments (three of seven medical faculties).

Postgraduate Training

After completing their 6-year studies and final examinations, students of medicine graduate and receive a Doctor of Medicine diploma. Graduates who wish to specialize in CAP are required to undergo an internship in psychiatry or pediatrics (24 months) and basic training in surgery, intensive care, and neurology (2 months each). After that, candidates have to complete training in CAP for at least 3 years (12 months for outpatient service and 24 months for inpatient unit) as well as basic training in pediatric neurology and pediatrics (2 months each). Clinical facilities where training is carried out have to be accredited by the Ministry of Health of the Czech Republic.

Candidates who complete their training in pediatrics and not in psychiatry have to pass a 9-month fellowship in adult psychiatry and 1 month in pediatric neurology before they enter training in CAP.

Furthermore, at least 160 h of education and training in psychotherapy is required. Candidates may choose the school of psychotherapy that fits best with their interests and professional orientation. For documentation of the different aspects of specialist training, the Institute issued a logbook for postgraduate education in medical professions.

After requirements for the specialist training are completed, an oral examination (theoretical and practical) has to be passed at the university where the final part of training has taken place. Defending the dissertation is part of the examination procedure.

Acknowledgments

The author would like to thank Vladimir Hort, Petra Uhlikova, Blanka Starkova, and Jaroslav Matys for their helpful comments on the preparation of the manuscript, and Michaela Holla for her assistance in language editing.

Child and Adolescent Mental Health in Germany: Knowledge, Services, and Practice

Helmut Remschmidt

INTRODUCTION

Definition

The field of child and adolescent psychiatry and psychotherapy (CAPP) in Germany is comprises "the diagnosis, non-operative treatment, prevention and rehabilitation of psychiatric, psychosomatic, developmental and neurological diseases or disorders as well as psychological and social behavior disturbances during childhood and adolescence" (German Medical Association, 1994). This definition has been modified several times and was first used in 1968, when CAP became an independent specialty. At that time, the specialty was called "child and adolescent psychiatry." Psychotherapy was added to the title in 1993, taking into account the importance of psychotherapeutic treatment methods. The postgraduate training program to become a child and adolescent psychiatrist and psychotherapist requires 5 years of training, 1 year of which can be completed either in pediatrics or general psychiatry. The training curriculum for child and adolescent psychiatrists and psychotherapists can be completed in all 16 states of the Federal Republic of Germany and ends with an oral board examination at the Office of the Medical Association (*Landesärztekammer*) of each state.

Historical Development

German CAP is closely connected to European and international developments. Its roots go back to several other disciplines, especially pediatrics and psychiatry, but also clinical psychology, pedagogy (therapeutic education), and, with regard to many regulations, social sciences and law. However, these influences did not lead to a type of CAP as a mixture of other heterogeneous disciplines, but rather as an independent specialty that has integrated all of these influences to give psychiatrically ill and disturbed children and adolescents and their families the best possible support.

An important milestone in the history of German CAP was the textbook by Hermann Emminghaus (1887) entitled *Psychic Disturbances in Childhood*, which was called the "hour of birth" of child psychiatry (Harms, 1960).

Further development was characterized by the books by Wilhelm Strohmayer (1910), *Psychopathology of Childhood*; Theodor Ziehen (1915), *Mental Disorders in Childhood*, August Homburger (1926), *Lectures on Childhood Psychopathology*; and Moritz Tramer (1942), *Textbook of General Child Psychiatry*. After the Second World War, the handbook article by Stutte (1960), the textbook by Jakob Lutz (1961), and the *Textbook of Special Child and Adolescent Psychiatry* by Harbauer, Lempp, Nissen, and Strunk (1971) were influential. These textbooks were followed by several others and by the three-volume handbook *Child Psychiatry in Clinic and Practice*, edited by Helmut Remschmidt and Martin Schmidt (1985, 1988).

As far as the journals are concerned, three developments were important:

1. In 1898, the journal *Children's Faults* (*Die Kinderfehler*) was founded, which was continued as *Journal for Child Research* (*Kinderforschung*) and ceased to appear with its 50th volume during the Second World War in 1944. After the war, this journal was continued as *Yearbook for Youth Psychiatry* (founded in 1956) and has been running since 1973 under the title *Journal of Child and Adolescent Psychiatry* (*Zeitschrift für Kinder-und Jugendpsychiatrie*). According to the change in the name of the specialty, this title was changed to *Journal of Child and Adolescent Psychiatry and Psychotherapy* in 1996.
2. In 1934, Moritz Tramer founded the *Journal of Child Psychiatry* (*Zeitschrift für Kinderpsychiatrie*), which was continued until 1984 as *Acta Paedopsychiatrica* and ceased to appear in 1994.
3. As a third journal with a more psychoanalytic, and later, more interdisciplinary orientation, *Practice of Child Psychology and Psychiatry* was founded in 1951 by Annemarie Dührssen and Werner Schwidder. It continues to exist and has a large readership.

Professional Organizations

The establishment of a new discipline, however, is possible only with the foundation of scientific and professional organizations that push forward the development of the discipline.

The official foundation of a German association for CAP took place on September 5, 1940, in Vienna as the German Society for Child Psychiatry and Therapeutic Education. Its first president was Paul Schröder, head of the Department of Psychiatry at the University of Leipzig. During the Second World War, under the Nazi regime, German child psychiatry was also involved in the euthanasia program, and thousands of mentally handicapped and psychiatrically ill children were murdered with its cooperation.

In 1950, the German Association for Youth Psychiatry was refounded as a medical association, but with intensive cooperation with other disciplines such as therapeutic education, law, clinical psychology, psychiatry, and pediatrics.

German CAP has developed from four traditions:

1. the neuropsychiatric tradition going back to roots in neurology and psychiatry, from which child psychiatry evolved at several points. This tradition was pronounced in the former German Democratic Republic, where the specialty was called "child and adolescent neuropsychiatry." It continues through neuropsychological approaches in several fields of child psychiatry;
2. a tradition in therapeutic education developed mainly in pediatrics; this can be considered a precursor of the departments of psychosomatics in pediatric hospitals;
3. the psychodynamic-psychoanalytic tradition, based on psychoanalytic theories, which goes far back to the beginning of psychoanalysis and was also responsible for including psychodynamic psychotherapy in the curriculum for child and adolescent psychiatrists as well as for establishing "psychagogues," who changed their name to "psychoanalytic child and adolescent psychiatrists";
4. and the empirical-epidemiological tradition. This orientation was established in the 1960s and 1970s and was influenced to a great extent by empirical research from England and the United States.

After the German reunification, the Society for Neuropsychiatry of Childhood and Adolescence was founded in February, 1990, in East Germany; it was later integrated into the German Society for CAP. This society, whose name was changed to the Society for CAPP in 1994, organizes official meetings every second year in different places in Germany. Two other organizations of CAP exist in Germany: one is a professional organization

(*Berufsverband*), which was founded in 1978 and has about 700 members. This organization represents the group of child and adolescent psychiatrists and psychotherapists in private practice. The other organization is the Conference of Directors of Child and Adolescent Psychiatric Hospitals in Germany, which was founded in 1990 and has about 177 members.

These organizations have established close cooperation and have joint working groups for quality assurance, training, and research.

KNOWLEDGE

Advances in knowledge resulted from reliable classification systems such as the ICD and DSM. Epidemiological studies found that about 8%−10% of children and adolescents experience psychopathological disorders. Genetic studies and magnetic resonance imaging studies brought new insights regarding the etiology of disorders and brain functions. New psychotherapy methods and medications remarkably improved treatment activities. However, all of this progress of the past decades can have an impact only if it reaches all of those who need treatment, care, prevention, and rehabilitation at a population level.

With regard to the goal of improving child and adolescent mental health in general, four developments have been decisive:

1. the *Psychiatry Enquête* of the Federal Government of Germany (report 1975),
2. the model program "Psychiatry" of the Federal Government of Germany (1980−5),
3. the Psychiatry Personnel Equipment Act (stepwise introduction between 1991 and 1995), and
4. the inclusion of psychotherapy into the training curriculum and the name of the specialty, which has been since 1992: "child and adolescent psychiatry and psychotherapy."

These four developments have notably influenced current CAPP. The *Psychiatry Enquête* inaugurated by two members of the parliament opened a broad inquiry into psychiatry and CAP across West Germany. After the report of the commission (1975), a model program "Psychiatry" was created, which was carried out in 14 regions of the Federal Republic of Germany, evaluated different types of services, and created new ones. One region (Marburg) was devoted exclusively to evaluating and establishing child and adolescent psychiatric services. Many newly created services could be continued. The Psychiatry Personnel Equipment Act was responsible for more satisfactory staffing of psychiatric hospitals and services; it led to great improvement in everyday work. The inclusion of psychotherapy into the curriculum for child psychiatrists and for general psychiatrists was not only important for the individual professional training of each child and adolescent psychiatrist, it improved the status of CAP.

STRUCTURE OF SERVICES AND PRACTICE

Guidelines for Services for Children and Adolescents With Psychiatric Disorders

The Expert Commission of the Federal Government of Germany proposed guidelines for services based on the following general principles (Report of the Expert Commission, 1988, pp. 383–385). These guidelines are current:

1. Services for psychiatrically disturbed children and adolescents should have parity with services for children with other disorders or diseases. Ideally, children with psychological disturbances and their parents should pass through the same door as children with an infectious disease or a broken leg or those who need an operation.
2. This parity requires integration of the relevant services in the medical field, although there is a broad overlap with other nonmedical services.
3. The services should be community-based, avoiding too-long distances for access and too-high thresholds for consultation. It was proposed to define a region of approximately 250,000 inhabitants for outpatient services and a region between 500,000 and 750,000 inhabitants for inpatient and complementary services. It should be the aim of service planning to treat most children and adolescents within their home region.
4. The services should be qualified and respect age and developmental stage, the individual nature of each child and his or her family, as well as risk factors and protective factors for the patient and his environment.

Types of Services

Table 12.3 gives an overview of the different types of child and adolescent psychiatric services in Germany. On the whole, there are enough inpatient places, but they are not well-distributed over the whole country. There are not enough outpatient services. This applies to outpatient services associated with hospitals as well as private practice. Child psychiatry is one of the few medical disciplines in Germany in which private practice still offers good prospects and is not restricted.

TABLE 12.3   Services for Psychiatrically Disturbed Children and Adolescents in Germany

I. Outpatient services
   1. Child and adolescent psychiatrists in private practice (n = 963)
   2. Analytical child and adolescent psychotherapists in private practice (around 1000)
   3. Outpatient departments at hospitals
   4. Child psychiatric services at public health agencies
   5. Child guidance clinics and family counseling services (n = 1.056 in 2010)
   6. Early intervention centers, social pediatric services
II. Day patient services (3.441 treatment places, 817.489 treatment days per year)
   1. Day patient clinics
   Two types: Integrated into inpatient settings or independent
   2. Night clinic treatment possibilities
III. Inpatient services (144 inpatient departments with 6.148 beds; average duration of treatment: 36.2 days, use rate: 92.9%)
   1. Inpatient services at university hospitals
   2. Inpatient services at psychiatric state hospitals
   3. Inpatient services at general community hospitals or pediatric hospitals
IV. Complementary services
   1. Rehabilitation services for special groups of patients (e.g., children with severe head injuries, epilepsy, etc.)
   2. Different types of homes
   3. Residential groups for adolescents

There is also a shortage of day patient facilities and a paucity of complementary services (rehabilitation programs and programs for chronic patients and for special groups such as drug-dependent children and adolescents, or delinquent adolescents).

Personnel

Great progress was made for all psychiatric services, particularly for child and adolescent psychiatric services in the Psychiatry Personnel Equipment Act, which was introduced in steps between 1991 and 1995. The main advantage of this new personnel act is that personnel needed for a certain ward or institution are no longer calculated in relation to the number but to the specific needs and requirements of patients. Therefore, patients are subdivided into several groups according to the amount of care, support, supervision, and treatment they need. The time required for every activity of personnel with regard to different patients' groups is registered, and on this basis the adequate number of staff members (doctors, psychologists, nurses, etc.) is calculated.

In 2016, the number of child and adolescent psychiatrists was 2259. Among those, 1004 were working in hospitals and 167 in leading positions; 963 were engaged in private practice.

Funding of Services

In Germany, inpatient, outpatient, and day patient facilities are paid for by the state. Germany has a compulsory insurance system. All patients and families are insured and the insurance usually pays the costs for outpatient, day patient, or inpatient treatment directly to the hospitals. This applies to all acute treatment necessary. Responsibility for chronically ill psychiatric children and adolescents is taken over by the youth welfare system and the social security system, depending on the kind and severity of the disorder, e.g., for multiply disabled children and adolescents in the sense of combined somatic and psychiatric disorders, usually the social security system is responsible. For children and adolescents with chronic psychiatric disorders, however, the youth welfare system has been responsible since 1991. This change in responsibility has imposed a heavy burden on youth agencies which were not prepared to deal with these problems.

As far as the complementary services are concerned, the same funding agencies are responsible (youth welfare system and social security system). Several of these functions are in the hands of nongovernmental welfare organizations and charities, which receive financial support from different sources, mainly the youth welfare system and the social security system.

Rehabilitation services are paid partly by insurance and partly by the social security system.

Evaluation of Treatments and Services

Evaluation of Treatments

As a rule, treatment in CAP is multidimensional. This philosophy was the basis for the development of the so-called component model of treatment. Based on this model, treatment procedures in a university department of CAP were analyzed out of a sample of 4545 patients in different settings (inpatient, day patient, and outpatient settings) by applying five different treatment components (individual psychotherapy with the patient, functional therapies, parent- and family-oriented interventions, other environmental interventions, and psychotropic medication).

These five components were applied in variable combinations to different disorders and in various settings. Based on therapists' ratings, treatment success was investigated with regard to nine diagnoses. Effect sizes were calculated for outpatient treatment (total sample: 1682) and inpatient treatment (total sample: 1490). The effect size in the outpatient setting was 1.01 for normal completers versus dropouts, 1.27 for normal completers versus non-beginners, and 0.34 for non-beginners versus dropouts.

Corresponding effect sizes for inpatients were: normal completers versus dropouts: 0.74, normal completers versus non-beginners: 1.27, and non-beginners versus dropouts: 0.84. Despite a few methodological limitations, the results of this naturalistic study can be used to improve empirically based treatment procedures under real everyday conditions (Remschmidt & Mattejat, 2001).

Evaluation of Services

Not many studies in Germany have evaluated psychiatric services for children and adolescents. In the region of Marburg, which was the only region to evaluate child and adolescent psychiatric services within the Model Program Psychiatry of the Federal Government, we had the unique opportunity to carry out a comprehensive evaluation study of all services of three counties within a specified time frame (Remschmidt & Walter, 1989; Remschmidt, Walter, Kampert, & Hennighausen, 1990; Walter, Kampert, & Remschmidt, 1988).

Within this program, psychiatric services for children and adolescents were evaluated in three rural counties composed of 575,000 inhabitants. Over 1 year, the referred population was almost completely recorded (n = 5307). According to these data, the use of outpatient services was influenced by the local provision of outpatient care. In well-equipped areas, the referral rates reached a comparatively high level. However, they did not exceed 3.8% of the total population of children and adolescents in the area. Markedly higher rates were found in community surveys, where the prevalence estimates amounted to at least 7%. Attendance at child and adolescent psychiatric hospitals depended on the availability of community-based outpatient care as well the distance between the living place and the place of residential care. With increasing distance, admission rates decreased, whereas the duration of hospital stays increased. The provision of specialized outpatient services was correlated with a high percentage of hospital referrals from that area whereas the duration of hospital stay was reduced. Inpatients from counties not appropriately served by outpatient facilities had significantly longer stays in the hospital. Over 42 months, hospital admissions (in relation to the number of inhabitants) were reduced in counties where outpatient services for children and adolescents had improved (Walter et al., 1988). There is no recent comparable study in Germany.

COOPERATION WITH OTHER MEDICAL AND NONMEDICAL DISCIPLINES

Table 12.4 gives an overview of the cooperation network of child and adolescent mental health services in Germany. Within the medical field, there is intensive cooperation, especially with departments of pediatrics and general psychiatry, and with doctors in private practice. However, it is a specific characteristic of CAP to establish cooperation with a large number of nonmedical institutions and professionals. Among them, the

TABLE 12.4   Cooperation Network With Other Medical and Nonmedical Services (Common Fields of Activity)

Cooperation with departments of pediatrics
- Pediatric liaison and consultation services
- Chronic physical diseases, neonatology intensive care
- Psychosomatic disorders

Cooperation with departments of general psychiatry
- Adolescent psychiatry
- Family psychiatry
- Forensic psychiatry

Cooperation with doctors in private practice
- General practitioners
- Pediatricians
- Child and adolescent psychiatrists

Cooperation with nonmedical institutions and professionals
- Child guidance clinics
- Local youth agencies (responsible for extra-familiar placement of psychiatrically disabled children and adolescents)
- School psychological services
- Special schools (for children with learning disabilities, speech and language disorders, conduct disorders, mentally disabled and autistic children)
- Child psychotherapists in private practice (among them analytic child and adolescent psychotherapists)
- Residential homes for children and adolescents with chronic psychiatric disorders or special disabilities

more than 1000 child guidance clinics have an important role, as well as the local youth agencies. Because the latter are responsible for extrafamilial placements and family support, good relationships with these agencies are extremely important. Of course, the cooperation network demonstrated in Table 12.2 varies greatly and depends on the readiness of personnel in the different institutions to accept the multidimensional approach in the field of child mental health, and also on financial considerations.

TRAINING AND CONTINUING MEDICAL EDUCATION

Undergraduate Training: The Role of Medical Faculties

CAP is represented by a separate department or chair in 28 of 38 medical faculties in Germany. This means that in 10 medical faculties, there is no formal teaching program in CAPP for medical students. This is compensated in some faculties by lecturers coming from other universities, but it is still urgently necessary to establish a department of CAP in every medical faculty.

Child psychiatry is also included in bedside teaching. As far as questions for multiple choice examinations are concerned, approximately 25% of questions in psychiatry and 15%−20% in pediatrics are on CAP topics.

Postgraduate Training: A Joint Effort

To become a specialist in CAP, after the final medical examination and the practical phase of training, which ends with the so-called "approbation" (certificate to practice medicine independently), a candidate has to spend 4 years in CAPP and 1 year in either general psychiatry or pediatrics. It is also possible to spend half a year in neurology. Of the 4 years of training in the field of CAPP, 2 years in inpatient services are obligatory. Two years can also be completed in a specialist private practice.

A substantial part of the training curriculum is concentrated on psychotherapy (since 1993).

After all requirements are completed for specialist training, an oral examination has to be passed at the office of the medical society of the state (Land) where the training has taken place.

Training Programs for Other Disciplines

Child and adolescent psychiatrists and psychotherapists are included in several training programs for other medical and nonmedical specialists. The main programs are carried out in the field of psychotherapy (especially with pediatricians and general practitioners), for psychologists, teachers, nurses, pedagogues, and social pedagogues.

RESEARCH

Worldwide trends in mental health research can be characterized into three strands:

- by increased consideration of the biological basis of psychiatric disorders at all ages. Main topics are molecular biology, genetics, and new imaging techniques;
- by greater consideration of the principles of development. Main topics are developmental psychopathology, developmental psychology, developmental neurology, and developmental biochemistry; and
- by the introduction of rational, effective, and evidence-based patient diagnostic and therapeutic approaches. Main topics are standardized diagnosis, development of guidelines, quality assurance, and evaluation.

These perspectives are also represented in child mental health research in Germany. A review of the achievements based on publications between 2003 and 2008 (Hebebrand et consortium, 2009) reveals the following results:

Among the *disorder-specific* publications, research on ADHD ranked first, followed by publications on eating disorders (2), obesity (3), schizophrenia (4), and autism (5). Among the *research field-specific publications*, the ranking order was: somatic disorders (1), infant psychiatry (2), forensic psychiatry (3), developmental disorders (4), and basic research (5). With regard to the *methodological approach*, publications on genetics and molecular biology were most numerous, followed by treatment research and studies on brain imaging. The authors of the report regret the small number of treatment studies. A more recent report on child and mental health research in Germany has not been carried out.

Child and Adolescent Psychiatry and Psychotherapy in Switzerland

Patrick Haemmerle

INTRODUCTION

Definition

CAPP is a medical specialty in which psychological, psychosomatic, psychosocial and development-related illnesses and disorders in childhood and youth until adolescence are examined, treated and assessed. It also deals with prevention and rehabilitation. CAPP is a neighbor discipline of other disciplines dealing with children and adolescents and their families such as pediatrics, neuropsychiatry, social or developmental pediatrics, general psychiatry, psychotherapy, but also education.

Historical Development

There are important milestones in the development of CAP in Switzerland:

- 1921: foundation of the first psychiatric children's institution, the "Stephansburg" in Zurich, by H.W. Maier, close to the "Burghölzli," the famous adult psychiatric clinic where Forel, C.G. Jung, and the Bleulers, Eugen and Manfred, worked;
- 1933: May 19: Birthday of child psychiatry (Leo Kanner, 1935): First use of the term *Kinderpsychiatrie*, by Tramer. Two years later, it became the title of Kanner's textbook, Child *Psychiatry*;
- 1938: creation of a commission for child psychiatry within the Swiss Society of (adult) Psychiatry;
- 1938: publication of the first Swiss book on general child psychiatry: Moritz Tramer, *Allgemeine Kinderpsychiatrie*;

- 1938: Foundation of a private clinic for the psychiatric treatment of children in Lausanne (Garibian, 2015);
- 1954: official recognition of the specialist title in CAP;
- 1957: foundation of the Swiss Society for Child and Adolescent Psychiatry (SSCAP), only 3 years later completed with the addition "and psychotherapy";
- 1960: the first European Symposium for CAP in Magglingen (Prof. A. Friedemann), which gave birth to the "European Union for Pedopsychiatry," renamed ESCAP in 1970 in Paris;
- 1960: introduction of disability insurance (*Invalidenversicherung*) "which took over responsibility for psychiatric treatment, special schooling and educational measures for children with mental and physical defects or birth injuries" (Bettschart & Bürgin, 1999).

The Professional Organization

The two current co-presidents, Hélène Beutler and Alain Di Gallo, described the mission and functioning of the specialist professional organization thus: "The Swiss Society for Child and Adolescent Psychiatry and Psychotherapy (SSCAPP) focuses on postgraduate training, collaboration with crucial cooperation partners, the social and political recognition of our profession, and destigmatizing mental health problems. It is [currently] led by two co-presidents. The board consists of eight members who stem from both the private and public sectors and represent pivotal areas of work. The regular liaison between the society's members and the board is ensured by the delegates' meetings, which take place biannually. Delegates are elected by the local groups of the different regions (cantons). Communication between the board and the members is also fostered through the cooperation of three working groups, representing the practitioners, the clinic directors, and the trainees. This organization has proved to be useful in coordinating the support of political forces nationwide and encouraging cooperation among the different university departments regarding clinical postgraduate education and research." (Beutler & Di Gallo, 2013).

Because CAP itself is a close relative of other different disciplines (psychiatry, pediatrics, neurology, [developmental] psychology, special and remedial education, anthropology, etc.), it is natural to cooperate with the different partners active in childhood, adolescence, and family matters, embodied by the Foederatio Medicorum Psychiatricorum et Psychotherapeuticorum (FMPP).

In the words of the co-presidents: "In order to represent the interests of child and adolescent mental health in the social and political realms, the SSCAPP cooperates with various partner organizations."

KNOWLEDGE

Public Knowledge

In many countries, including Switzerland, mental and behavioral disturbances and illnesses are stigmatized. Although once in their life, one in two people will experience psychological problems (estimate of the World Health Organization), it is still less accepted to have psychological or mental problems compared with any physical illness. There are several organizations in public information committed to mental and psychological problems (e.g., Pro Mente Sana, Swiss Public Health, and their professional group for mental health for minors). Some of them focus specifically on children with ADHD or autism spectrum disorders. Another organization focuses on children of mentally ill parents: *Institut Kinderseele Schweiz* (Institute for the Children's Soul).

Specialist Knowledge

As a clinical and scientific organization, the SSCAPP organizes a scientific congress every year. According to cooperation with the main partners in the field, these annual scientific congresses are held jointly and alternately every 3 years with the FMPP or with the Federatio Paedomedicorum helveticorum. The SSCAPP informs their members and the interested public through a printed and an electronic newsletter.

International Exchange

Since the beginnings of the SSCAPP, our professional society was constantly involved in international CAP activities. The society has had delegates and representatives in ESCAP, as well as in the IACAPAP. Indeed, the 17th ESCAP Congress took place in Geneva in 2017, with strong international participation from IACAPAP members.

SERVICES

Review of Services

Almost all of the 26 Swiss cantons are equipped with a public CAP service. Because of their small population, five cantons cooperate with a service of a larger neighbor canton.

All CAP services have an outpatient facility (normally called *Poliklinik*, or, in French, *consultation ambulatoire*); 15 have an inpatient facility (*Klinik/Clinique*) and 12 have a day hospital (*Tagesklinik/hôpital de jour, centre thérapeutique de jour*). There is also a trend toward establishing mobile or outreach teams, which are available in five cantons. In the bilingual French- and German-speaking canton Fribourg, this offer is called *"Psy-Mobile,"* an original and meaningful name.

Besides these cantonal institutions, treatment of children with developmental disorders, and mental and psychological disabilities and illnesses is provided by about 600 child and adolescent psychiatrists and psychotherapists in private practice. In addition, a broad range of other professionals treat children with psychological and mental problems, e.g., speech therapists, school psychologists, occupational therapists, special needs educators. Many of them are embedded in so-called "school psychological services," whereas others work in private practice. The most important specific partners are undoubtedly clinical psychologists working in either institutions or private practice.

Unfortunately, there are no comprehensive statistical data about these school-based cantonal institutions and the cantonal child and adolescent psychiatric clinics in the country.

Given the current total population (8.431 million) of minors, i.e., children aged less than 19 years (1.69 million), in Switzerland there is theoretically one child and adolescent psychiatrist and psychotherapist available for about 2800 minors. With this number, Switzerland still seems to be the best-resourced country in terms of CAPP. However, because a significant percentage of these specialists work part-time (women as well as men) and many of them are approaching retirement, the SSCAPP is actively seeking to promote the training of new specialists.

Personnel Load and Coverage of Costs

The costs of child psychiatric treatment are covered by compulsory basic insurance, or, for inherited or genetic disorders, disability insurance (*Invalidenversicherung*).

The duration of child psychiatric treatment is not limited, although for a "monotherapeutic" intervention with psychotherapy, after 2 years or 60 h, the child psychiatrist will have to send a report to the health insurance to justify further treatment. This is not the case if psychotherapy is a part of multimodal treatment with different elements.

PRACTICE

Policy and Legislation

In Switzerland, there is no specific legislation for mental health for adults or for children and adolescents. One reason is that public health legislation belongs to the area of competence of the federal cantons. The federal office for health (*Bundesamt für Gesundheit/Office Fédéral de Santé*) has a more administrative function. Because Switzerland has a high rate of suicides, especially in young men, several specialists in CAPP are highly involved in prevention and training activities for this problem.

Therapeutic Approaches

Because psychotherapy has been an essential element in the training of child and adolescent psychiatrists since the foundation of the specialists organization, all candidates are also trained in at least one psychotherapeutic method. During the 4 years of specialization, psychotherapy is a mandatory and integral part in the training curriculum (see also the Professional Training—Structure and Challenges section).

In view of this, clinical practice in institutions as well as private practice is characterized by the application of different therapeutic modalities: individual psychotherapy (psychodynamic, behavioral, and systemic), family therapy (psychodynamic or systemic), group therapy, creative therapy (music and art therapy), relaxation therapy, pharmacotherapy, socio-psychiatric interventions, parent counseling or parenting, etc.

The range of therapies was demonstrated in the 2007 survey (Haemmerle, 2007). Table 12.5 shows the therapeutic approaches used in clinics and private practice. It is evident that family therapy, with its different approaches, group therapy, and special interventions, is used significantly more often in institutions than in private practice.

TABLE 12.5 Therapeutic Approaches in Institutions and Private Practices

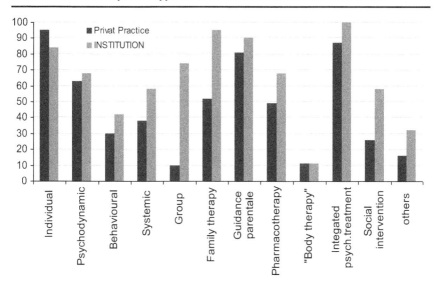

Following the medical approach, treatment should be based on a thorough diagnostic assessment. Therefore, it is interesting to know which diagnoses were most frequent in Swiss CAP. In the 2007 survey, we found a high proportion in the categories F9, F84, and F43 in institutions, as well as self-harm (X60 and X84), whereas in private practice, combined F9 disorders and F32 mood disorders were predominant, as well as certain autism spectrum disorders, such as Asperger syndrome (Haemmerle, 2007).

Specialized Consultations

Specialized services are concentrated on:

- infant psychiatry services (e.g., baby consultation)
- services for children with autism spectrum disorders (currently 38 specialized services, compared with zero in 2007)
- mobile outreach services, especially for so-called "multiproblem families"
- programs for (mental) health promotion. They do not belong strictly to the mental health system but have an important impact on the well-being of children and their families. Meanwhile, there are several evaluation studies regarding this approach.

Epidemiology

The only representative epidemiological study on the frequency of psychological disorders in children and adolescents was carried out in 1994 in the canton of Zurich. Over 6 months, 22.5% of interviewees had experienced a mental disorder. The most common were anxiety disorders, followed by tic disorders and ADHD.

The data of Steinhausen, Winkler Metzke, Meier, and Kannenberg (1998) or those of the Swiss Multicentric Adolescent Survey on Health study (Narring et al., 2004) are still relevant. According to these and some other European and international studies, we assume that approximately one in five children and adolescents (15–20%) has a psychological problem requiring treatment and that one in eight minors (about 12%) needs specific child psychiatric treatment.

In his 2007 survey, Haemmerle concluded, based on semiquantitative data, that Swiss child psychiatrists in both public services and private practice, treated approximately 3.3% of the minor population (treatment prevalence). This would mean that even in the best-resourced country with regard to CAPP, there exists an important gap between supply and demand.

Addiction and Forensic Child and Adolescent Psychiatry and Psychotherapy

Astonishingly, there are no addiction-specific institutions in Switzerland. Children with addiction problems are treated, if at all, in pediatric or adult psychiatry departments or in houses of education, often with no specialist know-how in the field of addiction.

Only recently, *forensic CAP* has become a subspecialty of its own in Switzerland. It is defined on the homepage of the SSFCAP: "Forensic CAP is a sub-specialty of children's and youth psychiatry. It includes child and youth psychiatric clinics, teaching and research in the context of criminal law, criminal and procedural law, civil law and insurance law. In addition, to the preparation of scientific-forensic expert opinions on delinquent minors, crime prevention, forensic therapies, as well as the child-care and juvenile psychiatric care of the prisons and the other institutions of the judiciary system are provided." In the German-speaking part of Switzerland, there are two clinics (with inpatient and outpatient facilities), in Zurich and in Basel, whereas in the French-speaking part, there is only one institution.

Research

The survey of European CAP of 1999 stated that research is not the task of the specialist organization, the SSCAPP, but has its place in the university departments and in some of the bigger cantonal institutions. Although a substantial amount of research is carried out on diverse themes, there is no common thread across the different centers. It can be stated that epidemiology and psychotherapy are and will remain the focus of research. Following an oral comment of the current president (Di Gallo, 2017), basic science has hardly been carried out in Switzerland and there have been only a few joint studies. This is starting to change. Indeed, a study of omega-3 fatty acid therapy in children and adolescents with depression is taking place at different centers.

COOPERATION WITH OTHER SERVICES

As mentioned, CAPP in Switzerland is essentially oriented toward social psychiatric issues. That means that cooperation with different partners and institutions relates to different tasks. The most important are, of course, adult psychiatry, pediatrics, and general practice, followed by school services, social and child protection services, and all other professionals working with children, adolescents, and families.

Another table from the 2007 survey shows the cooperation of Swiss CAPP with institutions and specialists (Tables 12.6 and 12.7).

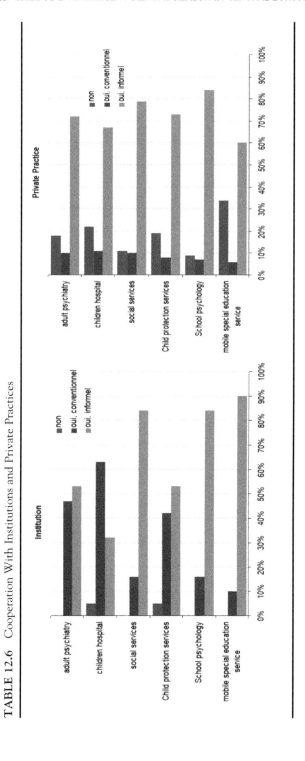

TABLE 12.6 Cooperation With Institutions and Private Practices

TABLE 12.7 Survey of Current Situation of CAP in Central Europe

	Country	Name of Association	Year of Foundation	University Departments in CP	Other Departments in CP	Doctor of Medicine in CP	Population (in 1000s)	Persons Aged <19 years (in 1000s)	Persons <19 Years (%)	Persons <19 Years per Doctor of Medicine in CP
1	Austria	CANP	1974	5	10	180	8,772	1,717	19.6	9,542
2	Czech Rep.	CAP	1960	3 (1 chair)	11	140	10,500	2,000[a]	19.6[a]	14,285[a]
3	Germany	CAPP	1940	28	116	2,259	82,067	13,270	18.25	5,874
4	Slovakia	CAP	1971	2 (1 chair)	4	50	5429	0–19: 1,120	20.6	22,400
5	Switzerland	CAPP	1957	5	11	603	8.430	1,690	20.0	2,802

CANPP, child-adolescent-neurology-psychiatry-psychotherapy; CAP, child and adolescent psychiatry; CAPP, child and adolescent psychiatry and psychotherapy; CP, Czech Republic.
[a]Czech Republic: Persons aged less than 18 years.

PROFESSIONAL TRAINING: STRUCTURE AND CHALLENGES

CAP is well-established in the curricula of Swiss medical schools at the university level in Berne, Basel, Geneva, Lausanne, Zurich, and Fribourg.

The revised postgraduate program still demands a minimum of 6 years of clinical training, four of which are specifically in CAP (at least 1 year in an inpatient and at least 2 years in an outpatient facility), 1 year in an adult psychiatry clinic, and 1 year in a somatic discipline.

Parallel to this clinical activity, candidates must be trained in at least one recommended psychotherapeutic approach (e.g., psychodynamically based, behavior, or systemic psychotherapy).

The candidate has to complete at least 500 items of theoretical courses and undergo a self-experience of at least 100 h. More details of the professional training can be found on the homepage of our professional society: http://www.sgkjpp.ch/fr.

PERSPECTIVES

In their programmatic paper from 2014, "Current Situation and Future Perspectives of CAP in Switzerland," a report drawing to the attention of the Federal Office for Health, Bundesamt für Gesundheit, the co-presidents of the SSCAPP worked out the mission and the challenges for contemporary Swiss child psychiatry. These proposals are intended to complete this chapter. The main issues of the paper are:

- promotion and training of young doctors in CAP. Compared with adult psychiatry, there is a lack of assistants (registrars) and senior child and adolescent psychiatrists in Swiss hospitals.
- ensuring and maintaining psychotherapeutic competence and method diversity in psychotherapy. Owing to medical, psychiatric, and psychotherapeutic training, child and adolescent psychiatry provides a comprehensive bio-psycho-social approach that cannot be offered by any other professional group.
- improvement in knowledge on causes, risks, and protective factors. Research on these factors and the transfer of results into clinical work will lead to the optimization of diagnostic procedures and treatment measures.
- improving access to treatment by reducing the access threshold for vulnerable populations (e.g., children from burdened families, migrant families).

- facilitating transitions: Human development is unavoidably accompanied by transitions. They offer opportunities for growth, but also comprise risks. Especially sensitive transitions are birth, nursery school, school entrance, and adolescence. Therapy transfer and the exchange of knowledge between youth and adult psychiatry require clearer and more integrated structures.
- promoting interdisciplinarity: Identification, diagnosis, and treatment of mental illnesses require close interdisciplinary cooperation. This mainly concerns the areas of child and youth psychiatry, psychology, pedagogy, and care.

CONCLUSIONS

Despite several similarities concerning child and adolescent psychiatry as an independent medical discipline and similar types of services, there are also remarkable differences among the three countries, presumably because of their different historical development:

1. the number of child and adolescent psychiatrists per population. In this regard, Switzerland is the leader with one child and adolescent psychiatrist (CAP) per 2802 persons aged less than 19 years, followed by Germany, with one CAP per 5874 and the Czech Republic with one CAP per 14,285 persons aged less than 19 years.
2. the number of beds for inpatients per population is larger in the Czech Republic than in the other countries, but there is a lack of inpatient beds for short-term patients. This applies also for day patient facilities, which are much more frequent in Germany and Switzerland.
3. training facilities at universities are also different. Whereas in Switzerland every university has a department of CAP, in the Czech Republic only three of seven medical faculties have a department of CAP; also, in Germany not every medical faculty has of a department of CAP. However, there are many nonuniversity hospitals that offer a complete training curriculum.
4. the training curriculum in the Czech Republic is the most extensive one and is composed of 24 months of internship in psychiatry or pediatrics, 36 months of outpatient and inpatient training in child psychiatry, and basic training courses in pediatric neurology and pediatrics.
5. training in psychotherapy of different durations is included in the training curricula of all three countries.

References

American Psychiatric Association. (2013). *Diagnostic and statistical manual of mental disorders* (5th ed). American Psychiatric Association. https://doi.org/10.1176/appi.books.9780 890425596.

Bettschart, W., & Bürgin, D. (1999). Child and adolescent psychiatry in Switzerland. In H. Remschmidt, & H. van Engeland (Eds.), *Child and adolescent psychiatry in Europe. Historical development — current situation — future perspectives.* Berlin: Springer.

Beutler, H., & Di Gallo, A. (2013). Child and adolescent psychiatry in Switzerland. *European Child and Adolescent Psychiatry, 22,* 519—520.

Di Gallo, A. (2017). Oral communication.

Emminghaus, H. (1887). *Die psychischen Störungen des Kindesalters.* Tübingen: Laupp.

Garibian, T. (2015). *75 ans de pédopsychiatrie à Lausanne. Du Bercail au Centre psychothérapeutique.* Lausanne: Éditions BHMS.

German Medical Association/Bundesärztekammer. (1994). *Musterweiterbildungsordnung Kinder- und Jugendpsychiatrie.* Köln: Verlag der BÄK.

Haemmerle, P. (2007). *Kinder- und jugendpsychiatrische Versorgung in der Schweiz — Ist-Zustand und Perspektiven.* Master thesis).

Harbauer, H., Lempp, R., Nissen, G., & Strunk, P. (1971). *Lehrbuch der speziellen Kinder- und Jugendpsychiatrie.* Berlin: Springer.

Harms, E. (1960). At the cradle of child psychiatry. *American Journal of Orthopsychiatry, 30,* 186—190.

Hebebrand, J., & et consortium. (2009). Forschungsleistungen der deutschen Kinder- und Jugendpsychiatrie. *Psychosomatik und Psychotherapie 2003—2008, 37,* 231—366.

Homburger, A. (1926). *Vorlesungen über Psychopathologie des Kindesalters.* Berlin: Springer.

Hort, V., Hrdlička, M., Kocourková, J., & Malá, E. (2000). *Dětská a adolescentní psychiatrie* (1st ed.). Praha: Portál. ISBN 80-7178-472-9.

Kanner, L. (1935). *Child psychiatry.* Springfield: Thomas.

Lutz, J. (1961). *Kinderpsychiatrie.* Zürich: Rotapfel Verlag.

Narring, F., Tschumper, A., Inderwildi Bonivento, L., Jeannin, A., Addor, V., Buetikofer, A., et al. (2004). *Gesundheit und Lebensstil 16-20jähriger in der Schweiz SMASH (2002).* Lausanne: raisons de santé. Retrieved from http://files.chuv.ch/internet-docs/umsa/umsa_smash_d_4.pdf.

Raboch, J. (1999a). *Doporučené postupy psychiatricke péče I.* Galén: Psychiatriská společnost ČLS JEP.

Raboch, J. (1999b). *Doporučené postupy psychiatrické péče I.* Praha: Galén. ISBN 80-7262-013-4.

Raboch, J., Anders, M., Hellerová, P., Uhlíková, P., & Šusta, M. (2014). *Doporučené postupy psychiatricke péče IV.* Prague: Psychiatriská společnost ČLS JEP. Česká psychiatrická společnost.

Remschmidt, H., & Mattejat, F. (2001). The component model of treatment in child and adolescent psychiatry. *European Child & Adolescent Psychiatry, 10*(Suppl. 1), 26—45.

Remschmidt, H., & Schmidt, M. H. (1988). *Vol. I, (1985) Vols. II und III. Kinder- und Jugendpsychiatrie in Klinik und Praxis.* Stuttgart, New York: Thieme.

Remschmidt, H., & Walter, R. (1989). *Evaluation kinder- und jugendpsychiatrischer Versorgung. Analysen und Erhebungen in drei hessischen Landkreisen.* Stuttgart: Enke.

Remschmidt, H., Walter, R., Kampert, K., & Hennighausen, K. (1990). Evaluation der Versorgung psychisch auffälliger und kranker Kinder und Jugendlicher in drei Landkreisen. *Der Nervenarzt, 61,* 34—45.

Report of the Expert Commission. (1988). Edited by the Ministry of Health. Bonn.

Signorini, G., Singh, S. P., Boricevic-Marsanic, V., Dieleman, G., Dodig-Ćurković, K., Franic, T., et al. (2017). Architecture and functioning of child and adolescent mental health services: A 28-country survey in Europe. *The Lancet Psychiatry.* https://doi.org/10.1016/S2215-0366(17)30127-X.

Steinhausen, H. C., Winkler Metzke, C., Meier, M., & Kannenberg, R. (1998). Prevalence of child and adolescent psychiatric disorders: The Zurich epidemiological study. *Acta Psychiatrica Scandinavica, 98*(4), 262–271.

Strohmayer, W. (1910). *Vorlesungen über die Psychopathologie des Kindesalters.* Tübingen: Laupp.

Stutte, H. (1960). Kinder- und Jugendpsychiatrie. In H. W. Gruhle, R. Jung, H. Müller, & W. Meyer-Gross (Eds.), *Psychiatrie der Gegenwart, Bd. 2* pp. S. 955–S.1087. Heidelberg: Springer.

Tramer, M. (1942). *Lehrbuch der allgemeinen Kinderpsychiatrie, einschließlich der allgemeinen Psychiatrie der Pubertät und Adoleszenz* (3rd ed.). Basel: Schwabe.

Walter, R., Kampert, K., & Remschmidt, H. (1988). Evaluation der kinder- und jugendpsychiatrischen Versorgung in drei hessischen Landkreisen. *Praxis der Kinderpsychologie und Kinderpsychiatrie, 37*, 2–11.

World Health Organization. (1992). *The ICD-10 classification of mental and behavioural disorders: Clinical descriptions and diagnostic guidelines.* Geneva: World Health Organization.

Ziehen, T. (1915). *Die Geisteskrankheiten einschließlich des Schwachsinns und die psychopathischen Konstitutionen im Kindesalter.* Berlin: Reuther und Reichard.

Further Reading

Bundesamt für Gesundheit, BAG, et al. (2015). *Psychische Gesundheit in der Schweiz. Bestandsaufnahme und Handlungsfelder.* Bern: BAG.

Di Gallo, A., & Beutler, H. (2014). *Gegenwart und Zukunft der Kinder- und Jugendpsychiatrie in der Schweiz.* Bericht zuhanden des Bundesamtes für Gesundheit (Not published).

Haemmerle, P. (2003). *Wo Europas Kinderpsychiatrie zur Welt kam – zur Geschichte, Aktualität und Perspektiven der schweizerischen Kinder- und Jugendpsychiatrie.* Oral communication, not published.

Mala, E. (1999). Child and adolescent psychiatry in the Czech Republic. In H. Remschmidt, & H. van Engeland (Eds.), *Child and adolescent psychiatry in Europe. Historical development – current situation – future perspectives* (pp. 55–69). Berlin: Springer.

Marmet, S., Archimi, A., Windlin, B., & Delgrande Jordan, M. (2015). *Substanzkonsum bei Schülerinnen und Schülern in der Schweiz im Jahr 2014 und Trend seit 1986: Resultate der Studie "Health Behaviour in School-aged Children" (HBSC).* www.suchtschweiz/Forschung/HBSC.

Remschmidt, H., & van Engeland, H. (1999). *Child and adolescent psychiatry in Europe. Historical development – current situation – future perspectives.* Berlin: Springer. http://www.sgkjpp.ch.

Schaffner-Hänny, E. (1997). *Wo Europas Kinderpsychiatrie zur Welt kam: Anfänge und Entwicklungen in der Region Jurasüdfuss (Aargau, Solothurn, Bern, Freiburg, Neuenburg).* Dietikon/ZH: Juris Druck + Verlag.

Schweizerische Eidgenossenschaft. (2016). *Die Zukunft der Psychiatrie in der Schweiz. Bericht in Erfüllung des Postulates von Philipp Stähelin.* Bern: Bundesverwaltung.

Stutte, H. (1974). Zur Geschichte des Terminus "Kinderpsychiatrie". *Acta Paedopsychiatrica, 41*, 209–215.

von Wyl, A., Chew Howard, E., Bohleber, L., & Haemmerle, P. (2017). *Psychische Gesundheit und Krankheit von Kindern und Jugendlichen in der Schweiz: Versorgung und Epidemiologie.* Eine systematische Zusammenstellung empirischer Berichte von 2006 bis 2016 (Obsan Dossier 62). Neuchâtel: Schweizerisches Gesundheitsobservatorium.

Child and Adolescent Psychiatry Training in Europe

Brian W. Jacobs[1], Elizabeth Barrett[2],
Henrikje Klasen[3],[†], Paul Robertson[4], Lucia Vašková[5],
Eva Šnircová[6], Ekin Sönmez[7]

[1] King's College London, London, United Kingdom; [2] University College, Dublin, Ireland; [3] Leiden University, Leiden, The Netherlands; [4] University of Melbourne, Melbourne, Australia; [5] INEP Institute of Neuropsychiatric Care, Prague, Czech Republic; [6] Insite Neuropsychiatrické Péče, Prague, Czech Republic; [7] Department of Psychiatry, Zonguldak Caycuma State Hospital, Caycuma, Turkey

INTRODUCTION

To understand the evolution of child and adolescent psychiatry (CAP) in Europe and the associated challenges in training, we need to review the historical development of the specialty. However, even before that, it is worth reminding ourselves why CAP is a medical specialty. In our view it is primarily to ensure that children, young people, and their families receive the best mental health treatment that can be provided, taking full account of the complex biopsychosocial context in which we all live. In addition to this fundamental objective, it is important to increase scientific knowledge and provide effective and skillfully delivered treatment to our patients. Finally, maintaining a thriving child and adolescent psychiatric profession requires ensuring that the processes and arrangements for training are realistic and, as far as possible, family friendly for our trainees. The training should not compromise standards, nor should it compromise the trainee's own family mental health.

[†] Very sadly, Dr. Henrikje Klasen died in July, 2017. She was a driving force in the CAP-STATE study and is a great loss to the work of IACAPAP.

To comprehend the evolution of CAP in Europe, it is necessary to understand the gradual and accelerating development of the subject, and then the medical specialty of the profession during the 20th century and the first part of the 21st century. It is also important to appreciate the various relevant organizations in Europe and their roles in contributing to efforts to develop a set of high training standards across the European countries, which pose diverse challenges.

To consider the challenges that we face, let us take the following vignette, which is based on a real interchange:

Two psychiatry trainees meet at an international training conference. They have spent the day in the same lectures as part of an organized young psychiatrists program, and they discuss what they have both learned, in particular some of the hot topics that came up. One reports that he has seen few cases of a particular psychiatric illness in his 2 years of practice, but he has 4 more years to go, so he may see more; the other agrees. The first trainee then complains about his long working hours and many examinations. He has to see up to eight families a day. The other listens, and then clarifies: he means only eight? She says, that is not very many. How does that work? She explains that she sees about 80 patients a day in the outpatient department of the mainly institutional setting in which she works. Aghast, he asks how she can possibly see 80 patients a day. Her role is not compliant with the European Working Time Directive. However, in 2 years, by the end of her training program, which is half as long as his, she will have seen a wide range of disorders. She will have managed many acute situations although she will not have had any examinations. By contrast, he explains, he will take four sets of examinations in all to complete training and will probably get a job near where he is now based. The second trainee explains that many of her colleagues plan to migrate to one of the Nordic countries, which she may consider. Another topic comes up: that of pharmaceutical company sponsorship. Whereas the male trainee thinks that funding by pharmaceutical companies to attend European meetings should be banned, this is not a view upon which they can agree. Like half of the trainees engaging in the young psychiatrists' program, she has managed to attend the conference only because of pharmaceutical company funding. The cost of the conference is more than her monthly salary.

Over several years of attending conferences, these trainees become friends. They begin to socialize with colleagues and develop training networks. They even conduct some small research studies with other trainees from the group. However, although they can agree about many aspects of working in psychiatry, neither can agree about whether the job they are doing is similar (whether they take the "same kind" of approach to patients), and (probably, secretly) each believes that the way they trained was better and that this makes them a better doctor.

How can this happen?

CHILD PSYCHIATRY IN EUROPE: ORIGINS

Child psychiatry gradually became a recognized branch of medicine in the first half of the 20th century. The Heidelberg University Clinic, established by August Homberger (1876–1930), was one of the very early child psychiatry clinics after the First World War (Bewley, 2008). He also wrote a groundbreaking textbook, *Die Psychopathologie des Kindesalters*, which brought together biological and environmental influences in relation to early-onset disorders (Hebebrand, personal communication). It was not until 1953 that the American Academy of Child and Adolescent Psychiatry (AACAP) was founded.

As Rey wrote in his interesting chapter on the history of child psychiatry, "The first child psychiatry shoots did not appear in the clinical tree until as recently as the 1920s with the child guidance movement. For example, what we now call the International Association for Child and Adolescent Psychiatry and Allied Professions (IACAPAP) started in 1937, the American Academy of Child & Adolescent Psychiatry (AACAP) was founded in 1953. The Union of European Paedopsychiatrists, which later became the European Society for Child and Adolescent Psychiatry (ESCAP), had its first meeting in October 1954. In many countries child psychiatry is not yet formally recognised as a specialty or subspecialty, not taught in medical schools, and no formal training is available." (Rey et al., 2015).

SOME KEY ORGANIZATIONS FOR CHILD AND ADOLESCENT PSYCHIATRY IN EUROPE

To understand what follows, we first describe some major European organizations that influence delivery, research, and training in medical aspects of child mental health.

Union Européenne des Médecins Spécialiste and Union Européenne des Médecins Spécialiste—Child and Adolescent Psychiatry

Shortly after the Treaty of Rome (1957), the Union Européenne des Médecins Spécialistes (UEMS) was founded in 1958. It now encompasses 37 nations and 43 specialty sections with some nations beyond Europe occupying an observer status. Its purposes throughout have been to advise the European Commission on harmony of specialist training in Europe and enhance the free movement of doctors in Europe on the basis of similar standards of training and ongoing professional development. CAP became a European-recognized specialty in its own right in Europe in 1994 (Hill & Rothenberger, 2005). Initially it was known as child and adolescent psychiatry and psychotherapy (UEMS-CAPP; more recently, UEMS-CAP), to recognize that a substantial part of treatment in this age range contains a strong psychological component.[1] This recognition as a separate specialty has been an important milestone to protect young patients by recognizing CAP as different from adult psychiatry with a different framework and also a strong, integral developmental perspective; it is also distinct from developmental pediatrics and pediatric neurology, although there is an overlap with both. It has also encouraged various countries in Europe to recognize the specialty so that now there are few countries in which CAP is not recognized as a separate medical specialty. CAP has always had a multidisciplinary ethos; CAP specialists work with clinical psychologists, specialist nurses, social workers, occupational therapists, speech and language therapists, and others to bring their various talents to bear effectively on the mental health of the child or young person.

With the recognition of CAP as a medical specialty, the issues of appropriate higher training became acute. From the outset, these have been challenged by the differing professional landscapes and responsibilities of neighboring medical professions in the different European countries.

European Society for Child and Adolescent Psychiatry

The European Society for Child and Adolescent Psychiatry (ESCAP) has the following goals:

1. To foster European knowledge and skills in child psychiatry
2. To facilitate and extend the bonds between European countries in mental health issues
3. To spread the results of research and experiences by publishing reports and organizing scientific conferences and meetings and to collaborate with international organizations with the same or related aims

Its organization includes three divisions (https://www.escap.eu/index/aims-and-goals). The academic division has the task: "To act as a forum for exchange of scientific research and to promote education and training, especially research training, in the field of CAP and mental health."

---

[1] More recently, it has adopted the more commonly used title of child and adolescent psychiatry (CAP), in keeping with much of the rest of the world.

The European Federation of Psychiatric Trainees

This is an independent organization founded in 1993 by trainees from across Europe. Delegates representing more than 30 member countries and their national training organizations meet annually. A CAP working group meets annually to explore issues in CAP training across Europe. The European Federation of Psychiatric Trainees (EFPT) has always valued CAP, with a permanent role on the parent board for the person chairing the CAP working group. The EFPT constitution supports the notion that whenever possible, countries should send both adult and CAP trainees to the EFPT annual meeting, and CAP trainees are well-represented in other aspects of the group, such as the international exchange and research groups (www.efpt.eu/ and http://efpt.eu/exchange/efpt-exchange/). In 2011, the EFPT-CAP section became a full member of UEMS-CAP, ensuring that European trainees are well-represented in that organization. This has been a bidirectional approach, with UEMS-CAP recognizing the important role of trainees in identifying strengths and gaps with regard to training on the ground. This has reflected the active role of trainees in contributing to the three research surveys of the provision of training across Europe that have been instituted since the creation of the first version of the UEMS-CAP logbook (Rothenberger, 2000, 2001).

Trainees as Adult Learners and the Role of Trainee Networks

Recognition of the role of trainees in their own learning as adult learners is a welcome development. They become active rather than passive recipients of training. This has additional benefits in increasing their skill set later as specialists and advocates for the profession on behalf of children and young people. There are also challenges for trainees and for those transitioning to be specialists in this (Nawka, Rojnic Kuzman, Giacco, & Malik, 2010; Riese, Oakley, Bendix, Piir, & Fiorillo, 2013).

The EFPT and the European Psychiatric Association (EPA) young psychiatrists' network endeavor to provide forums for trainees to explore and discuss the challenges of training, and may support them in articulating their needs (Giacco et al., 2014).

Trainee events are now common at international conferences and certainly foster collegiality, networks, and friendships. Examples include the IACAPAP Donald J. Cohen Fellowship (IACAPAP), the Italian Society of Psychopathology summer school, the European College of Neuropsychopharmacology's summer schools (Neuropsychopharmacology), and the young psychiatrists' programs at international conferences such as AACAP, ESCAP, and the European Psychiatric Association.[2] The UEMS-CAP initiative to provide a teaching seminar at the annual EFPT conference also supports this concept.

In many countries, trainees are included in feedback loops informing training standards, supporting service developments, etc. Trainees are uniquely placed as consumers of training to report on their experiences. Although supervisors can provide an overview of current training issues and crises, sometimes they may be less acutely familiar with the daily challenges experienced on the ground. Trainees may organize surveys. A survey for and by trainees stimulates less fear about reporting concerns or shortfalls in training (Kuzman et al., 2012).

Trainees have developed and encouraged their seniors to develop exchange schemes such as that organized by the EFPT. These schemes support the acquisition of experience in other countries (Dias, da Costa, & Bausch-Becker, 2012).

Each of these organizations, which comes from a slightly different perspective, contributes to an understanding of the evolving education of child and adolescent psychiatrists across Europe. This venture has several aims, among which are as follows:

- To improve the mental health of children and young people across Europe
- To aid scientific advance in the field of CAP by ensuring that we use similar concepts so that we can understand how these manifest variously by culture across Europe. This is likely to lead to a more rapid understanding of developmental psychopathology and to better evidence-based treatments that can be applied with appropriate cultural sensitivity in different places in Europe

[2] Useful resource sites for trainees include:

www.efpt.eu
https://www.ecnp.eu/junior-scientists/ecnp-school/Venice-child2017.aspx
http://www.europsy.net/education/summer-school/
http://www.fondazionechild.it/fondazione_child.php?sezione=173&id=320
http://iacapap.org/programs-campaigns/donald-cohen-fellowship
http://www.aacap.org/aacap/CME_and_Meetings/Annual_Meeting/61st_Annual_Meeting/Monitor_Program.aspx
http://www.europsy.net/early-career/congress-programme/

- To ensure that there is sufficient commonality of practice and training to allow clinical harmony of the profession across Europe, so that if patients and their families or the doctors who treat them move to different countries, they can expect a similar framework and standard of treatment

TOWARD UNIFORM TRAINING STANDARDS

Several initiatives have attempted to bolster training initiatives and raise standards. For example, the UEMS-CAP group has endeavored to support training by looking at curriculum guidance and the use of logbooks. MindEd has developed online training resources and information about child mental health for a variety of audiences including CAP trainees (MindEd). IACAPAP has developed an evidence-based textbook to support practice; it is readily available internationally (IACAPAP). Several international groups have advocated for training standards and competencies by using the guidelines and surveys of members to better understand the current situation in member countries, eg, in CAP (Hill & Rothenberger, 2005).

Training of Child and Adolescent Psychiatry

First Efforts: Developing a Logbook

In 2000, UEMS-CAPP developed a model training logbook (Rothenberger, 2000) in an effort to move toward harmonizing training of CAP across Europe. The appropriate length of training as a child and adolescent psychiatrist was set at 5 years; 4 of those years were used for "pure CAPP" training. Of those, it was thought that at least 24 months should be spent in outpatient work and 12 months in inpatient work/day care. It was noted that there should be a balance between practice with children and with adolescents. It was also thought important for CAPP trainees to have 12 months of training in adult psychiatry. Experience in pediatrics and neurology was suggested as optional. It was proposed that there should be 720 h of theoretical teaching over the 4 years of CAPP training. The view taken within UEMS-CAPP at that time was that a set of topical areas for theoretical knowledge and for developing practical skills should be listed, rather than developing a competency-based curriculum with detailed descriptions of each area using a "knowledge, skills, and attitudes" set of descriptors for each topic. Nineteen diagnostic areas were highlighted, together with 9 areas of knowledge that cut across diagnoses and were concerned with an admixture of topics; they included the application of a biopsychosocial approach to special situations such as crisis intervention, refugees, and issues of work and self-organization.

Other areas of diagnostic and intervention skills were covered. There were also areas of adult psychiatry practice that were thought to be important, as well as pediatric topics.

The 2000 logbook also addressed issues of organizing the training of child and adolescent psychiatrists across Europe. In this, it had to tread a delicate path. The responsibility for organizing higher training in medical specialties is held at a national level in each country in Europe; one might say that it is a devolved responsibility, or perhaps more properly, one that has never become centralized. This means that an organization such as UEMS-CAPP could point out the need for the following:

- Recognition of teachers and training institutions
- Quality assurance of training programs
- Quality and recognition of medical specialists
- Planning staff

Thus, UEMS-CAPP, in Chapter 4, entitled "EU Training Charter for CAPP," Articles 2–5, set out its vision for the organization of training. It is interesting, and unsurprising, that the language of this part of the document quickly slips from "requirements" to "should," ie, strong suggestions. The reason for this is clear. UEMS-CAPP had, and continues to have, some influence on what happens nationally, but it does not have the power to require European countries to comply with its suggestions. It also sets out the responsibility of trainees. In Chapter 5, the logbook skeleton is set out and the amount of time spent in the type of placement, the numbers of patients to be seen, and the hours that the trainee needs to demonstrate for each academic topic are also set. Forms to record this were not provided.

Comment: With the benefit of hindsight, what comes across is that the authors were attempting to grapple with the complexity of CAP and the myriad knowledge and skills that are needed to be a competent, sensitive clinician in this specialty.

UEMS-CAP Curriculum Framework 2012–14

This was initiated as a result of three strands of influence. First, the EFPT survey of CAP training had recently been completed (Simmons, Barrett, Wilkinson, & Pacherova, 2012) and its results showed the patchy implementation of the UEMS-CAPP 2000 curriculum. Second, UEMS as the parent body had decided that it wanted all medical training curricula to be revised in terms of both the curriculum content but and the organization of training institutions to represent advances in education thinking that had taken place since the last revision. Finally, some of the European countries (for example, Sweden and the United Kingdom) had moved to competency-based curricula in the intervening decade, and it was thought appropriate to examine whether this would be possible at a

European level. A curriculum working party was convened by the UEMS-CAP board president (Dr. Brian Jacobs). This group came to the conclusion that there was still too much diversity in the length of training and the context of other professions within which CAP existed, then and now, to allow the establishment of a demanding competency-based curriculum. Instead, it opted to develop a curriculum framework consisting of topics and skills that were, and are, regarded by all UEMS-CAP national representatives as essential for all specialists in the field. It also developed a larger set of knowledge and skills that should be acquired over time but that may not all be gained during formal CAP training, so that some would have to be developed as a process of continuing professional development (CPD) after reaching specialty status. The document also provided a fairly detailed model of organization of training. It was recognized at the time that this was, and remains, aspirational for some countries in Europe. It is represents high-quality practice with checks and balances in the system to ensure quality and appropriate external monitoring of that quality (UEMS-CAP & Jacobs, 2014b). A logbook for trainees to use was developed at the same time (UEMS-CAP & Jacobs, 2014a).

The UEMS-CAP curriculum framework envisages that the length of training in CAP itself will take a minimum of 3 years. It clearly states, "If training is proposed to take less time, then this must be robustly and evidentially justified in terms of the role of the consultant independent practitioner." The point of this threshold was to focus national training bodies on the normal minimum length of time that it takes a trainee to acquire sufficient supervised skills in case management and other aspects of becoming an independent child psychiatry practitioner. It assumes that placement in allied specialties such as adult psychiatry or branches of pediatrics will automatically extend this minimum period.

It also specified an ongoing caseload during training: "Number of procedures: An ongoing caseload of 25–35 cases is normally appropriate during training with an annual number of assessments of about 75 cases as a guideline. In inpatient settings, the caseload will be lower. Trainees should aim to see at least 10 cases of each common disorder and 5 cases of each of the less common disorders during their training." The rationale for providing these figures is to discourage high caseloads, which create situations in which the trainee has little chance to read about the patients and their problems. Equally, it is to discourage placements that will only yield a small caseload when valuable training time is likely to be squandered. However, it is recognized that for a limited time, inpatient experience may lead to a period with lower caseloads.

Trainees are also expected to "to be offered and to use regular weekly individual supervision of their work and of their training needs." Although not stated, it is assumed that this will normally be from the child psychiatry consultant on the team.

SURVEYS OF EUROPEAN TRAINING

Karabekiroglu, Doğangün, Hergüner, von Salis, & Rothenberger (2006)

These authors (Karabekiroglu et al., 2006) surveyed training of child and adolescent psychiatrists across Europe a few years after the development of the 2000 logbook. Their method was a structured descriptive survey using several approaches:

> In order to collect data on CAP training in European countries, we have communicated with UEMS-CAP and EFPT representatives of each country via e-mail. In addition, we used UEMS and EFPT annual forum minutes and web sites of national CAP societies to validate the data. Where there is conflicting information, we ranked the data's validity by considering the sources in the decreasing order as follows: web sites, personal communication and forum minutes. If the conflict was not resolved, that information is assumed as inconsistent and nor is it evaluated. Furthermore, recently published articles are also taken into consideration for this descriptive documentation.

Their results found much variability in training in CAP across European countries. In two-thirds of the countries, CAP was trained entirely separately from adult psychiatry, although there may have been some limited time spent there as placements. About 65% of 34 countries had an exit examination in CAP. The minimum duration of training to become a CAP specialist after leaving medical school (not the same as the time spent in CAP training) was also variable, ranging from 12 to 96 months (mean: 59.7 ± 17.1 months). They noted that CAP was a recognized specialty in 23 countries and a subspecialty in a further 8 countries, which left 5 European countries with no recognized specialty training in Europe in 2006. They also noted that there was great variability in the content of the training in the various European countries, so that, for example, experience in pediatric neurology was required in 13 of the 34 countries surveyed. A research or thesis was required by 9 of 25 countries where data were reliable.

In their discussion, the authors and ESCAP wanted to encourage the following:

- Broadening of experience in different psychotherapeutic methods, noting the need for funding of this training other than by the trainee themselves, because it often requires some form of personal therapy as a component of the training
- Greater experience in modern psychopharmacotherapy
- Training in research

They also noted that from its inception, EFPT has encouraged training exchanges between European countries as a way to broaden the trainee experience and encourage harmony of training.

Comment: The results of this survey clearly indicate some commonality across most European countries with regard to training but really emphasize the great variability in training, both in the length of post—medical school basic qualification as a doctor and in the structure and content of that training. We will return to this topic later in this chapter.

European Federation of Psychiatric Trainees Survey

The second survey was carried out by trainees themselves through the EFPT. It was conducted between 2010 and 2011.

This built on a smaller pilot study in 2009, when they gathering information from 27 countries in a short survey highlighting the variable duration of training, variable ability to attain a training post, and variable exposure to CAP at the undergraduate level. In this survey, CAP training was entirely separate from general psychiatry training 35% of the time (Barrett et al., 2011).

Using online survey methodology, these trainees aimed to gather information on current training and disseminate this to relevant organizations, with the overall goal of supporting trainees to support improvements in training standards. Overall, trainees hoped this would, in the longer term, lead to improved CAP training and service provision across Europe.

The questionnaire explored the structure and organization of training, training quality and content, working conditions, and recruitment. The group managed to collect full data sets on 28/34 participating countries. Subsequently they sought to triangulate information by presenting data gathered at the UEMS-CAP group, to check whether data submitted by country representatives were accurate, in workshop presentations at annual conferences, and again at the EFPT 2011 forum. When differences emerged between the trainee report and the UEMS perspective, discussions between representatives in individual countries ensued to ensure a best-shared understanding of the trainee experience was reached insofar as this was possible (Simmons et al., 2012).

The results of this survey will be presented compared, as much as possible, with the latest survey of European training. The Child and Adolescent Psychiatry - Study of Training in Europe (CAP-STATE) survey was carried out in 2016 and cited in the abstracts of the symposium on child psychiatry education presented at IACAPAP 2016 (Klasen, Jacobs, Herguner, Barrett, & Gaddour, 2016).

CAP-STATE

The idea leading to the CAP-STATE survey arose at the ESCAP Research Academy Meeting in Madrid in 2015. Johannes Hebebrand, who was the head of the ESCAP Research Academy and the editor-in-chief of *European Child and Adolescent Psychiatry* (ECAP), suggested that training in CAP should be a topic for research to be pursued by the early career investigators (ECI) as a survey to be published in the journal upon completion. Three senior investigators were identified who had a track record for research in CAP training: Henrike Klasen, Sabri Herguner, and Elizabeth Barrett. The group envisaged including all contributing ECI as coauthors of the article in an initial attempt to use national diversity assembled within the research academy and promote the careers of the ECI. The results of the CAP-STATE will be submitted to ECAP (Barrett et al., in preparation). The CAP-STATE survey was established as a 10-year comparison of, and extension to, the work of Karabekiroglu et al. that was already cited.

It aims to understand the current state of training in CAP across ESCAP member countries. A trainee or recently qualified child psychiatrist from each ESCAP member state and some additional European countries was recruited through ESCAP and asked to collect data on CAP training in their country. They were instructed to check national curricula and consult with residents and trainers from various university and peripheral training schemes, to collect reliable data on CAP training throughout their country (Barrett et al., in preparation). The final version of the survey covered the following:

- Country information (eg, regarding numbers of child and adolescent specialists and population ratios)
- Recruitment
- Training composition and duration
- Training of theory and practice, looking at the core components of training
- Supervision
- Assessment during training
- The role of senior clinicians as trainers
- Experiences of training institutions

Simmons et al. highlighted in the 2011 study that 28 of 34 countries had CAP training programs. At that time, there was no official training in Spain, Malta, Belarus, Bosnia, Ukraine, and Russia; the first two countries are in the European Union. Most commonly, in 68% of countries in 2011, training was in CAP alone as a separate specialty (in 25% there was a core trunk involving general psychiatry). As expected, the duration and composition of training were hugely variable. Most countries had national standards for training in CAP, although trainees reported implementation of these to be variable. This variability included intra-country variability (eg, between urban and less urbanized centers), as well as intercountry.

There were educational programs specific to CAP in 25 of 28 countries in the 2011 survey. Trainees reported that weekly supervision was provided in 19 of 28 countries.

Only 39% of the countries surveyed rigorously implemented their nationally documented training standards, with variable implementation elsewhere. A total of 29% of countries had introduced competency-based training; on a positive note, 89% of trainees reported that a theoretical CAP training program was available to trainees (Simmons et al.).

Psychotherapy training of some kind was obligatory in 19 of 28 countries. Research training was obligatory in 8 of 28 countries (Simmons).

By the time of the CAP-STATE survey of 34 countries, Bosnia was creating CAP training. The picture for Spain has been more complex, with a specialty created in 2014 but then deleted in December, 2016 by a court ruling that obstructed the development of trunk and branch training for medical and surgical specialties. Some of the more prominent specialties challenged this model because it would result in specialist trainees spending less time training in their specialty. The court ruling incidentally deleted the specialty from those recognized in Spain, taking the position back to that before 2014. It is unclear what the resolution to this difficulty will turn out to be. There are still four other countries surveyed with no CAP specialty or specialist training (Barrett et al., in preparation).

Length of Training

Length of training is defined as the time after initial qualification as a doctor. In four European countries, they could be recognized as CAP within about a year of qualifying. For a further six countries it would take trainees 6 years or longer. For most countries, the period after qualifying was 5 years (Barrett et al., in preparation).

Subspecialty Access

The range of subspecialty exposure in training, and indeed experience in allied disciplines such as neurology or pediatric medicine, is highly variable across Europe. For example, Simmons et al. (2012) reported that inpatient training time varied from none to a mandatory 5 years spent working in an inpatient setting. It appears that at that time there may not have been CAP outpatient child psychiatry in the country in question. For 15 of the 28 countries, the trainee would spend more than a half of the total training in an inpatient setting. We do not know whether this reflects the service provision in those countries.

Within training, exposure to subspecialities (Simmons) was hugely variable. In some countries, neurology experience was vital and mandatory. In others, this was not offered or recognized as training time. In 79% of respondent countries, trainees could access pediatric training; in 61%, they accessed neurology training; and in 89%, psychiatry experience. Substantial variation with subspecialties such as infant mental health or substance misuse were reported. Nordic countries, the United Kingdom, the Netherlands, and Germany tended to have better access to subspecialty experiences in general. This situation was much the same in the CAP-STATE survey.

Clearly, this may reflect both institutional culture and the systemic availability of psychiatry care within different health care systems across Europe. Given the move from institutional to community care in many countries, perhaps this will change in years to come.

Recruitment and Entry to Training

The CAP-STATE looked at this area in detail. In half of countries, selection is nationally based; in a third of countries, recruitment into psychiatry occurs through locally based training schemes.

Direct entry from medical school to CAP training schemes occurs in 13 of 33 of countries. Direct entry after an intern or registration year occurs in a further nine countries, so in total, in 22 of 33 countries, entry takes place directly from basic medical qualification or after an intern year.

The study found that in about one fifth of countries surveyed, trainees must complete some training in general/adult psychiatry (seven countries) before applying for training in CAP. In the remainder, there are a variety of different approaches.

Selection criteria for entry to training are clear at the outset in about three fifths of countries. Components included in selection include experience before application (one third), undergraduate examinations (about 50%), completion of postgraduate examinations (about half), doctoral research (one fifth), and various other requirements.

Training numbers are nationally determined in nearly three quarters of countries. At times, training numbers are set locally (in two countries) or by local training institutions (in eight). In the remaining two countries there are no set training numbers.

Seven countries reported that there were too few training places. In contrast, 10 countries reported that there were unfilled training placements and too few trainees were interested in this career.

Training part-time proves to be problematic in many countries. It is routinely available in about one quarter of countries.

In terms of gaining international experience, about one fifth of countries could provide this with ease. In most others it was difficult for a trainee to get this experience.

For most countries, trainees could attend international conferences (Barrett et al., in preparation).

Psychotherapy Training

This is not universally available across European countries, and even when it is, the amount of time, protected time, funding, orientation, and supervision arrangements are hugely variable. Simmons et al. (2012) found that this was an obligatory part of CAP training 68% of the time. Five years later, CAP-STATE found that it was required in 13 countries and recommended in a further six. Psychodynamic psychotherapy training and cognitive behavioral therapy were the approaches most commonly offered to trainees. Only half of countries fund this training for trainees. Few trainees are supported to access personal psychotherapy (Barrett et al., in preparation).

Research Training

Similarly, research training, which is considered crucial in some countries, is not universal. Simmons et al. highlighted in their 2012 report that this was compulsory in only 32% of countries. There was much intercountry variation. In 25% of countries, trainees were supported with some protected time to undertake some form of research during training. CAP-STATE participants reported about two fifths of the time conducting some research as a requirement during training (Barrett et al., in preparation).

Supervision

Supervision is not universally available, and the concept of an external educational supervisor (not the direct clinical supervisor) is far from common. Both CAP-STATE and the EFPT study by Simmons et al. highlighted gaps in supervision.

In 89% of countries, Simmons et al. reported that there was regular supervision, although this tended to vary across countries. Emergency duty supervision was available in 18 of 28 countries. Educational supervision occurred in 13 of 28 countries. It is worrisome that support and supervision for trainees undertaking emergency work was not always available: Only 64% of countries reported this to be available.

In 2016, CAP-STATE found that weekly supervision was required in about three fifths of countries. In 15% of them, there was usually no regular supervision.

Many countries have requirements or recommendations for supervisors, although there are few supports in place. In just over half of countries, trainers have protected, paid time dedicated to supervision of trainees (Barrett et al., in preparation).

Training Systems

CAP-STATE explored this area. To become a training supervisor, there are some requirements in many countries, although again these are not universal. Only a third of supervisors are required to have ongoing assessment of their own competencies. Only 15% of countries require their trainers to undertake CPD.

About 80% of countries have a formal recognition process for training centers. A national training body oversees this in about three fifths of the countries surveyed. Slightly less than a third of them use formal measures to assess training quality. Local experience is audited in some way in about a third of the countries. Trainee representation is sought in this in slightly fewer countries. Trainee perception of training quality matters: Half of respondents to the CAP-STATE survey noted variable training quality across countries; Slightly fewer felt that training was generally consistent across their country.

CAP-STATE reports that senior clinicians' perception of the training quality is monitored approximately a quarter of the time. However, in over half of the time, trainer perception of training is not monitored.

Around half of countries had set supervisor–trainee ratios. Most commonly, a supervisor supports one to three trainees; this is variable, and in around a fifth of countries it exceeds more than four trainees.

In some countries, trainees are routinely offered the opportunity to observe senior colleagues interviewing; this is a requirement in a third and is recommended in most of the remainder.

Senior colleagues observe trainees in "real-life" scenarios or using video technology in just over a third of countries as part of a workplace-based component to assess the quality of the trainee's skills.

In terms of physical supports available to trainees, there are often requirements regarding offices, library access, computer access, and equipment. For example, two-thirds of training schemes require trainees to access the Internet on a computer. Of course, this means this is not yet a requirement for one-third of European country trainees (Barrett et al., in preparation).

Assessment of Training

Assessing the standard attained by trainees is a complex area. There is much variability in approaches currently taken across European countries. Simmons et al. (2012) reported that oral examinations were the most common method of assessment; they were used in 68% of the 28 countries surveyed. Assessments based in the workplace were also common (in 57% of countries), and written examinations were used in 43% of countries. Six countries used other forms of assessment, including submission of a research thesis or curriculum vitae, or an analysis of a video recording of the trainee carrying out clinical interviews or treatment.

In the CAP-STATE study (2016), about two fifths had a written examination at some point during their training whereas about four fifths of countries reported an oral examination. A third had a clinical examination at the end of training. In just over a half of countries ongoing assessment was required in training, and there were many variable approaches to assessment during training. In 50% of countries there was some requirement to conduct ongoing assessment of patient care. Seniors observed this about half of the time. However, in only a fifth of the European countries was structured feedback to the trainee required.

An annual review of progress is required in training in 12 countries; 14 other countries recommend this without requiring it. In seven countries, this is neither required nor recommended.

Twelve countries include structured skills assessments as a requirement. In addition, presenting clinical cases is required in about two thirds of countries. A number of countries require none of these as part of training.

Feedback from multidisciplinary team members is uncommon. Completion of tasks or skills such as court reports and letters is required in just under one-third of countries. Objective structure clinical examination simulated scenarios are a requirement or recommended in only just over 10% of countries. Formal clinical skills assessments with participation of patients is required in seven countries.

In CAP-STATE, the two least-taught topics in child psychiatry training were the legal framework and the theory of teaching other adult learners (each slightly below 50% of countries where there was any teaching). Regarding the legal framework, this was compulsory or usually taught and compulsory in only 4 countries, whereas teaching of adult learners was taught regularly in only 7 countries. The number of countries setting a requirement for numbers of patients to be seen with particular diagnoses was poor (9 of 30).

CAP-STATE also highlighted that there is a remediation process of some kind in about two thirds of countries, including a feedback process for occasions in which trainees are struggling. Feedback does not always translate to action; Less than a half have some sort of process to support trainees in difficulty (Barrett et al., in preparation).

Undergraduate Teaching and Training

Undergraduate teaching and training and exposure to CAP are variable. This was highlighted in the EFPT pilot study in 2009, and again in CAP-STATE, in which countries reported that nearly three quarters of countries provide child psychiatry teaching to some degree for undergraduate medical students. A variety of approaches are seen to undergraduate teaching. Just over two fifths of countries require tutorial or small-group teaching in the subject with a similar proportion reporting that medical students gain clinical exposure to CAP. For interested undergraduates, a quarter of countries offered optional additional training electives in child psychiatry (Barrett et al., in preparation).

Conditions and Employment After Training

A total of 89% of countries reported that they were compliant with the European Working Time Directive (Simmons et al., 2012), and in most countries pay was similar to that of trainees in other specialities.

Simmons et al. reported that in general, trainees in psychiatry were paid comparably to those in other medical disciplines. CAP-STATE reported that in 27 countries most trainees in each country find a paid post at the end of training. Five countries reported that it is difficult to find paid employment. One country in the CAP-STATE cohort reported that there was no prospect of employment at the end of training (Barrett et al., in preparation).

BRIEF TRAINING EXAMPLES

The Czech Republic and Slovakia

Postgraduate training starting from basic medical qualifications in both of these European Union countries lasts a total of 5 years, full-time. In the Czech Republic, CAP training itself lasts 36 months. Trainees spend 20 months on a CAP ward. Then they can follow a course of 6 months of outpatient CAP, 9 months of adult psychiatry, and 1 month of pediatric neurology. Alternatively, they have 12 months of outpatient (ambulant) child psychiatry and then 2 months each of pediatrics and pediatric neurology.

In Slovakia, trainees have a total of 39 months to train as a CAP specialist, 27 months of which are spent in various types of inpatient setting and a further 12 months in a CAP outpatient setting. They spend an additional 12 months in adult psychiatry. They gain theoretical knowledge and practical skills while working in CAP departments. After all practice work is done, doctors take part in a 2-month internship in one of two clinics at the university to take the opportunity for additional experience. They also have 7 months in nonpsychiatric pediatric specialties.

The Slovak and Czech programs are both successfully completed by passing a final examination that contains both theoretical and practical components. The trainee also has to submit a relevant thesis. The topic of the final thesis must be approved by the senior lecturer of CAP. This thesis may provide a theoretical review of the latest knowledge on the chosen topic; alternatively, it can consist of the trainee's own clinical research with the clear methodology and aim of the study.

There is considerable commonality in the type of placement in the two countries, although there also some differences in emphasis. The Czech educational system specifies the theoretical knowledge and practical skills that a trainee should gain during the program. These requirements comply with the UEMS recommendations. Czech education requires a knowledge of the history of CAP as a subject, neurobiology, and the function of the central nervous system.

In Slovakia, the coverage of theoretical knowledge is similar. A compulsory part of the training in all medical specialization disciplines is the Course of Social Medicine and Organization of the Slovak Health Care, completed by examination.

Comparison With Australia and New Zealand

It is interesting to compare the developments that have taken place in the evolution of training for CAP in Australia and New Zealand with those in Europe. Is there convergence or has there been divergence? We provide a brief overview of the Royal Australian and New Zealand College of Psychiatrist (RANZCP) curriculum in Appendix 1. What emerges is a sense that both their curriculum and the European curriculum framework are trying to achieve similar aims. They have the advantage of fewer legislative frameworks within which they operate, so that they are able to specify a competency curriculum that is similar to those achieved in a few European countries such as Sweden and the United Kingdom, for example. Their approach to assessing trainees relies less on oral examination than in many European countries and may be a more modern approach in that it tests skill delivery regularly and in a form that is more likely to resemble day-to-day delivery of services by the child and adolescent psychiatrist. Their length of training appears to be shorter (24 months of specialist training after 6 months of more basic training in CAP) than that recommended by UEMS-CAP (36 months of specialist training). As the examples of two European states indicate in this chapter, it can be difficult to tease out from overall training lengths exactly how long trainees actually spend training in CAP itself rather than obtaining experience in adult psychiatry or allied medical professions.

DISCUSSION

This chapter illustrates the diversity of provision of CAP education across Europe. It describes the efforts to improve the harmony of training and raise standards. There really does not seem to be much disagreement about the need to achieve harmony of training and raise standards among child psychiatrists themselves. What is much more problematic is the project of bringing training systems into a more consistent framework. Each is tied to the country in which it exists and there is no real acceptance of some basic issues, such as the length of time it takes to train a basically qualified medical practitioner to be a specialist CAP. What seems likely is that countries that attempt to achieve this within a year or two of basic medical qualification will jeopardize the mental health care of their children and young people. There are always pressures to reduce the length of specialist training. It seems unlikely to us that this can be reduced beyond the 3 years required for CAP training by the UEMS-CAP curriculum framework. There is too much to learn and too many skills to acquire, some to a basic level but many to an advanced level to allow independent practice.

Beyond that, it becomes a question of balancing what the specialist needs to know to be a safe, senior, and most important, independent practitioner. There will always be more to learn about knowledge and skills for the qualified specialist that can be properly acquired through CPD, provided time away from direct patient contact and financial support are forthcoming to achieve it. The UEMS-CAP view remains that trainees need 3 years of uninterrupted exposure to CAP practice. There are two corollaries to this: The training program must provide a high-quality training environment with a variety of different practice settings including the community and inpatient or day patient settings. Spending more than a year in an inpatient setting is probably not helpful for training unless the practitioner is going to become an inpatient specialist. Many trainees can manage with less than 1 year.

There have been some developments in both the child and adolescent curriculums and some movement toward creating CAP as a specialty in one or two countries.

There are concerns that what is described as being required or firmly advised in documents is ignored with regularity. This cannot be good for patient care. It remains concerning that some European countries still do not have their own national curriculum to train in CAP.

Despite increasing evidence that psychological treatments can be effective and are often preferred by young people and their parents, the training commitment to these time-consuming approaches is variable across Europe. This does not arm the young specialist well.

More encouraging, there seems to be an increasing sense of the national organization of training across the countries of Europe. This can provide a basis for improving national standards of access to training of the training itself and of assessment and remediation over time.

CAP-STATE looked at supervisors and training institutions. It was evident that some trainers have little protected time or institutional support for training. Few objective measures are used to ascertain quality. There is reportedly good availability of local training directors and in some cases, there are good robust systems for trainees (Barrett et al., in preparation).

Concerns about supervision, protected time, and effective supervision are a major and surprising issue that arose in both the 2012 and 2016 surveys. Several studies including that of Jovanović and the BOSS study group highlighted this as an issue related to trainee burnout (and identifying some risk factors, including psychiatry not being the trainee's first career choice, an earlier stage of training and inadequate time for supervision, and long working hours). Burnout rates vary across Europe also (Jovanović et al., 2016).

Because of struggles to recruit in some countries, the increased number of women in medicine, and the purported role of training bodies in developing competent psychiatrists to provide the best possible mental health care for children and young people in their particular system, it is surprising these tangible messages evidently do not have an impact on various aspects of training in many places.

CONCLUSION

CAP is still a young specialty. It is vibrant and full of life.

It would be easy to be complacent and assert that the current inequalities in training and opportunity of training will even out over time. We are less sanguine about this. Many barriers to improving training lie at the national level among medical specialties, and perhaps even more important, at the governmental level. The latter are always subject to the pressures of needing to produce more specialists with the attraction of shorter training. There is also the risk that CAP will be regarded as either a less important medical specialty or, for trainees, as a less attractive option in which to train.

A collaborative approach between trainee organizations and their seniors who organize training is likely to be the best insurance alongside advocacy for our patients.

It is helpful for periodic surveys to remind us of the ongoing need to explore creative solutions to the problems of training. Comparing ourselves with other systems of training around the world will also help us to spot opportunities to develop creative solutions.

Acknowledgments

We would like to acknowledge the input of Professor Sabri Hergüner, Turkey. Unfortunately, we were unable to include Professor Hergüner as an author because we have been unable to contact him. He provided most of the preliminary analysis of the CAP-STATE data and would ordinarily have been an author.

The Early Career Investigator Group consists of 34 young investigators training in Child and Adolescent Psychiatry in countries across Europe.

References

Barrett, E. P., Nawka, A., Malik, A., Giacco, D., Rojnic Kuzman, M., Simmons, M., et al. (2011). P01-265-child and adolescent psychiatry training in Europe: Views of trainee representatives for 2009 − 2010 to the European federation of psychiatric trainees. *European Psychiatry,* 26(Suppl. 1), 266. https://doi.org/10.1016/S0924-9338(11)71976-9.

Bewley, T. (2008). *Madness to mental illness: A history of the Royal College of Psychiatrists.* London: Gaskell.

Dias, M. C., da Costa, M. P., & Bausch-Becker, N. (2012). P-1491-EFPT exchange programme: A new project towards a global future. *European Psychiatry, 27*(1). https://doi.org/10.1016/S0924-9338(12)75658-4.

Giacco, D., Bartoli, F., Puorto, C. d., Palumbo, C., Piras, S., Rubinacci, A., et al. (2014). Gli specializzandi possono contribuire a migliorare la formazione in psichiatria? I primi 20 anni della European Federation of Psychiatric Trainees. *Rivista di Psichiatria, 49*(1), 50−55.

Hill, P., & Rothenberger, A. (2005). Can we—and should we—have a neuropsychiatry for children and adolescents? *European Child & Adolescent Psychiatry, 14*(8), 466−470. https://doi.org/10.1007/s00787-005-0512-5.

IACAPAP. Donald Cohen IACAPAP fellowship. Retrieved from http://iacapap.org/programs-campaigns/donald-cohen-fellowship.

IACAPAP. IACAPAP textbook of child and adolescent mental health. Retrieved from http://iacapap.org/iacapap-textbook-of-child-and-adolescent-mental-health.

Jovanović, N., Podlesek, A., Volpe, U., Barrett, E., Ferrari, S., Rojnic Kuzman, M., et al. (2016). Burnout syndrome among psychiatric trainees in 22 countries: Risk increased by long working hours, lack of supervision, and psychiatry not being first career choice. *European Psychiatry, 32,* 34−41. https://doi.org/10.1016/j.eurpsy.2015.10.007.

Karabekiroglu, K., Doğangün, B., Hergüner, S., von Salis, T., & Rothenberger, A. (2006). Child and adolescent psychiatry training in Europe: Differences and challenges in harmonization. *European Child & Adolescent Psychiatry, 15*(8), 467−475. https://doi.org/10.1007/s00787-006-0599-3.

Klasen, H., Jacobs, B., Herguner, S., Barrett, E., & Gaddour, N. (2016). *Specialist training in child- and adolescent psychiatry: Towards more uniform standards?* Paper presented at the IACAPAP 2016 fighting stigma: Promoting resilience and positive mental health, Calgary, Canada   http://www.iacapap2016.org/wp-content/uploads/IACAPAP_Abstracts_web4.pdf.

Kuzman, M. R., Giacco, D., Simmons, M., Wuyts, P., Bausch-Becker, N., Favre, G., et al. (2012). Are there differences between training curricula on paper and in practice? Views of European trainees. *World Psychiatry, 11*(2), 135. https://doi.org/10.1016/j.wpsyc.2012.05.013.

MindEd. MindEd: A free educational resource on children and young people's mental health. Retrieved from www.minded.org.uk.

Nawka, A., Rojnic Kuzman, M., Giacco, D., & Malik, A. (2010). Mental health reforms in Europe: Challenges of postgraduate psychiatric training in Europe: A trainee perspective. *Psychiatric Services, 61*(9), 862−864. https://doi.org/10.1176/ps.2010.61.9.862.

Neuropsychopharmacology, E.C. o. Summer schools. Retrieved from https://www.ecnp.eu/junior-scientists/ecnp-school.aspx.

Rey, J. M., Assumpção, F. B., Jr., Bernad, C. A., Çuhadaroğlu, F.Ç., Evans, B., Fung, D., et al. (2015). History of child psychiatry. In J. M. Rey (Ed.), *IACAPAP textbook of child and adolescent mental health* (pp. 1−72). http://iacapap.org/iacapap-textbook-of-child-and-adolescent-mental-health: IACAPAP. Retrieved from http://iacapap.org/wp-content/uploads/J.10-History-Child-Psychiatry-2015.pdf.

Riese, F., Oakley, C., Bendix, M., Piir, P., & Fiorillo, A. (2013). Transition from psychiatric training to independent practice: A survey on the situation of early career psychiatrists in 35 countries. *World Psychiatry, 12*(1), 82—83. https://doi.org/10.1002/wps.20022.

Rothenberger, A. (2000). *UEMS section/board on child and adolescent psychiatry/psychotherapy (CAPP) working group on harmonization of CAPP-training.* Retrieved from http://www.uemscap.eu/uploads/14/Logbook_2000-pdf.

Rothenberger, A. (2001). The training logbook of UEMS section/board on child and adolescent psychiatry (CAPP) progress concerning European harmonization. *European Child & Adolescent Psychiatry, 10*(3), 211—213. https://doi.org/10.1007/s007870170030.

Simmons, M., Barrett, E., Wilkinson, P., & Pacherova, L. (2012). Trainee experiences of child and adolescent psychiatry (CAP) training in Europe: 2010—2011 survey of the European Federation of Psychiatric Trainees (EFPT) CAP working group. *European Child & Adolescent Psychiatry, 21*(8), 433—442. https://doi.org/10.1007/s00787-012-0275-8.

UEMS-CAP, & Jacobs, B. (2014a). *European training logbook for child and adolescent psychiatry (UEMS).* Retrieved from http://www.uemscap.eu/uploads/45/UEMS_Logbook_final__-_12-01-2014_-_no_password-pdf.

UEMS-CAP, & Jacobs, B. (2014b). *Training requirements for the specialty of child and adolescent psychiatry.* Retrieved from http://www.uemscap.eu/uploads/44/Training-Requirement-for-Child-adolescent-Psychiatry-approved_by_UEMS_Council_April_2014-pdf.

APPENDIX 1

Child and Adolescent Psychiatry Training in Australia and New Zealand

The RANZCPs is responsible for the training of psychiatrists, including child and adolescent psychiatrists. Successful completion of a minimum of 5 years within the RANZCP training program leads to Fellowship of the RANZCP and recognition as a specialist psychiatrist. In 2012, the RANZCP launched a redesigned training program, the Competency-Based Fellowship Program (CBFP), based on the Canadian Medical Education Directives for Specialists competencies (Box 13.1). Training uses an apprenticeship approach, with trainees working in a range of clinical settings under a supervising psychiatrist. The CBFP is divided into three stages with different knowledge and competency expectations at the end of each stage. Competency is assessed through a range of workplace assessments and centrally administered examinations. For more about the RANZCP CBFP, see www.ranzcp.org/Pre-Fellowship/About-the-training-program.aspx.

All RANZCP trainees complete 6 months of training in CAP in Stage 2. Trainees wishing to be recognized as child and adolescent psychiatrists complete Stage 3 (years 4 and 5) in credentialed CAP placements, which include a compulsory 6 months in a community setting and 6 months in an inpatient setting. Successful completion leads to the awarding of the Certificate of Advanced Training in Child and Adolescent Psychiatry as well as fellowship. All child and adolescent psychiatrists are recognized general psychiatrists.

BOX 13.1

FELLOWSHIP COMPETENCIES DESCRIBED THROUGH THE CANADIAN MEDICAL EDUCATION DIRECTIVES FOR SPECIALISTS ROLES

Medical Expert
Communicator
Collaborator
Manager
Health advocate
Scholar
Professional

Training in CAP requires 24 months in CAP clinical placements. Although a range of experiences is required and some, such a psychotherapy experiences, are mandated, training is primarily arranged around core CAP competencies. Competencies are skills, attitudes, and attributes, which are operationalized as 8 EPAs (Box 13.2). Two EPAs must be completed each 6 months, and a total of eight over 24 months. An EPA is completed when the supervisor judges the trainee has achieved competence at the level of a junior consultant. Work-based assessments (WBAs) (Box 13.3) are tools for evaluating competency; a minimum of three WBAs need to be completed for each EPA.

The observed clinical activity (OCA) is a particularly central WBA in which the trainee is observed undertaking an initial interview with a patient, and then follows by synthesizing and presenting the assessment and a diagnosis, formulation, and proposed management plan to the supervisor. At least one mandatory OCA is completed each 6 months.

A CAP trainee has a principal psychiatric supervisor within the workplace responsible for day-to-day training. Training is overseen by a director of advanced training (DoAT) CAP who represents the RANZCP. Training is monitored by in-term assessment (ITA) forms completed by the principle supervisor and submitted to the DoAT. For each 6 months, a formative midterm rotation ITA is completed at about 3 months. At the end of 6 months, a summative end-of-rotation ITA is complete. A logbook documenting clinical experiences is maintained as a formative tool but is not submitted for assessment.

Each CAP trainee completes a formal education program provided in each Australian state and New Zealand and guided by a central syllabus.

BOX 13.2

ROYAL AUSTRALIAN AND NEW ZEALAND COLLEGE OF PSYCHIATRIST STAGE 3 CHILD AND ADOLESCENT PSYCHIATRY ENTRUSTABLE PROFESSIONAL ACTIVITIES (EPAS)

EPA 1. Independently conducts an initial interview involving children and adolescents

EPA 2. Discussing a formulation and negotiating a management plan with a preadolescent child and/or family

EPA 3. Produces comprehensive psychiatric reports after initial assessment of children, adolescents, and their families

EPA 4. Commences psychopharmacological treatment for children and adolescents who have not previously been treated with psychopharmacology

EPA 5. Provides psychiatric consultation to the multidisciplinary team for the management of a child or adolescent in an inpatient setting

EPA 6. Conducts an assessment of culturally and linguistically diverse children and adolescents

EPA 7. Provides leadership in an interagency case conference focused on a child or adolescent

EPA 8. Assesses and implements a management plan for a complex clinical presentation in which there are ongoing child protection concerns

BOX 13.3

WORK-BASED ASSESSMENT TOOLS

Case-based discussion
Mini-clinical evaluation exercise
Observed clinical activity
Professional presentation
Direct observation of procedural skills

All psychiatric trainees complete training in leadership and management. For CAP trainees, this has a specific focus on CAP.

The centrally administered RANZCP examinations require successful completion to achieve fellowship. Although all CAP trainees complete these examinations, there are no specific examinations for CAP training.

Index